CON CHE SOAVITÀ

Con che soavità

STUDIES IN ITALIAN OPERA, SONG, AND DANCE, 1580–1740

EDITED BY

IAIN FENLON and TIM CARTER

CLARENDON PRESS · OXFORD

1995

Oxford University Press, Walton Street, Oxford OX2 6DP

Oxford New York
Athens Auckland Bangkok Bombay
Calcutta Cape Town Dar es Salaam Delhi
Florence Hong Kong Istanbul Karachi
Kuala Lumpur Madras Madrid Melbourne
Mexico City Nairobi Paris Singapore
Taipei Tokyo Toronto
and associated companies in
Berlin Ibadan

Oxford is a trade mark of Oxford University Press

Published in the United States
by Oxford University Press Inc., New York

British Library Cataloguing in Publication Data
Data available

Library of Congress Cataloging in Publication Data
Con che soavità : studies in Italian opera, song, and dance, 1580–1740
/ edited by Iain Fenlon and Tim Carter.
p. cm.
"Dedicated to Nigel Fortune on the occasion of his seventieth
birthday"—Pref.
Includes index.
1. Vocal music—Italy—History and criticism. I. Fenlon, Iain.
II. Carter, Tim. III. Fortune, Nigel.
ML1633.C66 1995 782'.00945'09032—dc20 94–49109
ISBN 0–19–816370–3

1 3 5 7 9 10 8 6 4 2

Typeset by Graphicraft Typesetters Ltd., Hong Kong
Printed in Great Britain
on acid-free paper by
Bookcraft Ltd.,
Midsomer Norton, Avon

For Nigel, from his friends

Preface

IN his celebrated *Paralèle des italiens et des françois, en ce qui regarde la musique et les opéra* (Paris, 1702), François Raguenet made strong claims for Italian music as being superior to French. The secret of Italian achievements, he said, lay above all in the skills brought to the task of fusing words and music so as to realize exhaustively and effectively the sentiments of the poetry. But there was surely another feature of the Italian style that Raguenet, like many of his predecessors, recognized in music from south of the Alps: its delicate combination of sweetness, subtlety, charm, and grace that the Italians called *soavità*. The notion of *soavità* became a benchmark of aesthetic quality and artistic craft in seventeenth-century commentaries on Italian music; it was also a quality deliberately invoked by contemporary poets and composers. Not for nothing did Monteverdi include a setting of Guarini's 'Con che soavità labbra adorate' in his *Concerto: settimo libro de madrigali* (Venice, 1619). And not for nothing did he set the poem for a striking combination of solo voice and nine instruments. As with the Seventh Book as a whole, it seems clear that Monteverdi was making some kind of statement about the new styles of Italian music that had emerged so significantly, and so surprisingly, during his own lifetime.

Whatever the merits of contemporary comparisons of French and Italian music, or the objectivity of the arguments they entailed, our choice of Italy as the central theme of these essays needs no apology. Although the country itself should be thought of more as a series of centres, each with distinct and changing traditions, rather than as a single entity, there can be no doubt that throughout the period covered by these studies the peninsula was of fundamental and lasting importance for the history of European music. It was in Italy that opera was established for the first time in the competitive and impresarial conditions that were to make it the dominant form of theatrical entertainment throughout the Continent for some 250 years. Equally, it was also in Italy that the concept of 'concerto', provocatively incorporated into the title-page of Monteverdi's Seventh Book, was first adopted and developed. And here, too, the new styles of the early decades of the century for solo voice(s) and basso continuo forged new paradigms of musical structure and expression of profound significance for years to come. The results inaugurated a wider trend that was to bring the *Musiche* of Sigismondo d'India to the bookshops of London, Lodovico Grossi da Viadana's *Centi concerti ecclesiastici* to the *Kantoreien* of Frankfurt, and Italian opera to the courts of Vienna and Warsaw.

For much of the seventeenth century and well into the next, developments in Italy remained at the centre of the musical world, as the travels of Heinrich Schütz and the writings of visitors from Thomas Coryate to Raguenet himself demonstrate. Yet while the broad outlines of music in Italy in the Seicento may seem clear, there remain notable gaps in terms both of sources and of our understanding of them. For example, while the apparent emergence of solo song and opera around 1600 is well documented, we have yet to come to terms with the complex interactions of production and consumption, and concomitant issues of taste and display, that explain the rather fragile history of opera in the north Italian courts, its transformation in Venice and elsewhere in the 1640s, and its relation (or not, as the case may be) to other forms of theatrical entertainment. Similarly, if the theoretical and aesthetic impulse towards the solo song and other text-focused musical styles in this same period seems well enough understood, we still tend to adopt a rather naïve view of musical progress, ignoring the delicate interplay of styles, structures, and affects encompassing all spheres of secular (and much sacred) music at this time, whether ostensibly 'old' (the polyphonic madrigal, say) or 'new' (the solo song or duet). And there remains the problem of how the new canons of verisimilitude—of being somehow 'true to life'—forged by the 'new music' could later encompass the evident shift in expressive and structural focus from the realistic speech-song of recitative to the melodious charms of the aria.

For the later Seicento and early Settecento, the important questions seem as much concerned with basic documentation as with critical interpretation. Indeed, Italian music of the second half of the seventeenth century is relatively unstudied, apart from some obvious exceptions, particularly in instrumental music. Some of the reasons for this neglect are clear, and include traditional preoccupations with matters of origins at the expense of later developments, as well as the poor survival rates of sources of key repertories: both points are well illustrated in the historiography of Italian opera. Still more to the point, many of the repertories and contexts for music in this period do not sit well with prevailing Romantic notions for judging artistic creativity, achievement, and significance that still inflect the way in which many music historians attempt to make sense of their pasts. Recent decades have seen a striking growth of interest in seventeenth-century studies on the part of European, British, and American musicologists. But much remains to be done.

In short, the essays in this volume aim to make a significant contribution to a richly diverse, patchily researched, and rapidly developing area of study. Our choice to limit the subjects to theatrical and secular vocal chamber music—for all the work still to be done on sacred and instrumental repertories—reflects the impulse that prompted us to conceive this collection. Dedicated to Nigel Fortune on the occasion of his seventieth birthday, these essays seek to reflect the range of his interests in an area of study which he did so much to pioneer in the 1950s, and which has been explored since by the many scholars influenced by his teaching and publications. Written by a group of friends, colleagues, and ex-pupils, they are offered in gratitude, admiration, and celebration.

IAIN FENLON
TIM CARTER

Contents

✢

List of Plates

1

Some Images of Monody in the Early Baroque

~✿~

BARBARA RUSSANO HANNING

MONODY, or accompanied solo song, was new at the end of the sixteenth century only in that it was being composed rather than improvised, written down by humanist-educated performers who believed in the power of the solo voice to move their listeners by conveying the words clearly and by imitating the affections underlying the text through purposeful vocal orna-mentation and graceful nuancing. This new style of art-song included a different type of accompaniment as well, which consisted of an instrumental rendering of a supporting line with some simple harmonies, unfettered by the competing contrapuntal parts that had been a feature of Renaissance vocal music. To be sure, monody had much in common with the Renais-sance humanist tradition of the improvised song recitations of courtly lyric and narrative poetry, which were self-accompanied on harp or lyre in the manner of Orpheus and other ancient bards. But it was also different enough and sufficiently celebrated to spark a new interest among the poets and painters of the early Baroque.

Among the poets, for example, was Giambattista Marino (1569–1625), whose attention to realism and descriptive detail leaves no doubt that he was a keen observer of contemporary musical practices. In Marino's retelling of the myth of Orpheus in his *Idillii favolosi* (1620), he describes how the singer, carrying his noble lyre in his arms, descended into Hades to retrieve his bride. Marino spends no less than ninety lines on a detailed depiction of his playing, and at the end of the passage gives a wonderfully accurate descrip-tion of the properties of contemporary monody, in which (according to the poet) the sense of the words, and the shape of their accents and rhymes, are not confused by or submerged in the roulades and ornaments of the song, but, rather, unfold clearly and distinctly.[1] This is precisely why the new style

---

[1] See *Orfeo*, ll. 114–85, in *Idillii favolosi,* ed. Gustavo Balsamo-Crivelli (Turin: UTET, 1928), 6–11. Further on *Orfeo,* see James V. Mirollo, *The Poet of the Marvelous: Giambattista Marino* (New York: Columbia University Press, 1963), 53 ff.

of solo singing was so widely acclaimed at the turn of the century, and this passage seems to be Marino's acknowledgement of its proponents and perhaps even of the inventors of opera, whose composers adopted the most radical kind of monodic declamation, *recitar cantando*, or speaking in song.

In the visual arts, images of monody would typically present a solo singer accompanying himself or herself on the lute, as in Plate 1, a recently rediscovered painting by Michelangelo Merisi da Caravaggio (1571–1610), dating from the 1590s, which was the centre-piece of an exhibition at the Metropolitan Museum of Art in New York in the spring of 1990, and on which this essay will focus. Another common representation is of a small group comprising one singer and one or more instrumentalists, as in Plate 2, a painting by Nicolas Tournier now at the Louvre dating from the 1630s, by which time it had become fashionable to use a solo instrument such as the violin in competition with the solo voice against the continuo accompaniment.

The conventional title of Caravaggio's *Lute Player* (Pl. 1) is not an accurate one, for the youth is clearly both playing and singing, like the young musician called simply Rainero who was eulogized in a poem by Marino as 'cantore e sonatore eccelentissimo'.[2] Caravaggio has painted the sensuous lips slightly parted, so that one can see some teeth and the tongue. While this has been considered an element of lascivious solicitation, the fact is that Giovanni Camillo Maffei's *Discorso della voce* of 1562 instructs performers to 'lay down the tongue so that its tip reaches and touches the base of the bottom teeth', and to 'open the mouth correctly and not more than is necessary to converse with friends',[3] advice to which Caravaggio's singer certainly seems to conform. These rules also seem relevant for other portrayals of singers, as, for example, *Il cantante appassionato* attributed to Giorgione (see Pl. 3). On the other hand, a portrait by Annibale Carracci of the lute-player Mascheroni (Pl. 4) bears no suggestion at all of singing; rather, the open score and pen placed on the table behind which he sits may indicate his reputation as a composer.

In comparing Caravaggio's and Giorgione's singers (Pl. 1, 3), one notes the similarity of their loosely fitting white blouses—gathered at the waist by an elegant sash in one instance—and, as I have already remarked, the comparable treatment of their mouths. Yet one is also struck by their differences, and principally by the androgynous, indeed effeminate appearance of Caravaggio's sitter; here and in some of his other musical paintings, this feature has been

---

[2] The sonnet appears among the *rime lugubri* in *La Lira I*, ed. Giovan Francesco Loredano (Venice: Francesco Baba, 1653), 169.

[3] See Nanie Bridgman, 'G. C. Maffei et sa lettre sur le chant', *Revue de musicologie*, 38 (1956), 3–34.

seen as an expression of Caravaggio's or his patron's sexual preference.[4] While this may have been a factor, other explanations have also been proposed that have more bearing on the relationship between Caravaggio's artistic choices and how he intended his subject to be perceived.

The art historian Franca Trinchieri Camiz conjectures that Caravaggio's sitter may actually have been a singer, a Spanish castrato named Pedro Montoya who was living in Rome in the same place where the painter also resided, in lodgings at the *palazzo* of Cardinal Francesco Maria del Monte (1549–1626), Caravaggio's first great patron and a well-known and respected figure in Roman art circles.[5] If this is Montoya, the androgynous quality of his appearance can be explained by the very fact that he was a castrato, one of many who were recruited during the last two decades of the sixteenth century to sing in the Sistine Chapel choir. Castration of boys before puberty resulted in androgyny, since male secondary characteristics such as muscular development and facial hair were suppressed along with the change in voice. Their bodies were often more fleshy, especially around the hips and thighs, and in the face as well. As to their musical accomplishments, their voices were valued for their greater power and endurance compared with women's voices, and praised for their agility, range, breath control, and ability to thrill the listener. Even the classicist Voltaire admitted that the castrato voice was more beautiful than that of a woman. Castratos were also trained as instrumentalists; in a letter of 1583, a list of qualities necessary for employment at the Mantuan court includes the comment that if a castrato were skilled at accompanying himself on the lute, he would be cherished even more.[6]

All Caravaggio's musical pictures date from between roughly 1595 and 1600, when he and Montoya were living in Rome in the household of Cardinal Francesco Maria del Monte.[7] In addition to housing and supporting young artists and musicians, the Cardinal was also a passionate music lover and collector of instruments and music books. Probably this painting was commissioned to show off del Monte's exceptional collection of expensive and beautiful instruments. The seven-double-course lute was one of at least four different lutes that he owned, and it is worth noting the meticulous way in which Caravaggio rendered the greater thickness of the two lowest courses

[4] See especially Donald Posner, 'Caravaggio's Homo-erotic Early Works', *Art Quarterly*, 34 (1971), 301–24.

[5] Franca Trinchieri Camiz, 'The Castrato Singer: From Informal to Formal Portraiture', *Artibus et historiae*, 18 (1988), 171–86, esp. 172; ead., 'Music and Painting in Cardinal del Monte's Household', *Metropolitan Museum Journal*, 26 (1991), 213–26, esp. 219–22.

[6] See Trinchieri Camiz, 'The Castrato Singer', 173–4.

[7] Keith Christiansen, *A Caravaggio Rediscovered: The Lute Player* (New York: The Metropolitan Museum of Art, 1990), 9–52, esp. 10, 23 ff.

of strings. The instruments arrayed on the oriental carpet covering the table
—a violin and bow, a tenor recorder, and a *spinettina* (a tiny, high-pitched
version of a harpsichord)—were all probably chosen for display with great
care, their small size perhaps intended to underscore the private and intimate
nature of the performances that took place in the Cardinal's apartments in
the Palazzo Madama. The Cardinal himself apparently sang and played the
Spanish guitar and was a close friend of Emilio de' Cavalieri, whose musical
pastoral, *Il giuoco della cieca*, he saw performed in Florence in 1595. He also
had very close ties with the Medici, and together with another notable
patron of music, Cardinal Montalto, he attended the second performance of
the first opera, Peri's and Corsi's *Dafne*, in Florence in early 1599. By the
time of his death in 1626, the Cardinal had had several monody collections
dedicated to him and had become *protettore* both of the Sistine Chapel choir
and of the Congregazione dei Musici, which later became the Accademia di
Santa Cecilia.[8] It is clear, then, that Caravaggio's patron was interested in
and informed about the newest musical trends and fashions of the period.

Given this wealth of information about the context of Caravaggio's painting
and its commission, is it in fact possible to know more about the performance—that is, exactly what the young musician is singing and playing?
Indeed, Colin Slim has identified the music lying open on the table as the
bass parts of two madrigals from a popular compilation of madrigals published more than sixty years earlier.[9] When this painting was executed, the
Cardinal was approaching his fiftieth year and Caravaggio was only about 25,
so one might question this choice of music from an earlier generation unless
one remembered that some of the madrigal repertory of the sixteenth century
was long-lived, and that, as Vincenzo Galilei testifies, the more popular examples of four- and five-part madrigals continued to be performed in versions
that approached the new style of solo singing with reduced accompaniments
at the end of the century. Also, this was the decade just before the earliest
published collections of monodies began to appear. Finally, as Cardinal del
Monte must have provided Caravaggio with a set of partbooks from his
prestigious collection, it is reasonable to assume that he would have chosen
one of his precious first editions to display in the painting. The works are

---

[8] For this and further information about Cardinal del Monte, see Christiansen, *A Caravaggio
Rediscovered*, 10 ff., and Trinchieri Camiz, 'La "Musica" nei quadri del Caravaggio', *Quaderni
di Palazzo Venezia*, 6 (1989), 198–221. About Cardinal Montalto, see James Chater, 'Musical
Patronage in Rome at the Turn of the Seventeenth Century: The Case of Cardinal Montalto',
Studi musicali, 16 (1987), 179–227 at 212–15.

[9] H. Colin Slim, 'Musical Inscriptions in Paintings by Caravaggio and his Followers', in
Anne Dhu Shapiro (ed.), *Music and Context: Essays for John M. Ward* (Cambridge, Mass.:
Harvard University Department of Music, 1985), 241–63. See also Trinchieri Camiz, 'La
"Musica" nei quadri del Caravaggio', 207–8.

in fact from Jacques Arcadelt's *Il primo libro di madrigali a quatro voci* (the first known edition dates from 1539). Arcadelt was one of the composers most in vogue during the Cardinal's youth, and one of the two pieces is a setting of a Petrarch sonnet which in its refined sensuality is typical of the early madrigal repertory.[10] The fact that only the bass part of a four-part madrigal is shown reflects the up-to-date performance practice of the singers of the time: the performer would have sung the soprano part and its text from memory, improvising ornamentation appropriate to the affections of the words, while at the same time rendering on the lute a simple accompaniment based on the printed music open before him or her. In this intimate type of performance, the other parts (alto and tenor) would have been suppressed, or their harmonies subsumed into the lute chords, one of which seems about to be struck in Caravaggio's painting; it might even be possible to see in the three instruments that lie unused in the foreground a reference to the earlier practice of performing these works as they were written, in four independent parts.

The highly specific character of the del Monte *Lute Player*, with its array of instruments and partbooks, strongly suggests that it was conceived both as a plausible representation of a musical performance, intended to evoke the private concerts del Monte held in his *palazzo*, and as a public record of these events, a kind of reminder for the friends and guests who visited him. But even though Trinchieri Camiz broaches the idea that the sitter actually was a musician, she concedes that this painting is hardly a portrait in the traditional sense; rather, it is 'more evocative and interpretive, underlining the beauty and eroticism of the castrato's manner of singing, which . . . strove . . . to be sweet, mellifluous, and womanlike. Moreover, it involves "dressing up" the sitter and "staging" the musical performance by means of a set of props that suggest a subtle allegorical context.'[11] Among the props that tie this picture to the tradition of allegorizing the art of music—a tradition which will be further explored below—are the instruments themselves and the caged songbird in the dark, upper left-hand corner of the canvas (Pl. 5) —perhaps the Cardinal's pet, or a reference to the sense of hearing, or even a poignant metaphor for the castrato condition. Whether portrait or allegory, the painting is surely a projection of its owner's aesthetic tastes, his wealth, and his pleasures.

But music's pleasures are never totally innocent or experienced in isolation

---

[10] 'Lassare il velo o per sole o per ombra' (sonnet 11), set here by Francesco de Layolle; see Slim, 'Musical Inscriptions', 246, and the appendix to the Metropolitan Museum's exhibition catalogue (see above, n. 7; pp. 90–1), which reproduces the texts of the madrigals and their English translations.

[11] Trinchieri Camiz, 'The Castrato Singer', 174.

from the larger cultural context, and the remainder of this essay will explore other ways in which this painting resonates with meaning. On the one hand, music is experienced as sound—in this case, sound evoked by the painter and dependent upon the memory of the present viewer but former hearer of the music—but on the other, it is also an embodied practice, a physical activity, perceived through the agency of human sight as well as hearing, and therefore an activity subject to the gaze. As a visual phenomenon, music is richly semantic, and the visual arts play an important role in helping us reconstruct the meanings that are encoded through the artistic conventions of a culture. Visual representation—of such things as how the performers look and gesture, how they are dressed, how they interact with their instruments and with one another, and how they regard the audience—summarizes and synthesizes the relationships within the context of which sound occurs and therefore in which music has meaning.[12]

In order to uncover the further meanings that are encoded in this painting, we need to examine some other works by Caravaggio and his contemporaries. In a painting by Bartolomeo Cavarozzi, entitled *The Lament of Aminta* (Pl. 6), which recalls a moment in Tasso's pastoral drama, the theatrical connection is more explicit;[13] but we also recognize among the Caravaggesque elements the *deshabillé* quality of dress, the languorous look in the eyes, and the sensuous, still-life atmosphere to which music lends its silent voice. But while Caravaggio's and Cavarozzi's paintings (Pl. 1, 6) seem to emphasize the sense of hearing, an earlier version of Caravaggio's *Lute Player*, executed for a different patron the year before (1595–6), includes all the senses (Pl. 7).[14] Taste and smell are represented by the fruit and flowers, touch by the manipulation of fingers on the instrument, sight by the open partbook with its musical notation that needs to be 'read', and hearing by the putative sound produced by the performer. Incidentally, it is worth noting that among all the senses in this painting, hearing is privileged by its spatial centrality and by its intended impact on the viewer; for among all the human senses, sight distances us from the objects perceived—and the fact that the performer's gaze does not directly engage us emphasizes this—whereas hearing (or in this case, its memory) envelops us, draws us into the painting, and

[12] In exploring these issues, I am guided by the recent work of Richard Leppert, the first real theorist of the role played by sight in the interpretation of musical meaning; see his *The Sight of Sound: Music, Representation, and the History of the Body* (Berkeley and Los Angeles: University of California Press, 1993).

[13] The musical notation is from a madrigal by Erasmo Marotta (1600) on a text from Tasso's *Aminta*; see Trinchieri Camiz, 'Music and Painting', 222 and n. 49.

[14] This painting, now at the Hermitage in St Petersburg, was commissioned by Vincenzo Giustiniani, another musical connoisseur, and was long confused with the related work executed for Cardinal del Monte; see Christiansen, *A Caravaggio Rediscovered*, 11, 28–38.

more than any other element makes us aware of our proximity and connectedness to the performer. The still-life representation of flowers and fruit is a traditional *vanitas* element, a reference to the ephemeral nature of all sensual stimuli, but especially of the pleasures of love, whose message is carried by the ethereal product of the performer's activity—musical sound which is lost as soon as it is gained.[15] The lute itself was often incorporated into Northern *vanitas* paintings of still life as an emblem of decay because its sound is so fragile that it evaporates almost instantly. And as if to reinforce the message, Caravaggio adds a crack between two of the ribs on the belly of this particular instrument, a further sign of temporality.

Thus the painting carries an allegorical message about the transitory nature of all of the senses. But how are we able to know that it warns us especially about the pleasures associated with love? Among the fruits are several that have potential sexual significance, like the cucumber and the overripe figs and pears. And once again, the musical notes have been deciphered and identified as belonging to madrigals whose texts are amorous declarations of love and undying devotion.[16] The position of the violin, pointing in the direction of the space towards which the performer also gazes dreamily, suggests his anticipation of a partner; and finally, as opposed to the oriental carpet depicted in the other painting, the marble slab which here separates him from the fulfilment of his desire has funerary associations and serves as a reminder that all things corporeal ultimately turn to dust.

And what of the performer? He is the same androgynous youth that Caravaggio used in the del Monte *Lute Player*; in fact, it is thought that the painter may actually have traced his contours on to a new canvas to serve as a point of departure for the later painting. But an altogether different interpretation of the Hermitage *Lute Player* was suggested by Maurizio Calvesi, who proposed that the sitter, in all his androgyny, was meant to represent the Divine Singer, Christ, and that the amorous content of his song was a metaphor for the Bridegroom–Saviour's love of his spouse, the Church, in all its humanity. In fact, although the bass parts of three madrigals are legible, the one that seems least obscured is the third, where the large (inverted) 'V' begins Arcadelt's 'Voi sapete ch'io v'amo' ('You know that I love you, even adore you, but you do not yet know that I die for you'). Calvesi believed that this painting was also destined for Cardinal del Monte, and he therefore allegorized the presence of flowers and fruit as well, imbuing each one with

---

[15] For a general treatment of the theme of music and love, see Albert Pomme de Mirimonde, 'La Musique dans les allégories de l'amour', *Gazette des Beaux-Arts*, 68 (1966), 265–90; 69 (1967), 319–46.
[16] See Slim, 'Musical Inscriptions', 243–4, and the texts and translations in Christiansen, *A Caravaggio Rediscovered*, 90.

religious symbolism. Finally, he noted the letter X formed by the crossing
of the bow on the violin and repeated on the neck of the instrument, and
he related it to the initial of Christ's name.[17]

Redeemer or not (and I think that Calvesi's interpretation is somewhat
strained), the lute-player's resemblance to the figures in another painting,
Caravaggio's *Musicians* (Pl. 8, the first of Cardinal del Monte's commissions
from his protégé) is striking. Here, Caravaggio was certainly drawing on a
tradition of north Italian and especially Venetian concert scenes, which
combine naturalism with allegory. Three youths, semi-clad in generic, loose-
fitting tunics that evoke without actually describing ancient dress, are shown
preparing for a performance: one studies the partbook from which he will
sing (and this time the music is not legible); another—who most resembles
the soloist in both versions of *The Lute Player*—tunes his lute; and the third,
at the back, usually identified as a self-portrait, turns from his cornett to gaze
at the viewer. A violin and open partbook lie on the cloth-covered ledge,
perhaps inviting our participation. But the nature of the concert in which
we would partake is clarified by the figure of Cupid on the left—one can
barely see the dark wings on his back and the quiver full of arrows behind
his right arm—whose presence identifies the subject as an allegory of Music;
the grapes he is gathering (a Bacchic motif) underscore this.

A similar painting of a group of musicians (also misnamed *The Concert*; see
Pl. 9) by Pietro Paolini, working in Rome in the 1620s, owes an obvious
debt to Caravaggio. Again, there are three musicians and a Cupid, whose
presence indicates (in the words of Vasari, describing a similar work from an
earlier generation) 'that Love is born from Music, or really that Love is
always in the company of Music'.[18] The grapes are gone in Paolini's painting, but instead Cupid offers a red carnation to one of the women, a pointed
allusion to the relationship between Love and Music: the women not only
inspire love through music but also become Love's object.

Another painter very much influenced by Caravaggio was Orazio
Gentileschi, and his *Lute Player* (Pl. 10), dating from between about 1610 and
1615, just after Caravaggio's premature death, owes a great deal to his work
in its use of an indeterminate and neutral space, illuminated by the diagonal
shaft of light, and in its exquisite attention to the details of costume and
texture and to the arrangement of instruments and music. But in the absence
of any overt allegorical elements, how can we know what it means? With
her back towards us, the sitter seems to be playing for herself and is therefore

[17] See Maurizio Calvesi, 'La realtà del Caravaggio: Seconda parte (i dipinti)', *Storia dell'arte*,
55 (1985), 227–87, esp. 264–7.
[18] Quoted by Andrea Bayer in the catalogue entry on Paolini's painting in Christiansen,
A Caravaggio Rediscovered, 70–1.

not only the agent or producer of the sound but also its receiver. No specific meaning is conveyed by the musical notation, which is indecipherable, but the performer's rapt expression indicates at once her contentment and her obliviousness to our presence. Perhaps, then, the painting may be interpreted as an allegory of hearing.

Another possible reading is derived from Cesare Ripa's anthology of emblems, *Iconologia*: its first edition (1593) was dedicated to the same Cardinal del Monte who was Caravaggio's patron, and the work was undoubtedly accessible to Caravaggio in the Cardinal's library. Emblems, which continued to be published in large collections, consisted of an image accompanied by a verbal gloss. With or without their text, emblems quickly found their way into the cultural vocabulary of other discursive practices, such as painting and poetry. In describing the attributes of Music, Ripa recommended that it be personified as 'a beautiful young woman who with both hands holds Apollo's lyre, and at her feet has various musical instruments'.[19] It is not too far-fetched, therefore, to see in Gentileschi's painting a beautifully simple representation of the personification of *La Musica*.

But is this painting really as innocent as it seems? Music was theorized from the time of Plato as possessing enormous sensual power. It was understood to act with dangerous immediacy on the sensate body, and therefore the musical gaze was charged with the potentiality of sexuality. And whose gaze was this painting intended to engage? When it was sold in Bologna in 1697 to Prince Johann Adam von Liechtenstein, it was described merely as 'a woman who plays'.[20] Before then, it undoubtedly decorated the private chamber of another wealthy, male consumer, who must have appreciated it much as any voyeur enjoys watching a woman unaware of being seen. And in the position of the violin, not to mention the loosened lacing of her dress, lies the titillating promise of a duet and other pleasures.

As an emblem, the lute was by itself often a marker for eroticism, for it connoted the potential of art-music for sexual arousal. One has only to think of the line from Shakespeare's *Twelfth Night*, 'If music be the food of love, play on!', or of Titian's famous paintings of 'Venus and the Lute Player'. The lute's reputation for debauchery is made explicit in the 1603 edition of Ripa's *Iconologia*, where the woodcut shown as Plate 11 represented one of the four humours or personality types of the Renaissance—sanguine temperament—personified by 'the gifted youth, overstimulated, who shuns proper

---

[19] Cesare Ripa, *Iconologia* (Rome: Gigliotti, 1593), 345, quoted by Bayer in Christiansen, *A Caravaggio Rediscovered*, 74. Most recently, see Nicoletta Guidobaldi, 'Images of Music in Cesare Ripa's *Iconologia*', *Imago musicae: International Yearbook of Musical Iconography*, 7 (1990), 41–68.

[20] See Bayer in Christiansen, *A Caravaggio Rediscovered*, 74.

behaviour and spends his days in play and amusement'. The youth is further described as blonde, rosy-cheeked, and rather fleshy. Wearing rich and fanciful garb and a wreath on his head, he is playing a lute at a music-stand. Behind him is a ram holding a cluster of grapes in his mouth, symbolizing the sanguine person's dedication to Venus and Bacchus. As a result of being so well supplied with good blood, the person of sanguine temperament is extroverted, given to pleasure and to the satisfaction of his appetites.[21]

This imagery conforms to an earlier, Northern Renaissance tradition in which Mary Magdalene was depicted as a musician, and specifically as a lutenist. Colin Slim has treated the theme of the Magdalene and has shown how she was visualized in mystery plays, song literature, and the graphic arts in the early sixteenth century as both dancer and singer before her conversion. In a series of paintings by the so-called Master of the Female Half-Length, the artist portrays her as a lute-player, probably choosing the lute 'because its hollow, rounded shape had widely understood erotic connotations in his society'.[22] And the Northerner Jan Breughel the Elder, whose Roman sojourn links him with Caravaggio, painted an Allegory of Hearing (Pl. 12) in which the lute is shown in the arms of Venus herself, who sings with Cupid as she accompanies them on her instrument.[23]

Returning to the del Monte *Lute Player* by Caravaggio (Pl. 1), one can now see that although the painting may be taken at face value, as a plausible representation of the performance of monody at the end of the sixteenth century, it also encodes a variety of clues about the cultural meaning of music as an embodied practice in the early Baroque period. For example, rather than attribute his effete appearance to the possibility that the sitter was a castrato, one can see echoes of Ripa's fleshy, overstimulated youth of sanguine temperament and fanciful dress. Or his suggestive tunic and the drapery over his right arm might be seen as a reference to the fabulous power of the music of antiquity—which the humanist musicians of contemporary solo song and opera sought to emulate—not to mention the generic pastoral garb of the theatrical nymphs and shepherds of contemporary *tragicommedia pastorale*, whose tearful laments were often expressed in melancholy solo song. Instead of merely a realistic display of items from Cardinal del Monte's collection, the instruments depicted in the foreground might represent the attributes of Ripa's personification of *La Musica*, or an allegory of the sense of hearing; and the yellowing pages of the music-book suggest not only a prestigious collector's item but also an allusion to the *vanitas* theme, a reminder of the transitory nature of the gratification derived from

---

[21] Ripa, *Iconologia* (1603 edn.), 76.

[22] Slim, 'Mary Magdalene, Musician and Dancer', *Early Music*, 8 (1980), 460–73 at 465.

[23] See Trinchieri Camiz, 'La "Musica" nei quadri del Caravaggio', 199–200.

all the senses, but especially of the elusive nature of musical sonority and the erotic pleasures it accompanies. After all, it is the lute which the performer embraces and not any of the other instruments in the painting—and with its silent strains he invites us to look, to listen, and to love.

And what of the caged bird, the poor little *uccellino* (Pl. 5) which, with the passage of time, has nearly been obliterated from the canvas? Although the nightingale, with its sweet and varied song, also served as an emblem of music, this is actually a finch, perhaps another of the Cardinal's possessions, for both were popular pets in the seventeenth century. Because of its emblematic significance, its presence may be seen to strengthen the interpretation of this painting as an allegory of music and to reinforce its sexual overtones, for a birdcage often symbolizes a brothel in Northern depictions of 'Merry Company' and 'Prodigal Son' scenes.[24] On the other hand, by juxtaposing the songbird and the musician, Caravaggio may have intended some sort of *paragone* between nature and art—a kind of visual analogue to the contest described by Marino in the seventh canto of his *Adone* (published in 1623). In that poem, Mercury beguiles Adonis with a lengthy narrative about the virtuosic encounter between a little nightingale and a lovelorn lutenist.[25] In their increasingly elaborate exchanges, the astonishing songbird combines the expressive qualities of a whole band of instruments, while the skilled musician demonstrates his mastery of the lute by the dextrous variations he produces with his nimble fingers. After twenty-five stanzas, during which the precision of Marino's extravagant language indicates his familiarity with the latest techniques of both singing and lute-playing, that marvel of nature, the unfortunate little bird, finally expires from its efforts to outperform the accomplished musician; and the lute-player, having vanquished his rival, is so remorseful that he lays the nightingale to rest in his instrument, transforming the once sonorous wood into a hollow tomb (stanzas 54–6):

> Poichè molte e molt'ore ardita e franca
> pugnò del pari la canora coppia,
> ecco il pover augel, ch'alfin si stanca,
> e langue, e sviene, e 'nfievolisce e scoppia.
> Così qual face, che vacilla e manca
> e maggior nel mancar luce raddoppia,
> da la lingua, che mai ceder non volse,
> il dilicato spirito si sciolse.

[24] Trinchieri Camiz, 'The Castrato Singer', 180; see also Slim, 'The Prodigal Son at the Whores': Music, Art, and Drama' (Distinguished Faculty Lecture, 1975–76, University of California at Irvine; pub. 1976), 10, 14.

[25] See *Adone*, ed. Giovanni Pozzi (Milan: Mondadori, 1976), vii. 34–56. Further on Marino and Caravaggio, see Elizabeth Cropper, 'The Petrifying Art: Marino's Poetry and Caravaggio', *Metropolitan Museum Journal*, 26 (1991), 193–212.

Le stelle poco dianzi innamorate
  di quel soave e dilettevol canto,
  fuggir piangendo, e da le logge aurate,
  s'affacciò l'alba, e venne il sole intanto.
  Il musico gentil per gran pietate
  l'estinto corpicel lavò col pianto,
  ed accusò, con lagrime e querele,
  non men se stesso, che 'l destin crudele.

Ed ammirando il generoso ingegno
  fin de gli aliti estremi invitto e forte,
  nel cavo ventre del sonoro legno
  il volse sepellir dopo la morte.
  Né dar potea sepolcro unqua più degno,
  a sì nobil cadavere, la Sorte.
  Poi, con le penne de l'augello istesso,
  vi scrisse di sua man tutto il successo.

(Thus for many, many hours bold and fearlessly | the songful pair fought as equals, | but lo the poor bird towards the end grows tired, | and languishes and faints, and grows weak and dies. | Just as the torch that flickers and fades | and redoubles its light as it fails, | from the tongue which never would yield | that delicate spirit freed itself. || The stars, shortly before enamoured | of that sweet, delightful song, | fled weeping, and from the golden loggias | dawn appeared, and the sun rose in the while. | The kind musician, for his great pity | washed the dead little body with his weeping, | and accused, with tears and complaints, | no less himself than cruel destiny. || And admiring the generous spirit | brave and unvanquished until its final breath, | in the hollow belly of the sonorous lute | he wished to bury it after its death. | Nor could Fate ever give a more worthy tomb | to so noble a corpse. | Then, with the feathers of the bird itself, | he wrote down the tale in his own hand.)

In the painting, the outcome of such a contest between musician and song-bird can only be imagined. It is likely, however, that Caravaggio would have wanted his audience to judge the victor to be neither the little prodigy of nature nor the artful music-maker, but rather the painter himself, who imparted through this silent image of music all the complex and multiple levels of meaning that the sonorous art derived from the culture which produced it.

2

The Origins of the Seventeenth-Century Staged *Ballo*

༄༅

IAIN FENLON

THE autumn of 1615 found Claudio Monteverdi at work on a new commission for his old masters, the Gonzaga. More precisely, a court official, Annibale Iberti, had recently been in touch with the composer through the Mantuan Resident in Venice, Camillo Sordi, with instructions that the composer should be commissioned to compose a *ballo* at the specific request of Ferdinando Gonzaga, who now found himself somewhat unexpectedly destined to become the sixth Duke of Mantua. The reasons for the commission are unknown, but it seems likely that it was intended for performance as part of the celebrations planned to mark Ferdinando's official installation early in the new year.[1] Yet beyond the fact of the commission itself, the Mantuans had given precious few details, unlike Ferdinando's direct predecessor (and Monteverdi's first employer at the court), Duke Vincenzo Gonzaga, who, as Monteverdi now put it (in his letter to Annibale Iberti of 21 November 1615), 'used to demand of me such productions either in six, eight or nine movements, besides which he used to give me some account of the invention, and I used to try to fit to it both the harmony and the metres that I knew to be most appropriate and similar'. Here, it seems, the composer was referring to the *Ballo delle ingrate* or to something similar, in which the choreography did not merely consist of a sequence of elaborate geometrical configurations, but operated within a narrative framework. However, Ferdinando had not even suggested appropriate subject-matter, despite his own experience as the author of theatrical entertainments during his student

---

[1] The events are described in Federigo Amadei, *Cronaca universale della città di Mantova*, ed. Giuseppe Amadei, Ercole Marani, and Giovanni Pratico (Mantua: CITEM, 1954–7), iii. 324; for the suggestion that the *ballo* was presented as part of the celebrations, see Leo Schrade, *Monteverdi: Creator of Modern Music* (New York, 1950; repr. London: Gollancz, 1972), 297.

days in Florence and Pisa.[2] Vincenzo had been, as contemporary commentators acknowledged, a great enthusiast for dance since his youth: he was, for example, one of the participants in the first performance of the *Ballo delle ingrate*.[3] Now, in the absence of any such detailed instructions from his son, Monteverdi had returned to the manuscript of another *ballo* in six sections ('mutanze') originally begun with the intention of presenting it to Ferdinando during a projected but unrealized visit by the composer to Mantua during the previous summer. Based on an episode from the pastoral story of Thyrsis and Chloris, written in a style strongly reminiscent of Marino,[4] it had now been completed by adding two more sections. With this text, now despatched to Iberti via Sordi, came Monteverdi's quite precise set of performance directions suggesting that the musicians should be disposed 'in a half-moon, at whose corners should be placed a theorbo and a harpsichord, one each side, one playing the bass for Chloris and the other for Thyrsis, each of them holding a theorbo, and playing and singing themselves to their instruments and to the aforementioned'. Then, 'having reached the ballet movement after they have sung a dialogue, there could be added to the ballet six more voices in order to make eight voices in all, eight *viole da braccio*, a contrabass, a *spineta arpata*, and if there were also two small lutes, that would be fine'.[5] As described, this arrangement implies at least a semi-staged performance: it was evidently intended that both singers and players as well as dancers should be visible, with the two principal continuo instruments spatially separated to support the introductory dialogue, while the vocal forces for the ballet itself were to be arrived at by augmenting the two

[2] For further details, see Antonio Bertolotti, *Musici alla corte dei Gonzaga in Mantova dal secolo XV al XVIII: Notizie e documenti raccolti negli archivi mantovani* (Milan, [1890]; repr. Bologna: Forni, 1969), 86; Stefano Davari, *Notizie biografiche di Claudio Monteverdi* (Mantua, 1885), 107; Edmond Strainchamps, 'New Light on the Accademia degli Elevati of Florence', *Musical Quarterly*, 62 (1976), 507–35; and Iain Fenlon, 'The Mantuan *Orfeo*', in John Whenham (ed.), *Claudio Monteverdi: 'Orfeo'* (Cambridge University Press, 1986), 11–12.

[3] See Federico Follino, *Compendio delle sontuose feste fatte l'anno 1608 . . . nella città di Mantova per le reali nozze del serenissimo prencipe D. Francesco Gonzaga con la serenissima infante Margherita di Savoia* (Mantua: Osanna, 1608), 124, the official Mantuan account of the 1608 festivities.

[4] Nino Pirrotta, 'Monteverdi's Poetic Choices', in id., *Music and Culture in Italy from the Middle Ages to the Baroque* (Cambridge, Mass., and London: Harvard University Press, 1984), 271–316 at 305. From 1608 until 1615 Marino was based at the court of Duke Carlo Emanuele of Savoy, a family united to the Gonzagas through the marriage, in 1608, of Margherita of Savoy to Francesco Gonzaga.

[5] The original letter, from Claudio Monteverdi, Venice, 21 Nov. 1615, to an unnamed court official at Mantua (Annibale Iberti) is preserved in Mantua, Archivio di Stato (Archivio Gonzaga)—hereafter ASM(AG)—Cassetta 6, fos. 136–7; for an English translation with commentary see *The Letters of Claudio Monteverdi*, trans. Denis Stevens (London and Boston: Faber & Faber, 1980), 106–8. Translations in the present essay are taken from this edition, with minor changes where necessary.

soloists with six more singers and a sizeable instrumental ensemble including additional continuo instruments and strings. The dancers presumably used the central area within the half-moon, an arrangement common in contemporary choreographies of set-piece *balli* and particularly reminiscent of Emilio de' Cavalieri's *ballo* which concluded the sixth *intermedio* of the set composed to accompany a performance of Bargagli's *La pellegrina* given in Florence to celebrate the wedding of Grand Duke Ferdinando de' Medici and Christine of Lorraine in 1589.[6] The coincidence is not casual, as we shall see, since the Cavalieri model provided the basis for the tradition of seventeenth-century large-scale danced spectacles, providing a structural framework dependent upon repetition, alternation, and variation on to which later composers grafted additional elements. Indeed, such structures may even have influenced opera performances: marginal notes in the copy of Marco da Gagliano's *Dafne* (Florence: Cristofano Marescotti, 1608) in the Biblioteca Nazionale Centrale, Florence, indicate that the five-part chorus, the *ballo*, and the three-part *risposta* sung by soloists are to be performed three times in succession with new texts.[7]

The manuscript of Monteverdi's *ballo* sent to Mantua by Sordi has not survived among the exceptionally well-ordered papers in the ducal archives; together with other such musical enclosures occasionally referred to in other letters there, it was presumably detached from the correspondence itself so that it could be put to practical use. But as has long been recognized, the work is preserved at least in some form or other in Monteverdi's Seventh Book of 1619, where it is described in the index as 'Tirsi e Clori Ballo. Concert[ato] con voci et Istrumenti a 5'.[8] Following an initial exchange ('Incominciano a parlar in Dialogo Tirsi e Clori') in which the two protagonists are assigned

[6] See the diagrams and accompanying explanation purporting to show the disposition of dancers and musicians on the stage as given in the *Nono parte* of Cristoforo Malvezzi's *Intermedi et concerti fatti per la commedia rappresentata in Firenze nelle nozze del Serenissimo Don Ferdinando Medici e Madama Christiana di Loreno Gran Duchi di Toscana* (Venice: Giacomo Vincenti, 1591), illustrated in *The New Grove Dictionary of Music and Musicians*, ed. Stanley Sadie (London: Macmillan, 1980), iv. 21, and transcribed in D. P. Walker (ed.), *Les Fêtes du mariage de Ferdinand de Médicis et de Christine de Lorraine, Florence 1589: I. Musique des intermèdes de 'La pellegrina'* (Paris: CNRS, 1963, repr. 1986), pp. lvi–lviii. Since the accompanying text is so ambiguous and riddled with errors that it is impossible to reconstruct the sequence of steps with any precision, it seems that the diagram was intended to be commemorative and decorative rather than functional.

[7] Denis Stevens, 'Monteverdi's Earliest Extant Ballet', *Early Music*, 14 (1986), 358–66 at 361.

[8] Claudio Monteverdi, *Concerto: Settimo libro de madrigali a 1. 2. 3. 4. et sei voci con altri generi de canti* (Venice: Bartolomeo Magni, 1619). The book was evidently popular, being reprinted by the original publisher no fewer than four times between 1622 and 1641. Comparison of all the surviving editions reveals no subsequent changes to what appears in the first edition; Magni's typesetters seem to have taken earlier editions as their models for the later ones.

alternate and contrasting strophes before uniting in a final duet (these are presumably the two additional movements which Monteverdi added to the basic structure), the *ballo* itself, sung by the chorus to instrumental accompaniment, begins. Scored in the traditional five parts (instead of the eight implied by Monteverdi's letter), it is cast in six sections, each of which sets one of the six *sestine* of the text; in musical terms, all have the structure and rhythmic characteristics of dance-songs and, with the exception of the final *mutanza*, all are to be repeated. In performance, each *mutanza* would have been accompanied by a different choreography.

Tirsi e Clori was not Monteverdi's last full-scale *ballo*; nor, of course, was it the first, a position occupied in all probability by his best-known work in the genre, the *Ballo delle ingrate* of 1608. The only other example of this kind to survive is 'Movete al mio bel suon le piante snelle', first published in the *Madrigali guerrieri, et amorosi* of 1638, but references in the composer's letters together with stray asides from other correspondents reveal that he must have originally composed many more such pieces, as well as more modest *balli* or *balletti*, such as that based on an episode from the story of Endymion, composed in 1604 and consisting of only four sections.[9] Since, as we now know,[10] Monteverdi remained legally bound to the Gonzaga throughout his career—a fact reflected in the dedications of his publications which appeared after his move to Venice in 1613—the composition of such occasional spectacles probably occupied much more of his time than is apparent from the sporadic remarks in the surviving letters. Already by the first decade of the seventeenth century, the large-scale *ballo* had become an established aspect of courtly spectacle which, as a free-standing independent entertainment making use of elaborate music, intricate choreography, costumes, machines, lighting, and special effects, retained all the readily appreciable 'wondrous' features of the *intermedio* tradition. Indeed, these are its precise historical roots, since as a genre it had evolved in Italy during the last decades of the Cinquecento alongside the more elaborate forms of *intermedi* and the earliest operatic experiments. As such, it had no place in the traditions of official Venetian republican ceremonial, even though Monteverdi is known to have occasionally put together such pieces for patrician patrons.[11] For the most

[9] See Monteverdi's letter to Duke Vincenzo Gonzaga in *The Letters of Claudio Monteverdi*, trans. Stevens, 46–7; the original is in ASM(AG), Cassetta 6, fo. 84. As Stevens notes in his introduction (p. 45), something similar to the plan for the Endymion *ballo* occurs in the *balletto* 'De la bellezza le dovute lodi', a Mantuan work published in the *Scherzi musicali* (Venice: Ricciardo Amadino, 1607). For a discussion of Monteverdi's authorship of this piece, doubted by most earlier writers, see Stevens, 'Monteverdi's Earliest Extant Ballet'.

[10] This will be discussed further in a forthcoming essay by Claudio Annibaldi.

[11] As in the final *ballo* of *Proserpina rapita*, composed to a libretto by Giulio Strozzi and performed in honour of the marriage of Lorenzo Giustiniani and Giustiniana Mocenigo in

part, it was in Mantua that Monteverdi first found himself constructing such elaborate danced spectacles, and it was the Gonzaga who remained his principal employers for this kind of work throughout his career.

In pride of place among these Mantuan 'productions either in six, eight or nine movements' is the *Ballo delle ingrate*, a work which though structurally more complicated than *Tirsi e Clori* still shows notable affinities with it. Specially written for the celebrations marking the marriage of Francesco Gonzaga and Margherita of Savoy in the early summer of 1608, it is set in the mouth of Hades, a scene strongly reminiscent of Monteverdi's *Orfeo*, first produced in Mantua the previous year, and something of a stock scenographical motif in the *intermedio* tradition.[12] As with *Tirsi e Clori*, the piece begins with a dialogue culminating in a duet; then, following a brief interjection from Pluto, the *ingrate* emerge in pairs from the flames and the *ballo* proper starts. Again, in common with the later work, the dance is arranged in six sections, each of which are distinguished by contrasting rhythmic patterns, all of which are to be repeated. At the end, Pluto points the moral of the story in a long *arioso* articulated by an instrumental ritornello, and as the *ingrate* return to the underworld, one of them sings a powerful lament punctuated by short chorus interjections. The interpolation of elements from opera and other new vocal styles is, characteristically, the main way in which Monteverdi secures yet further stylistic enrichment and temporal prolongation of a form which at its most basic consists of a series of instrumentally accompanied *mutanze* to which words were sometimes added. It was not necessary for the composer to have travelled to Flanders in 1599 to have encountered the French roots of this practice, as is sometimes suggested: the *ballet de cour* had already been assimilated by some Italian composers, notably Cavalieri, who had probably encountered it in the strongly Francophile atmosphere of the Medici court.

It is clear that the extant music for Monteverdi's two surviving Mantuan independent *balli* is altogether fragmentary and, at least in the case of the

April 1630. The Mocenigo family were important patrons of Monteverdi during the 1620s; it was for Girolamo Mocenigo (1581–1658), father of Giustiniana, that the *Combattimento di Tancredi et Clorinda* was written for performance in the old Palazzo Dandalo during the carnival season of 1624, and the lost setting of *Armida abbandonata* was also a Mocenigo commission. The music for the *ballo* in *Proserpina rapita* is also lost except for an isolated canzonetta, 'Come dolce hoggi l'auretta', which survives in the posthumous *Madrigali e canzonette . . . libro nono* (Venice: Alessandro Vincenti, 1615). For the text, in eight sections, see Giulio Strozzi, *Proserpina rapita* (Venice: Evangelista Deuchino, 1630), sig. [E3ᵛ].

[12] The music was published thirty years later in the *Madrigali guerrieri, et amorosi con alcuni opusculi in genere rappresentativo* (Venice: Alessandro Vincenti, 1638). For detailed contemporary descriptions of the performance of the *ballo*, see Follino, *Compendio delle sontuose feste*, 124 ff., and Federico Zuccari, *Il passaggio per Italia con la dimora di Parma* (Bologna: Bartolomeo Cocchi, 1608), 24 ff.

Ballo delle ingrate, is probably heavily revised. (As a number of writers have noted, the version in the *Madrigali guerrieri, et amorosi* is derived from a performance given in Vienna in the late 1620s or 1630s; comparison with the text printed in Follino's *Compendio* shows that the words have been altered (a reference to the Mincio is changed to the Danube), and some of the vocal music has evidently been recomposed. In stylistic terms, the music for Pluto is much closer to Seneca's ariosos than to the more formulaic bass writing for Charon or Pluto in *Orfeo*, and Venus' brief engagement with the *genere concitato* (at 'Invan gentil guerriero') can hardly have been composed in 1608.)[13] Yet despite their skeletal and elusive characters, further emphasized by the complete lack of set designs or descriptive choreographies in either case, these two works are among the major monuments to an Italian tradition of full-scale danced spectacle that is one of the most typical products of contemporary court culture. As separate and self-sufficient entertainments, they require large contingents of highly professional performers (dancers, instrumentalists, and singers) united under the direction of a skilled musician. Monteverdi's letter to Iberti speaks of *Tirsi e Clori* being 'directed with a beat suitable to the character of the melodies, avoiding over-excitement among the singers and players, and with the understanding of the dancing-master', and later in the century, Giovanni Battista Doni commended Cavalieri for being adept in both choreography and composition, the perfect combination, as he saw it at the distance of some decades, for those responsible for such elaborate spectacle:

> The *ballo* should be organized by a knowledgeable person, skilled in the one profession and in the other, as was that Signor Emilio del Cavaliere, inventor of that fine *ballo* and of the same air [*aria*] called the *Granduca*; he was not only an extremely expert musician but also a most graceful dancer. He invented that very beautiful dance called the Granduca or the Aria di Firenze, together with that musical pattern so much esteemed for the certain gravity and magnificence that it has.[14]

Although some of the individual musical and choreographic elements which characterize the large-scale *ballo* can certainly be found among the set-piece dances scattered among the more social kinds of dancing in sixteenth-century dance treatises,[15] and even among some of the more professional

---

[13] See, *inter alia*, Peter Holman, ' "Col nobilissimo esercitio della vivuola": Monteverdi's String Writing', *Early Music*, 21 (1993), 577–90 at 583.

[14] Giovanni Battista Doni, *Lyra Barberina . . . Accedunt eiusdem opera, pleraque nondum edita*, ed. Anton Francesco Gori (Florence: Stamperia Imperiale, 1763), ii. 95.

[15] On the similarities and differences between social and theatrical dances in late 16th- and early 17th-c. dance treatises, and in particular in Negri's *Le gratie d'amore*, see Pamela Jones, 'Spectacle in Milan: Cesare Negri's Torch Dances', *Early Music*, 14 (1986), 182–96.

court dances of the Quattrocento, in a work such as the *Ballo delle ingrate* they were fused into a free-standing spectacle of a new kind. Sometimes allied to the new style of *recitar cantando* (as in the case of both Monteverdi's Mantuan *balli*), sometimes interspersed with other musical features, and often laced with a strong dose of dynastic propaganda made almost inevitable through the commonplace Renaissance association (supported and facilitated by classical authority) of dancing with world harmony and order, this inde- pendent court *ballo* has its real roots not so much in the more elaborate court dances described in the pages of Caroso and Negri as in the Franco-Florentine culture of the late sixteenth-century Medici court. A further characteristic of many of the examples is that they were both sung and danced, a matter that was of some theoretical significance, as we shall see, even if composers might seem to be at times indifferent as to whether a *ballo* had words or not. But the most important element which marks off the new large-scale *ballo* from its antecedents is the introduction of a strong narrative element articulated by a variety of musical means, including choruses and solo song as well as through the *mutanze* of the *ballo* itself. In this sense, a work such as the *Ballo delle ingrate*, with its fusion of different musical textures and styles, represents the new genre in its mature form.

In this context, it is not irrelevant that Monteverdi's collaborator in writing the *Ballo delle ingrate* was Ottavio Rinuccini, a slightly older man of noble Florentine birth and classical education who had been involved in preparing entertainments at the Medici court since the age of 27. Rinuccini's involvement in the Mantuan wedding celebrations of 1608, not only as the author of the *Ballo delle ingrate* but also as the librettist of *Arianna*, is just one facet of that enthusiastic embrace of Florentine styles of composition and performance which is so characteristic of the arrangements as a whole. In part a reflection of the personal tastes of Ferdinando Gonzaga, who among other things was an amateur composer who had developed strong contacts with musicians in Florence during his years as a student at the University of Pisa,[16] this accentuation was also the product of the intense artistic rivalry that characterized relationships between the Gonzaga and the Medici. Ferdinando Gonzaga's enthusiasm for music and letters, an interest commented on specifically by the Venetian ambassador Giovanni da Mulla in 1615, took the form of distinct preferences not only for Florentine musicians and composers, but also for secular vocal music, theatrical pieces, and opera.[17]

---

[16] For Ferdinando's musical enthusiasms see the literature cited above, n. 2.

[17] Giovanni da Mulla's remarks are printed in Arnaldo Segarizzi (ed.), *Relazione degli ambasciatori veneti al senato* (Bari: Laterza, 1912–16), i. 140: 'Della poesia si diletta estra- ordinariamente: ha sempre, come si suol dire, per mani tutti li buoni poeti antichi e moderni, cosi volgari come greci e latini, e compone leggiadramente e gode di raccontar quello che

Opera in particular was ideally suited as a vehicle for the demonstration of 'conspicuous consumption', a concept which social historians have identified as central to their discussions of the behaviour of sixteenth- and seventeenth-century European élites.[18] In these formulations, Italian aristocrats of the period do not fit into the conventional model of 'economic man' in the sense that they were not concerned merely with profit and thrift, but, rather, with generating a steady income to spend on luxury goods. This behaviour, seen by both contemporaries and later moralizing historians as irrational and wasteful, was motivated by emulation, the need for socially rising groups to imitate the life-styles of those of a higher social standing.[19] In late sixteenth- and early seventeenth-century Italy, a key and related idea was that of *magnificenza*, which acted as a mechanism for converting wealth into status and power, and which, in turn, was merely one word in a rich vocabulary which contemporaries used to describe élite life-styles. In purely historical terms, the praise of magnificence seems to have begun with the defence of Cosimo il Vecchio's building projects by Florentine humanists, who invoked a Thomist–Aristotelian philosophy; it was St Thomas who had described magnificence as a virtue, while the *Nicomachean Ethics* clearly states that '. . . great expenditure is becoming to those who have suitable means to start with, acquired by their own efforts or from ancestors or connections, and to people of high birth and reputation, and so on; for all these things bring with them greatness and prestige'.[20] So, for families who had already arrived at the summit, conspicuous consumption was regarded as a duty, 'l'obbligazione di viver con fasto', as one contemporary put it, necessary to avoid loss of face and to sustain the honour of the dynasty;[21] the function of such consumption was to distinguish between two families who, as well as being dynastically linked, were also both rivals and equals at the same

ha composto e che sia commendate le sue composizioni. Ha gusto grandissimo della musica ed e in essa molto versato, mettendo egli stesso con molta facilità diverse delle sue composizioni in musica, che la fa poi cantare; e riescono stupendamente.'

[18] For a general introduction to the term, to its origins in the works of the American sociologist Thorstein Veblen, and to its use by later historians of the early modern period, see Peter Burke, *The Historical Anthropology of Early Modern Italy: Essays on Perception and Communication* (Cambridge University Press, 1987), ch. 10 ('Conspicuous Consumption in Seventeenth-Century Italy'); and id., *History and Social Theory* (Ithaca, NY: Cornell University Press, 1992), 67–9. For a classic instance of the deployment of the concept by a historian, see Lawrence Stone, *The Crisis of the Aristocracy, 1558–1641* (Oxford: Clarendon Press, 1965, repr. 1979).

[19] For a recent treatment of these ideas, see Richard A. Goldthwaite, *Wealth and the Demand for Art in Italy 1330–1600* (Baltimore and London: Johns Hopkins University Press, 1993).

[20] A. D. Fraser Jenkins, 'Cosimo de' Medici's Patronage of Architecture and the Theory of Magnificence', *Journal of the Warburg and Courtauld Institutes*, 33 (1970), 162–70.

[21] Burke, *The Historical Anthropology of Early Modern Italy*, p. 134.

time. In this process, awareness of the power of symbolic forms of expression
of precisely the kind with which contemporary courtly theatre is crowded
is fundamental to the struggle for higher status,[22] and competition is the un-
avoidable result. The popularity of the Orpheus myth in early court opera,
for example, or the close parallels between music, text, and drama in the
Peri–Rinuccini *Euridice* and the Monteverdi–Striggio *Orfeo* that have been so
frequently noted,[23] are to be understood in relation to these issues as well
as in terms of artistic emulation.

While the earliest phase of court opera occupies a central position in the
writings of those nineteenth- and twentieth-century music historians who
have judged the phenomenon to be the *fons et origo* of the entire operatic
tradition, the historical reality was different, as recent writers have reminded
us.[24] Furthermore, the critical reaction to the first operas was not over-
whelmingly enthusiastic, a point to which I shall return in detail, and it is
clear that the more familiar features of the *intermedio* tradition were thought
preferable by many in court circles. In this sense, too, early opera was probably a comparatively marginal entertainment in the eyes of contemporaries
when judged alongside the comedies, jousts, tournaments, and *naumachiae*
which normally made up most of the bill of fare in any extended sequence
of dynastic celebrations. The one exception, of course, was the Monteverdi–
Rinuccini *Arianna*, which enjoyed a good deal of well-documented popularity during the first half of the seventeenth century. Yet even in this case,
the enthusiasm was not so much for the complete opera *per se*, but, rather,
for its celebrated lament, as Severo Bonini's remarks and the surviving sources
reveal.[25] Ricciardo Amadino's apparently puzzling decision to issue a second
edition of Monteverdi's *Orfeo* was presumably made to satisfy the collectors'
market for music associated with exclusive environments and grand occasions; certainly the volume itself, which appeared without dedication and

---

[22] There is a large literature on the relationship between *magnificenza* and related concepts
(*pompa, splendore, liberalità, grandezza*, etc.) and court theatre; for a useful summary, see Roy
Strong, *Art and Power: Renaissance Festivals 1450–1650* (2nd rev. edn., Woodbridge: Boydell,
1984), esp. 98–125, 126–52, which deal with festivals at the Valois and Medici courts in the
late 16th c.

[23] See, *inter alia*, Nino Pirrotta, 'Monteverdi and the Problems of Opera', in id., *Music and
Culture in Italy from the Middle Ages to the Baroque*, 235–53; Barbara Russano Hanning, *Of
Poetry and Music's Power: Humanism and the Creation of Opera* (Ann Arbor: UMI Research
Press, 1980), ch. 3; and Gary Tomlinson, 'Madrigal, Monody, and Monteverdi's "via naturale
alla immitatione"', *Journal of the American Musicological Society*, 34 (1981), 60–108.

[24] See, in particular, Lorenzo Bianconi, *Music in the Seventeenth Century*, trans. David
Bryant (Cambridge University Press, 1987), 161–70.

[25] Writing in the 1640s, Bonini claimed that no musical household lacked a copy of the
lament; see his *Prima parte de discorsi e regole sopra la musica*, trans. MaryAnn Bonino (Provo,
Utah: Brigham Young University Press, 1979), 151.

which takes Amadino's first edition as its source and as the model for its typographical layout, shows scant sign of authorial corrections. In short, there is little to suggest that the earliest operas were anything more than rather recherché works of limited appeal; it may well be that a work such as the *Ballo delle ingrate*, shorter in length and more spectacular to watch, was able to amalgamate elements of older traditions together with the new song-styles in a more immediately accessible way.

Rinuccini was well prepared for his task as the librettist of the *Ballo delle ingrate*, having collaborated with Jacopo Peri in the 1590s, first in writing *Dafne* (the first drama to be sung in its entirety 'in the manner of the ancients', first performed privately at the Palazzo Corsi in 1598 and repeated in the following two years), and subsequently in putting together *Euridice*.[26] As far as the *Ballo delle ingrate* is concerned, Rinuccini's most relevant previous experience of writing for danced spectacle was as one of the team involved in putting together the *intermedi* for the 1589 Medici–Lorraine wedding celebrations in Florence, when he was alone responsible for writing the lion's share of the texts; this included the greater part of the first, fifth, and sixth *intermedi*, and all of the second and third. This places Rinuccini firmly in a precise intellectual context, since the texts of these *intermedi* are less a characteristic expression of the Florentine tradition of court entertainments than of the intellectual concerns of the Accademia degli Alterati, whose members included Girolamo Mei (the only non-resident member), Giovanni de' Bardi, and Jacopo Corsi. Founded in the late 1560s, and initially preoccupied with the study and spread of the Tuscan language and its literature, the Alterati later became concerned with dramatic theory and music. Rinuccini had joined the group in 1586 (the same year as Corsi) with the somewhat discouraging academic title of 'il Sonnacchioso' ('the Somnolent One'); among the other members at the time was Giovanni Battista Strozzi, author of the fourth *intermedio* of the 1589 set.[27] According to Bastiano de' Rossi's *Descrizione*, Rinuccini's own task also originally included responsibility for the text of the concluding *ballo* of the sixth *intermedio*, whereas Malvezzi's edition of the music (1591) prints different words 'fatte doppo l'aria del ballo, dalla Laura Lucchesini de Guidiccioni gentildonna principalissima della citta di Lucca'.[28] Since the composition of the choreography, and sometimes

[26] The collaboration between Rinuccini and Peri over *Euridice* is discussed in Tim Carter, 'Jacopo Peri's *Euridice* (1600): A Contextual Study', *Music Review*, 42 (1982), 83–103; for the first performance of the work, see the revised version of Claude Palisca's 'The First Performance of *Euridice*', in id., *Studies in the History of Italian Music and Music Theory* (Oxford: Clarendon Press, 1994), 432–51.

[27] On the Alterati, see Claude V. Palisca, 'The Alterati of Florence, Pioneers in the Theory of Dramatic Music', in id., *Studies in the History of Italian Music*, 408–31.

[28] Bastiano de' Rossi, *Descrizione dell'apparato e degli intermedi fatti per la commedia rappresentata in Firenze nelle nozze de' Serenissimi Don Ferdinando Medici e Madama Cristina di Lorena Gran*

1. Caravaggio,
The Lute Player.
Private collection

2. Nicolas Tournier,
Le Concert. Musée
du Louvre, Paris

4. Annibale Carracci, *The Lute Player Mascheroni.* Staatliche Kunstsammlungen, Dresden

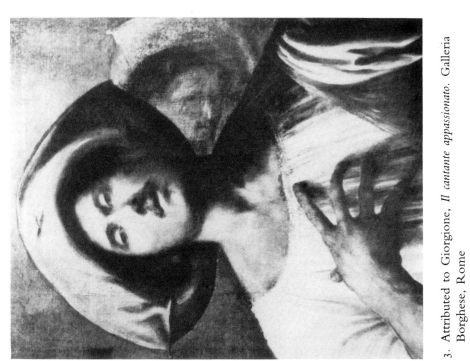

3. Attributed to Giorgione, *Il cantante appassionato.* Galleria Borghese, Rome

5. Caravaggio, *The Lute Player* (Pl. 1). Detail

6. Bartolomeo Cavarozzi, *The Lament of Aminta.* Private collection

7. Caravaggio,
   The Lute Player.
   Hermitage
   Museum,
   St Petersburg

8. Caravaggio,
The Musicians.
The Metropolitan
Museum of Art,
New York

9. Pietro Paolini,
The Concert.
J. Paul Getty
Museum,
Malibu

10. Orazio Gentileschi, *The Lute Player*. National Gallery of Art, Washington, DC

DI CESARE RIPA.

SANGVIGNO PER L' ARIA.

11. 'Sanguine Temperament': woodcut from Cesare Ripa, *Iconologia* (1603)

12. Jan Breughel the Elder, *Allegory of Hearing*. Museo del Prado, Madrid. Detail

13. Set for the sixth *intermedio* for Bargagli's *La pellegrina* (Florence, 1589): engraving by Epifanio d'Alfiano after the design by Bernardo Buontalenti

14. Woodcut from the beginning of Act III of Giovanni Battista Guarini's
Il pastor fido (Venice: Giovanni Battista Ciotti, 1602)

of the music too, often preceded that of the text in later large-scale independent *balli*, it may well be that Rinuccini's text was actually set to music,
particularly since the text remains in the second edition of Rossi's *Descrizione*,
the first edition of which was censored by the Grand Duke in order to give
a more favourable picture of Cavalieri's involvement.[29]

By the late sixteenth century, the interpolation of staged musical spectacles
between the acts of comedies had become a common theatrical practice;
the evidence is there in occasional references within the texts of plays,
and in the theoretical literature.[30] Equally traditional was the idea that the
last of a sequence of *intermedi* should finish with a dance, usually described
as a *moresca*. Yet common though the practice was, most of the examples for
which both music and text survive are of a kind that Nino Pirrotta has called
'aulic' or 'courtly' *intermedi*—elaborate, costly, and untypical versions 'intended to celebrate some particularly important event in the life of a court
and to impress all the guests with their inventiveness and extravagance'.[31]
Despite their obviously ephemeral character, these more elaborate and sophis-
ticated examples of a form of courtly entertainment with which the Medici
had become particularly associated (ever since the Florentine marriage celebrations of Cosimo I and Eleonora of Toledo just fifty years earlier)[32] had

Duchi di Toscana (Florence: Antonio Padovano, 1589), 63–4; see Walker (ed.), *Les Fêtes du mariage*, p. lvi.

[29] For the two editions of the *Descrizione*, see Ulderico Rolandi, 'Emilio de' Cavalieri, il Granduca Ferdinando e l'Inferigno', *Rivista musicale italiana*, 36 (1929), 26–37. At that time, Rolandi owned copies of both editions, which subsequently passed together with the rest of his extensive collection of librettos to the Fondazione Giorgio Cini, Isola di San Giorgio, Venice. Unfortunately, the Fondazione subsequently disposed of the rare first edition, believ-ing it to be a duplicate, and it can no longer be traced. I have not been able to find another copy; until one is identified, Rolandi's article remains the only guide to the textual differences between the two editions. Provisionally, at least, it would seem that since it was necessary to reset only the first gathering, the printer would have been able to salvage the rest of the sheets, making the two versions different states of the same edition.

[30] For a general survey, see the first section of the entry 'Intermezzo' (by Nino Pirrotta and Elena Povoledo) in the *Enciclopedia dello spettacolo*, vi (Rome: Le Maschere, 1959), cols. 571–6. That music was a recognized component of the phenomenon by the end of the 16th c. is evident from practical treatises such as Angelo Ingegneri's *Della poesia rappresentativa* (Ferrara: Vittorio Baldini, 1598), 78 ff.

[31] Nino Pirrotta and Elena Povoledo, *Music and Theatre from Poliziano to Monteverdi*, trans. Karen Eales (Cambridge University Press, 1982), 173. The first part ('Studies in the Music of Renaissance Theatre') of this classic account remains the most detailed and thoughtful introduction to the subject of the role and function of music in *intermedi*; see also the excellent article 'Intermezzo' (by David Nutter) in *New Grove*, ix. 258–69, which is particu-larly useful for the musical aspects of the Florentine court tradition.

[32] For general treatments of Florentine court *intermedi*, particularly in their propagandistic and scenographic aspects, see Alois M. Nagler, *Theatre Festivals of the Medici* (New Haven, Conn.: Yale University Press, 1964; repr. New York: Da Capo, 1974); the relevant entries in Mario Fabbri *et al.* (eds.), *Il luogo teatrale a Firenze: Spettacolo e musica nella Firenze medicea;*

a wide-reaching and long-lasting resonance, spawning a line of increasingly elaborate progeny stretching well into the seventeenth century, where the final monuments to the tradition coexisted alongside other courtly forms, including early court opera, danced spectacles, and equestrian ballets.[33] As has become increasingly clear, these temporally separated sets of *intermedi* are connected by a carefully elaborated common iconographical rhetoric in which myth, legend, state propaganda, and classical allusion were absorbed within a flexible language which, while constantly evolving to take account of new personalities and circumstances, nevertheless was highly dependent upon a strong sense of the past. The role of humanistically educated artistic advisers in this was central; men such as Vincenzo Borghini in 1565, and Bastiano de' Rossi in 1589, were not merely slavishly and unimaginatively reliant upon standard handbooks of *imprese* and other sources, as Seznec suggests;[34] on the contrary, they saw their task as a reinterpretation and re-arrangement of images in a virtuosic display of erudition and classical learning entirely characteristic of the time so as to forge a celebratory vocabulary made up of both universal and locally specific elements.[35] In this sense, the late sixteenth-century Medici *intermedio* tradition was a calculatedly political and dynastic objective long before it was an artistic one. For example, it was in order to pursue the essentially political dimension of the form that detailed descriptions were issued, their function not being that of a libretto intended to describe the meaning of the action to the necessarily restricted and élite audience (some of whom clearly only appreciated the immediately accessible elements of the spectacle rather than the often heavily allegorical

---

documenti e restituzioni (Milan: Electa, 1975), and Strong, *Art and Power*. The principal source for the 1539 *intermedi*, which accompanied a performance of Antonio Landi's comedy *Il commodo*, and which in many respects set the model for later Medici practice, is Pier Francesco Giambullari, *Apparato et feste nelle nozze dello illustrissimo duca di Firenze e della duchessa sua consorte, con le sue stanze, madriali, comedia et intermedij, in quelle recitati* (Florence: Giunti, 1539); the music was published separately, the first set of musical *intermedi* to be treated in this way, as *Musiche fatte nelle nozze dello illustrissimo Duca di Firenze il Signor Cosimo de Medici et della illustrissima consorte sua mad. Leonora da Tolleto* (Venice: Antonio Gardano, 1539). For a modern edition of both with commentary, see Andrew C. Minor and Bonner Mitchell, *A Renaissance Entertainment: Festivities for the Marriage of Cosimo I, Duke of Florence, in 1539* (Columbia, Mo.: University of Missouri Press, 1968).

[33] For which, see Nagler, *Theatre Festivals of the Medici*; Cesare Molinari, *Le nozze degli dei: Un saggio sul grande spettacolo italiano del Seicento* (Rome: Bulzoni, 1968); Fabbri *et al.* (eds.), *Il luogo teatrale a Firenze*.

[34] Jean Seznec, *The Survival of the Pagan Gods* (Princeton University Press, 1972), 279–85, and id., 'La Mascarade des dieux à Florence en 1565', *Melanges d'archéologie et d'histoire*, 52 (1935), 224–43, both of which emphasize the derivative character, as Seznec saw it, of the iconographical programmes of the 1565 and 1589 celebrations.

[35] See, for example, the corrective to Seznec's ahistorical reliance on later concepts of originality implicitly offered in R. A. Scorza, 'Vincenzo Borghini and *Invenzione*: The Florentine *Apparato* of 1565', *Journal of the Warburg and Courtauld Institutes*, 44 (1981), 57–75.

meanings),[36] but, rather, as a vehicle for propaganda, for disseminating beyond the immediate audience the sense of wonder which the performance, with its celebration of a familiar complex of princely virtues, had evoked. It is this, rather than facilitating further performances (which, stripped of their precise, local, dynastic meanings would make little sense anyway), that was also the principal function of engravings showing the sets, and indeed editions of the music, a practice which is continued with the publication of court opera.[37] All these memorial forms allowed much wider access to something which in their original versions had been devised for socially restricted use.

This becomes even clearer when it is realized that Grand Duke Ferdinando's Florentine wedding celebrations in 1589 were considered by the Medici to be as symbolically important as Cosimo I's had been in their time. This is evident from the sheer size and cost of the enterprise and from the months of preparation, much of it jealously guarded from the eyes of foreign observers, that were entailed.[38] Much as Cosimo's marriage had been intended at the

---

[36] For an instance of one anonymous observer who clearly failed to comprehend the extended series of classical allusions upon which Bardi had constructed the 1589 *intermedi*, see the account of his experiences in the copy of his diary now in Paris, Bibliothèque nationale, MS fr. 1550. In the first *intermedio*, for example, he did not recognize Armonia Doria but only 'une Donne qui estoit assise dans une nuee tenant ung lut en sa main'; in the third, simply 'ung homme armé d'un arc et flesche' instead of Apollo, and so on. I am grateful to Professor Margaret McGowan, who will be dealing with this material elsewhere, for sending me a copy of her transcription and allowing me to cite it.

[37] The model for Malvezzi's edition of the 1589 music was probably the *Musiche fatte nelle nozze dello illustrissimo Duca di Firenze il Signor Cosimo de Medici* printed in 1539 by Antonio Gardano; see Mary S. Lewis, *Antonio Gardano, Venetian Music Printer 1538–1569: A Descriptive Bibliography and Historical Study*, i (New York and London: Garland, 1988), 246–9, for a bibliographical description of the print, and Minor and Mitchell, *A Renaissance Entertainment*, for an edition of the music. Some of the issues contingent upon widespread access to élite music that print made possible are explored by Mary Lewis in the introductory first chapter of her study and in her contribution to the round-table discussion 'Produzione e distribuzione di musica nella società del XVI e XVII secolo' published in Angelo Pompilio *et al.* (eds.), *Trasmissione e recezione delle forme di cultura musicale: atti del XIV congresso della Società Internazionale di Musicologia* (Turin: EDT, 1991), i. 319–25.

[38] There is a considerable secondary literature dealing with the 1589 *intermedi*; the fundamental studies remain those of Aby Warburg, 'I costumi teatrali per gli intermezzi del 1589', in *Gesammelte Schriften: Die Erneuerung der heidnischen Antike; kulturwissenschaftliche Beiträge zur Geschichte der europäischen Renaissance*, ed. Gertrud Bing (Leipzig and Berlin: B. G. Teubner, 1932; repr. Florence: La Nuova Italia, 1980), 259–300, with important addenda and excerpts from the *Memorie e ricordi* of Girolamo Seriacopi, the engineer in charge of the stage machinery, on pp. 394–422; and, for the music, the relevant parts of Pirrotta and Povoledo, *Music and Theatre from Poliziano to Monteverdi*. See also Nagler, *Theatre Festivals of the Medici* and Fabbri *et al.* (eds.), *Il luogo teatrale a Firenze*. An account of the preparations, reconstructed from contemporary letters and diaries, is given in Iain Fenlon, 'Preparations for a Princess: Florence 1588–89', in Fabrizio Della Seta and Franco Piperno (eds.), *In cantu et in sermone. For Nino Pirrotta on his 80th Birthday* (Florence: Olschki, 1989), 259–81.

time to etch into the European consciousness the notion of the Medici as
the natural and undisputed rulers of Florence, so too did Ferdinando's represent an ambitious attempt (at precisely a half-century's distance from Cosimo's
marriage, an anniversary of considerable significance, the importance of which
would hardly have been lost upon the Medici and their advisers) to mark
out a new course and at least to temper traditional Imperial allegiances with
pro-French policies. Although in the end this proved to be a tightrope that
Ferdinando found impossible to walk, the political significance of the Lorraine marriage was impressive. Writing at the end of the eighteenth century,
Galluzzi astutely remarked that the 1589 wedding festivities were not simply
a visual spectacle, but also 'uno spettacolo' in a political sense as well.[39] To
the Italian princes and their representatives, and to the cardinals and foreign
ambassadors who gathered in the Pitti Palace where 'tutti applaudirono alla
novità, al genio dell'inventore e alla grandezza di Ferdinando, che giustamente
si meritò la gloria di aver superato in magnificenza tutti i principi d'Italia e
gl'istessi suoi antecessori' ('all applauded the novelty, the talent of the inventor, and the greatness of Ferdinando, who justly merited the glory of having
surpassed in magnificence all the princes of Italy and even his own ancestors'),[40]
the advent of a French princess to the grand-ducal palace seemed to stand
as a prelude to 'strange revolutions' in Italy. It was in part a sense of this mo-
mentousness of the event as much as the familiar pursuit of *magnificenza* that
led to the publicity that the celebrations received, unprecedented even by
Medici standards. Through books such as Bastiano de' Rossi's explanatory
account of the *intermedi* and Malvezzi's separate publication of the music, as
well as the less official accounts that proliferated from the presses of Florence
and elsewhere, a distant vision of these exclusive, private Medici splendours
was brought to an existing readership for such vicarious pleasures not only
in Italy but also beyond the Alps.[41] Somewhat in the same spirit, engravings
of the sets for all six *intermedi* not only brought the visual wonders of the
occasion to a wider audience, but also had a definite impact on later stage

---

[39] Jacopo Riguccio Galluzzi, *Istoria del granducato di Toscana* (2nd edn., Livorno: G. T.
Masi, 1781), iv. 157.

[40] Ibid., iv. 159.

[41] Accounts were published in a number of the major Italian cities; see e.g. Giuseppe
Pavoni, *Delle feste celebrate nelle solenissimi sposi, il sig. don Ferdinando Medici e la sig. donna
Christina di Lorena gran duchi di Toscana . . . Alli molto illustri e miei patroni osservandiss. li signori
Giasone e Pompeo fratelli de' Viziani* (Bologna: Giovanni Rossi, 1589); Simone Cavallino,
*Raccolta di tutte le solennissime feste nel sponsalitio della serenissima gran duchessa di Toscana fatte in
Fiorenza il mese di maggio 1589* (Rome: Paolo Blado, 1589); and the anonymous *Li sontuosissimi
apparecchi trionfi e feste fatti nelle nozze della gran duchessa di Fiorenza . . . Et la descrittione de
gl'intermedi rappresentati in una comedia nobilissima recitata da gl'Intronati senesi*, published in
Ferrara and Venice in the same year.

practice. As for Cavalieri's *ballo*, it developed a separate life of its own, not so much through the work itself (which can hardly have been repeated outside Florence, notwithstanding the appearance in print both of the music and of Cavalieri's schematic description of the choreography), but through the popularity of the *aria* on which it was based. Reworkings of this chordal–bass pattern have been noted in some 240 compositions written in the course of the following century.[42]

Whether or not Monteverdi was among the contingent of Mantuan court musicians lent by Vincenzo Gonzaga to his brother-in-law for the performances of the 1589 *intermedi*,[43] as has sometimes been suggested, there can be little doubt that he was aware of the fame of the *ballo* and of the way that it is constructed, if not of the music itself and its relationship to the political and theatrical context of the *intermedi* as a whole as originally planned. While whatever finally happened in performance is difficult to reconstruct, the dynastic resonances of the original conception are clearly given in Bastiano de' Rossi's authoritative outline in the *Descrizione*. After the comedy proper had finished, the heavens parted to reveal twenty pagan gods (Pl. 13). Seven clouds appeared, five of which slowly drifted to earth, leaving two aloft. The central descending cloud held Apollo, Bacchus, Harmony, and Rhythm, while on another stood the three Graces. The remaining clouds accommodated the Muses. As these came down, three madrigals were sung, the first by Apollo and his group, the second by the three Graces and three of the Muses, and the third by the six remaining Muses.[44] Twenty pairs of mortals in pastoral dress now appeared, enticed by the sound. When the clouds finally reached earth, the gods alighted and, taking the mortals by the hand, taught them how to dance. This Platonic scene, taken from the second book of the *Laws*, provides the pretext for Cavalieri's *ballo*:

[42] See Warren Kirkendale, *L'Aria di Fiorenza id est il Ballo del Gran Duca* (Florence: Olschki, 1972) for an account of the phenomenon, which shows that later composers ignored Cavalieri's upper parts and took the *aria* as the starting point for their own compositions. John Walter Hill, 'O che nuovo miracolo!: A New Hypothesis about the *Aria di Fiorenza*', in Della Seta and Piperno (eds.), *In cantu et in sermone*, 283–322, advances the argument that Cavalieri adapted earlier musical and literary traditions in constructing the *ballo* from the aria, which may be derived from a polyphonic *lauda* which in turn may be related to an earlier *strambotto*.

[43] See Iain Fenlon, *Music and Patronage in Sixteenth-Century Mantua* (Cambridge University Press, 1980, 1982), i. 128–32, where some of the Mantuan musicians who participated, including Alessandro Striggio *père et fils* and the Pellizzari sisters who were part of Vincenzo Gonzaga's *concerto di donne*, are identified. It is by no means certain that Monteverdi was in Gonzaga service at the time of the Florentine celebrations; for a review of the evidence, see Paolo Fabbri, *Monteverdi* (Turin: EDT, 1985), 32.

[44] Here, as in other places, Malvezzi's edition and Rossi's description are seriously at odds in their account of this first part of the sixth *intermedio*; for the differences, see Walker (ed.), *Les Fêtes du mariage*, pp. li–liii.

But the gods, in their compassion for the hardships incident to our human lot, have appointed the cycle of their festivals to provide relief from this fatigue, besides giving us the Muses, their leader Apollo, and Dionysus to share these festivals with us and keep them right . . . Now animals at large have no perception of the order or disorder in these motions, no sense of what we call rhythm or melody. But in our own case, the gods of whom we spoke as given us for companions in our revels have likewise given us the power to perceive and enjoy rhythm and melody. Through this sense they stir us to movements and become our choir-leaders. They string us together on a thread of song and dance, and have named our 'choirs' so after the delight [*chara*] they naturally afford.[45]

The choice of this passage as the basis for the scene is not casual; together with Lucian's *De saltatione*, Plato's *Laws* was the source of information about danced and sung choruses in the ancient world that was best known in the Renaissance. Interestingly, if Giovanni de' Bardi can be credited with the authorship of the anonymous *Trattato della musica degli antichi* printed by Doni in the *Lyra Barberina*, as Claude Palisca has proposed, then a conception of the chorus as dancing and moving while singing was clearly familiar in the very Florentine circles responsible for much of the 1589 *intermedi* as well as for the intellectual frameworks that supported them.[46] By this point in the century, knowledge of both Plato and Lucian's testimonies to ancient choral dancing would seem to have been quite widespread, and not merely among classical scholars who might have known the original texts or works such as Carlo Valgulio's proem to Plutarch's *De musica*, which clearly reveals a knowledge of Lucian;[47] Rinaldo Corso's *Dialogo del ballo* of 1554, for example, draws heavily on Lucian and also cites Plato's *Laws*, while Angelo Ingegneri is explicit on the point that choruses were both sung and danced in the ancient world.[48] It may well have been widespread knowledge of these sources that also prompted Guarini to experiment with sung and

[45] Plato, *The Laws*, trans. Alfred Edward Taylor (London: Dent, 1934), 30.

[46] For the Renaissance reception of Lucian, see Christopher Robinson, *Lucian and his Influence in Europe* (London: Duckworth, 1979), 81–2. Bardi's authorship of the *Trattato* is discussed in Claude V. Palisca, 'A Discourse on the Performance of Tragedy by Giovanni de' Bardi(?)', *Musica disciplina*, 37 (1983), 327–43; see also id., *The Florentine Camerata: Documentary Studies and Translations* (New Haven, Conn., and London: Yale University Press, 1989), ch. 5, where the *Trattato* is both edited and translated.

[47] On Valgulio, see Claude V. Palisca, *Humanism in Italian Renaissance Musical Thought* (New Haven, Conn., and London: Yale University Press, 1985), 88–110; and id., *The Florentine Camerata*, 13–44, where a facsimile of the 1507 edition and an English translation are provided.

[48] See G. Tani, *Storia della danza: Dalle origini ai nostri giorni* (Florence: Olschki, 1983), 432–4, where Corso's reliance on Lucian is demonstrated; and Evanghelos Moutsopoulos, *La Musique dans l'œuvre de Platon* (Paris: Presses Universitaires de France, 1959), 97–156, which discusses Plato's influence on the *Dialogo*. Ingegneri's remarks on the subject are in *Della poesia rappresentativa* (1598), 26.

danced choruses in the celebrated *Giuoco della cieca* in *Il pastor fido*. From his letters describing the attempts to rehearse and perform the play in Mantua in 1592, it is clear that the choreography of the *Giuoco* was planned first, then the music composed, and finally the text added. Moreover, in his own notes to Ciotti's authoritative edition of the play, published in 1602 together with seven illustrations by Francesco Valesio, one of which incorporates a moment from the dance itself (Pl. 14),[49] Guarini himself points out that the text of the *Giuoco* consists of lines of unequal length arranged to meet the requirements of the music, whose rhythm was in turn dictated by the dance steps.[50] These priorities are strikingly reminiscent of Cavalieri's 1589 *ballo*, and indeed, since the Mantuan attempts to mount the play in 1592 failed, it was Cavalieri himself who was the first to set the scene as a discrete entertainment in his lost version of 1595.[51] This was, in turn, just one of a number of independent sung and danced spectacles spawned by the text, including Gastoldi's music for the 1598 Mantuan production.[52] As for Cavalieri himself, the idea that a sung and choreographed *ballo* formed part of reconstructing ancient practice is implied in the preface to the *Rappresentatione di Anima, et di Corpo* of 1600, which finishes with just such a dance of this kind.[53]

[49] See Adriano Cavicchi, 'La scenografia dell'*Aminta* nella tradizione scenografica pastorale ferrarese del secolo XVI', in Maria Teresa Muraro (ed.), *Studi sul teatro veneto fra rinascimento ed età barocca* (Civiltà veneziana studi, 24; Florence: Olschki, 1971), 63–8, where it is argued that the illustration reflects the 1598 Mantuan performance of the play; and Ahuva Belkin, 'Leone de' Sommi's Pastoral Conception and the Design of the Shepherds' Costumes for the Mantuan Production of Guarini's *Il pastor fido*', *Assaph: Studies in the Theatre*, 3 (1986), 58–74.

[50] For further discussion of the difficulties surrounding the rehearsal of the *Giuoco* in 1592, see Fenlon, *Music and Patronage in Sixteenth-Century Mantua*, i. 149 ff.

[51] See Warren Kirkendale, 'L'opera in musica prima del Peri: Le pastorali perdute di Laura Guidiccioni ed Emilio de' Cavalieri', in *Firenze e la Toscana dei Medici nell'Europa del '500* (Florence: Olschki, 1982), ii. 365–95 at 373–4, and the literature cited there.

[52] Late 16th- and 17th-c. settings of the *Giuoco della cieca* are listed and discussed in Arnold Hartmann, Jr., 'Battista Guarini and *Il pastor fido*', *Musical Quarterly*, 39 (1953), 415–25 at 419–21, as part of a more general account of the importance of Guarini's play as a source of texts for madrigal composers. It cannot be assumed that any of these settings, even when they treat the complete scene, were actually written for theatrical performance, let alone to be danced. The one clear exception is Gastoldi's sequence of four madrigals designed to be interpolated between the speeches of Amarilli, Mirtillo, and Corisca in the Mantuan performance of 1598; see Fenlon, *Music and Patronage in Sixteenth-Century Mantua*, i. 152 for further details. Hanning, *Of Poetry and Music's Power*, 80–1, discusses Giovanni Ghizzolo's 'fully-fledged cantata in *stile rappresentativo*' from his *Madrigali et arie . . . a una, et due voci* (Venice: Alessandro Raverii, 1609).

[53] Emilio de' Cavalieri, *Rappresentatione di Anima, et di Corpo* (Rome: Niccolò Mutij, 1600), dedication: 'quello stile, co 'l quale si dice, che gli antichi Greci e Romani nelle scene, e teatri loro soleano a diversi affetti muovere gli spettatori'; 'a dar la perfettione, che si puotesse, a questo genere di musica affettuosa'. The passage is clearly principally concerned with the *stile recitativo*, but the final *ballo* presumably formed part of Cavalieri's conception of theatre 'all'antica'.

The choice of Plato's description of the gods' gifts of music and dance to humanity as the subject-matter for the *ballo* of the sixth *intermedio* is, then, drawn from a humanistically inspired tradition of theorizing about ancient choral dancing that must have been familiar to the Bardi circle, the question of the authorship of the *Trattato* notwithstanding. In its realization, Cavalieri's *ballo* presents a number of novel procedures. In terms of size alone, the conception is unparalleled in the repertory of sixteenth-century theatrical dance, as is the ingenious sequence of rhythmic variations on the simple musical material announced in the opening and closing sections of the piece, variations which also exploit textural contrast between full and three-voice material. As can be seen from F. W. Sternfeld's recent illustration of the overall design of the *ballo*, it is almost entirely symmetrical, with only the coda falling outside the scheme.[54] By devising this procedure, Cavalieri had essentially opened the way for more complex balletic scenes; by operating different permutations and variations much larger structures could be constructed. For all its apparent conflict with prevailing notions of the relationship of music and words within the *seconda prattica*, a conflict which, as in the case of some other categories of late sixteenth-century Italian music, can be arrived at only by misdirecting contemporary theorizing (including Monteverdi's own), the hierarchical ordering of choreography–music–words is not all that surprising. An obvious and traditional feature of all Renaissance choral dancing is that the function of the text was primarily metrical and not affective, a point that Monteverdi himself explicitly recognizes in a letter of February 1620 to his old collaborator, Alessandro Striggio. Once again, the Gonzaga had turned to their former employee for a staged *ballo*, presumably (in view of the date of the letter) for performance during Carnival alongside the composer's settings of Striggio's eclogue *Apollo* and Marigliani's *Andromeda*.[55] Since it had not yet been decided whether or not the work was to be sung, Monteverdi now asked for the words, if any, to be sent, 'for which I shall try (in setting them) to invent something in the metre that you gave me. But should there be one metre in all the verses, I shall certainly change the tempo from time to time.'[56] That questions of accentuation and rhythm took

[54] F. W. Sternfeld, *The Birth of Opera* (Oxford: Clarendon Press, 1993), 95.

[55] For the arrangements for the carnival of 1620, see Monteverdi's letters to Striggio (9, 16 Jan.; 1, 8, 15, 22 Feb. 1620) and to Ercole Marigliani (15 Feb. 1620) in *The Letters of Claudio Monteverdi*, trans. Stevens, 159–63, 167–78, and the commentaries printed there. All the originals are in ASM(AG), Cassetta 6. On *Andromeda*, once thought to have remained uncompleted and hence unperformed, see now Albi Rosenthal, 'Monteverdi's "Andromeda": A Lost Libretto Found', *Music & Letters*, 66 (1985), 1–8, and Iain Fenlon, 'Mantua, Monteverdi and the History of *Andromeda*', in Ludwig Finscher (ed.), *Claudio Monteverdi: Festschrift Reinhold Hammerstein zum 70. Geburtstag* (Laaber: Laaber Verlag, 1986), 163–73.

[56] ASM(AG), Cassetta 6, fos. 188–9, letter of Claudio Monteverdi, 1 Feb. 1620, to an unnamed recipient (Alessandro Striggio) in Mantua; the translation differs slightly from the one in *The Letters of Claudio Monteverdi*, trans. Stevens, 167.

priority over sense in the composition of choral *balli*, even to the extent that the existence of the literary text itself could be a matter of comparative indifference, is equally clear from another passage in Monteverdi's letter of 1615 to Annibale Iberti about *Tirsi e Clori*:

> While I am sending it [the ballet] off by the hand of the Resident [Camillo Sordi] to Your Lordship [Iberti], I also thought it a good idea to accompany it with a letter of mine addressed to Your Lordship, to tell you at the same time that if His Most Serene Highness [Duke Ferdinando Gonzaga] should want either a change of air in this [*ballo*], or additions to the enclosed [movements] of a slow and grave nature, or fuller and without fugues (His Most Serene Highness taking no notice of the present words which can easily be changed, though at least these words help by the nature of their metre and by imitating the melody), or if he should want everything altered I beg you to act on my behalf so that His Most Serene Highness might reword the commission, since, as a most devoted servant, and most desirous of acquiring His Highness's favour, I shall not fail to carry it out in such a way that His Highness will be satisfied with me . . .[57]

The 1589 *intermedi* are often categorized as the high point, if not virtually the final instalment, of a theatrical genre that was to be rapidly replaced by the opera in the early years of the seventeenth century. Such cosily Darwinian notions underestimate the inherent conservatism of the Italian courts and the easy appeal of the large-scale spectacles which they continued to mount; equally, they misrepresent the complex process of cross-fertilization between prevailing fashions for the pastoral, for aspects of the *intermedio* tradition, and for other current musical styles on the one hand, and for the more recent monodic styles on the other, that critically determined the language of early court opera. In this context, Cavalieri's *ballo* should be seen not merely as an idiosyncratic if gargantuan instance of the *moresca* which by convention closed the final *intermedio* of every set, but as a radical adaptation of existing court dance traditions. As such, it provided a model for a whole series of self-contained danced spectacles composed for the Italian courts, of which Monteverdi's Mantuan *balli* are simply the most prominent survivals in a tradition which became particularly popular in early seventeenth-century Florence with the work of Buonarroti, Salvadori, and Saracinelli.

Despite the evident success of the 1589 *intermedi* as a whole, Medici entertainments took a different and decidedly more adventurous artistic direction during the 1590s. Or rather, they were taken, since it was undoubtedly Cavalieri's position of pre-eminence at court, confirmed by his appointment

[57] ASM(AG), Cassetta 6, fos. 136–7; letter of Claudio Monteverdi, 21 Nov. 1615, to an unnamed recipient (Annibale Iberti) in Mantua; the translation differs slightly from the one in *The Letters of Claudio Monteverdi*, trans. Stevens, 107.

as overseer of artists, craftsmen, and musicians in 1588 and consolidated by his successful direction of what in effect had been the most lavish and prestigious series of *intermedi* ever produced, that set the tone. For the carnival season of the following year, Cavalieri organized three dramatic presentations: two pastorals, *Il satiro* and *La disperatione di Fileno*, for which he composed the music himself to texts by his collaborator in the *ballo* of the previous year, Laura Guidiccioni, and an elaborate production of Tasso's *Aminta* with sets and machines by Buontalenti. The new vogue for the pastoral was clearly in the ascendant, and it is no surprise that Guarini's *Il pastor fido*, still to be published in an authoritative edition sanctioned by the poet, was chosen as the source for the *Giuoco della cieca* adapted by Guidiccioni, set to music by Cavalieri, and presented in the Hall of Statues of the Palazzo Pitti for the visit of Cardinal Montalto in the autumn of 1595.[58] Yet by the time of the next important dynastic event, the wedding of Henri IV of France to Maria de' Medici in 1600, Cavalieri had started to lose effective control of artistic arrangements at court, partly because of his long absences in Rome and to some extent on account of the barely disguised hostility of the Medici musical establishment. In this sense, it is indicative of the shifting alliances among the main *animateurs* of court spectacle that the main theatrical event of the celebrations, *Il rapimento di Cefalo*, was the work of Giovanni de' Medici and Giulio Caccini, leaving Cavalieri the undoubtedly less prestigious task of setting Guarini's occasional piece *La contesa fra Giunone e Minerva* for performance during the official banquet.

Music historians might be inclined to attach more importance to *Euridice*, which Cavalieri was responsible for producing, but this was probably not a contemporary perception, even if the opera was subsequently printed, for although *Euridice* was presented before an audience of aristocrats and courtiers, it was promoted not by the Medici themselves but rather by Jacopo Corsi. As with Monteverdi's *Orfeo*, first presented before the members of the Mantuan Accademia degli Invaghiti largely at the instigation and with the active collaboration of Prince Francesco Gonzaga, who was responsible for some of the practical details including the borrowing of singers from Florence,[59] *Euridice* was designed to appeal to a refined intellectual audience, perhaps one rather different from that for the more immediately appealing performance of a comedy with *intermedi*, though even in this case those who were privileged enough to gain admittance, a group which evidently included foreigners of sufficiently elevated social rank, were often blissfully unaware

---

[58] Angelo Solerti, *Musica, ballo e drammatica alla corte medicea dal 1600 al 1637* (Florence: Bemporad, 1905; repr. Hildesheim: Olms, 1969), 19.

[59] For further details, see Fenlon, 'The Mantuan *Orfeo*', 1–19, and the documentation there in App. I.

of the complicated scaffolding of classical allegory and allusion on which *intermedi* were based. The gap, for example, between the detailed justifications of Bastiano de' Rossi's *Descrizione* of the 1589 set, in which even the colours of costumes are related to antique precedent, and the understanding of Barthold von Gadenstedt, who saw them, is considerable.[60] In this context, it is worth noting that for at least some of those accustomed to the imposing sonorities of the *intermedio* tradition, the new Florentine singing style could sound dry and sterile; one member of the audience for *Euridice* compared it to the 'chanting of the Passion', while one of Cardinal Aldobrandini's entourage who was present at the performance of *Il rapimento di Cefalo* candidly remarked that 'the style of singing easily led to boredom'. Inevitably, Cavalieri's view was different, and he later claimed that those who had seen both his *Rappresentatione di Anima, et di Corpo* in February 1600 and the more traditional celebrations in Florence later in the same year found the *Rappresentatione* 'more to their taste, because the music moved them to tears and laughter and pleased them greatly, unlike this music of Florence, which did not move them at all unless to boredom'.[61] This difference is perhaps more apparent than real (the *Rappresentatione* is full of solo music rather in the manner of Peri and Caccini), but the contemptuous phrase 'this music of Florence' gives the game away and reminds us that it was over the Medici wedding celebrations of 1600 that Cavalieri finally broke with Florence. On the one hand, he considered the chaotic presentation of everything except the banquet to be a sad reflection on his overall management, while on the other, Rinuccini's claim in the dedication to the libretto of *Euridice* that he and Peri had been the first to revive the ancient manner of reciting in music drove him to angry public refutation. Matters could only have been made worse by Caccini's extravagant remarks in the dedication of his own *Euridice*, published just two months later, that he had been composing dramatic

[60] Part of Barthold von Gadenstedt's journal (Wolfenbüttel, Herzog August Bibliothek, Cod. Guelf. 67.6 Extrav.) that relates to the 1589 *intermedi* is given in W. F. Kummel, 'Ein deutscher Bericht über die florentinischen Intermedien des Jahres 1589', *Analecta musicologica*, 7 (1970), 1–19. Von Gadenstedt's inability to recognize even the most obvious mythological references in the *intermedi* is paralleled by the observations of a French witness (see above, n. 36).

[61] Both quotes are taken from Claude Palisca's article on Cavalieri in *New Grove*, iv. 20–3; see also Tim Carter, '*Non occorre nominare tanti musici*: Private Patronage and Public Ceremony in Late Sixteenth-Century Florence', *I Tatti Studies: Essays in the Renaissance*, 4 (1991), 89–104. And note the remarks of Vincenzo Giustiniani (*c.*1628): 'This recitative style . . . proved to be so crude and without variety of consonances and ornaments that if the ennui that was felt had not been mitigated by the presence of such performers, the audience would have left the seats and the room quite empty' (in *Hercole Bottrigari, 'Il Desiderio . . .'; Vincenzo Giustiniani, 'Discorso sopra la musica'*, trans. Carol MacClintock (Musicological Studies and Documents, 9; American Institute of Musicology, 1962), 77.

monodies for the previous fifteen years. Whatever the effect on Cavalieri, this rather limited form of pamphlet war, conducted for the benefit of a small audience via the specialized literature of opera scores and librettos, can only have strengthened his resolve not to return to Florence after the débâcle of the Medici wedding.

While in artistic terms the marriage of Henri IV to Maria de' Medici marked the end of operatic experiment for public occasions, in political ones it signalled the high point in Grand Duke Ferdinando's Francophile policy, evident since the beginning of his reign in 1587 and fully expressed through his own marriage to Christine of Lorraine. At first, it had seemed that with the support of France—the 'unico riparo' that the Italian princes had against Spain—it would be possible to preserve the peace and what was left of the independence of Italy. That, at least, was the explanation for Ferdinando's new alliance offered by the Venetian ambassador, Francesco Morosini, in his report to the Senate made on his return to Venice in 1608. But in the years immediately after 1600, Ferdinando came to feel that his support for Henri IV had been at the expense of that balanced relationship with the leading European powers—France, Spain, and the Empire—which it was essential for any small Italian state to maintain. In an attempt to correct the disequilibrium, the Grand Duke now embarked on a strategy to secure the marriage of his eldest son, Cosimo, to the Archduchess Maria Magdalena of Austria, who, as daughter of the Archduke, first cousin to the Emperor, and sister to the Queen of Spain, embodied the possibility of an alliance which would conveniently unite the Medici with both the Spanish and the Austrian wings of the Empire. Negotiations began in 1602, soon became delayed by the endless Spanish and Austrian attempts to improve their bargaining positions, and finally seemed to be reaching some sort of agreement by the summer of 1607. By this time, the Florentines were sufficiently convinced of a successful conclusion that they took the first steps to prepare the usual series of celebrations to accompany the wedding; in the event, their plans did not reach fruition until over a year later.

Almost in tandem with these diplomatic manœuvres, the Gonzaga were separately pursuing their own ambitions to secure the marriage of Francesco Gonzaga, heir to the duchy, and Margherita, daughter of Duke Carlo Emanuele of Savoy. Discussions had begun as early as 1604, and at first the signs seemed auspicious. But when the possibility of an alliance between Mantua and Savoy became known, it posed a threat to other interests, not least to Emperor Rudolf II, who became alarmed by the union of two fiefs of the Holy Roman Empire, while another Habsburg, Philip III, was acutely conscious that his north Italian territories lay between Mantua and Savoy. These interests united to present the somewhat bizarre proposal that the aged Rudolf himself should become Margherita's suitor, principally in an attempt to forestall the Mantua–Savoy match. The history of delay and prevarication that ensued had the effect of postponing firm agreement until late 1607, by which time plans for celebrating the marriage could not be realized until the following year.[62] Originally, it had been intended that both the marriage and Ferdinando Gonzaga's elevation to the cardinalate should be celebrated during Carnival, but in the event the latter was marked by a performance of Marco da Gagliano's *Dafne*, while the wedding celebrations were deferred until late May, when some two weeks of festivities took place. The almost simultaneous conclusion of both sets of negotiations meant that lavish wedding celebrations of considerable dynastic importance were mounted in Florence and Mantua at more or less the same moment. And particularly since the Gonzaga and the Medici were themselves related through marriage, this also produced some strangely ambiguous artistic consequences, marked on the one hand by an apparent willingness to co-operate through the exchange of personnel, and on the other by an intense rivalry to secure the best artists, designers, engineers, musicians, and choreographers. Such ambiguities are a further potent reminder of the importance of the twin concepts of conspicuous consumption and the competitive model for a better understanding of the progress of events.

A brief history of those events makes the point even more clearly. In June 1607 one of the Grand Duke's secretaries wrote to Michelangelo Buonarroti 'il giovane', whose play *Il natale d'Ercole* had been presented in 1605, hoping to enlist his help in the search for 'qualche poesia o invenzione' that could be elaborated into a comedy, by convention the main entertainment on such occasions.[63] In passing, we should note that the request was not for a finished play, but for the idea on which such a work could be based. After some negotiation, it was decided to mount Buonarroti's *Il giudizio di Paride*, which ironically enough had originally been commissioned for the Gonzaga wedding as early as 1605 but had never been performed because of the subsequent delay caused by the protracted wedding negotiations. At the beginning of September the Grand Duke was able to write to his sister Leonora, Duchess of Mantua, that 'Le nozze con l'aiuto di Dio si faranno alla fine di questo mese' ('the wedding, with God's help, will be held at the end of this month'),[64] and even if, as things turned out, this prediction was over-optimistic, at the

[62] An excellent outline of the Mantuan negotiations and some of their musical consequences is given in Stuart Reiner, 'La vag'Angioletta (and others): i', *Analecta musicologica*, 14 (1974), 26–88.

[63] For much of what follows, see Tim Carter, 'A Florentine Wedding of 1608', *Acta musicologica*, 55 (1983), 89–107.

[64] Letter from the Grand Duke, Florence, 7 Sept. 1607, to his sister, the Duchess of Mantua, in Mantua; ASM(AG) 1093.

time it seemed appropriate to begin the initial preparations for *Il giudizio di Paride*. These started in late 1607, and by the beginning of December much of the music for the *intermedi* had already been composed, since separate requests from the Duke and Duchess of Mantua to the Grand Duke for the loan of Florentine court musicians were courteously refused 'perché essendo ancor'io vicino a simil bisogno' ('because I, too, am close to such a require-ment').[65] In the event, it was not until almost a year later, on 18 October 1608, that the Archduchess made her formal entry into Florence. At the cathedral, the traditional blessing by the ecclesiastical authorities was given, and music for four choirs, each of which descended from the cupola on a cloud, was performed. These spiritual decencies observed, the full ceremo-nial machine was started up, beginning with a banquet and *calcio* match in the Piazza Santa Croce and continuing via Francesco Cini's *La notte d'Amore* (a sequence of short scenes interspersed with dancing)[66] to finish with a *balletto de' cavalli* (something of a novelty, later to become a Florentine speciality), and finally a mock naval battle on the Arno.[67] Buonarroti's com-edy and its spectacular accompanying *intermedi* were presented in the middle of this seemingly endless series of events, and evidently with some success, since it was revived in November for the Duke of Mantua, who had been unable to attend the first performance.

The sixth and final intermedio for *Il giudizio di Paride* provides an im-portant part of the context for Monteverdi's *Ballo delle ingrate*. Perhaps with the miscalculations of 1600 still relatively fresh in the collective mind, the organizers of the 1608 celebrations returned not to the experimental spirit encouraged by Cavalieri but to the safer waters of more traditional theatrical

---

[65] Carter, 'A Florentine Wedding of 1608', 91, also citing earlier literature on this point.

[66] The music has not survived, but it seems from contemporary descriptions that the dancing in *La notte d'Amore* utilized choreographies taken from social dancing, a common practice in theatrical dances. See, for example, the letter of the Mantuan agent Gabriele Bertazzuolo to the Duke of Mantua cited in Solerti, *Musica, ballo e drammatica*, 55: 'quando era per finirsi l'atto, uscivano con li recittanti persone che havevano a ballare con le dame, le quali finito di cantare scendevano dal Palco et ballavano con varii modi di balletti . . .' ('when the act was about to end, there entered with the actors persons who were to dance with the ladies who, when they had finished singing, descended from the stage and danced with various types of dances'). The terminology is indicative. For Bertazzuolo, see also Paolo Carpeggiani, 'Studi su Gabriele Bertazzolo, i: Le feste fiorentine del 1608', *Civiltà mantovana*, 12 (1978), 14–56.

[67] For more on the festivities as a whole, see the standard accounts in Nagler, *Theatre Festivals of the Medici*; Angelo Solerti, *Gli albori del melodramma* (Milan: Sandron, 1904–5; repr. Hildesheim: Olms, 1969); and id., *Musica, ballo e drammatica*. Also useful is the material brought together in Fabbri *et al.* (eds.), *Il luogo teatrale a Firenze*. The principal contemporary printed source is Camillo Rinuccini, *Descrizione delle feste fatte nelle reali nozze de' Serenissimi Principi di Toscana D. Cosimo de' Medici e Maria Maddalena Arciduchessa d'Austria* (Florence: I Giunti, 1608); this survives in a number of different editions, at least one of which includes engravings.

spectacles. The parallels between the 1608 *intermedi*, composed to texts by all the major Florentine poets except Ottavio Rinuccini, and those for *La pellegrina*, which were almost entirely written by him, are otherwise strong. Nowhere is this more apparent than in the sixth *intermedio*, *Il tempio della Pace*, concocted by Buonarroti himself from a variety of sources. According to the original draft for the scene, it

> will show onstage the temple of Peace, made entirely of gold, full of statues and open to the audience. From underground will appear a throne, with a large number of priests and other people associated with Peace. Peace will descend from the heavens on a cloud with twelve Virtues to judge the competition between four gods each vying for the favour of the Prince. These gods, Bellona, Berecynthia, Pluto and Neptune, will descend from the heavens at the same time on their cloud to give the impression that they have come to find Peace. When Peace has reached the throne they will rehearse several arguments and she will decree that each of them should attend him, favouring him with their respective attributes. Then the stage will open to reveal two grottoes, one of minerals and gems in which sits Proserpine with many gods, and the other of mother-of-pearl, coral and other sea-treasures, containing Amphitrite and other marine gods. Pluto and Neptune each descend into their respective grottoes while Berecynthia and Bellona stay on the ground. The heavens open and a sung *ballo* is begun by zephyrs in the heavens and several people around the throne on the ground. At the end of this Bellona and Berecynthia each call up their own gods and goddesses, Bellona's military and Berecynthia's civil, who come to the new celebration. From one side of the stage Bellona's gods, and from the other Berecynthia's, appear in two groups to renew and augment the dancing and singing. With an epithalamium to the bride and groom, sung now by many, now by a few, now by solo voices, the celebration ends with great harmony.[68]

In the event, preparations for the sixth *intermedio* ran into difficulties, as Caccini reported:

> Finding myself yesterday evening in the Piazza S. Giovanni, numerous gentlemen told me that Most Serene Madame no longer wanted our *balli* of the sixth *intermedio* because Signor Don Grazia Montalvo had composed one to be danced by many Florentine gentlemen and this would suffice . . . Her Highness should be told that all the beauty was reserved for this sixth *intermedio*, in which Signora Ippolita, Signora Vittoria [Archilei] and Melchior [Palentrotti] the bass, all three belonging to my school, sing alone, and solo, as a duo and as a trio joining together one after the other. There is also a *ballo* of six ladies,

---

[68] Carter, 'A Florentine Wedding of 1608', 94, citing Buonarroti's scenario for the sixth *intermedio* from papers in the Archivio Buonarroti, Florence; for the final version of the *intermedio*, see Rinuccini, *Descrizione delle feste . . .* (1608), 52.

sung, played and danced to instruments, that is different from all others, and
then at the end there is another *ballo* performed by twenty or thirty dancing-
masters and sung and played by 64 musicians. Inform Her Highness that this
type of sung, played and danced *ballo* has always been prized above all other
balli and much more so than the morescas performed in Mantua as I described
them from an account by Signor Chiabrera, their author. Invention is more
necessary than dancing-masters in producing novel *balli*, and since Chiabrera
represented the Olympic Games in the Mantuan comedy the *ballo* of our sixth
intermedio cannot produce this effect, for the subject matter is different. If
Signor Don Grazia invents another, not for this will it be more beautiful than
the *ballo* performed in Mantua, for it will destroy our *ballo*, which needs nothing added to it. If Most Serene Madame will recall that the *ballo* most praised
in Mantua was the one devised by Signor Ottavio Rinuccini [the *Ballo delle
ingrate*] and performed outside the comedy, then she could take advantage of
the present occasion and of my advice, which if ignorant is not without good
intentions, so that the festivities may pass with the grandeur and nobility
appropriate to Their Highnesses and to the custom of this city.[69]

Caccini's position was, of course, a highly partisan one. Part of his objection
to these last-minute proposals for the final *intermedio* was that members of his
famous *concerto* would no longer be involved ('If Signor Don Grazia invents
another . . . it will destroy our *ballo*, which needs nothing added to it'). And
it is clear that, at least in Caccini's eyes, this trio of singers who 'sing alone,
and solo, as a duo and as a trio joining together one after the other' was one
of the highlights of the scene. This much one might expect, given all that
we know of Caccini's personality and of the troubled history of his Florentine
concerto since the 1580s. Of more interest in the present context, however,
are his remarks, unusually comparative for the period, about the various *balli*
presented in Mantua, since from the detail in Caccini's letter it is clear that
he is referring to the various staged entertainments given earlier that year to
mark the marriage of Francesco Gonzaga to Margherita of Savoy.

These Mantuan festivities had begun on 24 May with Margherita's *entrata*[70]
and had continued with Monteverdi's *Arianna*, allegedly given before 4,000
spectators in a specially constructed theatre, a naval battle with fireworks
(*Assedio di un castello sul lago*) devised by the court engineer Gabriele
Bertazzuolo,[71] Giovanni Battista Guarini's *L'idropica* (the principal theatrical

---

[69] Carter, 'A Florentine Wedding of 1608', 96.

[70] The principal sources are Follino, *Compendio delle sontuose feste*; Solerti, *Gli albori del melodramma*, i. 73–103; Amadei, *Cronaca universale*, ii. 222–49. For further discussion, see Fabbri, *Monteverdi*, 124–48.

[71] See, in addition to the general sources cited in the previous note, the detailed study of this aspect of the entertainments in Paolo Carpeggiani, 'Teatro e apparati scenici alla corte dei Gonzaga tra Cinque e Seicento', *Bollettino del Centro Internazionale di Studi di Architettura Andrea Palladio*, 17 (1975), 101–18.

presentation), given together with elaborate *intermedi*, and Prince Francesco's own tournament *Trionfo d'amore*, before arriving at the *Ballo delle ingrate* given by sixteen dancers, including both Duke Vincenzo and Prince Francesco Gonzaga, on 3 June. There was also another *ballo*, *Il sacrificio di Ifigenia* to a text by Alessandro Striggio.

The starting-point for Caccini's comparison is the *intermedi* devised by Chiabrera for Guarini's play, and particularly the fourth *intermedio*, which included a set of dances alluding to the Olympic Games. According to Follino's description of this scene, this fourth *intermedio* seems to have consisted of a sequence of *balli* interspersed with sung madrigals, before concluding with twenty-four dancers coming together for a battle-dance. The interest of Caccini's remarks lies in his distinction between this conventional kind of theatrical dance, to which he attaches the generic label *moresca*, and the 'type of sung, played and danced *ballo* [that] has always been prized above all other *balli*'. As an example of the latter type, he recalls 'the *ballo* most praised in Mantua . . . devised by Signor Ottavio Rinuccini and performed outside the comedy', that is, the *Ballo delle ingrate*. It is with this more elaborate kind of danced spectacle that Caccini associates the final *ballo* of *Il giudizio di Paride*. This evidently involved sixteen dancers, and about seventy-five musicians divided into two six-part vocal and instrumental choirs typical of late sixteenth-century *intermedi* in their scoring. Within this large group, there was a smaller one of six sopranos (singing two to a part), a bass, and instrumentalists who performed their own *ballo* within the *intermedio*. It is elements such as the structural contrast between large and small ensembles, both of whom sing, dance, and play, and even in smaller musical details such as high textures and the guitar accompaniment of the group of soloists that this *ballo* (of which the music, by Santi Orlandi, is lost) is strikingly reminiscent of Cavalieri's final dance for the 1589 *intermedi*.

In more general terms Caccini's letter reflects an important historical development in the history of dance. What seems to have happened is that towards the end of the sixteenth century a new type of danced *ballo* became popular in court entertainments given in Florence, beginning with Cavalieri's final *intermedio* for *La pellegrina*. This elaborate form of danced spectacle is distinguished both by being choral and by its reliance upon specially devised choreography rather than the stock formulas of court dance, or even newly written court dances for amateur performance. In essence, this was a professional enterprise which needed to be worked out by someone talented in the arts of both choreography and musical composition—'a knowledgeable person', as Doni later put it, 'skilled in the one profession and in the other, as was that Signor Emilio del Cavaliere, inventor of that fine *ballo* and of the same air [*aria*] called the *Granduca*; he was not only an extremely expert

Iain Fenlon

musician but also a most graceful dancer'. The idea of a lengthy and elaborately choreographed ballet as an integral part of court spectacle lies at the heart of the French *ballet de cour* tradition of the 1570s and 1580s, a tradition which was in essence an invention of an Italian choreographer (Balthazar de Beaujoyeulx) and a Medici queen (Caterina de' Medici).[72] Although numerous artists, dancers, musicians, and poets contributed to the final result, it was Caterina de' Medici who, with a highly developed notion of the *ballet* as a political instrument, was responsible for devising these entertainments, as Brantôme confirms. It is clear that these developments must have been known in Florence, where on the structural foundations established by Cavalieri the impressive and still largely unstudied tradition of court danced spectacle was founded.

[72] For further details of the French–Florentine connection, see Fenlon, *Music and Patronage in Sixteenth-Century Mantua*, i. 154 ff., and the literature cited there.

3

D'India the Peripatetic

᠀᠀᠀

GLENN WATKINS

DESPITE a rich chain of evidence to the contrary, it is frequently asserted that the birth of solo song coincided with the arrival of the Baroque. Even allowing for the special circumstances that prompted the renewal of solo singing towards the end of the sixteenth century, it is an especially confusing judgement that links its ascension at the dawn of the Baroque with the supposed demise of outworn polyphonic forms, figures, and textures. In addressing the dilemmas of similar stereotypes throughout the range of music history, musicologists have for some time been preoccupied with promoting a sense of continuity in those periods characterized by striking aesthetic shifts. If this desire to acknowledge formal and expressive reciprocity inevitably conscripts uncertainty in the location of a boundary line, the madrigal has none the less provided an exemplary testing ground. Although Monteverdi's significant status and justly acclaimed achievements in the domain of madrigal and opera have promoted both genres as ideal for observing the transferral of late Renaissance polyphonic techniques to early Baroque form and expression, the need to evaluate similar exchanges between generic and stylistic categories in the work of his contemporaries stems from the contention that no single figure ought to be required to stand for an age; that, indeed, only to the extent that the impulse is discoverable in the works of others can the dimension as well as the importance of such achievements be properly assessed. The music of Sigismondo d'India (born c.1582, died before 19 April 1629) offers an excellent opportunity for evaluating such questions. Nigel Fortune and Federico Mompellio were the first to pique our curiosity about this musician, laying the foundation for all work that followed.[1] Happily, the gradual appearance of d'India's music in modern editions and our

---

[1] Nigel Fortune, 'Sigismondo d'India: An Introduction to his Life and Works', *Proceedings of the Royal Musical Association*, 71 (1954–5), 29–47; Federico Mompellio, *Sigismondo d'India, musicista palermitano* (Milan: Ricordi, 1956).

increasing familiarity with it in the concert hall and through recordings in recent years now permit a somewhat amplified view.[2]

While d'India's first publication was a collection of five-voice madrigals of 1606, a collection of monodies appeared shortly thereafter in 1609, and the remainder of his career was devoted to producing works in both genres. His first book of madrigals reveals a composer not only soundly schooled in the techniques of late Renaissance polyphony but also in total control of its expressive means. The title-pages of these first collections proclaim the author as 'nobile palermitano', a title which he continued to use in his next five publications, that is to say, up to the time when he entered the employ of the Duke of Savoy at Turin in 1611. Following Mompellio, however, Paolo Emilio Carapezza has recently revived the notion that Sigismondo was perhaps the son of Carlo d'India, *nobile palermitano*, who lived in Naples around 1595.[3] If this is true, the composer may have been born there and received his early training at a time that saw Giovanni de Macque in residence. Whatever the force of d'India's early musical encounters with southern repertories, the fact that his *Delle villanelle alla napolitana, a tre voci . . . Libro primo* was published by Gio. Giacomo Carlino and Costantino Vitale in Naples in 1608 (a second book appeared in 1612) confirms his awareness of Neapolitan forms and styles, a sensibility that is further asserted in the musical language of his first collection of five-voice madrigals.

D'India's setting of 'Cruda amarilli, che col nome ancora' provides a rich illustration of the musical inheritance claimed by the composer in his *Primo libro de madrigali a 5 voci* (Milan: Agostino Tradate, 1606). Giovanni Battista Guarini's text (from *Il pastor fido*, I. ii) had already been set to music at least five times before d'India approached his task, and in each instance by a composer of the first rank. Giaches de Wert and Luca Marenzio head the list with pieces published at the ends of their lives (1595); Benedetto Pallavicino and Claudio Monteverdi follow with settings appearing respectively in 1600 (*Il sesto libro de madrigali a cinque voci*, Venice: Angelo Gardano) and 1605 (*Il quinto libro de madrigali a cinque voci*, Venice: Ricciardo Amadino). Arriving in Mantua in 1606, d'India wrote and dedicated his first book of madrigals to Duke Vincenzo Gonzaga, and his knowledge of the madrigals of Wert,

[2] D'India's *opera omnia* are being edited in the series 'Musiche rinascimentali siciliane' (Florence: Olschki): ix (1989), ed. John Joyce, including *Le musiche a una e due voci: Libri I, II, III, IV e V* (1609–23); x (1980), ed. Glenn Watkins, including the *Ottavo Libro de madrigali a cinque voci* (1624); xiv (1995), ed. Glenn Watkins, including *Il terzo libro de madrigali a cinque voci* (1615).

[3] Paolo Emilio Carapezza, '"Quel frutto stramaturo e succoso": Il madrigale napoletano del primo Seicento', in Domenico Alessandro D'Alessandro and Agostino Ziino (eds.), *La musica a Napoli durante il Seicento: Atti del convegno internazionale di studi, Napoli, 11–14 aprile 1985* (Rome: Edizioni Torre d'Orfeo, 1987), 17–27 at 25; Mompellio, *Sigismondo d'India*, 7–8.

Pallavicino, and Monteverdi, all of whom served at the Mantuan court, can surely be assumed.

> Cruda Amarilli, che col nome ancora
> d'amar, ahi lasso, amaramente insegni.
> Amarilli, del candido ligustro
> più candida e più bella,
> ma de l'aspido sordo
> e più sorda e più fera e più fugace,
> poi che col dir t'offendo,
> i' mi morrò tacendo.

(Cruel Amaryllis, whose very name | alerts us, alas, to the bitterness of love! | Amaryllis, paler and more beautiful | than the pale privet-flower, | but than the deaf adder, | more deaf, more wild, and more evasive, | since by speaking I offend thee, | I shall die in silence.)

The fact that Monteverdi's setting of 'Cruda Amarilli' comes from a time at least as early as Pallavicino's publication is known to all students of the Artusi–Monteverdi controversy.[4] Artusi had published extracts from it (minus the words) in 1600, ignoring the textual impulse and condemning its unbridled use of dissonance. Clearly, any decision to set this text after that date would have necessarily implied entrance into a continuing debate. Yet the earlier settings by Wert (in his *Undecimo libro de madrigali a cinque voci*, Venice: Angelo Gardano) and Marenzio (in his *Settimo libro de madrigali a cinque voci*, Venice: Angelo Gardano) were not ignored by later composers anxious to cite the authority of the past in announcing their own conservative or wayward solutions. Indeed, the relationship between these five pieces centres only partially on the varieties of dissonance singled out by Artusi. Thus Marenzio is obviously Monteverdi's model in a number of details, including texture and pitch in the opening and final lines. And as Mompellio noted almost forty years ago, d'India clearly borrows from Pallavicino for the initial suspensions used to portray the opening word (Ex. 3.1). But like Monteverdi, d'India also broadcasts his indebtedness to Marenzio at several internal points, as at 'Ma de l'aspido sordo' (Ex. 3.2), which is as near a direct quotation as anything could be. The most telling section, however, is the close, beginning with 'Poi che col dir t'offendo' (Ex. 3.3). The

---

[4] See Claude V. Palisca, 'The Artusi–Monteverdi Controversy', in Denis Arnold and Nigel Fortune (eds.), *The New Monteverdi Companion* (London and Boston: Faber & Faber, 1985), 127–58; Tim Carter, 'Artusi, Monteverdi, and the Poetics of Modern Music', in Nancy Kovaleff Baker and Barbara Russano Hanning (eds.), *Musical Humanism and its Legacy: Essays in Honor of Claude V. Palisca* (Festschrift Series, 11; Stuyvesant, NY: Pendragon Press, 1992), 171–94; Charles S. Brauner, 'The *Seconda pratica*, or the Imperfections of the Composer's Voice', ibid. 195–212.

Ex. 3.1. 'Cruda Amarilli': *a* Pallavicino; *b* D'India (upper voices only)

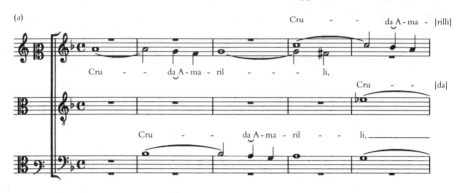

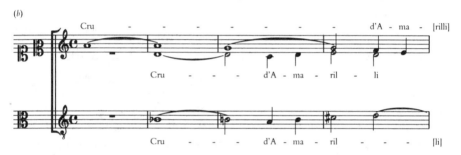

(Cruel Amaryllis . . .)

dissonance at 't'offendo' seems clearly addressed to Artusi and his followers —a wilful stance, so to speak, directed at securing d'India's position in the circle of *seconda prattica* composers. Similarly, the double chromatic inflections at 'io mi morrò' stand at the crest of an intense period of discovery and point to Gesualdo only as the nearest and most dramatic model. Moreover, the tetrachordal figures (marked *x*, *y*, *z*), both chromatic and diatonic, announce a familiarity with the arguments of Vicentino and the authority of the ancients, as well as with the solutions of Marenzio, Wert, Pallavicino, and Monteverdi at this precise point in the text (Ex. 3.4). They confirm in their rising and falling forms the multiple psychological perspectives perennially attendant on the word 'morrò', and they arguably prepare the way for the use of similar tetrachords in the later Baroque lament.[5]

---

[5] Vicentino, for example, used the descending chromatic tetrachord to set the opening of 'Jerusalem convertere' (from the Lamentations of Jeremiah) in his *L'antica musica ridotta alla moderna prattica* (Rome: Antonio Barré, 1555). See also Ellen Rosand, 'The Descending Tetrachord: An Emblem of Lament', *Musical Quarterly*, 65 (1979), 346–59, for a consideration

Ex. 3.2. 'Cruda Amarilli': *a* Marenzio; *b* D'India

(*a*)

Ma   de   l'a - - spi - do   sor - - do

(*b*)

Ma   de   l'a - - spi - do   sor - do

(. . . but than the deaf adder . . .)

Notice of such stylistic matters is undertaken not as pro forma musicological detective work. Rather, in establishing the credentials of *seconda prattica* composers according to the criteria of its formulator, we must constantly remind ourselves of its constituent ingredients. For if the recognition of a *seconda prattica* based upon text–music relationships is to have any bearing upon the arrival of what a later age has come to term the Baroque, then it is important that we do not perpetuate definitions of a new age limited only to the familiar perspectives of texture and form. The notion of a marriage between pioneering textural or dramatic perspectives and the valuable and hard-won techniques of the Mannerist polyphonists not only accentuates a sense of continuity but also, paradoxically, brings a fresh focus, and any consideration of one without the other may distort our view of the gradual emergence of new and striking orientations. Indeed, it is the Mannerist's awareness of multiple stylistic options that feeds an emerging Baroque sensibility. If the collage techniques of the Mannerist typically throw the spotlight on the seams between adjoining particles, the Baroque artist's tendency to conceal as he conflates ought not deflect us from observing the legacy.

of the influential role of the diatonic minor tetrachord as used by Monteverdi in his *Lamento della ninfa* (1638); and James Chater, '"Cruda Amarilli": A Cross-Section of the Italian Madrigal', *Musical Times*, 116 (1975), 231–4.

Ex. 3.3. D'India, 'Cruda Amarilli'

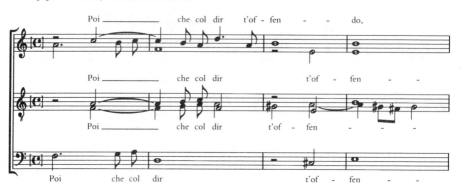

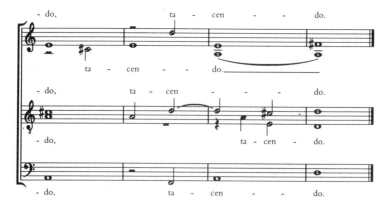

(... since by speaking I offend thee, I shall die in silence.)

Ex. 3.4. 'Cruda Amarilli': *a* Wert; *b* Marenzio; *c* Pallavicino; *d* Monteverdi

Ex. 3.4. (*cont.*)

(*c*)

(*d*)

(. . . I shall die in silence.)

D'India affords an ideal test case and virtually forces a comparison between fading Renaissance and emerging Baroque perspectives in his resetting of 'Cruda Amarilli' in the first book of *Musiche . . . da cantar solo* (Milan: Heirs of Simon Tini and Filippo Lomazzo, 1609).[6] Here he sets only the *prima parte* of the fuller text extracted from Guarini's *Il pastor fido* by Monteverdi, Wert, Marenzio, and Pallavicino. But just as his abbreviated text endorses the epigrammatic proclivities of the late polyphonic madrigal, so words like 'fugace' receive a more extended treatment in their monodic setting. D'India now introduces chromaticism at the close on 'offendo' instead of on 'morrò', and in so doing he proffers not so much a correction as an alternative. Although he endorses the breathless style and cross-relations of the polyphonists, he renounces the unadorned falling seventh in the *canto* of his 1606 setting for the final cadence of his monodic version. The invocation of this very interval elsewhere in the 1609 collection at internal points on words such as 'cruda', 'pietre', and 'nuovi tormenti', however, suggests that for his solo version of 'Cruda Amarilli' the monodic practice of notated diminutions at cadential points has taken precedence over other expressive alternatives.[7]

As one might expect, there are numerous instances of the re-elaboration of other composers' madrigals in d'India's *I a 5* of 1606, just as d'India himself appears to have been taken as a model by later composers such as Piero Benedetti and Lelio Bertani. Few collections of the period mirror more dramatically the ingredients of a rapidly changing aesthetic in Italian secular music. Its clear relation to a past tradition and its demonstrable connection with an emerging Baroque sensibility are only part of the fascination that resides in the music of virtually every page. D'India is as sure-handed as, if somewhat more inventive than, the youthful Schütz in his op. 1 of five years later. He employs the most advanced harmonic vocabulary of the masters of Ferrara and Naples without hesitation even as he discloses an interest in developing quasi-*parlando* textures that reveal an affinity with the canzonetta tradition, visible in his treatment of 'e con la rimembranza di quel giorno' ('and with the memory of that day') in the second madrigal of the collection, 'Al partir del mio sole'.[8] The use of specific vocal figurations, such as dotted quaver–semiquaver patterns that coalesce in parallel thirds (as in the final

[6] See d'India, *Le musiche a una e due voci*, ed. Joyce, 32–3.

[7] Indeed, it is possible to view the final cadence of 'Cruda Amarilli' as a pitch-specific ($d''–e'$) embellishment of the polyphonic version. The unembellished melodic seventh is to be found elsewhere in the 1609 volume in 'Donna, i' vorrei dir molto' (at 'guardo'), 'Là tra le selve in solitario orrore' (at 'cruda'), 'Piange madonna et io' (at 'nascer'), 'O se torna il mio sol di raggi adorno' (at 'pietre'), and 'Andate a mitigar, sospiri ardenti' (at 'nuovi tormenti').

[8] See Sigismondo d'India, *Madrigali a cinque voci, libro primo*, ed. Federico Mompellio (Milan: Ricordi, 1942), 6.

madrigal of the collection), also bespeak an awareness of the contemporary Monteverdi. Something of this eclecticism was to appear in future collections by d'India, but a tighter focus soon prevailed.

Indeed, in the *Libro secondo de madrigali a cinque voci* (Venice: Angelo Gardano &c., 1611) there is a decisive stylistic shift, and a few characteristics are used so repeatedly that their resultant effect seems to hover over the entire collection as an adopted *maniera*. These features include a high tessitura, readily confirmable in the choice of clefs; a general abandonment of linear chromaticism countered by an increased reliance upon cross-relations, especially in quaver motion; and a pronounced attraction to the cadence type familiar to Ferrarese madrigalists of the 1590s that 'evaporates' to a single pitch. But the most characteristic trait is the insistent use of syllabic patterns in quavers that show a pronounced proclivity to settle into *parlando* recitation. The first bars of 'Tempesta di dolcezza', which opens the collection, provide a good example (Ex. 3.5a). The effect speaks not only of a heightened attention to textual clarity or of an expansion of the short syllabic bursts of quavers that occasionally appeared in the First Book, but also of a purposeful investigation of the power of declamation that helps to clarify the transition from Wert to the new *stile recitativo*. This undoubtedly reflects not only d'India's familiarity with the polyphonic madrigals of Wert, which he could hardly have avoided encountering during his stay in Mantua, but also his growing experience as a solo singer and composer of monodies. In fact, it is a technique that Claudio Saracini was to remember in his monody on this very text published three years later in his *Le musiche. . . a una, e due voci* (Venice: Giacomo Vincenti, 1614; Ex. 3.5b). The poem is by Giambattista Marino, whose verses (including such favourites as 'Tornate, o cari baci' and 'O chiome erranti') dominate d'India's volume; his preferred poet for his First Book, Guarini, is now virtually abandoned.

The title-page of d'India's *Terzo libro de madrigali a cinque voci* (Venice: Bartolomeo Magni, 1615) contains the following statement: 'Con il suo basso continuo da sonar con diversi instromenti da corpo a beneplacito; ma necessariamente per gli otto ultimi'. This recalls the title-page of Monteverdi's Fifth Book (1605), where the final six numbers are similarly singled out. Indeed, the connection with Monteverdi becomes increasingly evident throughout the volume, for while the initial twelve pieces suggest an amalgamation of the various *maniere* of the first two books, the continuo here appears gratuitous and rarely moves beyond the role of a *basso seguente*. But before setting aside this group of madrigals as the conservative relics of a fashion now in decline, some brief comment is appropriate.

The first books of madrigals and of monodies that d'India published following the death of Gesualdo in 1613 were this Third Book of five-voice madrigals (1615) and *Le musiche . . . Libro terzo* (Milan: Filippo Lomazzo,

Ex. 3.5. 'Tempesta di dolcezza': *a* D'India; *b* Saracini

(A storm of sweetness pours over my soul . . .)

1618). In both, we find settings of 'Mercè! grido piangendo', a text which had already been set by Gesualdo (*Madrigali a cinque voci. Libro quinto*; Naples; Gio. Jacomo Carlino, 1611) and Pomponio Nenna (*Il quinto libro de' madrigali a cinque voci*; Naples: 'Gio. Battista Sottile, 1603) in their most progressive chromatic idiom: this prompts a consideration of Gesualdo's legacy. Alfred Einstein proposed d'India as one of the few genuine successors to Gesualdo, though his basis for a comparison of their styles was probably limited to d'India's *I a 5* as edited by Mompellio in 1942.[9] Although the stylistic

[9] Alfred Einstein, *The Italian Madrigal* (Princeton: Princeton University Press, 1949; 2nd edn., 1971), 717. It should be noted that Einstein's transcriptions now held at Smith College, Northampton, Mass., contain no polyphonic madrigals by d'India.

connection is confirmable in d'India's later works, it is as intermittent as it is conspicuous. Indeed, his setting of 'Mercè! grido piangendo' declines the audacious harmonies adopted by Gesualdo at 'morrò dunque tacendo', a passage which in 1635 still left Giovanni Battista Doni stupefied. Thus although the choice of text would appear to underscore d'India's southern origins and his Neapolitan connections, his rejection of exaggerated chromaticism and the lack of any reference to the parodic relationship of the Gesualdo–Nenna settings of this text announce the progress of a transforming aesthetic.[10] Although d'India's use of subtle chordal inversions (the hanging 6-4 at 'piangendo', for example) may betray a retrospective glance, the expressive melodic intervals in the *canto*—the falling minor seventh at 'tacendo' and diminished seventh at 'tesoro'—clearly betray his experience not only as a polyphonist but also as a monodist. Indeed, three years later d'India was further to dramatize his inclination through a setting of the same text as a monody. The adoption here of details from his polyphonic version affords a further opportunity to judge the effects of moving from one medium to another, and of transferring expressive aims to an only partially new form.[11] Moreover, there is perhaps another point to be made here. As I have noted, d'India's twin settings of 'Mercè! grido piangendo' appeared in his first two publications following the death of Gesualdo in 1613, and it is likely that they were written with the accusations of plagiarism made by Gesualdo in the preface to his *Madrigali a cinque voci. Libro quinto* of 1611 clearly in mind. Pointedly, 'Mercè! grido piangendo' is the twelfth and last number in d'India's *III a 5* for which the continuo part is optional; the remaining eight madrigals have an obligatory accompaniment. By resisting an instrumental support, d'India effectively challenged Gesualdo and Nenna on their own turf, and without resorting to the extreme chromaticism, 'luxuriant' melismas, or rhythmic posturing that typically results from such a juxtaposition.

But if the first twelve madrigals of this collection constitute a somewhat backward look, in the final eight settings d'India presents solutions, both technical and expressive, that surpass all his previous works, monodic as well as polyphonic. Here he adopts a true continuo that leaves the individual vocal parts free above an anchoring harmonic accompaniment. In addition, however, one can see a new formal ingredient involving *contrapposto*, the simultaneous juxtaposition of different texts, frequently with dramatic intent and not as the natural consequence of dovetailing phrases. This can involve the use both of short figures, as in '"Lasso", dicea Fileno' (Ex. 3.6), and longer ones, as in 'Ardemmo insieme, bella donna, et io'. The former, which

[10] For a discussion with musical illustrations, see Glenn Watkins, *Gesualdo: The Man and his Music* (2nd edn., Oxford University Press, 1991), 218–20.
[11] Ibid. 244.

Ex. 3.6: D'India, ' "Lasso", dicea Fileno'

('Alas', said Fileno to his beautiful Chloris: 'You said to me "die", and I . . .')

provides a dramatic portrayal of the sigh by isolating and reiterating the single word 'Lasso' in a chain of expanding and contracting intervals subjected to variable transposition, not only comes close to the spirit of ' "T'amo mia vita", la mia cara vita' of Monteverdi's Fifth Book or even the later *Lamento della ninfa* of the *Madrigali guerrieri, et amorosi*, but also reveals the capacity of manipulated textual elements to achieve notable formal as well as dramatic implications. Furthermore, it is immediately apparent that the intermittent solo voices are not self-sustaining and that they require the

harmonic support of the continuo. Although Monteverdi and others had
flirted with similar textures without an obligatory continuo, as in 'Che dar
più vi poss'io?' (in Monteverdi's Fifth Book), it is clear that the destruction
of homogeneous voice groupings and the new proportion and psychological
effect of d'India's setting derive directly from Monteverdi's discoveries in the
continuo madrigal.

Other structural devices such as sequence and refrain, familiar throughout
the Renaissance but now beginning to assume a new function and power,
are pursued by d'India in 'O rimembranza amara' (again in *III a 5*). Francesco
Rasi was the first to set this text to music in his collection of monodies published in 1608 (*Vaghezze di musica per una voce sola*, Venice: Angelo Gardano
&c.): given that he was also the author of the text, any future setting would
of necessity imply a direct artistic confrontation. D'India, having received his
first permanent employment at the court of Savoy in 1611, was obviously
anxious to exhibit his talents in anticipation of future patronage, and he may
well have felt that his expertise as both a polyphonist and a monodist could
best be demonstrated through the adoption of a concertato format. It is also
significant that Rasi's reputation had initially been cemented through his
participation in the first performances of Peri's *Euridice* and Caccini's *Il
rapimento di Cefalo* (both 1600), Marco da Gagliano's *Dafne* (1608), and
through the creation of the title-role of Monteverdi's *Orfeo* (1607). D'India,
who was vying for recognition as singer, lutenist, and composer in the north
Italian courts during this very period, could hardly have chosen a more
worthy target than Rasi in choosing to set both 'O rimembranza amara' and
another text set by Rasi, 'Indarno Febo il suo bell'oro eterno'. Rasi, proclaimed by Cavalieri as early as 1593 as a singer and chitarrone-player of rare
powers, had studied under Caccini and later served at Gesualdo's court from
*c.*1594 to 1596.[12] In 1597 his appointment to the Gonzaga court signalled the
beginning of a continuing relationship with Mantua for the remainder of his
life, including the period around 1606 when d'India was there and wrote his
first book of madrigals. Finally, d'India's Third Book is dedicated to Marcus
Sitticus, Archbishop of Salzburg. Half Italian and, like Gesualdo, a nephew
of Carlo Borromeo, Sitticus had vigorously promoted cultural exchange
across the Alps. Under his express encouragement, both monody and opera
were introduced to Salzburg through productions and by inviting foreign

[12] See Carol MacClintock, 'The Monodies of Francesco Rasi', *Journal of the American
Musicological Society*, 14 (1961), 31–6 at 31; Anthony Newcomb, 'Carlo Gesualdo and a
Musical Correspondence of 1594', *Musical Quarterly*, 54 (1968), 409–36 at 409; and especially
Warren Kirkendale, 'Zur Biographie des ersten Orfeo, Francesco Rasi', in Ludwig Finscher
(ed.), *Claudio Monteverdi: Festschrift Reinhold Hammerstein zum 70. Geburtstag* (Laaber: Laaber
Verlag, 1986), 297–335.

artists: Rasi went there in 1612. Thus, d'India's open challenge to Rasi seems clearly directed at Sitticus just as the archbishop was seeking appropriate candidates for his patronage.

A comparison of the distribution of time-honoured madrigalian approaches to key words confirms that it is more in larger formal issues that d'India demonstrates the crucial differences between his and Rasi's approaches. While d'India's setting of 'Indarno Febo' shares Rasi's elaborate melisma on 'suono' and similar figurations for 'il suo bell'oro eterno' and 'e Cintia mi disvela' at the opening, and presents an ornate treatment of 'vento' and dual melismas in thirds on 'argento' in place of Rasi's semibreves, it is in fact Gabriello Chiabrera's canzonetta-like refrain ('ch'io lontano da voi') that affords the opportunity for the most telling distinction.[13]

> Indarno Febo il suo bel oro eterno,
>   e Cintia mi disvela il puro argento,
>   ch'io lontano da voi nulla nón scerno.
> E mov'indarno lusinghevol vento,
>   e tra bell'erbe di ruscell'il suono,
>   ch'io lontano da voi nulla non sento.
> Ohimè, dell'esser mio poco ragiono:
>   ch'io lontano da voi nulla non sono.

(Though Phoebus unveils for me his lovely eternal gold, | and Cynthia her pure silver, | I see nothing when I am far away from you. | Though gentle breezes blow, | and the rivulet murmurs in the grasses, | I hear nothing when I am far away from you. | Alas, I speak little about myself, | for I am nothing when I am far away from you.)

While the invitation in the text for a musical reprise is accepted by both composers, d'India dramatizes the ritornello idea with a treatment that extends to twenty-five bars at each occurrence, characterized by a rising sequential figure and a change to triple metre that throws the text into bold relief. Architecture and expression have now been wedded in a new, symbiotic embrace that totally recasts earlier Renaissance approaches to the formulaic refrain (Ex. 3.7*a*).

The year 1615 saw the publication not only of d'India's *III a 5* but also of his *Le musiche a due voci* (Venice: Ricciardo Amadino). Here the common lineage of the newly constituted chamber duet and the older five-voice madrigal is dramatically confirmed by the use of triple-time aria and especially by the imitative episodes between the sopranos that coalesce into passages in

---

[13] For a transcription of Rasi's 'Indarno Febo', see Carol MacClintock (ed.), *An Anthology of Solo Song 1580–1730* (New York: Norton, 1973). I have used MacClintock's translation of the text here.

Ex. 3.7. D'India: *a* 'Indarno Febo'; *b* 'Langue al vostro languir'; *c* 'O leggiadri occhi'

(*a*)

(. . . and Cynthia unveils for me her pure silver, [I see] nothing . . .)

Ex. 3.7. (*cont.*)

(*b*)

(. . . O soul of Love too thieving . . .)

(*c*)

(. . . Beautiful eyes which I adore, look, look . . .)

parallel thirds. The degree of dependency between the two collections is most clearly revealed in 'Indarno Febo' (Ex. 3.7*a*), which conflates figures from both 'Langue al vostro languir l'anima mia' (Ex. 3.7*b*) and 'O leggiadri occhi' (Ex. 3.7*c*). From the last of these pieces, a triple-time aria, d'India briefly takes two voices as a metrically contrasting refrain in a composition in duple time for five voices and continuo. Yet the outright transfer of materials fails to carry any symbolic allusion and serves principally in the construction of an amplified design. Rasi's refrain is short by comparison, is never transposed, and is in the same metre as the preceding section. In contrast, d'India uses prolonged repetition, sequence, and contrasting metres in order to develop a new musical architecture. He has delivered himself of a sermon.

My emphasis earlier on both Rasi and Saracini is not unexpectedly corroborated in 'O rimembranza amara' (the text is by Rasi).

> O rimembranza amara
>   che somministri al core
>   infinito dolore,
>   homai partiti a volo,
>   e col'acceso stuolo
>   de gli alati sospiri
>   partans'i miei desiri.
>   O rimembranza amara,
>   fui ben per te felice,
>   hor sei del viver mio,
>   se non ti prend'oblio,
>   sola tormentatrice.

(O bitter remembrance | which provides the heart | with infinite sorrow, | at last depart on wings, | and with the enflamed multitude | of winged sighs | may all my desires thus take part. | O bitter remembrance, | I was indeed happy for thee, | and now you are of my life, | if I do not find you, forgetfulness, | my only tormentor.)

Saracini, a Sienese noted for his *bizzarie*, had published a setting of 'O rimembranza amara' the year before (in his 1614 *Musiche*), and d'India invites a comparison through the blatant approximation of his initial motif (Ex. 3.8). However, he refuses the traditional prolongation accorded the word 'infinito' by Saracini and the virtually mandatory melismatic flights of both Rasi and Saracini on 'volo': his attention lies elsewhere. And the resistance of all three composers to the standard rest for 'sospiri' broadcasts the passing of an era. But neither Rasi's thrice repeated 'O rimembranza amara' nor Saracini's transposed double statement of this text in his opening so much as hints at

Ex. 3.8. 'O rimembranza amara': *a* Saracini; *b* D'India

(*a*)

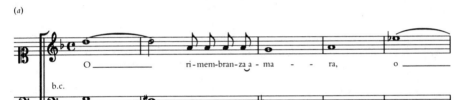

Ex. 3.8. (cont.)

(b)

(O bitter remembrance which provides the heart with infinite sorrow, at last
depart on wings . . .)

the psychological component inherent in d'India's setting: between each line of the text projected by the lower three voices, the upper two introduce the 'bitter remembrance', at progressively rising levels, as a compulsively insistent refrain. Here d'India not only recalls a technique exploited in '"Lasso", dicea Fileno' but also prefigures the extreme explorations of his own later monodic laments, where he precipitates a powerful drama through the alternating tension and relaxation of ascending and descending *parlando* phrases. The multiple constituent ingredients of an age now forming are gradually being displayed in the act of competitive settings of the same text. Factors attendant on the formation of all avant-gardes as well as the political tussling of rival protagonists are patently operating in the background.

Whatever the intended points of comparison, nothing can camouflage the evidence that in his *III a 5* d'India takes a step in a decidedly Monteverdian direction, though less through figurative modelling than through formal and textural layout. Perhaps this is the point of the collection: one may produce a critique of a venerable model in a slightly older style (the chromaticism of Gesualdo's 'Mercè! grido piangendo'), or momentarily ignore new directions (d'India's setting of 'Dovrò dunque morire' pays little heed to Caccini's solo song in *Le nuove musiche*),[14] but ultimately (as in the last eight madrigals) one is obliged to integrate, individualize, and even extend an emerging aesthetic not previously addressed. In so doing, d'India not only demonstrates fresh and vivid alternatives to the monodists but also secures his importance for the definition of a new musical age and previews the marvels of his final continuo madrigal collection, to be published in 1624. At the same time, he serves notice that one of the finest singers and monodists of the age understood that vocal polyphony could still serve as a powerful tool in the discovery of new modes of textual expression.

Although the dedications to d'India's *Quarto* and *Quinto libro de madrigali a cinque voci* (both Venice: Ricciardo Amadino, 1616) and his *Settimo libro de madrigali a cinque voci* (Rome: Gio. Battista Robletti, 1624) fail to explain why, the obligatory continuo of the final eight madrigals of *III a 5* disappears completely from these collections (d'India's *VI a 5* seems lost). Other characteristics, however, are endorsed which allow us to fix the essential features of d'India's musical personality and to trace its development. Mompellio has suggested that *IV a 5* witnesses a return to the contrapuntal aspects of d'India's *II a 5* and *III a 5*. He notes correctly that the themes are generally brief, marked by diatonicism and short imitative passages, and concludes that craft prevails at the expense of expression and that there are few memorable pages.[15]

---

[14] See the introduction to d'India, *Terzo libro de' madrigali a cinque voci*, ed. Watkins.

[15] Mompellio, *Sigismondo d'India*, 39: 'Sovente il mestiere prevale e rimangono senza risposta gli inviti della poesia al cuore del musicista; le pagine meritevoli di nota non sono dunque molte'.

There can be no question that it is initially difficult to reconcile d'India's stance in *IV a 5* with the developments of his first three books. Yet the harmonic chromaticism so securely employed in a number of his earlier works does find a single and singular demonstration in a setting of Marino's strained conceit, 'Strana armonia d'amore'.

> Strana armonia d'amore
>   anch'egli al tuo cantar forma il tuo core.
>   Son' del canto le chiavi
>   i begl'occhi soavi;
>   son' le not'e gli accenti
>   i miei pianti e i lamenti;
>   i sospiri acuti e gravi
>   son'anco i miei tormenti.

(Strange harmony of love | with your singing it also moulds your heart. | Beautiful eyes so gentle | are the keys of the song; | its notes and accents are | my tears and laments; | and sighs both high and low | are my pain and anguish.)

This is one of the curiosities of d'India's œuvre. For beyond the time-honoured introduction of rests in tandem with Marino's 'sospiri' and a toying with multiple stresses in the setting of 'accenti', it is the virtuoso manipulation of accidentals virtually demanded by the first line of the poem that marks the whole and easily earns for this madrigal recognition as the boldest chromatic statement in the composer's entire output. The use of conflicting or partial signatures (one flat in the *alto* and *basso* only) is decidedly old-fashioned in appearance and reminiscent of Rore's 'Crudele acerba inesorabil morte', although d'India promotes a language of consistently greater tension and expressive urgency. In this *tour de force*, d'India presses the implications of the conflicting signatures from the very beginning (Ex. 3.9) through a persistent endorsement of the cross-relation as an expressive device (E♭/E: bars 1–2, 11–12; F/F♯, C/C♯: bars 7–10; G/G♯: bars 11–12). Yet both here and later in the madrigal, his manipulations are anything but arbitrary and, indeed, are clearly motivated by the text: the G♯ sounded against the E♭ (Ex. 3.10), for example, not only mirrors the high/low binary of the text ('acuti e gravi') but through the simultaneous use of sharp and flat also recalls the linearly derived enharmonic spellings on the text 'muti una volta quel suo antico stile' ('once change its ancient style') found in Marenzio's madrigal 'O voi che sospirate a miglior note' (*Il secondo libro de madrigali a cinque voci*, Venice: Angelo Gardano, 1581). Although the complete passage clearly ranks among the most tortured expressions of an era, the ease with which tonal goals are secured announces a new command of old forces.

Ex. 3.9. D'India, 'Strana armonia d'amore'

Ex. 3.9. *(cont.)*

(Strange harmony of love . . .)

Ex. 3.10. D'India, 'Strana armonia d'amore'

Ex. 3.10. (*cont.*)

(. . . my tears and laments; and sighs both high and low . . .)

If the effect of the whole is so extreme as to border on the bizarre, giving the impression of a momentarily adopted *maniera*, the underlying commitment to textual expression virtually demanded by the poem clearly reigns supreme at every turn. It is as though the task of setting Guarini's precocious refinements had been replaced by a new challenge to address the brilliant and even more ambiguous marvels of Marino. Indeed, by combining the cumulative traditions of Rore, Marenzio, and Gesualdo, d'India surpasses his own earlier 'Cruda Amarilli' and forecasts the later, brilliant achievements of Michelangelo Rossi. At the same time, it is as well to remember that exploration of the multiple functions of accidentals—both melodic and harmonic, consonant as well as dissonant—had been consistently nurtured in some of the more rarified monodies of Saracini as well as by d'India himself from the time of his first book of *Musiche* of 1609.

If d'India seems to have bid farewell to the world of Gesualdo in 'Mercè! grido piangendo' and to have only obliquely recalled it in 'Strana armonia d'amore', it is his *Settimo libro de madrigali a cinque voci* of 1624 that provides final testimony to the memory of an approach now clearly in decline. Leaving the court of Savoy under the pressures of a personal scandal, he moved first to Modena, where, under the patronage of the Este (who had left Ferrara), he published his final two sets of polyphonic madrigals in the same year. In the preface to these two collections he speaks not only of entertainments at Turin but also of the virtuosity of the singers at Modena. *VII a 5*, published without even an optional continuo, contains d'India's final setting of a text also set by Gesualdo, 'Ecco morirò dunque'.[16] Here, too, d'India evinces another aspect of the chromatic revolution of the Renaissance with 'Udite lagrimosi | spirti d'Averno', which in its movement to E♯ and B♯ before returning to less esoteric tonal terrain offers a belated though explicit demonstration of a previous age's infatuation with harmonic spirals.[17] Having previously made a direct reference to Gesualdo's legacy in his *III a 5* of 1615, in 1624 d'India not only offers the faded and moribund tradition of the madrigal in both Naples and Ferrara a final sign of recognition and appreciation but also signals its importance in the securing of a new aesthetic. His signals are not only the chromatic extravagance of 'Ecco morirò dunque' and 'Udite lagrimosi' of *VII a 5* but also the announcement in the preface to his last book that he had created it at, and had dedicated its contents to, the Este court, still full of the memories of its former musical glory in Ferrara.

D'India's *Ottavo libro de madrigali a cinque voci* (Rome: Gio. Battista Robletti,

---

[16] For a transcription, see d'India, *Ottavo libro de' madrigali a cinque voci*, ed. Watkins, pp. xv–xvii.

[17] Transcribed ibid., pp. xx–xxiii.

1624), his virtuoso *opus ultimum*, sums up a career and retrospectively reviews the importance of *Il pastor fido* for the beginnings of the musical theatre. Eschewing Guarini's lengthy and impressive choruses, d'India, like most of his contemporaries, chose the soliloquies and narrative passages for his settings. Perhaps unexpectedly, he sets a *Pastor fido* text as a monody on only three occasions:[18] elsewhere he opts for polyphony. In *VIII a 5*, the underlying point is hammered home in a lengthy setting in five sections that opens the volume. In his opening of Silvio's 'Dorinda, ah, dirò "mia", se mia non sei', the *terza parte* of this cycle, he marries the breathless style punctuated by rests—already hinted at by Monteverdi in his setting in his Fifth Book—with a sequence of chromatic inflections, and follows it immediately with the *parlando* declamation in quavers initially exhibited in his own *II a 5*.[19] A similar combination of features is used at the opening of the extraordinary 'Ferir quel petto, Silvio', now coupled with dramatic punctuations freed from classical constraints on dissonance or loosely anchored by extended pedal-points.[20] But in the final piece of the set, 'Silvio, come son lassa', a hint of the language that d'India may have employed in his lost theatrical endeavours surfaces in the elaborate dialogue of the three characters. The *madrigale concertato* has taken the next step, joining monody and polyphony, verisimilitude of character with choral declamation, in what can only be described as a miniature operatic scene.

In the final bars of the piece, d'India sequesters the composite technical resources of an age (Ex. 3.11). The *parlando* tradition—recognized in d'India's first book of monodies,[21] accorded a dominant role in the polyphonic domain from the time of his second book of madrigals (see 'Tempesta di dolcezza', above), and adopted wholesale as the essential ingredient for recitative in opera's first decades—served numerous roles in the early seventeenth century. Not only did it provide the means of articulating large quantities of text quickly, but it also challenged composers and a new breed of singer to discover the expressive mode in the act of declamation. Though virtually all composers of the age knew its pitfalls—and in 1626 Domenico Mazzocchi could speak specifically of the need to 'break the tedium of the recitative'[22]—there was a keen awareness of its powers as well. In 'Silvio,

[18] 'Cruda Amarilli' and 'O primavera, gioventù dell'anno' in his first book of *Musiche*; 'Com'è soave cosa' in his third.

[19] D'India, *Ottavo libro de' madrigali a cinque voci*, ed. Watkins, 10–16.

[20] Ibid. 17–23 (cf, bars 4, 10–14).

[21] D'India's designations are specific in his first book of *Musiche*: 'Ferma, Dorinda mia, deh ferma il piede' is labelled a 'madrigale in stile recitativo', and 'Là tra 'l sangue e le morti egro giacente' an 'ottava in stile recitativo'.

[22] So he said in a note to the score of his *La catena d'Adone* (Venice: Alessandro Vincenti, 1626).

Glenn Watkins

Ex. 3.11. D'India, 'Ferir quel petto, Silvio'

Ex. 3.11. (*cont.*)

(... is indeed dear to me, and death, sweet.)

come son lassa', d'India's simultaneous engagement of the five-voice concertato ensemble in extended *parlando* declamation, protracted chromaticism, and extravagant vocal intervals (note the descending ninths in the upper two voices two bars before the end) effects a striking summation and a calculated announcement of some of the most expressive devices of an age. In the process, ingredients of the lament style, so tellingly forecast in the *madrigale in stile recitativo* 'Ferma, Dorinda mia' of d'India's first book of *Musiche* (1609) and elaborately developed in his recent *Le musiche . . . Libro quinto* (Venice: Alessandro Vincenti, 1623; Ex. 3.12) are absorbed and transcended.[23]

Various options put forward in the 1580s and 1590s—including Wert's *parlando*, Luzzaschi's 'luxuriant' melismas, Gesualdo's chromaticism, Monteverdi's structural use of *contrapposto*, the examples of the diminution

[23] See Tim Carter, *Music in Late Renaissance and Early Baroque Italy* (London: Batsford, 1992), 196–7. Attention should be drawn once again to Modena, Biblioteca Estense, MS Mus. F1530, which contains not only alto parts to 'Godea del sol i rai', 'Pallidetto mio sole', 'Lidia ti lasso, ahi lasso', and 'Se tu, Silvio crudel, mi saettasti' from d'India's *VIII a 5*, but also an alto part for 'Infelice Didone', which appears as a monody in *Le musiche . . . Libro quinto*. Just as Monteverdi made dual settings of the *Lamento d'Arianna*, d'India apparently confected monodic and polyphonic versions of his setting of Dido's lament.

Ex. 3.12. D'India, 'Infelice Didone' (*Lamento di Didone*)

(. . . Why do you flee from me? What did I do to you, my heart? Why deny me, alas, the last farewell? . . .)

treatises, Caccini's renewal of monody, and the power of dance rhythms to effect contrasting structures—have now melded with concertato textures. The net product is a hybrid of these multiple impulses that addresses the issue of dramatic accountability with a new accent. Much of this same sense of amalgamation took place in the world of opera among its finest practitioners, and few of them would have professed ignorance of the composite tradition. The surface distinctions between Marenzio, Wert, Gesualdo, Macque, Saracini, Rasi, and Monteverdi have now dissolved in a grand alliance, and the apparent opposition of late Mannerist gesture and proto-Baroque organicism is laid bare as a myth. Even if we did not know of the circumstances that placed Monteverdi, Mazzocchi, and d'India in direct competition at Parma as late as the summer of 1627,[24] it would be difficult to imagine that in creating at least some of the marvels of his final collection, the *Madrigali guerrieri, et amorosi* of 1638, Monteverdi could have been totally innocent of the beguiling synthesis of d'India's *VIII a 5* (1624). For as d'India—a vagabond musician who had travelled to and participated in the musical activities of numerous Italian cities—bids a last but affectionate farewell, he takes notice both of the expressive range of an age and of its main centres of musical activity. The collaborative traditions of music and theatre at Turin, Mantua, Florence, and Salzburg were all familiar to d'India, and

[24] To provide the music for the festivities celebrating the wedding of Odoardo Farnese and Margherita de' Medici; see Stuart Reiner, 'Preparations in Parma—1618, 1627–28', *Music Review*, 25 (1964), 273–301, esp. the letter of 13 Aug. 1627 given on pp. 286–7.

one can only regret the fact that if d'India made any forays into the realms of opera, the results are apparently lost today. None the less, the components available to d'India for such an undertaking are not in doubt.

The first impression of a musician long out of view invariably stems from a handful of pieces which tend to perpetuate themselves as iconic representatives. In time, the arduous task of preparing an edition of his collected works may lead to extensions and revisions of previously held views. Ultimately, however, the need to relate a composer to the larger impulses of an age requires the assessment of numerous factors. Rather than seeing the issue of style as a personal and rectilinear development within genres, we should accept that the interplay of repertories and the politics of art—factors of patronage, employment opportunities, an awareness of the competition and the need to address it—surface inevitably as natural extensions of the perennial humanist concern for and attention to multiple authorities in the formation of contemporary modes of expression. Recent attempts to spell out the parameters of text–music relationships and to claim ripening modes of discourse for such an assignment have only confirmed that the attendant issues are multifarious and that final clarification is destined to remain out of reach.[25] This is so because the colouring of our questions is subject to continuing reshading. Those interdisciplinary studies that have borrowed the arguments of literary criticism, that have attended to the issue of narrative archetypes both tonal and textual, and that have once again noted literature's perennial striving towards the condition of music and vice versa, not surprisingly leave us with the same fundamental questions asked by the ancients. Interest in positivist structural analysis that seeks to illuminate the mechanics of the frame for both music and its attendant texts, as well as to note the interaction of the two, seldom disappears for long, even as it rises and falls in reaction to the shifting attention accorded to cultural backgrounds and reception histories. The conclusion that to privilege now one angle and now another permits an endless round of appraisals only invites the corollary that the recovery of an *Ur*-perspective from a bygone age is no longer deemed possible or even desirable, and announces the elimination of one of history's former goals. We now appear to be content with the thought that our studies, packed with details, reflect a perspective at a single contemporary moment of reception destined one day to be absorbed in other new and provocative reassessments.[26] Whatever the future may hold for d'India's music,

---

[25] See the series of essays addressed to this general question in Steven Paul Scher (ed.), *Music and Text: Critical Inquiries* (Cambridge, Mass., and London: Harvard University Press, 1992).

[26] See Charles Hamm, 'Privileging the Moment of Reception: Music and Radio in South Africa', ibid. 21–37. I am grateful to the following seminar students for their critical appraisal of numerous points in the present essay: Todd Borgerding, Derek Bermel, Mark Jannello, Gregory Marion, and Rose Pruiksma.

recognition of its importance has increased significantly since the initial studies of Fortune and Mompellio some forty years ago. Although the appearance of his complete works in modern edition remains a continuing goal, the best news of all is that his music is now beginning to be widely performed and recorded. In time, however, we may anticipate that performance practices will also be subject to modifications as significant as recent changes to our critical perspectives.

4

Lamenti recitativi da camera

◥❀◤

WILLIAM V. PORTER

'LASCIATEMI morire': 'Let me die . . . Turn back, my Theseus . . . But with gentle breezes, you happily depart while I weep here . . . Where, where is the faith that you so much promised to me? O storms, o tempests, o winds, drown him beneath your waves! . . . Ah, what am I saying? Am I delirious? . . . It was my distress speaking, and my pain; yes, my tongue did speak, but not my heart . . . O mother, o father, o splendid palaces of the ancient realm . . . look where pitiless fate has led me! Such is the destiny of one who loves too much and trusts too deeply.' Thus cries the abandoned Ariadne in the words of Monteverdi's poet Ottavio Rinuccini, as her distraught mind races across a wide spectrum of conflicting thoughts and emotions—inconsolable despair, piteous calls for Theseus' return, Theseus' joy as opposed to her own weeping, recollections of broken promises, angry calls for his destruction, reconsideration as she acknowledges her abiding love for him, calls for the sympathy of her parents, and finally, realization of the consequences of excessive love and trust. Monteverdi produced three settings of Ariadne's lament in recitative style for accompanied solo voice: first as a climactic scene to his opera *Arianna* (premièred in 1608; music lost), where the vocal solo is punctuated by choral commentary; then as an independent piece for chamber performance (published in 1623); and finally as a spiritual work with Ariadne's words reworked and reassigned to the Virgin (published in 1640).[1] These settings became models for countless

---

[1] Modern editions of Monteverdi's surviving solo versions are in *Tutte le opere di Claudio Monteverdi*, ed. Gian Francesco Malipiero (2nd edn., Vienna: Universal Edition, 1954–68), xi. 161–7, xv. 757–62. See also the facs. edn. of the chamber lament of 1623 in Gary Tomlinson (ed.), *Italian Secular Song 1606–1636* (New York and London: Garland, 1986), vii. 1–21. In 1623, the chamber version was also published in *Il maggio fiorito: Arie sonetti, e madrigali, à 1.2.3. de diversi autori* (Orvieto: Michel'angelo Fei and Rinaldo Ruuli), but only the voice part (without continuo) survives. Monteverdi's arrangement of the lament as a five-voice madrigal cycle, not discussed in this essay, was printed in his Sixth Book of madrigals in 1614. Although the score for the opera *Arianna* does not survive, the solo portions of the lament are essentially recoverable from the Venetian print of 1623 and from contemporary manuscripts.

composers of the early seventeenth century. The operatic scene was proto-
typical of laments in Roman and Venetian operas until the early 1640s, at
which time the recitative lament was gradually replaced by the aria lament
over a descending tetrachord.[2] The independent solo version of 1623, undoubtedly intended for intimate chamber concerts, may especially be viewed
as the germinating force in a genre of secular pieces popular until around the
middle of the seventeenth century. The words of these laments were those
of abandoned or widowed heroines (or more rarely, of distraught males)
from both classical and Renaissance literature, of contemporary political
figures or their survivors, or even of anonymous afflicted souls. And finally,
Monteverdi's sacred contrafactum, the lament of the Madonna, gave rise
to additional laments of bereft religious figures.[3] In Monteverdi's original
lament for Ariadne as well as in the countless works it inspired, the newly
developed recitative style was a superb medium for representing the impassioned speech not only of one who has suffered a profound loss, but also of
one whose agitated mind moves swiftly through a wide range of ideas and
moods.

In this essay I review the essential features of Monteverdi's famous work
and then trace its impact upon recitative laments by numerous other
composers of his time who set the words of grieving individuals. Although
examples abound in early opera and sacred music, the scope here is limited
to chamber laments by secular figures from classical literature or from
Renaissance epics. It will be seen that Monteverdi's *Lamento d'Arianna* had
its greatest influence on recitative laments written for courts and cities of
northern Italy through the 1620s. With the emergence of early cantatas,

The 1623 print gives the accompaniment as a basso continuo, but the operatic lament was
said by the Mantuan official Federico Follino to have been accompanied by a consort of viols
and violins ('accompagnato da viole et violini'). For a further interpretation of this remark
and for background concerning ensembles as accompaniments for solo songs in theatrical
productions of the time, see Gary Tomlinson, *Monteverdi and the End of the Renaissance*
(Oxford: Clarendon Press, 1987), 138–9. At least two manuscript copies of the lament
(Florence, Biblioteca Nazionale Centrale, Banco Rari 238, and London, British Library, Add.
MS 30491) extend Ariadne's music beyond its ending in the print.

    [2] The legacy of Ariadne's lament in early 17th-c. opera has been discussed in detail in
Margaret Murata, 'The Recitative Soliloquy', *Journal of the American Musicological Society*, 32
(1979), 45–73, and Ellen Rosand, *Opera in Seventeenth-Century Venice: The Creation of a Genre*
(Berkeley and Los Angeles: University of California Press, 1991), esp. ch. 12. See also
Rosand, 'The Descending Tetrachord: An Emblem of Lament', *Musical Quarterly*, 55 (1979),
346–59; F. W. Sternfeld, *The Birth of Opera* (Oxford: Clarendon Press, 1993), ch. 6.

    [3] For an overview of the chamber genre (both sacred and secular), see Lorenzo Bianconi,
Il Seicento (Storia della musica, 4; Turin: Edizioni di Torino, 1982; 2nd edn., 1985), trans. by
David Bryant as *Music in the Seventeenth Century* (Cambridge University Press, 1987), ch. 23.
See also Silke Leopold, *Claudio Monteverdi und seine Zeit* (Laaber: Laaber Verlag, 1982), trans.
by Anne Smith as *Monteverdi: Music in Transition* (Oxford: Clarendon Press, 1991), ch. 4.

especially those by Roman composers in the 1630s and 1640s, the lament exclusively in recitative style yielded to a new type of lament with mixed styles, still predominantly recitative-like but with short arioso or aria-like sections. My study ends with a discussion of these cantata laments in mixed styles: I do not consider the important repertory of mid-century laments which are set completely in aria style, characteristically over a descending tetrachord.

ARIADNE LAMENTS

Ariadne's lament, in one or more of Monteverdi's settings, has become one of the composer's most-discussed compositions in modern scholarship.[4] Commentaries have focused on the music, on the special characteristics of Rinuccini's poetry, and on possible meanings of the work for seventeenth-century audiences. Although Ovid's accounts of Ariadne, in his *Metamorphoses* and *Heroides*, provided the prime sources for the poem, Rinuccini undoubtedly relied on Italian Renaissance versions, frequently with enlargements and embellishments of the original texts; his language also seems closely related to the grieving women of Ariosto (Olimpia) and Tasso (Armida and Erminia).[5]

Despite the numerous possible sources for elements of the poem, Rinuccini's own contributions were clearly of utmost importance to the eventual effectiveness of Monteverdi's music, as Gary Tomlinson has so ably

---

[4] See Peter Epstein, 'Dichtung und Musik in Monteverdis "Lamento d'Arianna"', *Zeitschrift für Musikwissenschaft*, 10 (1927–8), 216–22; J. A. Westrup, 'Monteverdi's "Lamento d'Arianna"', *Music Review*, 1 (1940), 144–54; Anna Amalie Abert, *Claudio Monteverdi und das musikalische Drama* (Lippstadt: Kistner & Siegel, 1954), 29–32; Guido Pannain, 'Studi monteverdiani: viii', *La rassegna musicale*, 29 (1959), 310–21; Claudio Gallico, 'I due pianti di Arianna di Claudio Monteverdi', *Chigiana*, 24 (1967), 29–42; Carolyn Gianturco, *Claudio Monteverdi: Stile e struttura* (Pisa: Editrice Tecnico Scientifica, 1978), 99–115; Gary Tomlinson, 'Madrigal, Monody, and Monteverdi's "via naturale alla immitatione"', *Journal of the American Musicological Society*, 34 (1981), 60–108, and id., *Monteverdi and the End of the Renaissance*, 125–31; Ulrich Michels, 'Das "Lamento d'Arianna" von Claudio Monteverdi', in Werner Breig *et al.* (eds.), *Festschrift für Hans Heinrich Eggebrecht zum 65. Geburtstag* (Beihefte zur Archiv für Musikwissenschaft, 23; Wiesbaden: Steiner Verlag, 1984), 90–109; Leopold, *Monteverdi*, ch. 4; Eric Chafe, *Monteverdi's Tonal Language* (New York: Schirmer, 1992), ch. 8; and Suzanne G. Cusick, 'There Was Not One Lady Who Failed to Shed a Tear', *Early Music*, 22 (1994), 21–41.

[5] For a discussion of Rinuccini's possible sources, see Gary Tomlinson, 'Rinuccini, Peri, Monteverdi, and the Humanist Heritage of Opera' (Ph.D. diss., University of California, Berkeley, 1979), 182–91; and Lorenzo Bianconi and Thomas Walker, 'Production, Consumption and Political Function of Seventeenth-Century Opera', *Early Music History*, 4 (1984), 209–96 at 254–7. Bianconi and Walker point especially to the numerous editions of the *Metamorphoses* in the *ottava rima* translation/expansion of Giovanni Andrea dell'Anguillara, and to editions of the *Heroides* in the translation into blank verse by Remigio Fiorentino. Anguillara based his version of Ariadne not on Ovid's original text, but on Ariosto's Olimpia (itself deriving from the *Heroides*).

shown. The 1608 libretto, incorporating the diverse thoughts of Ariadne quoted above, divides the lament into five sections, all but the last concluded by a choral commentary on the preceding monologue. Within each section, Ariadne's words unfold with simplicity and forcefulness, and with a great sensitivity to the sound of the poetry; these qualities, along with periodic repetitions of ideas and structural parallelisms, make the text ideal for a musical setting. The first (and shortest) section, ending with the choral comment 'In boundless sorrow, the mortal tongue can offer no comfort', creates the opening mood of inconsolable despair. Ariadne's calls for death ('Lasciatemi morire') frame her brief remark about her hopeless situation. Rinuccini's second section, the longest of the five, has Ariadne calling for Theseus' return and then comparing her deplorable state with his presumed happiness; it concludes with the commentary 'How sad to see you rushing towards a wretched end'. This section is particularly rich in parallelisms and contrasts, most notably with Ariadne's three calls to Theseus, and her three contrasts of her own despair with Theseus' joy; Rinuccini also heightens Ariadne's emotional state with the introduction of frequent interjections ('O' and 'oimè'). In the third section, Ariadne poses a series of questions as she reviews incredulously Theseus' promises made to her earlier, and wonders how it is possible that he can now leave her to die. The commentary adds, 'The unfortunate one does not realize that her prayers and sighs go unheard'. Here, Ariadne's questions are again put into parallel formats as she repeats her earlier calls to Theseus and her pleading for death. Rinuccini's fourth section brings the most dramatic moments of the lament, as Ariadne flies into her fit of rage against Theseus but then realizes that this outburst does not represent her true feelings about her beloved; the choral commentary adds, 'The world admires one who in bitterness does not seek revenge'. In the final section, Ariadne calls to her parents and friends to observe the cruel fate of one who loves and trusts too much.

Monteverdi's music in the chamber version everywhere brings out and enhances the fine qualities of Rinuccini's text, and enables the singer to deliver the unfolding drama in the manner of an impassioned actress. Examples 4.1–3, from the surviving chamber version without the choral commentaries, illustrate the wide range of declamatory styles which the composer matches to different sections of the text. In the opening bars of the lament (Ex. 4.1), Ariadne utters her first piteous cries for death. In these two phrases, her ascent from a' to d'', with two dissonances between the voice and the bass (in both statements of 'lasciatemi', on the second syllable), may be seen as representing her increasing anguish. The upward direction of the melody is twice broken by downward leaps of a fourth and sixth respectively followed by a stepwise descent. This fall into the lower register suggests Ariadne's

Ex. 4.1. Monteverdi, 'Lasciatemi morire' (*Lamento d'Arianna*)

(Let me die, let me die. . . .)

emotional collapse and ultimate resignation to her fate.[6] After a literal repetition of these two phrases to conclude the first section of the lament, they beçome a musical motto for the rest of the composition, returning in varied forms to punctuate other parts of the piece: for the text 'et io più non vedrovvi | o madre, o padre mio' at the end of the second section; for 'Lasciarmi in abbandono' and 'lascierai tu morire' within the third section, and for 'parlò l'affanno mio' and 'parlò la lingua sì, ma non già il core' at the end of the fourth section. Elsewhere, Monteverdi makes less significant use of short motives from the opening of the lament: for 'che mio pur sei' and 'in solitarie arene' in the second section, 'mi ripon degl'avi' in the third, and 'non son quell'io' in the fourth.

In other sections of the lament, Monteverdi has longer successions of repeated pitches in the voice, accompanied by relatively static harmony. Several times, Ariadne calls to or rhetorically questions Theseus in monotonal declamation. In the second section of the lament, when she calls to Theseus for the third time (Ex. 4.2), the initial pedal *d* is interrupted only to under-score the exclamations in the text: for the second 'o Teseo' (*c♯*); and then for 'o Dio' (*e*) and 'oimè' (*c♯*) at the ends of parallel phrases of text ('se tu sapessi, o Dio, | se tu sapessi, oimè'). These exclamations receive further emphases through the downward leaps of a diminished fifth and minor seventh respectively in the vocal line, which otherwise rises through the notes of the prevailing D major chord. The accompaniment changes to a sustained harmony on G minor as Ariadne turns her thoughts to herself ('come s'affanna | la povera Arianna'), but then back to D major with the vain hope of Theseus' return. Later, in the third section, when Ariadne repeatedly questions her present state in the light of Theseus' earlier pro-mises, her recitation again unfolds primarily through a sustained D chord,

---

[6] Chafe, *Monteverdi's Tonal Language*, 164–82, provides numerous illustrations of the dualism of Ariadne's pain and her subsequent collapse, which he sees as represented in the hexachordal/tonal dualism of these opening bars and then presented in various parallel ways throughout the lament.

Ex. 4.2. Monteverdi, 'Lasciatemi morire' (*Lamento d'Arianna*)

O Te - seo,   o ___ Te - seo mi - o,   Se tu sa-pes-si o ___ Di -

- o,   Se tu sa - pes - si oi - - mè __ co-me s'af-fan - na La po - ve-ra A - ri -

- an - na,   For - se, for - se pen - ti - to   Ri-vol-ge-re-sti an-cor la pro-ra al li - to.

(. . . O Theseus, o my Theseus, if you knew, o God, if you knew, alas, how poor Ariadne suffers, perhaps, perhaps repentant would you turn your ship back to shore. . . .)

allowing the singer to press each new thought with increasing agitation: 'Così ne l'alta fede | tu mi ripon degl'avi? | Son queste le corone | onde m'adorn'il crine? | Questi gli scettri sono, | queste le gemme, gl'ori?'

Ariadne's outburst of anger in the climactic fourth section (Ex. 4.3) again has declamation mostly on repeated notes (rising from *a'* to *d''*) until the height of her rage at the words 'le voragini profonde'. The increasing intensity of the passage is created not only by the rising pitches but also by a gradual increase in the rate of speed for the declamation, ending with semiquavers. The supporting harmonies underscore the unusual climactic function of these bars, since Monteverdi departs from the basic tonal orientation of the lament (d) and moves successively through a, B, G, and a (where lower case indicates minor 'keys' and upper case major). With Ariadne's

Ex. 4.3. Monteverdi, 'Lasciatemi morire' (*Lamento d'Arianna*)

sudden change of heart, following the moment of silence, she resorts to a less animated vocal style, in which her distraught state of mind is underscored by rests, by the chromatic rise from g' to $g\sharp'$, by the leaps for the two exclamatory words 'ahi' and 'oimè', and by the continuing tonal shifts (g, A, and finally a return to d, the basic tonality of the lament). True, many stylistic features shown in these three examples had roots in earlier polyphonic madrigals by Monteverdi and his contemporaries, and can be seen in

Ex. 4.3. (*cont.*)

(. . . Ah, he replies not; ah, he is deafer than an asp to my laments. O clouds, o gales, o winds, sink him beneath those waves. O orcs and whales, rush and fill the deep abysses with his foul limbs. What do I say, ah, what am I dreaming? Wretched, alas, what do I ask for? O Theseus, o my Theseus, I am not, I am not she, I am not she who said such harsh things. My suffering spoke, my grief spoke, my tongue spoke, yes, but not my heart. . . .)

the solo vocal music of the decade preceding the première of *Arianna*.[7] But in this work, Monteverdi's exquisite matching of musical details to Rinuccini's poetry has created a powerful musical–poetic language for the grieving soloist. Monteverdi and Rinuccini's lament also succeeds because of its overall structural integrity. The composer carefully follows the refrains, parallelisms, and other syntactical devices built into the poetry by using musical recurrences, sequential patterns, and varied repetitions. The general tonal orientation of D minor is reinforced by the fact that each of the five sections ends in this key; furthermore, the first, second, and fourth sections end with similar music, although different text. Within the individual sections, Monteverdi's tonal designing seems to operate not only on the local level but also throughout the section.

Musical and textual features of Monteverdi's work recur in the numerous laments of classical characters by other composers over the next few decades; often the *Lamento d'Arianna* seems the clear model. Especially susceptible to imitation is the climactic rage of anger and vengeance, followed by a sudden change of mind as the grieving one regains composure and becomes resigned to the situation. Also frequent are contrasts of present despair with former happiness, as the bereft one repeatedly calls for the lover's return. But rarely, if ever, do the later recitative laments display so skilful a combination of musical and textual ingredients as Monteverdi's masterpiece, and thus rarely do they make the same powerful cumulative impact on the listener. For example, two additional solo settings of Rinuccini's text survive in contemporary prints, by Severo Bonini (1613) and by Francesco Costa (1626).[8] Although Bonini greatly praised Monteverdi's setting in his later treatise on music and counterpoint dating from the 1640s,[9] his music seems not to be modelled on Monteverdi's.[10] Bonini begins his setting at an earlier point in

[7] See the examples in Tomlinson, 'Madrigal, Monody, and Monteverdi's "via naturale alla immitatione"', 60–80.

[8] Bonini, *Lamento d'Arianna . . . posto in musica in stile recitativo* (Venice: Bartolomeo Magni, 1613), facs. edn. in Tomlinson (ed.), *Italian Secular Song*, i. 33–64; Costa, *Pianto d'Ariana: Madrigali, e scherzi . . . a voce sola* (Venice: Alessandro Vincenti, 1626), facs. edn. ibid., iv. 281–6.

[9] *Prima parte de discorsi e regole sopra la musica*, trans. MaryAnn Bonino (Provo, Utah: Brigham Young University Press, 1979), 151.

[10] A point made by Tomlinson in *Italian Secular Song*, i, p. x. Lelia Galleni Luisi, 'Il "Lamento d'Arianna" di Severo Bonini (1613)', in Raffaello Monterosso (ed.), *Congresso internazionale sul tema 'Claudio Monteverdi e il suo tempo': relazioni e communicazioni* (Verona: Valdonega, 1969), 573–82 at 576–80, discusses some similarities between the two settings (in rhythm, melodic writing, and the general correspondence of styles and moods), but I believe that her examples are not sufficiently convincing to prove Bonini's *musical* indebtedness to Monteverdi. Marianne Danckwardt, 'Das Lamento d'Olimpia "Voglio voglio morir": Eine Komposition Claudio Monteverdis?', *Archiv für Musikwissenschaft*, 41 (1984), 149–75 at 163 and 165, adds two more examples of correspondence between Bonini and Monteverdi, which

Rinuccini's libretto, and includes a chorus of soldiers, two choruses of fishermen, and solo sections for Theseus and Ariadne. The five sections of the lament itself are punctuated by choral settings of Rinuccini's commentary. Many expressive moments of Ariadne's monologue are heightened by Bonini's use of dissonances, chromatic writing, leaps for exclamations, and unusual chord progressions:[11] this last feature is more prominent than in Monteverdi's setting. The most dramatic part of the monologue comes, as might be expected, with Ariadne's spiteful rage at Theseus, followed by her sudden return to grief (Ex. 4.4). Bonini begins the passage by sequential treatment suggested by the parallelism in the poetry: 'Ahi che pur non risponde, | ahi che più d'asp'è sord'à miei lamenti'. Here Ariadne's distress is underscored by the chromatic inflection of the voice over the unsettling harmonic progressions. Her rage is then depicted through a patter of repeated notes over more stationary notes in the bass. But in contrast with Monteverdi's setting of the same text (Ex. 4.3), Bonini fails to match Ariadne's ever increasing agitation through gradually rising pitches. Particularly notable is the loss of tension at the end of the passage, with the full cadence and drop in vocal register for the words 'empiete le voragini profonde'. With Ariadne's poignant change of mood, Bonini returns to the slower note-values and unusual harmonic progressions, before eventually cadencing in A minor. Despite some effective passages, Bonini's lament ultimately lacks the cumulative power of Monteverdi's chamber setting. Bonini's failure to match many parallelisms and recurrent lines in the poetry with musical sequences and refrains, his more relaxed tonal designing, and his inclusion of the choral interludes all contribute to a less integrated composition. In contrast, Costa's setting is closer to the general style and approach of Monteverdi, and at times seems directly indebted to him.[12] Its slow-moving bass, often changing only once or twice for a line of poetry, and its predominantly stepwise or monotonal vocal part allow a more flowing, lyrical declamation of the text. Costa, however, makes two sizeable cuts in Rinuccini's poem, immediately before and after Ariadne's rage. Her anger is put into a musical section by itself, thereby reducing the effectiveness of her sudden change of heart.

In 1623, after (I assume) issuing Monteverdi's *Lamento d'Arianna*, the Venetian publisher Bartolomeo Magni printed another Ariadne's lament by

---

may be isolated instances where the two composers were led to similar music by the syntax of the poetry.

[11] Especially root progressions by thirds, a feature frequently found in the Florentine settings of Rinuccini's *Euridice* (by Peri and Caccini) and in Monteverdi's *Orfeo*.

[12] Danckwardt, 'Das Lamento d'Olimpia', 164–5 provides three examples to illustrate the point. Unlike Monteverdi, however, Costa uses a few embellishments, including the *trillo*; exploits a curious cadential cliché, comprising a dotted rhythm and slur for the last syllable of a poetic line; and provides a short section in triple metre.

Ex. 4.4. Bonini, 'Lasciatemi morire' (*Lamento d'Arianna*)

(. . . Ah, he replies not; ah, he is deafer than an asp to my laments. O clouds, o gales, o winds, sink him beneath those waves. O orcs and whales, rush and fill the deep abysses with his foul limbs. What do I say, ah, what am I dreaming? Wretched, alas, what do I ask for? O Theseus . . .)

Pellegrino Possenti, setting an abridged version of Giambattista Marino's poem *Arianna* published a few years earlier.[13] In the parts of Marino's lament used by Possenti, Ariadne expresses some of the same thoughts as Rinuccini's heroine. She momentarily curses Theseus; she contrasts her piteous fate with his more fortunate turn of events; she continues to love him despite his betrayal; she contemplates death; and she cautions any woman who too deeply trusts an impetuous youth. But her language is far more discursive and less dramatic than Rinuccini's. Before pronouncing her curse on Theseus ('sen va da me lontano | abbia al suo corso iniquo | l'onde contrarie e i venti, | le stelle e gli elementi'), she devotes twenty-six lines of poetry to asking who was responsible for her abandonment, considering as possibilities Boreas, Zephyrus, Eurus, and Notus (the north, west, east, and south winds) respectively. In contrasting her fate with that of Theseus, she has eighteen lines which relate his insensitivity to her past deeds that saved his life: 'I gave you the thread by which you freed yourself from the labyrinth, and you abandoned me in these deserts; I rescued you at the risk of the horrible minotaur, and you leave me to the wild beasts . . .'. And in expressing her continuing love for Theseus, she spends twenty lines promising to be a servant to him and even to his new wife if only he will return to her. Through these long commentaries on various topics, Marino's poetry provides few opportunities for Ariadne to display sudden shifts of mood or thought. Possenti's music occasionally highlights words in the text by means of dissonant leaps and embellishments in the voice, and by unexpected harmonic progressions, but more often the voice has a monotonal declamation over a static bass. Despite the composer's reference to Monteverdi's lament in the preface to his collection, Possenti's setting shows little of Monteverdi's skill in treating individual dramatic details or achieving overall coherence throughout the monologue. Ex. 4.5 is a rare instance of rising tension depicted by a gradually rising vocal line. After Ariadne's initial references to trickery and betrayal, with the two high-pitched exclamations ('O'), her voice gradually rises from e' to g'' through sequential phrases as she recalls

[13] Marino's poem was published in his collection *La sampogna* (Paris: Abraam Pacardo, 1620; Milan: Gio. Battista Bidelli, 1620; Venice: I Giunti, 1621). A modern text of the complete poem is in *Opere scelte di Giovan Battista Marino e dei Marinisti*, ed. Giovanni Getto (Turin: UTET, 1949), i. 286–309. Possenti's lament appeared in his collection *Canora sampogna*; see the facs. edn. in Tomlinson (ed.), *Italian Secular Song*, vii. 33–70. Marino's complete *Arianna* is 781 lines long and features a narration of mixed seven- and eleven-syllable lines, which four times gives way to monologues in different verse structures, for Bacchus (100 lines of five-syllable lines) and Ariadne (298 lines of seven-syllable lines), plus a second song for Bacchus (twelve stanzas, each with six lines, primarily *ottonari*), and a third (30 lines of alternating seven- and eleven-syllable lines). Of Ariadne's 298 lines, Possenti chose 155 for his setting.

Ex. 4.5. Possenti, 'Misera, e chi m'ha tolto' (*Lamento d'Arianna*)

(. . . O evil trickery, o perverse betrayal. Are these the nuptials, these the
promises, these the oaths, when you gave me your faith with a proud marriage
to seek to make me blessed? O foolish and desperate woman, who submits
herself to a lover who begs. . . .)

Theseus' false promises and her ill-fated hope; her voice falls back in pitch as she realizes the foolishness of her trust.

LAMENTS OF OTHER CLASSICAL FIGURES

Within the repertory of early seventeenth-century laments, relatively few chamber works treat the grieving words of classical male characters, which is perhaps an indication of the growing importance of female soloists for concerts, but also one of the prevailing image of the weeping woman in contemporary society.[14] As exceptions, Sigismondo d'India's three examples of lamenting men—Orpheus (1621), Apollo (1621), and Jason (1623),[15] each with the composer's own texts—provide extraordinary settings for tenor voice, which may well have been performed by the singer-composer-poet himself. In Orpheus' lament, the text makes clear that his grief is in response to his second loss of Eurydice, as he reviews the events of her sudden disappearance and the harsh law which has governed her death. At first he resolves to seek mercy from the underworld, but he eventually concludes that Eurydice is lost for ever and senses the ebbing of his own life. Although there is no apparent reason for revenge, and thus no cause for raging against a traitorous beloved or other enemy, Orpheus does express a moment of great anger as he resolves to go among black waves and horrible monsters: d'India's rising pitches and semiquaver declamation appropriately accompany the text 'Ah, che dall'ire ultrici | agitato n'andrò fra l'ombre spente, | precipitando il volo a l'onde nere | del fiammeggiante et atro Flegetonte'. But following a long pause, Orpheus' mood is abruptly reversed as he realizes that his delirious outburst has no useful purpose: 'Ma che vaneggi, Orfeo,

---

[14] See especially Cusick, 'There Was Not One Lady Who Failed to Shed a Tear', 37: 'As it was gradually gendered feminine, the musical (and the literary) genre of the lament allowed the whole of early modern society to displace the suffering of forced submission onto women ... Women themselves—real women who impersonated Arianna and her sisters in chamber music, and who witnessed Arianna and her sisters received with ecstasy as models of desirable womanhood—learned to repress the flashes of anger they might feel, to stylize their responses to life's griefs into laments. Finally they learned to understand their femaleness and their beauty as inextricable from, even dependent on, their ability to lament, to "not fail to shed a tear".'

[15] In *Le musiche . . . a una et due voci . . . libro quarto* (1621) and *Le musiche . . . Libro quinto* (1623), both published in Venice by Alessandro Vincenti. For the best discussions of d'India's laments in the context of his musical career, see Nigel Fortune, 'Sigismondo d'India: An Introduction to his Life and Works', *Proceedings of the Royal Musical Association*, 81 (1954–5), 29–47; and John Joyce, *The Monodies of Sigismondo d'India* (Ann Arbor: UMI Research Press, 1981). The three settings are edited in Sigismondo d'India, *Le musiche a una e due voci: Libri I, II, III, IV e V*, ed. John Joyce (Musiche rinascimentali siciliane, 9; Florence: Olschki, 1989), 249–57, 274–82, 306–14. For facsimile editions, see Tomlinson (ed.), *Italian Secular Song*, iv. 108–11, 122–6, 145–8. D'India's text of Orpheus' lament was also set by Dionisio Bellante in his *Concerti accademici* (Venice: Bartolomeo Magni, 1629).

| così dunque disperi, | così dunque ne peri?' Throughout the lament, d'India's music shows all the hallmarks of the composer's highly expressive style, which is particularly effective in capturing sudden shifts of mood.[16] The voice makes dramatic use of wide leaps, chromatic motion, gradually rising pitches over several lines of text, sequential phrasing, rapid monotonal declamation, and unexpected rests. The continuo effectively introduces unusual harmonic progressions, chromatic lines, and sharp dissonances against the voice. The overall tonal focus of the lament is D minor, although changes to other 'keys' match temporary changes in subject or mood.

In the laments of Apollo and Jason, d'India introduces two-line refrains which recur several times in terms of both text and music:[17] this technique was used increasingly to integrate recitative laments in the early seventeenth century. Both works include all the above-mentioned musical devices characteristic of Orpheus' lament. But for Apollo, the progression of events and states of mind are essentially different from those of Orpheus.[18] A highly distraught Apollo begins with a frantic search for his beloved Daphne; deprived of her joy and comfort, he will die. But he considers the consequences of his death for mankind and the world, and concludes that, although in deepest grief, he must *not* die. Without the sun-god, nature would be deprived of life-giving light. As he accepts the reality of his loss, his healing begins when he commands that the garland of leaves from Daphne's transformed hair shall become a symbol of victory in contests. Jason's lament, however, is an almost unbroken expression of profound grief upon his discovery of the broken bodies of his two sons. Only once does he direct a volley of anger at Medea, the perpetrator of the double murder: 'Wicked Medea, perfidious beast! Why did I not kill you, rip your heart from your breast?'

[16] In the preface to his first book of *Musiche . . . da cantar solo* (Milan: Heirs of Simon Tini and Filippo Lomazzo, 1609), d'India identifies two key techniques used to enhance the expressiveness of his solo music: 'I found that one could compose in the true manner with unusual intervals and pass with utmost novelty from one chord to another, following the changing sense of the words' (trans. Joyce).

[17] Apollo: 'Ahi, che morir non posso; e per dolore | languisce al mio languir e piange Amore' ('Ah, I cannot die; and for grief | Love languishes at my languishing and weeps'). Jason: 'Ancidetemi pur, doglia e martire! | Trafigetemi pur, ch'io vuò morire!' ('Kill me, grief and torment! | Pierce me through, for I wish to die!'). At the beginning of Jason's lament, an additional line ('Poiché non trovo loco al mio languire') is placed between the other two lines of the refrain.

[18] D'India's text introduces two sections of stanzaic poetry within the otherwise blank verse. Both stanzaic sections present two four-line strophes, rhyming *abba*, all with eleven-syllable lines. In the first of these sections, Apollo speaks dispassionately of the potential disaster which would follow his death; and in the second, he commands that the laurel wreath shall become the symbol of victory. For both stanzaic sections, d'India avoids any suggestion of more lyrical aria style; he continues in declamatory recitative, with a sustained continuo line.

D'India's two remaining laments from *Le musiche . . . Libro quinto* (1623) are the words of grieving women.[19] Both Dido and Olimpia, like Ariadne, were abandoned by their lovers on the seashore, and like Rinuccini's Ariadne, both of d'India's heroines frantically call for their lovers' return, finding incomprehensible any possible reasons for their betrayal. They finally seek vengeance, but their rage is suddenly broken off, as Olimpia, like Ariadne, thinks of her abiding love for her departed beloved, while Dido thinks only of her approaching death. In these two works, d'India gives his finest examples of how expressive recitative can represent the volatile mind of a distraught heroine. Thus Dido's lament has four notable episodes, each marked by a gradual rise and sudden fall of tension. First, she questions Aeneas' motives for leaving her, but then implores him not to hate her. Next, she rails against him, but suddenly calls for him to return. Then she considers dying scorned and despised, but abruptly changes her line of thought. And finally, she calls for the raging furies to wreak vengeance, but suddenly feels symptoms of her own ebbing life. In each case, the sudden change of mind is matched by an abrupt pause and change of declamatory speed. The first of these episodes is given as Ex. 4.6. Beginning with 'Dove ten vai?', the successive phrases rise in pitch from $f\sharp'$ to e'' in a prevailing quaver declamation; then comes the long rest, followed by the fall of a minor seventh and declamation in crotchets. Although d'India's piece has no textual or musical refrains to unify the entire work, the poem has many parallelisms and repeating words which are then matched by the music. Obvious examples are in Ex. 4.6:

> Enea, mia vita, Enea, dove ten vai?
> Dove ten vai, crudele?
> Perchè sola mi lasci?
> Perchè da me ten fuggi?
> Che ti feci, cor mio?
> Perchè negarmi, ohimè, l'ultimo addio?

Also, the full lament is integrated by a tonal centre on D, with an auxiliary focus on E. As for d'India's Olimpia, she sings with similar passion and rapidly changing moods. More than in any of the laments considered earlier, her desperate state is constantly emphasized through sighs and exclamations ('ahi', 'ohimè', 'ciò', 'deh', 'aiuto', etc.) which are represented musically by rests, leaping pitches, syncopations, and dissonances. One characteristic passage, seen in Ex. 4.7, presents four sighs of 'Ohimè' followed by cries for help. Olimpia's final pleas in the example, 'Chi, lassa, mi soccorre? aita,

[19] Tomlinson (ed.), *Italian Secular Song*, iv. 138–42, 151–5. For modern editions, see d'India, *Le musiche a una e due voci*, ed. Joyce, 295–304, 317–26.

Ex. 4.6. D'India, 'Infelice Didone' (*Lamento di Didone*)

E - nea, mia vi-ta, E-nea, do - ve ten va-i? Do-ve ten vai, cru-de-le? Per-chè

so - la mi la - sci? Per-chè da me ten fug - gi? Che ti fe - ci, cor mi - o?

Per-chè ne-gar-mi, ohi-mè, l'ul - ti - mo ad-di - o? Non m'o-di tu, mio so - le?

Deh, por - tas - se-ro i ven - ti, Co-me por-tan le ve - le i miei la-men - ti!

(. . . Aeneas, my life, Aeneas, where are you going? Where are you going, cruel one? Why do you leave me alone? Why do you flee from me? What did I do to you, my heart? Why deny me, alas, the last farewell? Do you not hear me, my sun? Ah, let the winds carry my laments as they do your sails! . . .)

Ex. 4.7. D'India, 'Misera me, sia vero' (*Lamento d'Olimpia*)

Ohi - mè, ohi - mè ch'io mo-ro! Ohi - mè, ohi - mè,

chi mi da vi - ta, _____ Chi, las- sa, mi soc-cor-re? a - i - ta, a - i - ta!

(. . . Alas, alas I die! Alas, alas, who gives me life, who, alas, brings me aid? Help, help! . . .)

aita!', comprise a refrain heard in two other places in the lament, each time reinforcing the heroine's sense of general hopelessness.

Another lament of Olimpia, 'Voglio, voglio morire', attributed to Monteverdi in its only extant source but surely by another (as yet unknown) composer, is clearly modelled on Monteverdi's *Lamento d'Arianna*.[20] Divided into three parts, the text treats various thoughts and emotions found in the earlier Rinuccini poem. The first seven lines are very similar (same versification and subject-matter), with the heroine calling for death ('Lasciatemi morire'/'Voglio, voglio morir'); she then continues with piteous calls for Bireno's return and with references to her abandoned parents and homeland. The second part focuses on Bireno as a traitor and the third on Olimpia's burst of anger, followed by her reconsideration and realization that her heart remains with her beloved. Olimpia's final lines are 'Perdona, ohimè perdona, | perch'altro il cor, altro la lingua suona' ('Forgive, alas forgive, | for the heart speaks differently from the tongue'); she does not go on to express Ariadne's closing thoughts of death and the futility of love and trust. Although the musical setting has some isolated parallels with Monteverdi's

[20] London, British Library, Add. MS 30491. See Danckwardt, 'Das Lamento d'Olimpia'. Danckwardt finds the attribution to Monteverdi highly doubtful on grounds of artistic inferiority and demonstrates clearly the work's parodistic relationship to Monteverdi's *Lamento d'Arianna*. A modern edition of the lament is in *Claudio Monteverdi: 12 composizioni vocali profane e sacre (inedite) con e senza basso continuo*, ed. Wolfgang Osthoff (2nd edn., Milan: Ricordi, 1978).

lament, it lacks Monteverdi's masterful attention to details in the text and his overall command of tonal design. The most dramatic moments come in the second and third parts, with gradual rises and falls of pitch to match the corresponding stages of Olimpia's rage and subsequent remorse. Elsewhere, Olimpia delivers the text with much repetition of single pitches over a slowly changing continuo.

Apart from these two laments of Olimpia by d'India and pseudo-Monteverdi, characters from Ariosto's *Orlando furioso* inspired no other large-scale chamber laments strictly in recitative style.[21] But from Tasso's more recent *Gerusalemme liberata*, the pitiable Erminia, grieving over the seemingly lifeless body of her beloved Tancredi, was the subject for three such laments. The earliest appears in three manuscripts which are associated with Cardinal Montalto in Rome and datable mainly from 1611 to 1619.[22] Ascribable to the Sicilian organist and composer Ottavio Catalani, the work sets four stanzas of Tasso's text,[23] including all but the final two lines of Erminia's monologue. She bewails the irony of finally seeing her beloved again but not being seen by him (first stanza); she questions where signs of his vibrant life have gone (second stanza); and then she decides to kiss his lifeless body

[21] Giovanni Francesco Anerio (1611) and Antonio Cifra (1615 and 1617) each have settings for solo voice of one or two single stanzas from Ariosto. 'Mortalmente ferito', a lament of Zerbino by Mario Savioni to a text by Domenico Benigni, is a long cantata inspired by the Ariosto character Zerbino who laments his dead Isabella. The music, however, is mainly in aria style, and therefore not considered here; for a discussion of the poem and Savioni's setting, see Robert Rau Holzer, 'Music and Poetry in Seventeenth-Century Rome: Settings of the Canzonetta and Cantata Texts of Francesco Balducci, Domenico Benigni, Francesco Melosio, and Antonio Abati (Ph.D. diss., University of Pennsylvania, 1990), 307–14.
[22] Venice, Conservatorio di Musica Benedetto Marcello, Fondo Torrefranca, MS 28600, fos. 45ᵛ–48ʳ; Bologna, Civico Museo Bibliografico Musicale, CC.225; and Rome, Biblioteca Universitaria Alessandrina, MS 279 (attrib. Ottavio Catalani). The three manuscripts, all copied by the Roman Francesco Maria Fucci, were among seven discussed by John Walter Hill in a paper, 'Early Roman Monody from the Circle of Cardinal Montalto', delivered at the annual meeting of the American Musicological Society, Boston, in 1981. For a further discussion of styles within these manuscripts, see Hill's 'Frescobaldi's *Arie*', in Alexander Silbiger (ed.), *Frescobaldi Studies* (Durham, NC: Duke University Press, 1987), 157–94, also published as 'Le arie di Frescobaldi e la cerchia musicale del cardinal Montalto', in Sergio Durante and Dinko Fabris (eds.), *Frescobaldi e il suo tempo: Girolamo Frescobaldi nel IV centenario della nascita* (Florence: Olschki, 1986), 215–32. The Venice MS, which also has an early copy of Monteverdi's *Lamento d'Arianna*, is also discussed in Irving Godt, 'A Monteverdi Source Reappears: The "Grilanda" of F. M. Fucci', *Music & Letters*, 60 (1979), 428–39, which includes a transcription of the lament of Erminia. In the 1940s, Fausto Torrefranca attributed Erminia's lament to Monteverdi on stylistic grounds, but the attribution has been rejected by most Monteverdi scholars. In the Venice MS, the music is headed 'Lamento cantato dalla Sig.a Olimpia Saponara nella comedia del Ill.mo Sig.r Cardinal Savelli'.
[23] XIX. 105–8, beginning with the third line of stanza 105 (the first two lines belong to the preceding narration).

once more (third and fourth stanzas). Catalani's composition comprises a
series of four short sections of music which are variously repeated with
different texts over the course of the four stanzas.[24] The entire work is set
as a declamatory recitative, with many repeated notes in the voice over
generally slow-changing harmonies. Although the vocal line is sensitive to
textual rhythms and syntax, and makes appropriate adjustments for new texts
in repeated sections, it offers few interpretations of poignant moments in
Erminia's monologue. Indeed, the schematic design of the piece, which
makes repeated use of standard harmonic progressions (especially i–iv–V–i,
and i–VII–VI–V), and the generally restricted vocal range (a third either side
of *d'*, with few melismas except for word-painting or rhetorical emphasis)
suggests the well-known formulaic approach to singing *ottave rime* in the late
Renaissance and early Baroque periods, in which the performer adds indi-
vidualized nuances and embellishments to a pre-existing pattern.[25]

In Biagio Marini's *Le lagrime d'Erminia*, printed in Parma in 1623 by
Anteo Viotti, a short prose synopsis before the music tells of Erminia's earlier
travels and woes, and informs the reader that she has finally found Tancredi
by the Jordan and believes him to be dead. The poem itself is by Guido
Casone and consists of twenty six-line stanzas, alternating *settenari* and
endecasillabi with the rhyme *ababcc*. The first six stanzas, set for a tenor in the
role of a narrator, tells of the pitiable and weeping Erminia. In the remaining
fourteen stanzas, sung by a soprano, Erminia addresses Tancredi, presenting
a variety of grievances: how cruel he was to take away both her soul and
her hope! She laments her lost liberty, country, family, and above all, her
rejected love. Formerly a noble queen, she is now a homeless citizen of the
forests, seeking consolation from compassionate shepherds. Throughout the
monologue, Erminia sustains an unrelenting mood of self-pity and despair,
and never lashes out in anger. Marini sets the entire composition in recitative style, disregarding the stanzaic structure of the poem. From time to
time, individual words are given short expressive embellishments, but there
are few dissonances or other musical gestures to add drama to the overall
work.

Similar in concept is Giovanni Rovetta's *Le lagrime d'Erminia*, included in
his *Madrigali concertati . . . libro primo* (Venice: Bartolomeo Magni, 1629).[26]
The anonymous paraphrase of *Gerusalemme liberata*, XIX. 104–8, is in five

[24] See the analysis in Godt, 'A Monteverdi Source Reappears', 433.

[25] For a discussion of formulaic patterns for singing *ottave rime*, see James Haar, 'Arie per
cantar stanze ariostesche', in Maria Antonella Balsano (ed.), *L'Ariosto, la musica, i musicisti:
Quattro studi e sette madrigali ariosteschi* (Florence: Olschki, 1981), 31–46. The various 'arie'
given as Haar's Ex. 2 (pp. 36–9) have bass lines which are particularly suggestive of the
patterns found in the Catalani lament.

[26] Facs. edn. in Tomlinson (ed.), *Italian Secular Song*, vii. 74–83.

stanzas, the first assigned to a narrator, and the other four to Erminia. But in fact, the entire work, including Erminia's monologue, is sung by a tenor, in recitative style. Erminia's words focus only on grieving images of Tancredi's lifeless body and make no reference to her past experiences. Her final stanza is typical:

> Morte ch'a me ti tolse, hor mi conceda
> in difetto d'amor gli estremi baci,
> freddi e languidi baci, infausta preda,
> di sfortunato Amor larve fallaci.
> Così ne' baci miei l'alma posseda
> fra le tue labbra l'ultime sue paci,
> sì ch'io morendo à la tua bocca unita
> sol viva in te fin ch'i miei baci han vita.

(May death that took you away from me now grant me | in default of love the last kisses, | cold languid kisses, ill-omened booty, | deceitful ghosts of unhappy love. | Thus in my kisses may my soul possess | in your lips its last sensations of peace, | so that in dying united to your mouth, | I may live only in you as long as my kisses have life.)

Rovetta's recitative is newly composed for each stanza and introduces some virtuoso flourishes to emphasize or illustrate certain words in the poem (e.g. 'tremante', 'fiamme', 'ahi', 'larve', 'baci', etc.). But since the text has no sudden dramatic changes of mood, Rovetta's music provides few opportunities for an impassioned performance.

Among the last chamber laments in the emotionally charged tradition of Monteverdi and d'India are Jacopo Peri's lament of Iole and Benedetto Ferrari's lament of Andromeda. Peri's work may have been intended for an opera *Iole ed Ercole*, with a libretto by Andrea Salvadori, which was planned for the 1628 wedding festivities of Margherita de' Medici and Odoardo Farnese of Parma.[27] Even from the opening lines it is clear that Peri's text is closely modelled on Rinuccini:

Rinuccini	*Salvadori?*
Lasciatemi morire,	Uccidimi, dolore,
lasciatemi morire.	uccidimi, dolore.
E che volete voi che mi conforte	E qui mi veggia l'idolo mio spietato
in così dura sorte,	per soverchio martire
in così gran martire?	innanzi a lui morire.

---

[27] The most recent modern edition is in *Jacopo Peri: 'Le varie musiche' and Other Songs*, ed. Tim Carter (Recent Researches in the Music of the Baroque Era, 50; Madison, Wis.: A–R Editions, 1985), 92–100.

Although the circumstances of Iole's abandonment are different from those of Ariadne, she nevertheless raises questions of how a lover who had once lavished such affection upon her could now leave. Does he value her kisses less than the wrathful commands of Mars? Instead of going to battle, could he be searching for another love? Iole flies into a rage, with the expected curses of her misfortune and Hercules' treachery. But with a sudden reconsideration, she confesses her delirious state of mind and her abiding love for Hercules. Peri's setting uses the various expressive devices of Monteverdi's Ariadne: irregular dissonances for poignant words or exclamations, changes in rhythmic pacing to underline changing moods, and moderate chromaticism within an essentially diatonic idiom.

Benedetto Ferrari's monologue of Andromeda was published in the first book of his *Musiche varie a voce sola* (Venice: Bartolomeo Magni, 1633);[28] the text is by the composer. Andromeda is not specific about the cause of her dire plight but simply blames cruel fate that she must satisfy the gluttonous wishes of beasts and gods. Chained to the rocky cliff, her most impassioned moments come as she imagines in her terror the horrible monster tearing her to pieces (Ex. 4.8). Over a slow-moving bass, Ferrari's vocal part captures Andromeda's distraught condition through wide leaps, dissonances, frequent pauses, and repetitions of text. In the last sections of the lament, she lashes out at the transitory state of worldly happiness: 'O fleeting beauty of nature, o most bitter sweetness of the world; how near the sunset of human splendours is to the sunset of pains and grief . . . Foolish is the one who trusts this world that seems so strong and is as fragile as glass.'

The numerous works so far discussed come predominantly from northern Italy in the first third of the seventeenth century, and they illustrate the power of early Baroque recitative in imitating the impassioned speech of a distraught figure who pours out a succession of mixed emotions over the loss of a loved one. With the exception of the two Erminia laments by Marini and Rovetta, each of which has a narrator as well as direct speech, any of these laments could have served (and indeed Monteverdi's and perhaps Peri's did serve) as monologue scenes within operatic productions, and not just as effective chamber pieces. Gradually rising tensions in the character's speech are matched to increasing speed of declamation and higher pitches, often involving sequential repetitions of text and musical motifs. Conversely, feelings

---

[28] Facs. edn. in Tomlinson (ed.), *Italian Secular Song*, v. 299–304. The myth of Andromeda and Perseus became the subject of the opera *Andromeda* with music by Francesco Manelli and libretto by Ferrari, premièred at the Teatro S. Cassiano in Venice in 1637. An earlier *Andromeda* by Girolamo Giacobbi (music lost), to a text by Ridolfo Campeggi, dates from 1610 in Bologna.

Ex. 4.8. Ferrari, 'Lassa, lassa che veggio'

O ____ Dio, già di mortal cru - do spa - ven - to

Im - pal - li - di - sco, e nel - le fi - bra il san - gue S'ap - pren - de, e si con -

- ge - la. Già, già di sen - tir par - mi, Già di ve - der mi sem - bra L'hor - ri - bil mo - stro in -

- sa - no Strac - ciar - mi, strac - ciar - mi à bra - no à bra - no, Ne ba - sta al mo - rir mi - o

Lo stral di mor - te do - lo - ro - - so e fie - - ro

Ex. 4.8. (*cont.*)

(. . . O God, already am I growing pale from deadly, cruel fear; and in my
nerves blood takes fire and freezes. Already I seem to feel—to see—the horrible
insane monster tearing me, tearing me to pieces, nor is the arrow of painful
and violent death enough for my dying, which deprives me of life and also
thought. . . .)

of growing depression are created by falling pitch and slower motion, as well
as by dissonances and chromatic progressions. Gasps, interjections, and sudden
changes of mood are highlighted through the use of rests and abrupt shifts
of register. In these many ways, the flexibility of a continuous recitative style
was superbly suited to the musical outpouring of a grieving individual in the
early decades of the Baroque, an observation made by the Florentine theorist
Giovanni Battista Doni in his treatises *Il compendio del trattato de' generi e de'
modi della musica* (1635) and *Trattato della musica scenica* (*c.*1633–5); Doni,
in fact, used Monteverdi's *Lamento d'Arianna* as his example of expressive
recitative.

RECITATIVE LAMENTS IN EARLY CANTATAS
During the second quarter of the seventeenth century, however, fundamen-
tally new approaches changed the character of the recitative lament as a
chamber composition, particularly as the increasingly popular arias in operas
and vocal chamber music diminished the role of expressive recitatives. A
singing narrator, found only rarely in the earlier laments from northern Italy
(e.g. the Erminia laments by Marini and Rovetta), now normally framed the
monologue of the grieving character in order to provide a setting before the
lament and then to tell of the character's fate afterwards. This same singer
then had to transmute into the role of the grieving character for the purpose
of presenting the monologue. Within the monologue itself, the character sang
in speech-like recitative style (at least in the laments continuing the recitative-
lament tradition), but often broke into an arioso passage or even into a short
independent aria in order to sustain a single emotion, or to punctuate a
section of the discourse. The recitative lament thus lost its original character
as a pure monologue, stageable in an operatic production, and became a

concert piece no longer restricted to the representation of impassioned speech; it was thereby free to encompass a greater variety of musical styles.

The Roman cantata composers Luigi Rossi, Marco Marazzoli, and Mario Savioni, each of whom set at least one lament of a classical figure, provide fine examples of the new trends. Rossi composed two recitative laments on characters from ancient literature (Deïaneira and Arion), both most likely composed before 1641.[29] Each work opens and closes with a narrator, who creates the setting for the central monologue. In Deïaneira's lament 'All'hor ch'il fort'Alcide',[30] the opening narration informs the listener (but not Deïaneira) that Alcides' (Hercules) return home is long overdue because of his dalliance with the beautiful Iole. Unaware of the reason for his delay, Deïaneira in her monologue expresses her anguish at being separated from her beloved, and three times pleads for his return in a single-line refrain: 'Return to Deïaneira, Alcides'. In the concluding narration, we are told that she runs to the beach in the mistaken belief that she hears his approach. Rossi's music is predominantly a declamatory recitative, with infrequent chord changes; expressive dissonances within the vocal line or between the voice and the continuo are rare. But occasionally Rossi makes significant departures from this prevailing recitative style. One such place comes at the end of Deïaneira's monologue (Ex. 4.9) as she sees visions of Alcides, first a victim of a wild beast and then in pursuit of a shameless woman. She then dismisses her fears and concludes her lament with a final repetition of her refrain ('Return to Deïaneira, Alcides'). In Rossi's music for this section, the recitative is intensified through several wide leaps in the voice ('e lo trafigga, ohimè' and '. . . la fede antica. | Ma di tal vaneggiare'), dissonances between voice and bass, and a gradually rising vocal line ('e con rigor maggiore' to 'la fede antica'). In the refrain (at the end of Ex. 4.9, and heard twice earlier in the cantata), the singer shifts to a lyrical arioso, perhaps to suggest the urgency of Deïaneira's plea but also to serve as a punctuating device for a section of the monologue. Finally, Rossi expands the last line of the concluding narration ('come havesse d'Amor l'ali à le piante'; 'as if she had the wings of Love at her weeping') by repeating the text, changing to triple metre, and embellishing 'l'ali' with virtuoso passagework. Deïaneira's monologue (but not the framing parts for narrator) is often centered on B minor, and at times it features a descending fourth in the bass (see the refrain at the end of Ex. 4.9), the descending tetrachord known to be an 'emblem of lament', in Ellen Rosand's memorable phrase.

In Rossi's lament of Arion, 'Al soave spirar d'aure serene', to a text by

---

[29] The dating is suggested by the Paris MSS listed in nn. 30 and 31.
[30] Paris, Bibliothèque nationale, Rés. Vm⁷ 102, fos. 87ʳ–90ᵛ.

Ex. 4.9. Rossi, 'All'hor ch'il fort'Alcide'

Ma non mo - re col gior - no il mio tor - men - to,   Per-chè

par - mi tal - hor ch'Er - co - le e - stin - to E da fe - ra cru - del à ter - ra

ca - da,   E lo tra - fig - ga, ohi - mè,   più ___ d'u - na ___

___ spa - da,   E con ri - gor mag - gio - re Ge - la po - scia nel

Giulio Rospigliosi, the opening narration tells of Arion's horror as his life is threatened by the angry sailors accompanying him on his voyage.[31] In his following monologue, Arion gives repeated cries for help and asks why his

---

[31] The work survives in at least seven manuscripts: Rome, Biblioteca Apostolica Vaticana, Chigi Q VII 99 (facsimile in *Cantatas by Luigi Rossi*, ed. Francesco Luisi (The Italian Cantata in the Seventeenth Century, 1; New York and London: Garland, 1986), 91–5); Paris, Bibliothèque nationale, Rés. Vm⁷ 59, fos. 1ʳ–8ᵛ; London, British Library, Harley 1265, fos. 125ʳ–42ʳ; Rome, Biblioteca Casanatense, MS 2477, fos. 13ʳ–22ᵛ; Rome, Biblioteca Apostolica Vaticana, Chigi Q IV 3, fos. 39ᵛ–51ᵛ; Naples, Conservatorio di Musica S. Pietro a Majella, MS 33.5.18, fos. 59ʳ–70ᵛ, and 33.3.11, fos. 85ʳ–92ʳ.

Ex. 4.9. (*cont.*)

cor l'a - ni - ma mi - a. Al - l'hor che va - neg - gian - te Io Io ri -

- mi - ro in fem - mi - nil sem - bian - te Se - guir don - na im - pu - di - ca A

me rot - ta in - fe - del la fe - de an - ti - ca. Ma di tal va - neg - gia - re A-mor sen

ri - de. Tor - na, deh tor - na a Dei-a - ni - ra Al - ci - de.

(. . . But my torment does not cease with the day, for it now seems to me that Hercules is dead and is felled to the ground by a wild animal, and more than one sword transfixes him, and with greater harshness my soul freezes in my heart. Now, delirious, I see him pursuing a shameless woman in female guise, the faithless one having broken his former vow to me. But Love laughs at such delirium. Return, ah return to Deïaneira, Alcides. . . .)

former friends have suddenly turned against him. Near the end of the
lament, he has an outburst of anger followed by a sudden change of mind
and mood, in a manner recalling Monteverdi's and d'India's great laments.
After the frantic monologue, the concluding narration tells us that Arion fell
into the turbulent sea but was subsequently rescued through the power of
his passionate singing, heard by a friendly dolphin which then nudged him
to shore. The narrator concludes with a contemporary message: 'Now if
harmonious accents can accomplish such a marvel, can[not] the singing of
a beautiful woman with lovable pain bind every soul?' Much of Rossi's
cantata is set in a recitative style close to that of Deïaneira's lament, where
text declamation is skilfully handled but without sudden changes of mood.
However, when Arion flies into his rage and then regrets his words, the
recitative is more reminiscent of Monteverdi and d'India, with an abrupt
change of register, of speed of declamation, and of tonal orientation (Ex.
4.10). However, significant portions of the cantata depart from the recitative
style. Brief ariosos occur twice for the refrain 'Ahi, chi mi porge aita' ('Ah,
who offers me help'), and for three other single lines of affective text: 'o
pensier troppo folli' ('o thoughts too insane'), 'mostri di crudeltà' ('monsters
of cruelty'), and 'o pianti, o doglie, o pene' ('o weeping, o suffering, o
torments'). The cantata also has two short independent arias. The first is at
the beginning of Arion's monologue, and incorporates two additional presentations of the refrain as its first and fifth lines of text: 'Ahi, chi mi porge
aita? | Chi da morte mi toglie? | S'alcun pietade in gentil cor accoglie, |
sia scudo alla mia vita! | Ahi, chi mi porge aita?' ('Ah, who offers me help?
| Who takes me away from death? | If any pity is granted to a gentle heart,
| be the shield of my life. | Ah, who offers me help?'). Rossi's reason for
setting this section of text as an aria is later made clear by the second aria
of the cantata, sung at the end of the work as the narrator tells about the
effects of 'harmonious accents'. It was through the power of Arion's singing
that he was saved by the kindly dolphin, just as through the power of singing a beautiful woman can conquer every soul. Although the texts for both
arias are in *versi sciolti* and as such might well have been set in the recitative
style that prevails elsewhere in the lament, both arias convey the extraordinary power of music (as opposed to that of speech) and thus appropriately
call forth more musical settings.

Three additional cantatas attributed to Rossi present laments by characters
from the Renaissance epics: Olimpia ('Fra romite contrade'),[32] Armida ('Potesti

---

[32] Paris, Bibliothèque nationale, Rés. Vm⁷ 59, fos. 67ʳ–69ᵛ. Although the singer twice
cries out to Bireno, she does not specifically identify herself as the Olimpia of Ariosto's epic.
That she is, however, is suggested by a reference to a ship setting sail, thereby abandoning
her on a deserted island.

Ex. 4.10. Rossi, 'Al soave spirar d'aure serene'

Ex. 4.10. (*cont.*)

(. . . I will agitate the clouds, I will clash with the winds, and against the fragile
ship, in imitating wrath, I will break the voracious waves. Quiet, miserable one,
quiet; your mind is delirious. Do you not know that all anger is in vain and
without force? Indeed, friends, pardon my grief; it speaks, not I. . . .)

i lini sciogliere'),[33] and Erminia ('Erminia sventurata').[34] In all three the
music is predominantly in recitative style, with slow harmonic rhythm, few
dissonances, and relatively few imposing rhetorical flourishes in the vocal
line. 'Fra romite contrade', to a text by Antonio Abati, is the shortest of the
five Rossi laments considered in this essay; it comprises only the words of
the abandoned Olimpia, without a framing narration. Apparently having
found solace in nature, she finally issues a warning to other girls to beware
of the perils of love: 'naïve young girls, who are at the same time both pre-
dators and prey of false lovers, extinguish your ardours; do not trust your-
selves . . .'. Rossi's only significant departures from recitative style come in
an arioso refrain which is heard twice during the cantata at 'un ingrato
Bireno | mi rapì, mi tradì, | m'allettò, mi scernì' ('an ungrateful Bireno |
abducted me, betrayed me, | ensnared me, scorned me').

   Armida's lament, 'Potesti i lini sciogliere', to an anonymous poem of six
stanzas each with identical versification, is set entirely in recitative style. The
basic pattern is established in the first stanza:

> Potesti i lini sciogliere
>   e me cruda lasciar su l'erme arene,
>   de la mia fede a cogliere

[33] Evanston, Illinois, Northwestern University Library, Music MS 1, cantata no. 14.
This source was acquired in 1977 and is the subject of my 'Northwestern University's
Seventeenth-Century Manuscript of Roman Cantatas', forthcoming in *Essays in Memory of
John F. Ohl.* So far as I am aware, this anthology of thirty-nine cantatas, most likely compiled
between the mid-1630s and 1660, is the sole source of this Armida lament, here attributed
to Luigi Rossi.

[34] Rome, Biblioteca Apostolica Vaticana, Barb. lat. 4200, fos. 67ᵛ–72ʳ; Oxford, Christ
Church, MS 946, fos. 91ʳ–96ᵛ; London, British Library, Harley 1265, fos. 143ʳ–152ᵛ; Naples,
Conservatorio di Musica S. Pietro a Majella, MS 33.4.12, fos. 75ʳ–84ʳ; Rome, Biblioteca
Casanatense, MS 2478, fos. 4ʳ–8ᵛ.

fior di vano sperar, frutto di pene.
Va pur e sian con tè
de l'aria tutti i turbini,
del mare tutti i fremiti,
del cielo tutti i fulmini,
poiche legge d'amore in te non è.

(You were capable of opening the sails, | and of leaving me unprotected on the solitary shores, | to gather from my faith | the flower of vain hope, the fruit of suffering. | Go then, and let there be with you | all the whirlwinds of the air, | all the roaring of the sea, | all the lightning of the sky, | since the rule of Love is not in you.)

The mixture of line-lengths and line-endings, including *versi sdruccioli* and *tronchi*, are features normally thought to be associated with the light-hearted *canzonetta* tradition, but here they are made to suit the serious mood of the lament.[35] The first four lines state Armida's deplorable condition, while the remaining five give her reaction to it as she places Rinaldo at the mercy of the elements. Her alternation of self-pity and rage continues through the first three stanzas, which are set as modified strophic variations. However, in the fourth stanza, with completely new music, she abruptly begins to pray for mercy for Rinaldo, using the familiar words of earlier laments: 'Ma dove, ahi lassa, spronami | il furor, il dolor che l'alma accora? | Idolo mio, perdonami: | se la lingua t'offese, il cor t'adora' ('But where, alas, am I driven | by the fury, the grief that overwhelms my soul? | My idol, forgive me: | if my tongue offended you, my heart adores you'). Rossi's setting continues with new music for the fifth stanza, when Armida prays for mercy for herself, and for the sixth, when the narrator tells of Armida's sorrowful departure.

In 'Erminia sventurata', the narrator's lines at the end tell that the love-sick Erminia is languishing by the Jordan, but nowhere in her monologue does she mention Tancredi by name. She only questions the cruelty of her fate, which now leaves her abandoned and alone. The prevailing recitative is twice broken by a more lyrical refrain, partially over a descending chromatic tetrachord, in which Erminia asks who will now comfort and console her. Her monologue concludes with a short aria-like section in triple metre (Ex. 4.11) which reinforces her utterly hopeless mood. For this section, the descending tetrachord returns as a sevenfold ostinato, heard four times chromatically and three times diatonically. The ground bass ends on the

---

[35] Holzer (in 'Music and Poetry in Seventeenth-Century Rome') dispels the commonly held view that canzonettas always treat light subject-matter, and provides numerous examples of serious subjects presented in stanzaic poetry with diverse versification schemes. See especially his chs. 2 and 3.

William V. Porter

Ex. 4.11. Rossi, 'Erminia sventurata'

Mo - ri, in - fe - li - ce, mo - ri, mo -

- - ri Cer - ta di tue ru - i - - ne;

et ha - vran fi - ne__ Con un so - lo do - lor_____ tan - ti do -

- lo - - ri. Mo - ri, in - fe - li - ce,

mo - ri, mo - - - ri.

(... Die, unhappy one, die certain of your ruin; and with one sole grief so
many sorrows will have an end. Die, unhappy one, die, die. . . .)

dominant, thus denying the section the status of a completely independent aria. Immediately following, the narrator returns in recitative style in duple metre for concluding remarks about Erminia's pitiable state. Rossi's use of the descending tetrachord, first within the arioso refrains and then for the ostinato in the aria-like section—but both times closely connected to the surrounding recitatives—closely parallels the use of the emblematic tetrachord in operatic laments during the early 1640s.[36] In both chamber and operatic scenes, the flexible recitative sections allow the exploration of quickly or even subtly changing thoughts, while the more lyrical sections over the symbolic bass patterns produce moments of immutable despair.

Two cantatas, both attributed to Marazzoli and dated in the 1640s, are among the last of the recitative laments on ancient classical subjects: 'La dov'Etna contesse', a lament of Galatea,[37] and 'A pena udito havea | la bella Cleopatra'.[38] Both works introduce an independent aria near the end which summarizes one or two basic moods already expressed more diffusely in earlier recitatives of the cantata. In 'La dov'Etna contesse' the narrator appears only in the opening section, telling of the cruel stoning of Acis by the monster Polyphemus, and of gentle Galatea's frantic search for her beloved. In her monologue, Galatea learns gradually of Acis' fate and his murderer through questions answered by Echo, who identifies himself as the spirit of her deceased lover.[39] She then laments her loss, which is reinforced by a single-line refrain 'Sventurata beltade' ('Unfortunate beauty'). Next, her thoughts turn to revenge as she appeals first to Jupiter and then to the wild beasts of the forest. Finally, she sings a concluding aria, with two stanzas using essentially the same music (Ex. 4.12 gives the second stanza). The aria has two sections which successively depict the discrete moods of despair and vengeful rage: the opening, marked 'adagio', with its lyrical vocal line, sharply contrasts with the following 'presto', with its rapid quaver patter. In Marazzoli's 'A pena udito havea' the opening narration tells that Cleopatra has just heard the bitter news of the death of her lover. After reviewing the earlier glories of her reign, she resigns herself to her own impending death

[36] See Rosand, *Opera in Seventeenth-Century Venice*, ch. 12, and compare Rossi's cantata with Rosand's Ex. 79, Deidamia's lament from Francesco Sacrati's *La finta pazza* (1641), in which the descending tetrachord is heard only twice in each of two presentations of a refrain.

[37] Northwestern University Library, Music MS 1, cantata no. 2. This manuscript, which ascribes the piece to Marazzoli, appears to be its only source.

[38] Biblioteca Apostolica Vaticana, Chigi Q VI 81, fos. 41ᵛ–45ʳ. Wolfgang Witzenmann ('Autographe Marco Marazzolis in der Biblioteca Vaticana (II)', *Analecta musicologica*, 9 (1970), 203–94 at 215) dates the manuscript *c.*1642?–5.

[39] The character Echo also appears in Loreto Vittori's opera *La Galatea*, premièred in Naples in 1644. Here, however, Echo is Cupid in disguise, and has taken the side of Acis' murderer, Polyphemus.

Ex. 4.12. Marazzoli, 'La dov'Etna contesse'

Il mio bel l'A - ci è mor - to, Po - li -
fe - mo il tra - dì, On - d'io sen - za con - for - to
Pian - ge - rò not - te e dì, pian - ge - rò not - te e dì.

Sù, sù pren - de - te - lo, Fie - re uc - ci - de - te - lo, Que -

and feels the poison of the asp as it runs through her veins. Then in a short aria of two stanzas, set in triple metre, she projects a final mood of serenity. The narrator returns in a brief recitative to announce that Cleopatra is dead.

Marazzoli's lament of Armida, 'Dove fuggi, crudele? | Crudele amato e non più dolce amante', is one of my latest examples (dated *c*.1655–6).[40] The

---

[40] Biblioteca Apostolica Vaticana, Chigi Q V 69, fos. 69ᵛ–74ʳ. I take the dating from Witzenmann, 'Autographe Marco Marazzolis', 281. For a facs. edn., see *Cantatas by Marco Marazzoli*, ed. Wolfgang Witzenmann (The Italian Cantata in the Seventeenth Century, 4; New York and London: Garland, 1986), 222–31.

Ex. 4.12. (*cont.*)

(. . . My beautiful Acis is dead, Polyphemus betrayed him, thus I without comfort will weep night and day. Up, up, take him, wild animals kill him, this wicked monster who murdered him.)

text exploits most of the stereotypical topics of the genre, comprising a free mixture of rage, sorrow, and continuing love. The latter part of the poem presents many opportunities to depict the troubled mind of the heroine.

> O mio diletto, o mio caro, o mio vago,
> ed è pur vero, ahi lassa,
> che mi t'involi, oh Dio?
>
> Deh, quali empi costumi
> il cor ti trasformaro?
> E chi t'invoglia,
> là fra barbare turbe,
>
> Vanne, empio, vanne, e 'l cielo
> e l'onde e' nembi e le tempeste e' venti
> s'armin di tetro velo!
> Voi folgori, voi lampi,
> voi turbini e procelle
> ch'ergeste il pondo de' cerulei campi
> fin all'aurate stelle,
> entro all'algoso lido
> sommergete quest'empio e quest'infido!
> Ma che parlo? che dico?
> Vanne con cielo amico,

abbia l'aure seconde,
abbia tranquille l'onde,
e s'armasti di strali i tuoi begl'occhi,
arma di ferro il petto!
Vattene, o mio diletto, e fa' ch'il core
nelle fiamme di Marte arda d'amore!

(O my delight, o my dear, o my love, | is it indeed true, alas, | that you leave me, o God? | . . . | Indeed, what impious manners | have transformed your heart? | And who tempts you | there among the barbarous hordes? | . . . | Go, impious one, go; and let the sky, | waves, clouds, tempests, and winds | arm themselves with a veil of loathly murk! | You lightning, you thunder, | you storms and whirlwinds | who bore the weight of the cerulean plains | up to the golden stars, | in sight of the wracky shore | sink this impious and faithless one! | But what am I speaking? What am I saying? | Go with a friendly sky, | have favourable winds, | have calm waters, | and if you armed your beautiful eyes with arrows, | arm your breast with iron! | Go, o my delight, and make your heart | in the flames of Mars burn with love!)

Marazzoli's music, however, shows little of the expected treatment of rage and a subsequent change of heart. This section has only a few vocal dissonances and mostly unfolds over a slowly changing accompaniment until 'Ma che parlo? che dico?'. From here to the end, Armida forgets her troubles and sings a light aria in triple metre which focuses only on her best wishes for her departed lover.

In the same manuscript as Marazzoli's lament of Armida is his lament of Artemisia, 'Già celebrato havea | la Regina di Caria al morto sposo', to a poem by S. Casino.[41] On the basis of its framing narration, set in recitative style, the work appears to derive from the tradition of the earlier recitative laments. But within Artemisia's monologue—the core of the cantata—she expresses her state of mind in three independent arias with virtuoso elements, each separated by less imposing recitatives. In the poetry, Casino clearly distinguishes the verses for recitatives (*versi sciolti*) from those for the arias (almost entirely *ottonari*, with systematic rhyme-schemes). Both composer and poet have obviously shifted the emphasis away from the potentially frenetic recitative style, so dominant in earlier chamber laments, and have yielded to the growing fascination with the aria as a means of sustaining a single emotion.

One final cantata will illustrate how far from the intensely expressive language of Monteverdi's Ariadne the recitative lament has travelled within a few decades. Savioni's lament of Dido, which dates before 1641, is essentially

---

[41] Chigi Q V 69, fos. 64ʳ–69ʳ.

a comic parody of the heroine's death, set to a text by Francesco Melosio.[42] Melosio's style is immediately apparent in the narrator's introduction, with its convoluted syntax and verbal tricks.

Quando ch'il buon *Troiano*	assonance
ch'in Cartago arrivò pieno di stracci,	
onde pareva appunto	
ch'*a far carta in Cartagin* fosse giunto,	assonance; word-play
quando in somma il guidone	
dal hostessa Didone	
si risolse di corsela pian piano,	
e non hebbe vergogna,	
chi lo fece sguazzar com'in cuccagna	
pagar con una volta di calcagna?	
La povera figliola	
cominciò disperata	assonance
com'una spiritata	
a darsi i pugni al volto	
ed *a grattarsi* il capo	internal rhyme
c'havrebbe dett'ogn'un questa ha la tigna,	
e contr'il galant'huom che la tradì,	
si morse *il dito, e disse,* alfin così:	word-play

(When the good Trojan | who arrived in Carthage completely in rags, | whence it seemed precisely | that he had come to Carthage to make cartonnage, | when in short, the leader | from the hostess Dido | decided to sidle softly away, | and had no shame, | who made him wallow as if in the land of pleasure | and pay with a turn of the heel? | The poor girl | began desperate | as one possessed by demons | to strike her face with her fists | and to tear at her head | so that everyone might have said 'She's got ringworm', | and against the gentleman who betrayed her, | she bit her finger and finally said:)

Dido hurls insults at the departed Aeneas, continuing to speak with word-plays and double meanings. She eventually shifts her thoughts to her own forthcoming death by stabbing and fire. Not even the tragic subject-matter

[42] For the music, see Paris, Bibliothèque nationale, Rés. Vm⁷ 102, fos. 33ʳ–40ᵛ; Naples, Conservatorio di Musica S. Pietro a Majella, MS 33.3.11, fos. 41ʳ–46ᵛ; San Francisco State College Library, Frank V. de Bellis Collection, Misc. *M2.5, vol. 68, pp. 70–92; Evanston, Illinois, Northwestern University Library, Music MS 1, cantata no. 36. The text was printed in *Poesie e prose di Francesco Melosio da Città della Pieve* (I consulted the printed edition issued in Venice by the Heirs of Francesco Baba in 1673; there were numerous editions published between 1672 and 1704), in the section entitled 'Poesie di Francesco Melosio, recitativi varii, e possono adattarsi per musica'. Melosio is the subject of D. Gnoli, 'Un freddurista nel Seicento', *Nuova antologia di scienze, lettere ed arti*, 56 (1881), 575–95; but for a more balanced, sympathetic view, see Holzer, 'Music and Poetry in Seventeenth-Century Rome', ch. 5.

of this section escapes Melosio's verbal conceits. Dido's final utterance matches her name to the sound of the bells which will toll her death:

> E quando sentirai
> da questo torrione
> sbatachiar le campane, à più non posso,
> dì pur, che il mesto suono
> ch'à te l'aria trasporta
> vuol dir con quel dindon Didone è morta.

(And when you will hear | from this tower | the ringing of the bells, ah, I can do no more, | say then that the sad sound, | which the air transports to you, | would say with that ding-dong, 'Dido is dead.')

Up until this point in the text, the cantata unfolds entirely as a declamatory recitative, giving the singer full opportunity to project to the audience any shifting moods in the poem and, probably more important, its verbal puns. But with the return of the narrator who sings of the heroine's fate, Savioni provides a sprightly aria, immediately dispelling any sense of pathos which may have been felt in the latter portions of Dido's monologue. By the end of the cantata, there seems little doubt that Melosio and Savioni intended a work that focuses on clever word-play and turns of phrase, rather than on the impassioned speech of a tragic heroine.

5

Aspects of Aria

৴৵

F. W. STERNFELD

THE present discussion expands some passing remarks on 'aria' and 'number' in my monograph on *The Birth of Opera* (Oxford: Clarendon Press, 1993), notably in chapters 2, 6, and 7, where various recent interpretations of Monteverdi's letter to Alessandro Striggio of 9 December 1616 concerning 'parlar cantando' are discussed in greater detail. See also Nino Pirrotta and Elena Povoledo, *Music and Theatre from Poliziano to Monteverdi*, trans. Karen Eales (Cambridge University Press, 1982), ch. 6 ('Early Opera and Aria'). For a more literary discussion of the principle of repetition from Homer to T. S. Eliot, see my 'Repetition and Echo in Renaissance Poetry and Music', in John Carey (ed.), *English Renaissance Studies Presented to Dame Helen Gardner* (Oxford: Clarendon Press, 1980), 33–43.

In the history of Italian music, such terms as 'aria' or 'aer' (or other derivatives from the same root) are often met from the fourteenth century on. Sometimes they refer to a skeleton of a bass or of a melody, or both, suitable for the recitation of a stanza or several stanzas of a text: At other times, 'aria' seems to function as synonym for music, but usually vocal solo music, involving the structural principle of repetition. Strophic form is quite frequently encountered, as are sectional designs (such as ABA, AAB or ABB), and in Cavalli and Cesti these two types of repetition may be combined so that each stanza repeats the same design. To define aria is wellnigh impossible because the term has changed so much over the centuries, and even in operas of the seventeenth and eighteenth centuries one must distinguish between the neat separation of aria and recitative in Metastasian opera and the fluidity with which composers shift from recitative to arioso and aria within the *stile recitativo*. It is difficult for the modern historian to unburden himself of his knowledge of Metastasian or Mozartian number opera and to

This essay was handwritten, and in part dictated, by Dr Sternfeld during his final illness: it represents his last published work. We decided not to revise or expand his text—although the author intended to add footnotes—feeling that significant editorial intervention was both inappropriate and, in the end, unnecessary. (Eds.)

regain a 'period' perspective which does justice to the almost imperceptible transitions of the *stile recitativo*. In the following pages, an attempt will be made to clarify at least two aspects of aria in early opera, namely the role played by the structural principle of repetition (notably strophic repetition), and the relative importance of words and music, i.e. the contrast between 'recitar cantando' (or 'parlar cantando') and 'cantar recitando' (or 'cantar parlando').

Strophic lyrics, which are perceived as numbers, do occur in the operas of Peri and Monteverdi. They are perceived as such usually with the help of instrumental ritornellos which frame or punctuate them and differentiate them from the surrounding music, accompanied only by a basso continuo. Also, the repetition of the vocal melody is sufficiently obvious to be perceived by a lay audience. Strophic variations over an instrumental bass are not sufficiently conspicuous. For example, one could argue that in Monteverdi's *Orfeo* (1607) the prayer-lament 'Possente spirto' has a strophic text and that its vocal melody displays, at least in five of its six stanzas, a recurring skeleton. But that underlying unity is obscured by so much ornamentation that the average spectator or listener would not recognize it. Indeed, 'Possente spirto', like the *Lamento d'Arianna* (1608), is perceived by the average listener as an impassioned plea for pity, whose craggy irregularity intensifies the emotion it conveys. On the other hand, both Peri's *Euridice* (1600) and Monteverdi's *Orfeo* contain pastoral strophic lyrics whose repetitive structures are readily apparent. These strophic lyrics are not necessarily important pillars of the dramatic structure, like 'Possente spirto', but, rather, pleasant foils for the more serious stations of the dramatic action. For instance, in *Euridice* Tirsi sings 'Nel puro ardor', which clearly falls into two stanzas in duple time, framed by an instrumental ritornello in triple time. A modified strophic text is sung by Orpheus near the end of *Euridice*. The first stanza ('Gioite al canto mio, selve frondose') consists of three *endecasillabi*; the third line speaks of rebounding echo ('Eco rimbombi dalle valli ascose'), which—predictably— induces Peri to repeat the line. The melodic similarity of the second stanza ('Risorto è 'l mio bel sol di raggi adorno') to the first is readily perceived and does not require study of the score. Rinuccini extends the second stanza to four *endecasillabi*, the third of which speaks of 'redoubling' ('raddoppiare'), which like 'echo' almost invariably provokes further repetition on the part of composers of madrigals or early operas. Consequently, the same phrase of music is heard three times, not just twice as in the first stanza. Nevertheless, the strophic structure is perfectly clear, even if the section is not framed or punctuated by an obbligato ritornello: the melody is simple and catchy, in triple time, and is instantly recognized. (The majority of arias in early opera are fairly simple and syllabic. Florid virtuoso solo song is encountered more rarely: Gluck's 'Che farò senza Euridice' is a more typical descendant than Mozart's arias for the Queen of the Night, its effects being achieved not by melismatic expression but by contrasts of tempo and dynamics.)

Before leaving Peri's *Euridice*, it would be useful to look briefly at the irregular structure of one of the composer's impassioned ariosos: for instance, at the plea to the underworld pronounced by Orpheus, 'Funeste piagge, ombrosi, orridi campi', which consists of three sections, containing ten, eight, and twelve lines respectively. Such irregular lengths of the component sections of a lyric are quite characteristic of the non-arias of early opera: note the analogous organization in Orpheus' echo-lament at the beginning of Act V of Monteverdi's *Orfeo* and in the *Lamento d'Arianna*. Musically, too, the three sections of 'Funeste piagge' start differently. Melodically, they are not even similar, let alone identical. And the bass of the first section starts with a G held for nine semibreves, a static quality not typical of early aria but quite characteristic of climaxes of expression in the *stile recitativo*. On the other hand, these three irregular components of 'Funeste piagge' are somewhat held together by a single-line refrain, 'Lacrimate al mio pianto, ombre d'inferno' ('Weep at my lament, shades of Hades'), which concludes each section: the identity of melody and bass is unmistakable and instantly noted by the layman.

A somewhat similar unity is achieved in Monteverdi's *Il ritorno d'Ulisse in patria* (1640), where at the beginning of Act I Penelope's lament falls into three sections, irregularly shaped by the composer but held together by the recurring refrain 'Torna, [torna, torna,] deh torna, [torna,] Ulisse' ('Return, ah return, Ulysses'). Considering the fivefold occurrence of the word 'torna' in the refrain, which in turn is stated three times, and the frequency with which 'torna' and 'tornar' permeate the entire lament (to express Penelope's impatient desire for the return of Ulysses), this is indeed a most striking example of the structural principle of repetition. Certainly, the return of the refrain in melody and bass is unmistakable, but it is equally obvious that Penelope's long and impressive plaint is not an aria. Yet she does have an aria in the opera's finale. This finale consists of two sections: it starts with the jubilation of Penelope at the happy resolution of the action and continues with a duet for Ulysses and Penelope, affirming their conjugal love; the libretto then concludes with a chorus for the people of Ithaca, for which, however, no music is extant.

Like at least one version of Monteverdi's *L'incoronazione di Poppea* (1643)— if for different reasons—the libretto of *Ulisse* provides two kinds of finale: the more forward-looking love-duet, and the more traditional 'choral' or ensemble finale. Penelope's lyric which precedes the duet falls into four

stanzas of three lines each. Monteverdi sets the first three stanzas as a modified strophic aria in C major, and utilizes the fourth stanza, in A minor, as
a bridge to the duet. The first stanza ('Illustratevi, o cieli'; 'Shine forth, o
heavens') is set off from the preceding and succeeding portions of the score
by two factors: it has a memorable tune (one of the best in the opera) in
triple time, and is accompanied by a typical (and not static) aria bass. After
this initial statement, the principle of repetition produces an orchestral echo:
a ritornello of four obbligato instrumental parts reiterates melody and harmony over the same bass. The same C major tune (later slightly modified)
over the same bass opens the second stanza ('Gli augelletti cantando') and
is again echoed ('plugged', to use the vocabulary of show business) by an
orchestral ritornello. Finally, the third stanza ('Quell'herbe verdeggianti';
again, the melody is slightly modified) lets us have a third vocal statement,
again repeated in the orchestral ritornello. One could analyse the strophic
form of Penelope's aria in greater detail, dealing also with the second strain,
which receives its orchestral echo in the first and second stanzas. (In the
third stanza it is omitted to make room for a fourth stanza in A minor,
which leads to the final duet, also moving from C major to A minor;
possibly the chorus for the Ithacans would have returned to C major.) But
for present purposes, the establishment of the strophic form by the opening
strain, and by its orchestral ritornellos, is the most important point of this
aria. Penelope, whom the composer has denied an aria even when action
and libretto would have permitted it, finally receives her musical due, a
memorable melody with an expressive vocal line, suitably 'set off'. In later
Venetian opera, the 'diva' would be given more set-pieces, more so-called
numbers. Similarly, much could be said about the final duet for Penelope
and Ulysses, not least its repetitive design and vocabulary. Certainly, its
much repeated 'yes' ('sì, sì') is an important factor in establishing the 'lieto
fine', and it reminds the modern listener of Molly Bloom's monologue concluding Joyce's *Ulysses* (Molly is a deliberate modern descendant of Homer's
Penelope). But we had better return to the solo arias of the first decade of
the seventeenth century.

   In view of the importance we have attached to strophic organization, it
may be helpful to enquire whether this aspect of the aria was recognized in
the early seventeenth century. Here an anthology such as Caccini's *Le nuove
musiche* of 1602 is helpful in that it collects twelve 'madrigals', followed
by the finale of the opera *Il rapimento di Cefalo* (1600), and then ten 'arie'.
All the arias have strophic texts, ranging from three to ten stanzas. They
are usually in duple or common time, but occasionally (in three out of ten
pieces) triple or compound time is encountered (it becomes more customary
in later songs). More often than not the music for one stanza serves also for

the succeeding ones, but occasionally strophic variation masks the under-lying similarity. Usually, these pieces are scored for high voice, with the exception of the last aria ('Chi mi confort'ahimè', also from *Il rapimento di Cefalo*), which is for bass and whose range and melismatic ornamentation make it more a virtuoso piece than a memorable and expressive tune. Still, in Caccini's terminology, strophic organization and various aspects of repeti-tive articulation seem germane to the term 'aria'.

Let us now consider Monteverdi's *Orfeo*. In Act II, Orpheus' pastoral aria 'Vi ricorda, o boschi ombrosi' is set off from the preceding chorus and the succeeding solo of a shepherd by an orchestral ritornello, notated in five parts for bowed and plucked strings. This ritornello frames all four stanzas, each one consisting of four *ottonari*. Both ritornello and aria trip along merrily in compound time; the mood is pastoral rather than tragic, the diction syllabic rather than florid, the bass moving at a speed comparable with that of the melody. One would not hesitate to call the melody itself catchy: it certainly is easily remembered, particularly since it is heard not only at the beginning of each stanza, but also at the end, where the com-poser repeats the first line after the fourth to achieve an ABA design within all stanzas.

Towards the end of Act IV, Orpheus again sings a seemingly merry song in three stanzas of four lines each: it is as if he wanted to exhort himself to courage before looking back and losing Eurydice a second time. And when he begins to have doubts, the strophic organization stops immediately:

> Ma mentre io canto (ohimè) chi m'assicura
> che ella mi segua? . . .

(But while I sing (alas), who assures me | that she follows? . . .)

The subdivision into stanzas is less obvious than in the previous examples. True, the ritornello which opens each stanza, notated on three staves for bowed strings and basso continuo, remains unchanged, and so does the bass which accompanies the vocal melody. But the melody itself is slightly varied, apart from its characteristic and memorable incipit. Monteverdi employs less 'plugging', no doubt intent on avoiding undue delay before reaching the catastrophe of the act. The strophic organization is perceived without re-course to a score, but is less conspicuous. What is noticeable, however, is that the lively motion of the bass during the three stanzas of the aria and its framing ritornello stops, and that over long-held notes in the bass irregularly repeated words, like the expletive 'ohimè' with its diminished fifth, receive the kind of emphasis more associated with the *parlando* sections of the *stile recitativo*.

Perhaps we are now in a better position to approach assessing the relative importance of voice and verse in 'cantar parlando' and 'parlar cantando'—in aria and recitative, to use Metastasian terminology for the century before Metastasio. It can fairly be said, I think, that the delight in aria is primarily associated with voice, rather than with verse. The attractiveness, euphony, and beauty of the vocal line are the focus, rather than the verbal expression of the situation of the plot, or even of the affection behind that situation. Needless to say, the choice of diction and prosody are crucial to find the right musical tone for the basic emotion, but once these decisions have been made, the aria stands or falls according to its musical merits. We are translated to another level of aesthetic perception, and various signals (ritornellos, triple time, strophic organization) alert us to the fact that we are proceeding to another realm with another set of conventions for vocal solo melody over a bass, punctuated possibly by preludes, interludes, or postludes. 'Cantare' refers to music, and 'cantar parlando' means that 'poetry must be altogether the obedient daughter of the music', to quote Mozart. (Since our discussion is at present systematic rather than historical, the anachronistic introduction of such luminaries of the genre of opera as Metastasio or Mozart will not be amiss.) In early operas such as *Euridice* and *Orfeo*, the opportunities for such musical or lyrical concentration were rare within the dramatic structure. But with the rise of institutional opera and of professional librettists such as Giovanni Faustini and Nicolò Minato, the emphasis changes. In the operas of Monteverdi's pupil Cavalli, the occasions for awarding the leadership to music increase, particularly as the composer sets to music texts by Faustini and later poets. In these arias, music comes first, and the text seems a set of words of secondary importance. However, whereas the incidence of these lyrical islands may be increased, an exclusive diet of set-pieces with a hegemony of voice over verse must be avoided for aesthetic as well as practical reasons. Exigencies of timing, for instance, require the occasional preponderance of 'parlare', 'recitare', 'favellare': hence the 'parlar cantando' from Monteverdi to Mozart, with its unpredictable irregularities, its dramatic impact, and its variety of musical organization from *parlando* to arioso. 'Parlar cantando' (or 'recitar cantando') is neither a stopgap to gain time, nor a poor relation of 'aria'. It is one of the necessary foils for the musical glories of the beautiful solo song (another such foil being the choral or ensemble finale). 'Parlare' is concerned not only with the literary and prosodic aspects of verse, but also—last but not least—with the emotions expressed in the text. It is in the judicious assessment of the affective properties of both 'aria' and 'recitative' that these two building-blocks fit into the structure of the *stile recitativo*, that 'cantar parlando' and 'parlar cantando' complement each other and provide the bulk of the edifice of opera, a genre whose fascination is based, *inter alia*, on its accommodation of contrasting ingredients.

Perhaps one could derive most of the aspects of aria sketched above, and the differences between aria and recitative, from one decision, namely to concentrate on a single emotion. The pastoral arias of Tirsi in *Euridice*, of Orpheus in *Orfeo*, are sung when an idyllic stage (or 'station') of the action has been reached, and during the aria the music does not deviate from the 'affetto', reflected in melody, bass, and instrumentation. No such 'unity' of action pervades the various irregular structures superficially held together by a refrain discussed earlier. For instance, the 'torna, torna' refrain in Penelope's lament cannot hide the fact that at some moments Penelope expresses grief over her condition, and at others gives vent to her desire for the return of her husband. It is the shifting from one 'affetto' to another, the fluidity of transition, that makes recitative (and arioso) such an indispensable carrier of dramatic action, even in the Metastasian operas of Hasse and Mozart. What does change, however, in the course of the period from Peri to Mozart is the relative incidence of 'parlar cantando' and 'cantar parlando'. As time marches on, arias become more frequent, orchestral ritornellos and accompaniments more *de rigueur*. Also, the arias become longer, and the structural principle of repetition cannot manifest itself in strophic organization but is accommodated by sectional design. But that is another story.

6

Resemblance and Representation:
Towards a New Aesthetic
in the Music of Monteverdi

TIM CARTER

By the mid-1620s, Claudio Monteverdi had been *maestro di cappella* of St Mark's, Venice, for over a decade. He was widely recognized as the leading composer in Italy, was head of a prestigious musical establishment, and was supported by gifted assistants who could carry the day-to-day burdens of administering, rehearsing, and directing music in the Basilica. As the composer entered middle age, his thoughts turned to more relaxing endeavours. There was still the unfinished business of the treatise he had (perhaps foolishly, he now felt) promised Artusi in his famous polemic with the Bolognese theorist in the early 1600s—we know that the treatise was still on his mind from two letters to Giovanni Battista Doni written in 1633–4[1]—but Artusi had died in the year Monteverdi moved to Venice (1613), and the composer claimed the satisfaction of seeing him reconciled with the modernist position.[2] For the moment, Monteverdi put all that aside in favour of a more

A first version of this essay was presented as a paper ('Monteverdi's *via naturale alla immitatione*: New Light on Opera and Song in Early Seventeenth-Century Italy') at the Conference on Seventeenth-Century Music, Washington University, St. Louis, Mo., in April 1993. It was then read by Susan McClary and Massimo Ossi. I am indeed grateful for their illuminating comments and criticisms which undoubtedly had their effect in various revisions, even if I have perhaps too stubbornly adhered to my original thesis.

[1] The letters to Doni of 22 Oct. 1633 and 2 Feb. 1634 are in *The Letters of Claudio Monteverdi*, trans. Denis Stevens (London and Boston: Faber & Faber, 1980), 406–16. According to the composer's eulogist, Matteo Caberloti, the composer was still working on the treatise at his death; see Paolo Fabbri, *Monteverdi* (Turin: EDT, 1985), 62.

[2] In his letter to Doni of 22 Oct. 1633; see *The Letters of Claudio Monteverdi*, trans. Stevens, 410: 'he calmed down in such a way that from thenceforward not only did he stop overruling me—turning his pen in my praise—but he began to like and admire me'. There may be a degree of wishful thinking here: we have no writings from Artusi directly praising the composer.

intriguing hobby, alchemy: five letters to the Mantuan court secretary Ercole Marigliani written between August 1625 and March 1626 (23 August and 19 September 1625, 15 and 24 February, and 28 March 1626)[3] suggest a lively exchange of ideas, materials, and equipment all the more surprising given that we have no other evidence of the composer being interested in much besides music.

This is not the place to discuss why Monteverdi should have gained so sudden an enthusiasm for his new hobby (nor, for that matter, where and how he learnt of it). But it is worth considering what benefits the composer might have drawn, however tangentially, from his pastime. For example, in the first of these five letters, Monteverdi discusses how to calcinate gold with lead (with a drawing of the necessary pot). Also:

> I must tell you how I shall be able to make mercury from unrefined matter which changes into clear water, and although it will be in water it will not however lose its identity as mercury, or its weight; because I have tested it by taking a drop, and have put it on a brass spoon and rubbed it, and it became all tinged with silver colour. From this purified water I shall hope to make something worthwhile, inasmuch as it is a powerful solvent of silver.[4]

The lesson is an interesting one. Something precious (*il mercurio*) can be made from something base (*del vulgo*), and it can look like something else (*acqua chiara*). Given its misleading appearance, some other test must be adopted for purposes of identification (*l'ho posta sopra un chuchiaro di ottone et fregatolo*). Nevertheless, Monteverdi's new cocktail has a powerful effect (*solve l'argento galiardamente*), suggesting that something useful might come of it.

Monteverdi's music is rich in examples of his making something precious from something base. But the question of appearances, however, is more intriguing. It was precisely in this decade that Monteverdi focused particular attention on the imitation of appearances in music, whether for serious (the *Combattimento di Tancredi et Clorinda* of 1624) or for comic (the unfinished *La finta pazza Licori* of 1627) effect. Such imitation, in turn, was predicated upon notions of (some might say, too literal) resemblance: witness the *concitato genere* or the dislocated succession of mimetic gestures that Monteverdi proposes to represent Licori's feigned madness.[5] Here a rather laboured concept

---

[3] Nos. 83, 84, 86, 87, and 89 in *The Letters of Claudio Monteverdi*, trans. Stevens.

[4] Ibid. 291. For the original, see *Claudio Monteverdi: Lettere, dediche e prefazioni*, ed. Domenico de' Paoli (Rome: De Santis, 1973), 222–4.

[5] It seems to me that there are distinct dangers in extrapolating from the well-known letters on the unfinished (uncomposed?) *La finta pazza Licori* (1627) evidence of a serious new aesthetic in Monteverdi's Venetian secular music, *pace* Gary Tomlinson, *Monteverdi and the End of the Renaissance* (Oxford: Clarendon Press, 1987), 204–5: it is, after all, a comedy. Moreover, all this needs grounding in 'mad scenes' on the contemporary stage (see below, ch. 8).

of verisimilitude—indeed, one easily open to ridicule—provided the touch-
stone of what might be called a homologous approach to the *rappresentatione
degli affetti* and consequently to emotional arousal: musical gestures should
resemble as closely as possible the tenor of the words that they accompany,
thereby facilitating and securing their action upon the senses. Of course, this
was by no means a new idea—it provided the conceptual underpinning for
much word-painting in, say, the Renaissance madrigal—and indeed it gives
much of the music in which Monteverdi explores such an approach a somewhat conservative air, for all its seeming adoption of modern elements. Not
for nothing has this music received something of a bad press in the recent
literature.

The importance of representation in early seventeenth-century musical
endeavour goes without saying: witness the term *stile rappresentativo*, which
could be, and was, applied widely to monody or to polyphony, and to music
for the theatre, chamber, and church.[6] Exactly what is represented in the *stile
rappresentativo* (the emotions, the text, the act of representation itself?) is
open to debate. But one can usefully ask whether representation is best
achieved by such resemblances or by some other means. Indeed, Monteverdi's
little alchemical experiment suggests a different solution. His two substances
(mercury and 'clear water') have no overt resemblance one to the other—
their shared identity has to be discovered by experiment—and yet the visu-
ally innocuous *acqua chiara* can have potent effects.

Today, the term *stile rappresentativo* is most often identified with the new
music for the stage, which Giovanni Battista Doni called the 'stile detto
recitativo'. He subdivided this style into three categories—'narrativo',
'recitativo' (or 'recitativo speciale'), and 'espressivo'. But for all his humanist
enthusiasm for the recitative, Doni was somewhat less keen on its effects in
the modern theatre, particularly the narrative style, which so often bored the
listener due to its limited musical interest: at one point he suggested that
such narrative recitative should be abandoned and replaced by speech delivered over an instrumental accompaniment.[7] (Of course, Doni was by no
means alone in objecting to 'the tedium of the recitative'.)[8] The expressive

---

[6] See my entry on 'Stile rappresentativo' in *The New Grove Dictionary of Opera*, ed. Stanley
Sadie (London: Macmillan, 1992), iv. 543–4.

[7] For example, in Doni's *Discorso sesto sopra il recitare in scena*, published in his *Annotazioni
sopra il Compendio de' generi e de' modi della musica* (Rome: Fei, 1640), transcribed in Claudio
Gallico, 'Discorso di G. B. Doni sul recitare in scena', *Rivista italiana di musicologia*, 3 (1968),
286–302 at 295–6. Doni goes on to discuss the problem of mediating between speech and
song.

[8] See Carolyn Gianturco, 'Nuove considerazioni su *il tedio del recitativo* delle prime opere
romane', *Rivista italiana di musicologia*, 17 (1982), 212–39; Tim Carter, '*Non occorre nominare
tanti musici*: Private Patronage and Public Ceremony in Late Sixteenth-Century Florence', *I
Tatti Studies: Essays in the Renaissance*, 4 (1991), 89–104.

style was somewhat more powerful—Doni cited Monteverdi's celebrated *Lamento d'Arianna* in support (although much of its power, he said, was due to the poet, Ottavio Rinuccini), not least for being 'more than the others delightful, adorned and rich in varied intervals, which the stage requires both to avoid tedium and engender greater delight in the listeners, and to be able to express better all those diverse affects which underpin this type of poetry and musical imitation'.[9] But Doni's preferences reveal a serious problem in his conception (and in fact, most conceptions) of the ideal music for the theatre. What happens when the need for delight and variety supersedes the no less important need for verisimilitude on the dramatic stage?

Doni cites Plutarch in support of a style of theatre music that was 'variata e artifiziosa', and in so doing he invokes a surprising model. He says that the Florentine inventors of opera made a serious error in assuming

> that madrigalian music (which is today the most esteemed and artful) is worth little in producing those effects which one reads of ancient [music], and they persuaded themselves that this occurred because it was too *arioso* and scarcely similar to common speech, and not because of other, truer reasons, that is, because of the brevity of the verses, the frequent repetitions, and chiefly of the interweaving of so many airs together instead of forming one only, with the most beautiful flow of melody possible; and in having different words sung together, with great loss to the understanding, as well as the harm caused by the affected artifices of direct and retrograde fugues, and the excessive sprinkling of such lengthy and incessant passagework.[10]

[9] Doni, *Trattato della musica scenica* (1633–5), cited in Maurizio Padoan, 'Nature and Artifice in G. B. Doni's Thought', *International Review of the Aesthetics and Sociology of Music*, 23 (1992), 5–26 at 17: 'più degli altri vago, e adorno, e ricco di variati intervalli, i quali richiede la Scena sì per evitare il tedio, e recare maggior diletto agli uditori, come per poter meglio esprimere tutti quei diversi affetti, che soggiacciono a questa sorte di Poesia, e Musicale imitazione'. For Doni and Rinuccini, see Gary Tomlinson, 'Madrigal, Monody, and Monteverdi's "via naturale alla immitatione"', *Journal of the American Musicological Society*, 34 (1981), 60–108 at 86. Tomlinson is tempted 'to trust Doni's emphasis on Rinuccini's role in the creation of *L'Arianna*' (ibid. 87), although it was doubtless coloured both by a dim view of composers' intellectual abilities (even Monteverdi's; see Fabbri, *Monteverdi*, 292–3) and by a degree of Florentine chauvinism.

[10] Doni, *Discorso sesto sopra il recitare in scena*, in Gallico, 'Discorso di G. B. Doni sul recitare in scena', 294: 'che la musica Madrigalesca (ch'è oggi la più stimata e artifiziosa) poco vale in produrre quegli effetti che dell'antica si leggono: onde si persuasero che ciò avvenisse per essere troppo ariosa, e poco simile alla favella comune, e non da altre più vere ragioni: cioè dalla brevità de' versi; da tante ripetizioni; e principalmente dall'intessere più arie insieme, in vece di formarne una sola, con quel più bel procedere di melodia che si può; e nel far cantare insieme parole diverse, con molta perdita dell'intelligenza; oltre il danno che recano gl'affettati artifizii di fughe dritte e rovesce ecc., e i soverchi condimenti di passaggi tanto lunghi e frequenti'.

But in fact

> experience shows us that to move the affects, this *arioso* music similar to madrigals (especially when it touches the notes of various modes) is much more effective than that simple and scarcely varied music which for the greater part is heard in the recitative. Whenceforth, just as I judge that the former should be perfected and applied to those parts of dramas that are appropriate, so do I believe that that other [style] which takes the place of real speech is to be spurned.[11]

Considering the arguments against the madrigal style that had formed so crucial a context for early opera and solo song in Florence, Doni's present argument marks a striking volte-face, however necessary it might have been in the changing musical climate of the 1620s and 1630s.

Doni's preference for a 'musica ariosa e simile a i Madrigali' did not necessarily extend to polyphonic madrigals—he made the usual criticism that counterpoint obscured the words—or to the *ariette* with which some composers were filling their stage music.[12] But he clearly wanted something more structured and more varied than the declamatory recitative that had played so great a part in early opera. So too, it seems, did a number of composers in the early seventeenth century. For example, Giulio Caccini and his successors had laid down important parameters for the solo song, consisting of declamatory solo madrigals on the one hand, and on the other, the 'canzonetta à uso di aria per poter usare in conserto di più strumenti di corde' (to use Caccini's own curious terminology for the strophic dance-songs that became characteristic of contemporary arias).[13] But these distinctions were being modified significantly by the second decade of the century. Indeed, Caccini's own stylistic boundaries were not always so clear-cut: his madrigals, while sometimes owing a debt to contemporary operatic recitative, often invoked more structured (and more melodic) *arioso* writing; and some of his arias could be only loosely strophic in any musical sense of the term, adopting a number of stylistic traits of the solo madrigal. By the late

[11] Ibid.: 'l'esperienza ci mostra che per muovere gl'affetti questa musica ariosa e simile a i Madrigali (massime quando tocca corde di varii Tuoni) è molto più efficace di quella semplice e poco variata, che per la maggior parte si sente nel Recitativo. Laonde, quanto più stimo che si debba perfezionare questa, e applicarla a quelle parti de Drammi, che ne sono capaci, altrettanto credo che sia da disprezzare quell'altra, che tiene il luogo del vero parlare.'

[12] Doni, for example, took significant exception to Cavalieri's *Rappresentatione di Anima, et di Corpo* (1600) because of its 'ariette con molti artifizi di ripetizioni, echi e simili, che non hanno che fare niente con la buona e vera musica teatrale' (*Trattato della musica scenica*, in Angelo Solerti, *Le origini del melodramma* (Turin: Bocca, 1903; repr. Hildesheim: Olms, 1969), 208).

[13] The description comes from the preface to Caccini's *Le nuove musiche* (Florence: I Marescotti, 1601 [= 1602]), sig. B1r.

1610s, however, the influence seems to have been moving the other way, as aria styles (for example, structured triple- or duple-time writing) started to have a significant influence on contemporary madrigals. Such stylistic cross-overs also become apparent in the increasing number of solo songs and duets—whether formal arias or formal madrigals (and there is an increasing lack of musical distinction between the two)—which involve shifts in style between declamatory writing and more focused passages in aria style. Nigel Fortune has already discussed one key example, Sigismondo d'India's 'Torna il sereno Zefiro' published in his *Le musiche . . . Libro quinto* (Venice: Alessandro Vincenti, 1623),[14] and I have pointed out some others (for example, by Jacopo Peri).[15] However, two specific duets by Monteverdi are particularly useful in the present context, another 'Zefiro' piece published by Monteverdi in the 1632 *Scherzi musicali* (Venice: Bartolomeo Magni), 'Zefiro torna, e di soavi accenti', and 'O sia tranquillo il mare, o pien d'orgoglio', published in his *Madrigali guerrieri, et amorosi . . . Libro ottavo* of 1638 (Venice: Alessandro Vincenti).

The well-known 'Zefiro torna, e di soavi accenti' sets a sonnet by Ottavio Rinuccini:

> Zefiro torna, e di soavi accenti
> l'aer fa grato e 'l pié discioglie a l'onde,
> e mormorando tra le verdi fronde,
> fa danzar al bel suon su 'l prato i fiori.
> Inghirlandato il crin Fillide e Clori
> note tempran d'amor care e gioconde;
> e da monti e da valli ime e profonde
> raddoppian l'armonia gli antri canori.
> Sorge più vaga in ciel l'aurora, e 'l sole
> sparge piú luci d'or; piú puro argento
> fregia di Teti il bel ceruleo manto.
> Sol io, per selve abbandonate e sole,
> l'ardor di due begli occhi e 'l mio tormento,
> come vuol mia ventura, hor piango hor canto.

(Zephyrus returns, and with sweet accents | makes the air pleasing and loosens his foot from the waves, | and murmuring among the green branches, | he makes dance to his sound the flowers in the meadows. || Phyllis and Chloris, garlands on their brow, | temper their sweet and joyous notes of love; | and from the mountains and the valleys low and deep | sonorous caverns echo

---

[14] In Nigel Fortune, 'Italian Secular Monody from 1600–1635: An Introductory Survey', *Musical Quarterly*, 39 (1953), 171–95.

[15] See Tim Carter, *Music in Late Renaissance and Early Baroque Italy* (London: Batsford, 1992), 250–1.

their harmony. ‖ Dawn rises more lovely in the heavens, | and the sun
spreads forth more rays of gold; | [while] purer silver adorns Thetis' fair
cerulean mantle. ‖ Only I, [wandering] through abandoned, lonely woods,
| the brightness of two lovely eyes and my torment, | as my fortune wills
it, now I weep, now I sing.)

Rinuccini's poem is a close imitation of Petrarch's sonnet 'Zefiro torna e 'l
bel tempo rimena' (no. 310 in the *Canzoniere*)—set by Monteverdi in his
Sixth Book of 1614—and there are also echoes of the nature imagery of
Tasso (compare the *ottava rima* 'Vezzosi augelli infra le verdi fronde' from
Gerusalemme liberata, XVI. 12, a popular text for sixteenth-century madrigalists);
indeed, the resonances are clear enough to permit some syntactic obscurity
in the present verse. The poem seems ready-made for musical setting, even
if Monteverdi felt it necessary to clinch the point by changing the first *parola
rima* (Rinuccini's first line is 'Zefiro torna, e di soavi odori', rhyming with
'fiori', 'Clori' and 'canori'). The composer's new 'accenti' prompts a setting
for the most part over the syncopated *ciaccona* bass pattern in a jaunty triple
time.[16] Nor does he lose any opportunity to 'paint' the specific images of the
text—the 'sweet accents' 'murmuring' through the branches, the flowers
made to 'dance' to the wind, the 'sweet and joyous notes' of the nymphs,
and the (high) mountains, low valleys, and echoing caverns. But for the final
tercet Monteverdi shifts to a dissonant madrigalian style, contrasting the joys
of spring with the pains of the lover (Ex. 6.1): triple time returns only at the
end as the poet counterpoints weeping and singing, the reference to 'canto'
providing the final justification for the use of the two gestures that most
obviously invoked 'song' in the early seventeenth century, triple-time writing and (in the final cadence) ornamental roulades. Thus Monteverdi's 'Zefiro
torna' conventionally plays off aria styles (for the delights of spring) against
'recitative' (for the grieving lover). He also resorts to the literal mimetic
gestures so redolent of sixteenth-century word-painting, and so criticized by
some Monteverdi scholars in the composer's Venetian secular music. It is
not entirely clear whether this is done seriously or in jest (the duet is, after
all, one of a group of *scherzi musicali*, 'musical trifles'),[17] and whether we

[16] The technique is discussed in Massimo Ossi, '*L'armonia raddoppiata*: On Claudio
Monteverdi's *Zefiro torna*, Heinrich Schütz's *Es steh Gott auf*, and Other Early Seventeenth-
Century *Ciaccone*', *Studi musicali*, 17 (1988), 225–53.

[17] Massimo Ossi makes the point (private communication) that perhaps one should not
be misled by the title (whose?) of the 1632 collection, *Scherzi musicali* (and the term 'scherzo'
is notoriously difficult to translate), which is followed by an explicative subtitle, 'Cioè Arie,
& Madrigali in stil recitativo, con una Ciaccona A 1. & 2. voci' ('that is, Arias, and Madrigals
in recitative style, with a *Ciaccona*[,] for one and two voices'). Also, the last piece of the 1632
Scherzi musicali, 'Armato il cor d'adamantina fede', was later published in Monteverdi's *Madrigali
guerrieri, et amorosi . . . Libro ottavo* (1638), and for that matter, both 'Zefiro torna, e di soavi

Ex. 6.1. Monteverdi, 'Zefiro torna, e di soavi accenti'

(. . . fair cerulean mantle. Only I, [wandering] through abandoned, lonely woods, the brightness . . .)

should be amused or moved (or both). But for all its modern medium (a duet), style (dancing triple time), and technique (the ground bass), this seems an essentially old-fashioned piece evoking, like Rinuccini's resonant sonnet, a past emotional world.

'O sia tranquillo il mare, o pien d'orgoglio' also plays off madrigalian 'recitative' against triple-time 'aria', but to very different effect. Again, the text is a sonnet (the poet is unknown):

> O sia tranquillo il mare, o pien d'orgoglio,
> > mai da quest'onde io non rivolgo il piede;
> > io qui t'aspetto, e qui de la tua fede,
> > tradito amante, mi lamento e doglio.
> Spesso salir su queste rupi io soglio
> > per veder se il tuo legno ancor se 'n riede.
> > Quivi m'assido e piango, onde mi crede
> > il mar un fonte, e 'l navigante un scoglio.
> E spesso ancor t'invio per messaggieri,
> > a ridir la mia pena e 'l mio tormento,
> > dell'aria vaga i zeffiri leggieri.

accenti' and 'Armato il cor d'adamantina fede' appeared in the posthumous *Madrigali e canzonette . . . Libro nono* (Venice: Alessandro Vincenti, 1651). But the same piece can, perhaps should, be 'read' differently in different contexts. It seems to me, too, that we have yet to reach an adequate sense of genres and their likely influence on critical interpretation for this period.

Ma tu non torni, o Filli, e 'l mio lamento
l'aura disperge; e tal mercè ne speri
chi fida a donna il cor e i prieghi al vento.

(Whether the sea is calm or haughty, | I never turn away from the waves; | here I await you, and here I, | a betrayed lover, lament your ill faith. ‖ Often I climb these cliffs | to see whether your ship returns. | Here I sit and weep, so the sea believes me | a fountain, and the sailor a rock. ‖ And often I send you as messengers | to tell of my pain and torment | the light breezes of the air. ‖ But, o Phyllis, you do not return, and my lament | is scattered by the air; such is the reward | of him who entrusts his heart to women and his prayers to the wind.)

Here we have another representation of the pains of an abandoned lover, but now things seem more serious: the piece is one of a set of *madrigali amorosi*, not *scherzi musicali*. Moreover, the text lacks the binary oppositions (for example, happy nature/sad lover) characteristic at various levels of Rinuccini's pastoral verse. As a result, Monteverdi seeks a different motivation for the equivalent binary oppositions available to him in musical terms. The first two-thirds of Monteverdi's setting is in a conventional madrigalian/recitative style, but at line 12—'Ma tu non torni, o Filli'—the composer devotes some fifty bars of expansive triple-time writing for the most part to just half a line of verse (Ex. 6.2), returning to 'recitative' for the final ironic epigram. In contrast to 'Zefiro torna, e di soavi accenti', the use here of triple time—and the shift between 'recitative' and 'aria'—certainly does not seem motivated by any desire for literal word-painting or pictorial madrigalism. Moreover, it gives the text a musical weight seemingly disproportionate to its role in the sonnet as a whole, a weight further emphasized by the function of this triple-time section in initiating the large-scale structural octave descent of the piece. The long first section is an effective prolongation of d' ($\hat{8}$), the upper final of the modal octave reinforced by the main cadences (and no less significantly, by the arrival of the two voices on a unison): this explains its static feel. The triple-time section begins with a striking harmonic shift to F, then C, the C cadence providing support for c' ($\hat{7}$) in the voices (again emphasized by a unison) that is effectively prolonged for the bulk of the section until the conclusion on a major triad on E, supporting b ($\hat{6}$). The remainder of the structural descent (a–d = $\hat{5}$–$\hat{1}$) is passed over quickly in the final lines, as the poet realizes the consequences of his situation. I have argued elsewhere that this use of aria styles to provide a rhetorical and emotional climax to a given setting marks a significant shift in early seventeenth-century musical aesthetics, and obviously one with

Ex. 6.2. Monteverdi, 'O sia tranquillo il mare'

(. . . the light breezes of the air. But, o Phyllis, you do not return . . .)

significant resonances for the later Baroque period.[18] It also recovers the ground for music as music, rather than as some spurious form of speech. In this case, one interpretation of the result is that it transcends the text to produce a palpably real representation of grief.

Monteverdi well knew that dance-derived aria styles articulated the relationship between the triumvirate of *oratione*, *harmonia*, and rhythm that together made up *melodia* (the whole art of composition) in ways very different from the formula proclaimed as the credo of the *seconda prattica* in the 1600s (the oration as mistress, not servant, of the harmony). In a letter to Alessandro Striggio of 21 November 1615 Monteverdi discusses the recent commission

[18] Carter, *Music in Late Renaissance and Early Baroque Italy*, 253. Most recently, I have discussed the issues in '*Possente spirto*: On Taming the Power of Music', *Early Music*, 21 (1993), 517–23.

arrived from Mantua for a *ballo* in music. When Duke Vincenzo I Gonzaga used to commission such works in six, eight, or nine *mutanze*, Monteverdi says, he

> used to give me some account of the invention, and I used to try to fit to it both the harmony and the metres [*tempi*] that I knew to be most appropriate and similar.

The present commission, however, lacked any such detail, so the composer had come up with a *ballo* of six *mutanze* (a version of *Tirsi e Clori*, later published in the Seventh Book of madrigals of 1619). He also tells Striggio that:

> if His Most Serene Highness should want either a change of air in this [*ballo*], or additions to the enclosed [movements] of a slow and grave nature, or fuller and without fugues (His Most Serene Highness taking no notice of the present words which can easily be changed, though at least these words help by the nature of their metre and by imitating the melody [*canto*]), or if he should want everything altered I beg you to act on my behalf so that His Most Serene Highness might reword the commission . . .[19]

The notion that the present words 'can easily be changed'—although their metre is appropriate and they imitate the melody—is striking in the context of Monteverdi's earlier protestations over the *seconda prattica*. Of course, this is dance music—so the requirements are different—but Monteverdi's statement is easily applicable to many arias of the early (and for that matter, later) seventeenth century. The relative unimportance of the individual words of canzonetta texts and the dominance of metre and stereotyped subjects perhaps inspired a more compatible and less competitive relationship between poetry and music. The issues go beyond simple matters of genre to raise profound questions concerning the status of musical expression as the Baroque period came into its own.

In 'O sia tranquillo il mare', one textual (as opposed to affective) cue for the shift to triple time seems provided retrospectively in the poem by the reference to 'my lament' scattered by the air (and 'e 'l mio lamento' actually appears in the triple-time section).[20] But this is no tragic lament in the grand manner of the *Lamento d'Arianna* and its numerous imitations: even if the

---

[19] My translation differs slightly from the one in *The Letters of Claudio Monteverdi*, trans. Stevens, 107–8.

[20] I am grateful to Silke Leopold for suggesting (private discussion) that one common textual cue for triple time would seem to be notions of 'return' (as here: 'Ma tu non torni . . .'), and it is certainly true that 'tornare' and its derivatives can often be found in Monteverdi's and other's triple-time music, or is somehow present by implication (for example, in a nostalgic evocation of past pleasures). The whole issue seems to require fuller, and systematic, exploration.

apparent situations are similar—Ariadne, too, was left abandoned on a rocky beach—the laments of shepherds and their nymphs are cast in a more discrete vein. But they are no less impassioned, and the affective musical codes are equally clear. 'O sia tranquillo il mare' is one of the *canti amorosi* in Monteverdi's Eighth Book, and as in many of its counterparts, triple-time writing becomes one trait of the *molle* ('soft' or 'tender') *genere* that in the preface to the *Madrigali guerrieri, et amorosi* Monteverdi contrasts with the *temperato* and the *concitato*. The first madrigal in the Eighth Book further emphasizes the point: 'Altri canti d'Amor, tenero arciero', 'Let others sing of Love, the tender archer'. This begins in a sensuous triple time, and the descending tetrachord ($d'-c'-bb'-a$) implied in the bass through the opening turns into a true ground bass at the second line, 'i dolci vezzi, e sospirati baci' ('the sweet charms and sighed-for kisses'; Ex. 6.3)—here, it seems, less an 'emblem of lament' than of that which so often gives rise to lament.[21] As numerous passages in Monteverdi's late madrigals and operas make clear, the triple-time aria is the musical language of love.[22]

The processes whereby particular kinds of triple-time writing come to signify 'love' in early seventeenth-century secular music have yet to be traced, although the poet Gabriello Chiabrera had already made the connection between the pleasures or pains of love and the poetry most frequently associated with triple-time in the period, the canzonetta (often in metres other than the seven- or eleven-syllable *versi piani* of contemporary madrigals).[23] But whatever the case, the semiotic works in ways very different from the traditional associations of signifier and signified: having a lamenting lover sing in triple time is scarcely a plausible mimetic gesture, nor for that matter a particularly verisimilar one. In the Renaissance, the relationship between signifier and signified had been straightforwardly conceived in terms of the elaborate chains of resemblance dominating the Renaissance worldview. In a cosmos saturated by webs of analogy, the place of any element was fixed within a hierarchy from macrocosm to microcosm by virtue of its resemblance to elements both higher and lower on the scale. Identities were thus forged by similarities (whether revealed or hidden) that allowed the

[21] Compare Ellen Rosand, 'The Descending Tetrachord: An Emblem of Lament', *Musical Quarterly*, 55 (1979), 346–59.

[22] For example, see Tim Carter, '"In Love's harmonious consort"? Penelope and the Interpretation of *Il ritorno d'Ulisse in patria*', *Cambridge Opera Journal*, 5 (1993), 1–16.

[23] Gabriello Chiabrera's dialogue *Il Geri* of 1624–5 offers some useful suggestions; see most recently Robert R. Holzer, '"Sono d'altro garbo . . . le canzonette che si cantano oggi": Pietro della Valle on Music and Modernity in the Seventeenth Century', *Studi musicali*, 21 (1992), 253–306. I have no doubt that the ideas presented in the present essay will eventually mesh with those suggested in Massimo Ossi, 'Claudio Monteverdi's *Ordine novo, bello et gustevole*: The Canzonetta as Dramatic Module and Formal Archetype', *Journal of the American Musicological Society*, 45 (1992), 261–304.

Ex. 6.3. Monteverdi, 'Altri canti d'Amor'

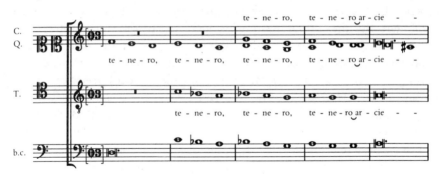

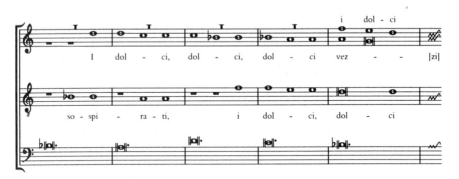

(... the tender archer, the sweet charms and sighed-for [kisses] ...)

Renaissance to make sense of its world. Music reflected the harmony of the spheres; texts set to music were to be 'imitated' by musical homologues through word-painting; even the Florentine 'new music' sought validation on the grounds of resemblance (in this case, to oratorical speech), making it (in more than just the humanist sense) a profoundly 'Renaissance' genre.

The new modes of scientific endeavour and of philosophical thought in the seventeenth century encouraged an alternative construction of the relationship of signifier to signified as instead being one of difference, for all its possible grounding in similarity and identity: *x* 'represents' *y* but is (because it is?) different from *y*. The link was now forged less by resemblance—although that could still be an issue—than by conventions fostered by tradition or created by invention, establishing a code to be learned by and shared complicitly between producer and receiver. In contemporary terms, such notions of difference—and the emotional and other effects that such juxtapositions could produce—were intimately linked to the *concettismo* and *meraviglia* central to Marinist aesthetics. But they also had more far-reaching implications, for the increasingly autonomous sign also took on a life of its own, permitting an ever deeper exploration of its intrinsic nature and effects. As Foucault argues, the conceptual divorce of resemblance and representation was an intensely liberating experience: 'the sign . . . is charged no longer with the task of keeping the world close to itself and inherent in its own forms, but, on the contrary, with that of spreading it out, of juxtaposing it over an indefinitely open surface, and of taking up from that point the endless deployment of the substitutes in which we conceive of it'.[24] This, it seems to me, offers significant potential for viewing in a more positive light the aesthetic and other tendencies of the second, third, and fourth decades of the seventeenth century that have tended to receive so negative a press in recent years.[25]

The play of signs in Monteverdi's Venetian secular music—and for that matter, later music as well—can variously depend on both 'Renaissance' and 'Baroque' modes of signification. It should be clear from the above discussion that 'Zefiro torna, e di soavi accenti' seems to rely on the former, the composer perhaps being influenced by Rinuccini's echoes of older poets, not least Petrarch and Tasso. Of course, Tasso also inspired the development of the *stile concitato* in the *Combattimento di Tancredi et Clorinda* (based on an episode from *Gerusalemme liberata*). It is perhaps revealing that when

---

[24] Michel Foucault, *The Order of Things: An Archeology of the Human Sciences* (London: Tavistock Publications, 1970; repr. London: Routledge, 1989), 61. The original of this text, *Les Mots et les choses*, was published in 1966. I am not the first to use Foucault in this context: see, for example, Jeffrey Kurtzman, 'A Taxonomic and Affective Analysis of Monteverdi's "Hor che'l ciel e la terra"', *Music Analysis*, 12 (1993), 169–95; and note the comment on Tomlinson below, n. 28. I am indeed grateful to Professor Kurtzman for giving me a copy of his unpublished paper 'Monteverdi's Changing Aesthetics: A Semiotic Perspective' (presented at the Fifth Biennial Conference on Baroque Music, University of Durham, July 1992): we are moving on slightly different, if related, lines.

[25] For example, in Tomlinson's *Monteverdi and the End of the Renaissance*. I raised some of the issues in my review in *Early Music History*, 8 (1988), 245–60.

Monteverdi sought consciously to 'invent' a new *genere*—'In all the works
of the former composers I have indeed found examples of the 'soft' [*molle*]
and the 'moderate' [*temperato*], but never of the 'agitated' [*concitato*], a genus
nevertheless described by Plato . . .'[26]—he adopted a conservative tack, using
conventional mimetic gestures predicated upon their putative resemblance to
the emotions being expressed (as Foucault says, 'keeping the world close to
itself and inherent in its own forms'). The composer found it hard to play
the intellectual, and the results ring false in an increasingly alien context (as
many commentators on the *Combattimento* have claimed). But Monteverdi's
musical instincts were much more assured. His exploration of the *molle genere*
certainly seems to have been more intuitive, drawing on a wealth of experience (both from the work of 'former composers' and in his own output) in
new conceptions and articulations of notions of representation, juxtaposing
signs 'over an indefinitely open surface' with the possibility of an 'endless
deployment' of new styles, sounds, and gestures.[27] Realizing such possibilities
was, of course, the chief task of the years to come.

The fruits are apparent in 'O sia tranquillo il mare'. They are still more
so in the most famous of the *canti amorosi* in Monteverdi's Eighth Book,
the *Lamento della ninfa*.[28] Here a nymph laments her betrayal by her lover,

[26] From the preface to Monteverdi's *Madrigali guerrieri, et amorosi*, translated in Oliver
Strunk, *Source Readings in Music History* (London: Faber, 1952), 413–15.
[27] Compare also Foucault, *The Order of Things*, 61–2: 'It had long been known—and well
before Plato's *Cratylus*—that signs can be either given by nature or established by man. Nor
was the sixteenth century ignorant of this fact, since it recognized human languages to be
instituted signs. But the artificial signs owed their power only to their fidelity to natural signs.
These latter, even at a remove, were the foundation of all others. From the seventeenth
century, the values allotted to nature and convention in this field are inverted: if natural, a
sign is no more than an element selected from the world of things and constituted as a sign
by our knowledge. It is therefore strictly limited, rigid, inconvenient, and impossible for the
mind to master. When, on the other hand, one establishes a conventional sign, it is always
possible (and indeed necessary) to choose it in such a way that it will be simple, easy to
remember, applicable to an indefinite number of elements, susceptible of subdivision within
itself and of combination with other signs; the man-made sign is the sign at the peak of its
activity. It is the man-made sign that draws the dividing-line between man and animal; that
transforms imagination into voluntary memory, spontaneous attention into reflection, and
instinct into rational knowledge.'
[28] See the discussion in Gary Tomlinson, *Music in Renaissance Magic: Toward a Historiography
of Others* (Chicago and London: University of Chicago Press, 1993), 229–46, which I read
after presenting my paper. Tomlinson's use of Foucault here is somewhat similar to mine—
I am happy to acknowledge his precedence (along with Kurtzman's; see above, n. 24), and
indeed his virtuosity—although we disagree on the extent to which Monteverdi 'lied—
extravagantly, resonantly, and with rarely matched force—in the *Lament of the Nymph*' (ibid.
242). Tomlinson also praises 'Renaissance' notions of resemblance in Monteverdi's earlier
madrigals (in particular, 'Sfogava con le stelle' from the Fourth Book of 1603) without acknowledging that (in my view) such notions underpin the mimetic gestures that he formerly
criticized as anti-Renaissance in the Venetian music.

watched by three shepherds, who comment wryly on the situation. The opening narration exploits standard mimetic gestures (close imitation for the nymph trampling the flowers; a trenchant dissonance for her 'dolore'). But the nymph's complaint itself is set as the most sensuous triple-time aria over a descending tetrachord ground bass: here the focus is less on the words (which Monteverdi contorts freely) than on the raw power of the human voice, using melody, not the text, to achieve emotional representation and arousal. Again, one cannot imagine a greater contrast to that archetypal lament so lauded both by Monteverdi and in the literature, the *Lamento d'Arianna* of 1608. Yet both settings are avowedly in the *stile rappresentativo*, and both seek to represent the pains of love. In the *Lamento d'Arianna*, the success of the representation was to be judged by its adherence to Renaissance notions of verisimilitude, by its recognizable resemblance to heightened oratorical speech. However, the success and power of such new representations as the *Lamento della ninfa* must be judged not according to a Renaissance canon but instead by their immediate effect on the senses. Now the acid test is one of experiment and experience, whether rubbing 'clear water' on the back of a brass spoon or feeling ourselves moved to new heights by the power of a new kind of song.

The different world of the *Lamento della ninfa* may be conditioned not just by a new aesthetic but also by new constructions of gender.[29] The *molle genere* is itself explicitly gendered ('Io canto d'Amor'—'*I* sing of Love'—says the soprano in the counterpart to 'Altri canti d'amor, tenero arciero' in the *Madrigali guerrieri, et amorosi*, 'Altri canti di Marte e di sua schiera'); and there is some play to be made of the notion that 'old' modes of resemblance versus 'new' modes of representation can somehow carry 'masculine' and 'feminine' connotations. After all, the *Combattimento di Tancredi et Clorinda* is nothing if not a male show-piece, in several senses of the term; and the *Lamento della ninfa* offers a dramatic realization of different male (the shepherds) and female (the nymph) responses to emotional upheaval that in turn reifies the otherness of the lament, whether to signify madness (following Susan McClary) or (as I perhaps prefer) to emphasize the sense of distance newly required for true emotional expression. No less significant, however, is the question of genre: as with 'O sia tranquillo il mare' (and much of Monteverdi's other secular music) we are in the realms of the pastoral, where the problem of nature

---

[29] Compare, for example, the discussion of the *Lamento della ninfa* in Susan McClary, 'Excess and Frame: The Musical Representation of Madwomen', in ead., *Feminine Endings: Music, Gender, and Sexuality* (Minneapolis and Oxford: University of Minnesota Press, 1991), 80–111, although again I seem to be moving in a somewhat different direction. How my view meshes with Suzanne Cusick, 'Gendering Modern Music: Thoughts on the Monteverdi–Artusi Controversy', *Journal of the American Musicological Society*, 46 (1993), 1–25, is a matter for further study.

versus art comes to the fore. Pastoral conventionally extolled the virtues of nature, but any self-respecting pastoral poet knew full well that the art-less 'nature' praised in verse conformed less to nature in 'real life' than to a nature modified and indeed improved by art: thus pastoral defined a space amenable to artistic experimentation of various kinds, and one of some significance for early Baroque endeavours in drama, poetry, and music. And Monteverdi must surely have realized that his 'via naturale alla immitatione' ('natural path to imitation')[30] was scarcely 'natural' in any realistic sense: his task, too, was to use art to improve upon nature. If that was not obvious enough in musical terms, it was clearly made apparent in alchemy, where art did indeed offer the possibility of creating things anew from the base substances of the real world.

Did Monteverdi learn some lessons from his little alchemical experiments? Perhaps we should not take them too seriously, for the composer ended his last letter on the subject (28 March 1626) on a whimsical note:

> I am at present engaged in making a fire under a glass urinal with its cover on, to extract from it an I-don't-know-what and then make of it an I-don't-know-what so that (please God) I may then cheerfully explain this I-don't-know-what to my Lord Marigliani.[31]

One also wonders about the danger of taking Monteverdi's music a mite too seriously, ignoring the whimsy and fancy arguably at the heart of all musical entertainment in this (and perhaps any other) period. In other words, too intense a reading of, say, 'O sia tranquillo il mare' and the *Lamento della ninfa* might well be accused of gloriously missing the point: 'Ben, bene, tutto è zolfa, tutto è zolfa' ('Well, well, it's all sol-fa, it's all sol-fa'), Monteverdi would say benignly on looking over the feeble music of an aspiring pupil.[32] In the end, the composer left us in the dark, never completing the treatise to 'cheerfully explain this I-don't-know-what' that made his music work. But his delicate play of signs and his changing approaches to resemblance and representation were surely of profound significance for his time. They are also what challenge us most in his music today.

---

[30] The comment comes from Monteverdi's letter to Doni of 22 Oct. 1633; see *The Letters of Claudio Monteverdi*, trans. Stevens, 410; Tomlinson, 'Madrigal, Monody, and Monteverdi's "via naturale alla immitatione"'.

[31] My translation differs slightly from the one in *The Letters of Claudio Monteverdi*, trans. Stevens, 302–3.

[32] See the anecdote from Antimo Liberati, *Lettera scritta . . . in risposta ad una del sig. Ovidio Persapegi* (Rome: Mascardi, 1685), given in Fabbri, *Monteverdi*, 297.

7

'Aria' in the Madrigals
of Giovanni Rovetta

❧✿❧

JOHN WHENHAM

THE *concertato* madrigals of Giovanni Rovetta, who was Monteverdi's assistant at St Mark's, Venice, from 1627, and his successor there in 1644, have not yet achieved a modern edition; nor have they been studied in the round. Specific aspects have been noted, mainly in theses,[1] and Jerome Roche offered some judicious comments on Rovetta as composer in his article in the *New Grove Dictionary of Music and Musicians*, including praise of the madrigal 'A che bramar, a che aventar i dardi' (1640). However, Rovetta's significance in the development of new styles and formal structures in the 1620s has not been fully appreciated, chiefly, one suspects, because he published only one solo song, the lament *Le lagrime d'Erminia*, to a text modelled on

In the absence of an agreed terminology which is concise, elegant, and neutral, the terms 'duple metre' and 'duple time', and 'triple metre' and 'triple time', are used in this essay to denote music written under the mensuration signatures **C** and 3/1 respectively. These are the only signatures used in the works under discussion, and it is quite clear that Rovetta intended the usual proportion (three semibreves in 3/1 equals one semibreve in **C**) to exist between them, except on the very few occasions when he qualifies the speed of a 3/1 section by using a tempo marking (as in Ex. 7.2, for instance). Since the *tactus* normally remains constant from one section to another, it can be used as an absolute measure of the durations of sections written in duple and triple metre/time, as has been done here.

---

[1] Nigel Fortune included discussion of Rovetta's only solo song—the lament (or 'cantata', as it is called on the title-page) *Le lagrime d'Erminia* from the first book of madrigals (1629)— in his unpublished, but highly influential study of Italian monody, 'Italian Secular Song from 1600 to 1635: The Origins and Development of Accompanied Monody' (Ph.D. diss., University of Cambridge, 1954). Other aspects of Rovetta's madrigal collections have been studied in more recent theses: John Whenham, *Duet and Dialogue in the Age of Monteverdi* (Ann Arbor: UMI Research Press, 1982), and Margaret Mabbett, 'The Italian Madrigal, 1620–1655' (Ph.D. diss., King's College London, 1989). See also A. W. Ambros, *Geschichte der Musik*, 3rd edn., vol. iv, rev. Hugo Leichtentritt (Leipzig and Breslau: F. E. C. Leuckart, 1909), 877–9.

Canto XIX, stanzas 104–8 in Tasso's *Gerusalemme liberata*.[2] The monograph in which one might have hoped for a more wide-ranging and balanced study—Einstein's *Italian Madrigal*—contains only the dismissive statement that Rovetta and Alessandro Grandi, his predecessor as Monteverdi's assistant, 'lived off Monteverdi's patrimony: untroubled by his scruples, they are less imposing and less interesting but at the same time more progressive and more versatile than their great contemporary, who had by this time become a sort of patriarch'.[3]

For Einstein, of course, Rovetta's work represented the post-classic phase of the madrigal—a period of decline and decay—and it has to be said that his view both of Rovetta's music and of the relationship between Monteverdi and his younger contemporaries begs a number of questions. It is interesting, however, to find him condemning Rovetta for being a 'progressive' madrigalist, a judgement that might appear paradoxical when we consider that Rovetta was publishing polyphonic madrigals as late as the period 1629 to 1645. This paradox is explored in the present essay, taking examples from Rovetta's first two books of madrigals (1629 and 1640).

Neither the place nor the date of Rovetta's birth is certain, although it seems likely, as James Moore pointed out, that he was born either in Venice or in the Veneto.[4] At his death on 23 October 1668, he was reported in the necrology of the Venetian Provveditori della Sanità as being 72 years old, and in the *Libro dei morti* of St Mark's as being 71.[5] These records, then, suggest a date of birth somewhere between 24 October 1595 and 23 October 1597. The earliest hard evidence concerning Rovetta's life and career, however, dates from 1614, when on 7 December, aged probably between 17 and 19, he was listed as an instrumentalist at St Mark's. He was, evidently, an ambitious man. In August 1617 he competed unsuccessfully for the post of *capo dei concerti* at St Mark's in succession to Giovanni Bassano, and he soon began to set his sights even higher, a process which he described with remarkable frankness in the preface to his *Salmi concertati*, op. 1, of 1627 (1626

---

[2] There is, in fact, a good deal more music for solo voices in Rovetta's madrigal books than is apparent from a simple listing of the contents. The dialogue in Book I, the strophic arias in Books I and II, the *ottava* setting 'Rosa, riso d'amor del ciel fattura', and the cantata 'Spieghi i contenti suoi' all contain extended solos. The contents of all three books are listed in the Appendix, below. The list of contents for the Second Book given in *Il nuovo Vogel* is inaccurate in several respects and is corrected here.

[3] Alfred Einstein, *The Italian Madrigal* (Princeton University Press, 1949), ii. 867.

[4] *Vespers at St Mark's: Music of Alessandro Grandi, Giovanni Rovetta and Francesco Cavalli* (Ann Arbor: UMI Research Press, 1981), i. 11–18. Moore's biographical study of Rovetta remains the fullest and most up-to-date review of the known evidence. I have included here (with occasional slight adjustments) only the biographical material relevant to the present study.

[5] Ibid., i. 11–12.

more veneto), a document evidently conceived in response to malicious gossip following his *de facto* promotion to the post of vice-*maestro* at St Mark's.

> For many years past my profession was that of a player of all kinds of instruments, both string and wind, and though I laboured not a little at these, nevertheless I did not neglect the study of composition; and desiring to employ my talent in this field I sought from the Most Illustrious and Most Excellent Lord Procurators to be admitted to the brotherhood of the other gentlemen musicians [*Signori Musici*] of Their Excellencies at St Mark's; and of this I was deemed worthy. I hoped later to be able, in the absence of the *maestro di cappella*, to exercise the function of vice-*maestro* should the said position already have become vacant; and my hopes in this matter did not prove vain, since the need arose shortly after my entry [and] I was honoured with that charge by the Most Illustrious and Most Excellent Lord Procurators pending a new election. But since it seemed strange to some people that I should pass so quickly from the profession of instrumentalist to that of composer, and that I should direct music on various feasts, they made the ill-founded judgement that such church music [as I provided] could not have been composed by me. Anticipating that such objections could very soon make a bad impression on those by whom I am not known, I have taken the opportunity of sending these sacred songs to the press, so that the Most Illustrious and Most Excellent Lord Procurators will actually see that I, having obtained favour through their kindness, have the same foundations of skill as others who have obtained the said position before me; and let it also be known that these are really my compositions and not those of other people; nor will I refuse to demonstrate this on any day, through any kind of test, to anyone who believes otherwise: and let it not be marvelled at that I should at first have exercised the profession of instrumentalist, and then put myself to the practice of composition, for Signor Striggio, Signor Priuli, Signor Valentini, and almost all the best school of composers have followed this path. On the contrary, with this knowledge I might rightly aspire to the said position of vice-*maestro di cappella* at St Mark's since one finds in this Most Serene service not only thirty and more singers, but also twenty and more players of wind and string instruments.[6]

In order to bolster his credentials as a potential vice-*maestro*, then, Rovetta had seen that it would be necessary both to establish himself as a composer and to raise his status from instrumentalist to singer, the 'Signori Musici' being not the 'musicians' of St Mark's in general, but more specifically the singers in its choir. The surviving facts confirm his account. His sacred

---

[6] The Italian text is given in Claudio Sartori, *Bibliografia della musica strumentale italiana stampata in Italia fino al 1700* (Florence: Olschki, 1952), 305, and Moore, *Vespers at St Mark's*, i. 233, Doc. 7.

compositions began to appear in print in Venetian anthologies from 1620,[7] and he was appointed a bass singer in the choir of St Mark's on 2 December 1623. By the date of publication of the *Salmi*, early in 1627, he was already standing in for Alessandro Grandi as vice-*maestro di cappella*. Grandi must have vacated this post officially by 18 March 1627, when he was appointed *maestro di cappella* at Santa Maria Maggiore in Bergamo, and Rovetta was appointed in his place on 22 November of the same year, aged between 30 and 32.

Rovetta published the *Salmi concertati* clearly with the intention of establishing his competence as a composer of sacred music. His first book of *Madrigali concertati*, another very substantial volume, dedicated to Paolo Giordano II Orsini, Duke of Bracciano,[8] followed two years later, in 1629 (the dedication is dated 10 October 1629); it was presumably intended to stake a similar claim for recognition in the field of secular music. These two volumes may, perhaps, be seen as marking the end of Rovetta's apprenticeship, and they are followed by a six-year gap before the next group of his publications, bounded by the *Motetti concertati* of 1635 and the *Salmi* for eight voices of 1644, a volume dedicated to the procurators of St Mark's in gratitude for their having appointed him *maestro* in succession to Monteverdi. This group of publications includes the second book of *concertato* madrigals (1640), a volume dedicated to the Venetian lawyer and musical patron Francesco Pozzo.[9] I suspect that most, if not all, of its contents belong to the 1630s, partly on stylistic and technical grounds, and partly because Rovetta, with an eye to the Monteverdian succession, would probably have wished to include in it only the best of his most recent and mature work. One possible exception may be the three-voice madrigal 'La giovane bellissima

---

[7] The earliest in *Symbolae diversorum musicorum binis, ternis, quaternis, et quinis vocibus cantandae*, ed. Lorenzo Calvi (Venice: Alessandro Vincenti, RISM 1620²).

[8] There is no obvious connection between Rovetta and Orsini except, perhaps, through Monteverdi, who was in correspondence with the Duke in 1619–20 and knew him as a patron of music; see *The Letters of Claudio Monteverdi*, trans. Denis Stevens (London and Boston: Faber & Faber, 1980), 153–5.

[9] The dedication is dated 15 Mar. 1640. In it, Rovetta reveals in passing that Pozzo was a lawyer—he is 'V. S. Eccellentissima, che con tanta eleganza difende le cause de' suoi clienti' ('Your Most Excellent Lordship, who with such elegance defends the cases of your clients')— and that music was performed at his house, noting 'Il sollievo, che V. S. Eccellentissima, frà la numerosità de suoi principali, e gravissimi affari, suol tal volta ricevere dalla Musica con arrichir questa Città bene spesso del tesoro d'angeliche armonie, per lo valore di pregiatissimi soggetti da lei favoreggiati, e raccolti' ('The relaxation which Your Most Excellent Lordship, amid the great number of your main and most burdensome affairs, is occasionally wont to receive from music, often enriching this city with the treasure of angelic harmonies thanks to the worth of the most highly prized individuals favoured and gathered together by you'). Two other Venetian composers—Martino Pesenti and Giovanni Antonio Rigatti—also dedicated volumes of music to Pozzo, both in 1641.

Hadriana', a virtuoso celebration of the vocal skills of Adriana Basile, who had visited Venice in 1623 in the retinue of the Duke of Mantua.[10]

The three volumes of Rovetta's music published between 1645 and 1650, beginning with his third and last book of madrigals, were all collected for publication by his nephew, Giovanni Battista Volpe. The third madrigal collection includes music almost entirely for two and three voices, and its settings are on average shorter than those contained in the earlier books: the madrigalian settings range in length from 59 to 128 *tactus*, with a mean length of 86, as against a range of 73 to 143 *tactus* and a mean length of 106 for Book I, and a range of 62 to 226 *tactus* and a mean length of 122 for Book II. It is not clear whether smaller-scale madrigals represent a new direction in Rovetta's work, or whether (and more likely) in the aftermath of his appointment as *maestro* he felt a need to maintain a healthy publication record and thus simply allowed his nephew to gather together any settings which were to hand, whether newly composed or not. At all events, the Third Book lacks the general sense of progression that I think is detectable between the first two and is certainly not so clearly the work of a composer wishing to cut a *bella figura*.

Although Rovetta mentions his composition studies, which presumably began before 1620 and his first forays into print, he does not say who his teacher was. The dedication of the 1627 *Salmi*, however, includes a generous tribute to Monteverdi and reveals that at the very least Rovetta took Monteverdi's work as his model.[11] That he was indeed a pupil of Monteverdi seems to be confirmed by a report on the Monteverdian succession at St Mark's sent on 7 January 1645 by the Modenese Resident Giovanni Pietro Scalabrini in reply to an enquiry made by the Duke of Modena: 'Giovanni Rovetta, a Venetian musician and pupil of Monteverdi, who was in his time *sotto maestro di cappella*, was substituted by the procurators.'[12]

Rovetta's reception of Monteverdi's ideas can be pursued at several levels in his madrigal books. There is, for example, a superficial resemblance between the layout of Rovetta's First Book and that of Monteverdi's Seventh Book, published in 1619. And the inclusion of several large-scale settings in Rovetta's Second Book—for up to eight voices and violins—could be seen as aping the appearance of similar settings in Monteverdi's *Madrigali guerrieri, et amorosi* (1638), especially if one takes the view that such pieces were outmoded by

[10] See Alessandro Ademollo, *La bell'Adriana ed altre virtuose del suo tempo alla corte di Mantova* (Città di Castello: Lapi, 1888), 271–87; John Whenham, 'The Gonzagas Visit Venice', *Early Music*, 21 (1993), 525–42.

[11] The text of the dedication is given in Sartori, *Bibliografia*, 304.

[12] Modena, Archivio di Stato, Cancelleria estero, Venezia, Busta 98, letter 116.X.69.

1640. On the other hand, similarities between the output of the two composers could simply reflect the fact that they served the same musical public.
There is some evidence to support the view that during the 1630s Rovetta
began to shoulder public duties that might otherwise have fallen to
Monteverdi. In 1632, for example, he was in charge of the musicians
who sang at the installation of Cardinal Cornaro as Patriarch of Venice;[13] and
in 1638 he composed and directed the music for the celebrations at San
Giorgio commissioned by the French ambassador to mark the birth of the
Dauphin.[14] It is possible, too, that he occasionally substituted for Monteverdi
in writing secular music for state occasions or for patrons requiring large-
scale madrigals.[15]

Some aspects of Rovetta's style do suggest Monteverdian associations,
though this is not the element of his work in which the older composer's
influence is most apparent. The enjoyment of voices singing in parallel
seconds, a familiar feature of Monteverdi's madrigals from Book IV onwards,
colours the end of Rovetta's setting of 'Quella fede leal ch'io consecrai' for
alto, tenor, and bass (1629; Ex. 7.1); and the same setting begins with an
extended passage over a 'walking' bass which then gives way to declamatory
recitative in a manner analogous to Monteverdi's 'Augellin che la voce al
canto spieghi' (1619). Occasionally, too, and particularly in his later work,
Rovetta uses contrary motion to produce dissonant textures of a kind that
Monteverdi employed in both secular and sacred contexts. It has to be said,
however, that these are relatively isolated instances within a musical language
which otherwise seems to be held in common by Monteverdi, Grandi, and
Rovetta.

An interesting facet of Rovetta's work, and one that does seem to owe

---

[13] See Giulio Strozzi, *Lettera . . . famigliarmente scritta ad un suo Amico, oue gli dà conto del solenne possesso preso dall'Eminentissimo Signor Cardinal Cornaro Patriarca di Venetia li 27. di Giugno 1632* (Venice: Giovanni Pietro Pinelli, 1632), 27.

[14] See the dedication to Rovetta's *Messa, e salmi* (Venice: Alessandro Vincenti, 1639); and Ciro Fausto, *Venezia festiva per gli pomposi spettacoli fatti rappresentare dall'illustrissimo et eccellentissimo sig. d'Hussé ambasciatore di S. M. christianissima per la nascita del Reale Delfino di Francia* (Venice: Francesco Baba, 1638), 24.

[15] Margaret Mabbett has suggested that Monteverdi's late large-scale madrigals may reflect Viennese, rather than Venetian musical taste, and given that he dedicated his Eighth Book to the Emperor, there is merit in this argument. So far as I know, Rovetta had no direct dealings with the Viennese court, though in the preface to his *Salmi* of 1627 quoted above he mentions Giovanni Priuli and Giovanni Valentini, who were both composers in the service of the Emperor and whose large-scale *concertato* madrigals were published in Venice between 1619 and 1625 and may have been known by Rovetta. There were, however, state occasions in Venice for which large-scale madrigals might have been appropriate, and (un-worthy thought!) the larger the ensemble the larger the number of singers from St Mark's who would have been eligible for the tips and extra pay brought in by participating in such events.

Ex. 7.1. Rovetta, 'Quella fede leal'

(. . . to repay faith with ingratitude.)

something to Monteverdi, is his concern with the problems of generating coherent structures, and an occasional willingness to tamper with the word order of a text in order to achieve this. His attempts at integration are not all equally successful. In the large sonnet setting 'Taccia il cielo e la terra al novo canto' (1629), for example, the motif with which the introductory sinfonia begins is brought back rather artificially for the setting of the third line of text, and then again in a triple-time variant for instruments just before the setting of the final tercet. But in the four-part setting 'Udite, amanti, udite' (1629), the phrase 'è fatta amante', which is really the nub of the text—the previously reluctant maiden has now succumbed—is repeated several times out of its original context to underline its pervading importance.

One of the elements which distinguishes Rovetta's style from Monteverdi's is the lyrical—one might almost say 'tuneful'—impulse that underlies much of his writing. In this respect, he seems as much a disciple of Alessandro Grandi as of Monteverdi. But where Grandi was content to remain a miniaturist, at least in his madrigals, Rovetta uses melody—particularly triple-time aria styles—to create extended structures, and in this lies something of his originality and the 'progressive' quality of his settings.

The 'aria' styles that Rovetta uses—in duple time over a walking bass, and in a broad triple metre—are most often discussed nowadays as styles found in the strophic solo songs of Venetian composers like Grandi and Giovanni Pietro Berti, and both styles also figure prominently in the strophic pieces that Rovetta included in his first madrigal book—triple time in 'Pur al fin di mia fè' and 'Giovinetta fastosa', and the walking-bass style in 'Vivo in foco amoroso', a duet with two violins that owes more than a little to Monteverdi's 'Chiome d'oro' (1619). In the same book, however, both styles also appear in a dramatic context—in the setting of Giulio Strozzi's dialogue *La gelosia placata*, where they are used to construct short aria-like passages contrasted with declamatory recitative[16]—and in madrigals. In the latter, Rovetta generally uses a walking bass simply to vary the pace of his duple-time arioso. This is a stylistic trait that can be compared with similar examples in Grandi's First Book of madrigals (1615). The only real exception in Rovetta's First Book is the opening of the three-part 'Quella fede leal', cited earlier, where the whole of the opening section is constructed over such a bass line.

However, the use of triple-time 'aria' in the madrigals of Book I is much more significant, though it is localized particularly in the two-voice settings. As far as the three- and four-voice madrigals of the book are concerned, triple-time writing appears in only three of the eight settings, and here its appearance is generally explicable in terms of the meaning of the texts. In 'Ove ch'io vada, ove ch'io stia tal hora', for example, triple-time passages lasting no longer than two *tactus* are used to slow the prevailing pace to underline the rhetorical cry 'Ahi folle'; and in 'Anime pellegrine che bramate', a short motif in triple metre is treated in close imitation as a musical metaphor for 'confusion' in setting the lines 'Sian confusi voleri | le speranze, i pensieri'. 'Quante volte giurai ferm'e costante' is the only three-voice setting in Book I to employ an extended passage of triple-time melody, and this 'aria', lasting 45 *tactus*, occurs at the main point of articulation of the

[16] For a fuller discussion of Strozzi's text and Rovetta's setting, see Whenham, *Duet and Dialogue*, i. 207–16; the dialogue is transcribed ibid., ii. 414–37.

Ex. 7.2. Rovetta, 'Quante volte giurai'

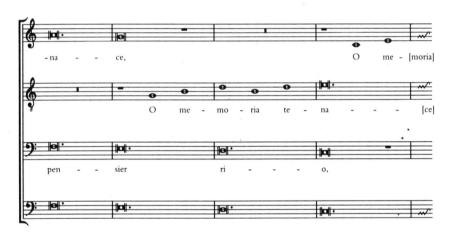

(. . . O stubborn memory, o harsh thought . . .)

sonnet—lines 9–11—as the lover looks back to the 'stubborn memory' and 'harsh thought' of his beloved's cruelty (Ex. 7.2).

This use of triple-time melody to draw attention to an important juncture in the text, though rare in the three- and four-voice settings, appears in no fewer than seven of the ten two-voice madrigals in Book I. In these cases, the introduction of a triple-time 'aria', with text and melodic phrases repeated several times and developed through imitation and sequence, seems not so much a matter of word- or mood-painting as a solution to the problems that Rovetta encountered in trying to build extended structures with only two voices at his disposal. Thus in two of the duet settings—'O rubella d'amor cruda a l'amante'[17] and 'Quel neo ch'appar nel viso'—Rovetta makes the first two lines of text function as a refrain. In both cases this produces an $xAxBxB'$ structure, where x represents the refrain.[18] Otherwise, the two settings are quite different from each other. 'Quel neo', set (unusually) entirely in triple metre, is lyrical, while 'O rubella d'amor' contains dramatic declamatory writing of a kind which Rovetta otherwise employs only in the dialogue setting *La gelosia placata*.

The remaining five duets in this group all employ extended triple-time 'arias' for substantially the same reason: to draw attention to focal points within the text. This is most clearly illustrated in the fourth and sixth madrigals of the book—'Ardi contento e taci' and 'Stanco di lacrimar a voi rivolgo', where the focus is the final 'point' of the madrigal. In the setting of 'Stanco di lacrimar', a text of thirteen lines, Rovetta allots the first eleven lines 46 *tactus* in duple rhythm. The final couplet is then set to 62 *tactus* of melodious triple-time aria and a final 9-*tactus* envoi in duple time.[19]

The treatment of 'Ardi contento' is a little more complex. In this nine-line madrigal the lover, wishing to keep his love secret, tries to suppress the sighs that would betray him:

> Ardi contento e taci,
> o di secreto amore
> secretario mio core;
> e voi sospiri, testimoni ascosi
> de' miei furti amorosi,
> che per uscire ad hor ad hor m'aprite
> le labra, ah, non uscite:
> ch'ai saggi, oimè, de l'amorosa scola
> il sospiro è parola.

(Burn happy and be silent, | thou of my secret love | the guardian, O my heart; | and you, sighs, hidden witnesses | of my amorous thefts, | which in order to escape now and again open | my lips, ah do not issue forth: | for to the sages, alas, of the school of love | a sigh is as good as a word.)

Rovetta sets the first six lines in 31 *tactus* of duple metre and the last three in a complex lasting no fewer than 113 *tactus* and set mainly in triple-time aria style:

---

[17] Transcribed ibid., ii. 272–9.

[18] In 'O rubella d'amor', line 1 of the refrain is set in triple time, and line 2 in duple; when the refrain is repeated, the two lines are given in reverse order.

[19] 'Uccidetemi pur, bella tiranna' also ends with a eleven-*tactus* envoi following an 'aria' of 22 *tactus*, but the 'point' is set in duple metre. This is an exceptional text, however, in that its first and last lines are identical, and the use of a duple-time ending simply reflects a repetition of the opening of the setting.

text	signature	no. of tactus
ah, non uscite:	C	5
ch'ai saggi, oimè, de l'amorosa scola il sospiro è parola.	3/1	59
Ah, non uscite:	C	5
ch'ai saggi, oimè, de l'amorosa scola il sospiro è parola,	3/1	35
il sospiro è parola.	C	9

The first two madrigals of Book I appear at first sight not to belong to this group, since triple-time writing appears in the body of the setting rather than at the end. 'Chi vuol haver felice e lieto il core'[20] falls into three main sections of 29, 35, and 31 *tactus* respectively:

text	signature	no. of tactus
Chi vuol haver felice e lieto il core non segui il crudo Amore, quel lusinghier ch'ancide quando più scherza e ride;	C	29
ma tema di beltà, di leggiadria l'aura fallace e ria;	3/1	29
al pregar non risponda, a la promessa non creda;		6
e se s'appressa, fugga pur, chè baleno è quel ch'alletta nè mai balena Amor se non saetta.	C	31

(He who would have a happy and joyful heart | should not follow cruel Love, | that flatterer who kills | when most he jests and laughs; | but let him fear of beauty and grace | the impression deceiving and harsh; | let him not respond to entreaty, and in promises | let him not believe; and if he [Love] approaches | flee, yes, for it is the flash that charms | and Love never flashes when he does not shoot.)

The first section is based on an opening gambit familiar from, and perhaps pioneered in, the duets of Alessandro Grandi's first madrigal book, and which is also found in the duets that Monteverdi published in 1619:[21] that is, Rovetta invents a broad span of melody comprising three constituent phrases, the last of which, in particular, lends itself to extension by imitation and sequence (Ex. 7.3). Just as the semiquavers of the last of these phrases

---

[20] Transcribed in Whenham, *Duet and Dialogue*, ii. 266–71.
[21] See ibid., i. 157, 165.

Ex. 7.3. Rovetta, 'Chi vuol haver felice'

(He who would have a happy and joyful heart should not follow cruel Love,
that flatterer who kills when most he jests and laughs . . .)

Ex. 7.4. Rovetta, 'Chi vuol haver felice'

(. . . the impression deceiving and harsh . . .)

must have been suggested by the words 'scherza e ride' ('jests and laughs'), so, in the last section of the setting, the words 'fugga' ('flee'), 'baleno' ('flash'), and 'saetta' ('shoot') also provoke musical metaphors. The change to triple metre in the second section is a different matter. It is just possible, though not very convincing, to argue that the suave aria-like writing, in which line 6 of the text in particular is repeated over and over again (Ex. 7.4), suggests the false blandishments of beauty mentioned in the text. It seems more important, though, that the change of rhythm serves to articulate the syntax of the text; the extended 'aria' then reinforces what is essentially the first 'point' of the madrigal. (The setting of line 7 and the first part of line 8, though still in triple metre, is declamatory in style and serves to initiate the second part of the setting, culminating in the 'point' proper.) Similarly, in the second of these two madrigals, 'Io mi sento morir quando non miro', a duple-time setting of the first two lines—'Io mi sento morir quando non miro | colei ch'è la mia vita' ('I feel myself die when I do not see | her who is my life'; 26 tactus)—gives way to a triple-time setting of the third—'poi se la miro anco morir mi sento' ('then if I see her, again I feel myself die'; 22 *tactus*)—offering a similar, if simpler instance.

What is happening in these madrigals seems analogous to the contrasts of recitative, arioso, and aria styles that Nigel Fortune noted in solo songs like Sigismondo d'India's 'Torna il sereno Zefiro' (1623) and Giovanni Pietro Berti's 'Da grave incendio oppresso' (1627).[22] The difference lies in the much larger scale of the canvases on which Rovetta was working, the fact that he was writing in the form of the madrigal rather than the strophic song, and the consistency with which he employed this approach. And it does not detract from the significance or originality of his work to suggest that he might have derived the idea of using triple-time aria to emphasize focal points within a madrigal from a setting like Monteverdi's 'Non vedrò mai le stelle' (1619), which has just such a passage at its centre to the words 'O luci belle, | deh siate sì rubelle' ('O beautiful eyes, | ah you so rob').[23]

Aria styles also feature prominently in Rovetta's Second Book of madrigals, though there are also settings which contain no extended passages in aria style at all, such as 'Sovra il carro stellato in ciel sorgea'—whose *ottava rima* stanzas are set as a freely constructed group of strophic variations entirely in duple-time arioso—or the virtuoso 'La giovane bellissima Hadriana' and the splendid 'A che bramar' for six voices and two violins. The last involves a particularly interesting structure, and one which explores in a new way the type of solo–ensemble setting employed by Monteverdi in 'Ahi come a un vago sol cortese giro' (Book V, 1605) and 'Qui rise, o Tirsi, e qui ver me rivolse' (Book VI, 1614). Following an introductory sinfonia, the first six lines of the text are set for solo tenor and continuo and then repeated in a varied form for the remaining five voices. The next five lines are set for tenor solo accompanied by strings and continuo while the ensemble continues to interject phrases from lines 1–4, producing juxtapositions such as the ensemble's 'A che bramar?' (line 1: 'What do you long for?') followed by the tenor's 'Tutto languisce e cade' (line 10: 'Everything languishes and falls'). Voices and strings then join for the 'point' of the madrigal.

However, settings of this kind are in the minority in Book II, for no fewer than nine of the fourteen settings make extended use of aria styles, and a tenth—'Voi partite, crudele, ah voi partite?'—hints at a recitative–aria division when its highly charged opening section gives way to a more lyrical arioso initiated by writing over a walking bass. Triple-time writing again predominates, although the book includes one aria over a ground bass moving

[22] 'Italian Secular Monody from 1600 to 1635: An Introductory Survey', *Musical Quarterly*, 39 (1953), 171–95 at 190–1.
[23] Discussed in Tim Carter, *Music in Late Renaissance and Early Baroque Italy* (London: Batsford, 1992), 251–3.

mainly in crotchets. This is the setting of 'Rosa, riso d'amor del ciel fattura', the well-known set-piece in praise of the rose from the third canto of Marino's *Adone*.[24] This ground bass appears to be an original invention of Rovetta's, although its harmonic outline is not unlike that of the so-called 'chaconne' bass found in a number of books of solo songs and madrigals during the 1630s.

The reasons which seem to prompt Rovetta to write extended 'aria' passages in the madrigals of Book II are essentially the same as those identified in the duets of Book I. 'O quante volte, o quante',[25] for example, employs a triple-time refrain heard three times during the setting; in 'Lacrimosa beltà', the first thirty-two lines of text are set in 75 *tactus* of duple metre, and the last two lines—the 'point'—in 34 *tactus* of triple-time melody with a duple-metre envoi of 10 *tactus*; and similarly, in 'Hor lieto rido e canto', the point is set in triple time (marked 'presto') within an ABA'B' structure (where B is the section in triple metre).

The chief novelty in Book II is the inclusion of triple-time aria writing in three works scored for five and more voices, the madrigal 'Venga dal ciel migliore' and the two sonnet settings, 'Tutto lieto cantai benigno amore' and 'Io torno, amati lumi, al caro oggetto'. The two larger-scale works are rather schematic in structure. 'Venga dal ciel migliore', scored for five voices, two violins, and continuo, is a setting of a fourteen-line madrigal. Rovetta divides his setting into four sections. The first, lasting 19 *tactus*, consists of two statements for solo voice, each followed by a homophonic restatement for all the voices plus violins. The second and third sections, too, each begin with a short solo, this time accompanied by the violins. In the first, the solo dissolves into showers of semiquavers for various groupings of the full ensemble representing the descent of joy and laughter from the heavens. The second section employs the dotted rhythms and triadic figures of the *concitato genere* to represent the 'warlike trumpet' and the noise of battle. All this occupies 65 *tactus*. The remaining 92 are given over to the 'point', an ABA'B' complex in which the line 'Sia festoso ogni dì, lieta ogni sera' ('be festive every day, happy every evening') is set to a total of 71 *tactus* of triple-time 'aria' tinged by mild dissonances (Ex. 7.5), which are complemented by a total of 21 *tactus* of duple-time writing for the remaining two lines, 'Sian grati i nostri canti | e a più felice, e a più funesti amanti' ('May our songs be welcome | both to happier and to sadder lovers'). In this case, the triple-time 'aria' both lends weight to the end of the setting and functions as word-painting.

---

[24] See Ambros, *Geschichte der Musik*, iv. 879.
[25] Transcribed in Whenham, *Duet and Dialogue*, ii. 291–5.

Ex. 7.5. Rovetta, 'Venga dal ciel'

(. . . be festive every day, happy every evening . . .)

'Io torno, amati lumi' is a massive setting in which the ensemble of eight voices and two violins is used sometimes as a block, producing, as it were, harmonized monody, and sometimes as two choirs each of four voices and a violin, used for short, dialogue-like exchanges. The underlying conception of the setting seems to have been suggested by the fact that the two quartets and the two tercets of the sonnet can each be seen as a complementary pair. In the first quartet, the poet refers to the beloved's eyes as 'cruel' and 'proud'; in the second, they become 'blessed', and he wishes to kiss them. In the first tercet, he asks that loving eyes should not turn into eyes of hatred; and in the second, he reflects that 'where such beauty is, hardness cannot be'. Triple-time writing occurs only in the second of each pair, and the relative lengths of the sections—35, 82, 21 (a section for solo voice), and 88 *tactus* respectively—show how aria writing is used to develop and extend these sections while at the same time underpinning the more optimistic tone of their text.

The five-part 'Tutto lieto cantai' is both the most madrigalian of these settings and the most assured in its grasp of overall structure. The text takes sunset and sunrise as metaphors for the death of one love and the prospect of a new one. The octet of the sonnet is treated as a single unit, with the transition from lines 4 to 5 covered by the use of a recitative-like phrase overlapping the cadence.[26] Within this unit, however, Rovetta attends to all the musicable details of the text—singing, sighs, laughter—containing them at first within balancing periods of arioso over a carefully controlled harmonic scheme, but then allowing an abrupt silence as the early morning light (the recitative-like phrase just cited) 'disappears into sunset' and night comes, represented by a five-part 6-3 chord reminiscent of the setting of the same word in Monteverdi's 'Hor che 'l ciel e la terra e 'l vento tace' (Eighth Book, 1638). The first passage of triple-time writing occurs at line 9, with the emergence of the new sun; and although the passage is relatively short, it contains no fewer than four statements of the poetic line—a genuine little five-part aria. The end of the setting is again dominated by triple-time writing, appropriate to the meaning of the last line—'m'invita un nuovo Apollo a nuovo canto' ('a new Apollo invites me to a new song'). For the most part, this is set for alternating pairs of voices; but the final statement, for five voices, produces the most richly dissonant passage in Rovetta's madrigalian output (Ex. 7.6).

Rovetta's continuo madrigals, like those of Monteverdi from the Fifth Book onwards, represent an exploration of the problems and possibilities raised by incorporating the new resources of continuo song into a polyphonic context

[26] See Ambros, *Geschichte der Musik*, iv. 878–9.

Ex. 7.6. Rovetta, 'Tutto lieto cantai'

(. . . a new Apollo invites me to a new song.)

and attempting to build large-scale structures from them. More specifically, Rovetta is one of the earliest composers of large-scale secular music fully to absorb and exploit the walking bass and languorous triple-time aria styles that we tend to think of as having been developed in books of solo songs. Thus his madrigals are crucial to the process that Nigel Fortune perceived in the development of solo song during the 1620s and early 1630s, and those of the 1629 book in particular actually seem to pre-date corresponding developments in solo song. It is tempting, with benefit of hindsight, to see the contrast of duple- and triple-time passages in these madrigalian structures as forerunners of the recitative–aria divisions in the cantata; and so, in a sense, they are. But the texts that Rovetta set are madrigals and sonnets, not cantatas—they do not usually exhibit a clear division between narrative and reflection, still less clear divisions in metrical structure —and Rovetta's use of the new triple-time aria styles in particular must be seen as a response to specific problems in the setting of madrigalian texts.

If the forerunners of Rovetta's style are, on the one hand, the arioso madrigals of Alessandro Grandi's *Madrigali concertati* of 1615, and, on the other, settings by Monteverdi like 'Augellin che la voce al canto spieghi' and 'Vaga su spina ascosa', which use walking basses, and 'Non vedrò mai le stelle', which incorporates an aria-like passage of triple-time writing, then the madrigals of these two older composers must also be seen as belonging to the mainstream of stylistic change in early seventeenth-century Italy. At the very least it is no longer adequate to think in terms of the formula 'solo song = progressive; polyphonic madrigal = conservative'; and any future study of Italian secular music up to about 1640 which does not take account of the *concertato* madrigal will omit a crucial dimension of the subject.

APPENDIX

The Madrigal Books of Giovanni Rovetta

*Madrigali concertati a 2. 3. 4. & uno a sei voci, & due violini. Con un dialogo nel fine,
& una cantata a voce sola . . . libro primo, opera seconda* (Venice: Bartolomeo Magni,
1629)

Incipit	Scoring	Text type	Poet/source
Taccia il cielo e la terra al novo canto	6vv (SSATTB), 2 vns, bc	sonnet	G. B. Guarini
Chi vuol haver felice e lieto il core	2vv (SS), bc	madrigal	Guarini
Io mi sento morir quando non miro	2vv (SS), bc	madrigal	Guarini
Ardi contento e taci	2vv (TB), bc	madrigal	
Uccidetemi pur, bella tiranna	2vv (SB), bc	madrigal	
Stanco di lacrimar a voi rivolgo	2vv (TT), bc	madrigal	
Oimè, chi mi ferisce?	2vv (TT), bc	madrigal	
È partito il mio bene	2vv (TT), bc	madrigal	G. B. Marino
O rubella d'amor cruda a l'amante	2vv (TT), bc	?madrigal	
Portate onde correnti aure volanti	2vv (TT), bc	madrigal	
Quel neo ch'appar nel viso	2vv (TT), bc	madrigal	
Piangea donna crudele	3vv (ATB), bc	madrigal	
Quella fede leal ch'io consecrai	3vv (ATB), bc	madrigal	
Quante volte giurai ferm'e costante	3vv (ATB), bc	sonnet	
Ove ch'io vada, ove ch'io stia tal hora	3vv (STB), bc	sonnet	
Sì mi dicesti et io	3vv (TTB), bc	madrigal	Guarini
Pur al fin di mia fè	3vv (TTB), bc	strophic	
Udite, amanti, udite	4vv (SATB), bc	madrigal	Guarini
Credetel' voi che non sentite amore	4vv (SATB), bc	madrigal	Guarini
Anime pellegrine che bramate	4vv (SATB), bc	madrigal	Guarini
Giovinetta fastosa	4vv (SATB), bc	strophic	

Incipit	Scoring	Text type	Poet/source
Vivo in foco amoroso	2vv (SS), 2 vns, bc	strophic (canzone)	Guarini
Rattenete le destre (La gelosia placata)	Licori (S), Titiro (T), Coro (ATB), 2 vns, bc	dialogue	Giulio Strozzi
La bella Erminia sconsolata amante (Le lagrime d'Erminia)	iv (T), bc	ottave rime	after Tasso, Gerusalemme liberata, xix. 104–8

Madrigali concertati a due e tre voci, & altri a cinque, sei, & otto con due violini et nel fine una cantata a quattro, libro secondo . . . opera sesta (Venice: Alessandro Vincenti, 1640)

Incipit	Scoring	Text type	Poet/source
Voi partite, crudele, ah voi partite?	2vv (SS), bc	madrigal	
O quante volte, o quante	2vv (SS), bc	madrigal	
Sovra il carro stellato in ciel sorgea	2vv (TT), bc	ottave rime	
Hor lieto rido e canto	2vv (TB), bc	madrigal	
Ah mio bene tu mori	2vv (TB), bc	madrigal	
Lacrimosa beltà	3vv (ATB), bc	madrigal	
La giovane bellissima Hadriana	3vv (STB), bc	madrigal	
Rosa, riso d'amor del ciel fattura*	3vv (STB), 2 vns (optional), bc	ottave rime	G. B. Marino, Adone, iii. 156–61
Che cosa è amor? ch'il sa?	3vv (STB), bc	strophic	
Tutto lieto cantai benigno amore	5vv (SSATB), bc	sonnet	
Venga dal ciel migliore	5vv (SSATB), 2 vns, bc	madrigal	
A che bramar, a che aventar i dardi	6vv (SSATTB), 2 vns, bc	madrigal	
Io torno, amati lumi, al caro oggetto	8vv (SSAATT BB), 2 vns, bc	sonnet	
Spieghi i contenti suoi chi vive amando (Cantata)	4vv (SSTB), bc	irregular strophic	

* 'E ben saran tra voi conformi voglie', listed as a separate work in *Il nuovo Vogel*, is, in fact, the fifth stanza of 'Rosa, riso d'amor'.

Madrigali concertati a due, tre, e quattro voci, libro terzo . . . raccolti da Gio. Battista Volpe (Venice: Alessandro Vincenti, 1645)

Incipit	Scoring	Text type	Poet/source
S'avien ch'in piaggia aprita o in colle ameno	2vv (SB), bc	*ottava rima*	
Con quel vago augellin ch'in chiusa gabbia	2vv (SB), bc	madrigal	
Qual'hor Florinda per baciar mi porge	2vv (SB), bc	madrigal	
Vaga e cruda è costei che sia l'adoro	2vv (TB), bc	madrigal	
Prodiga ove non dei	2vv (SS), bc	madrigal	
Ardi tu, Eurilla, anch'io	2vv (SS), bc	madrigal	
Quanto di me più fortunate sei	2vv (SS), bc	madrigal	
Soavissime rose	2vv (SA), bc	madrigal	attrib. Orafi in *Il nuovo Vogel*
Eran le vostre lagrime nel viso	2vv (TT), bc	madrigal	
Sdegnato amor che 'l tuo gelato petto	2vv (TT), bc	madrigal	
Dorme colà su fresch'e molli herbette	3vv (STB), bc	madrigal	
Se vuoi pur che sian spine	3vv (STB), bc	madrigal	
Vedi il lampo, odi il tuono, ecco diserra	3vv (STB), bc	sonnet	
Mio ben mentre porgesti	3vv (ATB), bc	madrigal	
Spiritelli incostante	3vv (ATB), bc	madrigal	
Son fatto tempio de la dea d'amore	3vv (ATB), bc	madrigal	
O mie fatali stelle	3vv (ATB), bc	madrigal	
Sono in bellezza e Roma e Lilla eguali	3vv (TTB), bc	sonnet	
Questa riva tempestata (Canzonetta)	3vv (ATB), bc	strophic	
D'uscir da crudo impaccio (Canzonetta)	4vv (SATB), bc	strophic	
O quanto lieto io torno (*Il Maggio*)	Tirsi (T), Choro di Ninfe (ATB), bc	strophic	

8

On the Origins
of an Operatic Topos:
The Mad-Scene

༄༅

PAOLO FABBRI

THE Venetian poet and librettist Giulio Strozzi (1583–1652) exploited the theme of feigned madness at least twice on the musical stage: in *La finta pazza* (1641) written for Francesco Sacrati (the long-lost opera rediscovered by Lorenzo Bianconi); and in *Licori finta pazza innamorata d'Aminta*, a text offered to Claudio Monteverdi more than a decade earlier. The latter is mentioned for the first time in Monteverdi's letter of 1 May 1627 (L. 91 [92]).[1] On 2 January 1627 (L. 89 [90]), Monteverdi had noted that on a visit to Venice the Mantuan singer Francesco Campagnolo raised the possibility of a commission for the composer from Mantua: this should probably be associated with the forthcoming coronation of Duke Vincenzo II Gonzaga. Monteverdi made a number of suggestions, including 'a little play by Signor Giulio Strozzi, very beautiful and unusual, which runs to some 400 lines, called *Licori finta pazza innamorata d'Aminta*, and this—after a thousand comical situations—ends up with a wedding, by a nice touch of strategem' (L. 91 [92]). Strozzi had written this short text 'to provide entertainment at a musical evening which a certain Most Illustrious Signor Mozenigo, my lord,

I am grateful to Tim Carter for his skilled handling of this material, and to Leofranc Holford-Strevens for his invaluable assistance with classical sources.

---

[1] *Claudio Monteverdi: Lettere, dediche e prefazioni*, ed. Domenico de' Paoli (Rome: De Santis, 1973). Hereafter the letters are cited by the numbering L. 91, etc. used in this edition, although reference is now perhaps better made to Claudio Monteverdi, *Lettere*, ed. Éva Lax (Studi e testi per la storia della musica, 10; Florence: Olschki, 1994). Additional numbers in square brackets refer to *The Letters of Claudio Monteverdi*, trans. Denis Stevens (London and Boston: Faber & Faber, 1980), from which the translations are drawn (with some minor changes in styling). On the loss of this opera by Monteverdi, see Gary Tomlinson, 'Twice Bitten, Thrice Shy: Monteverdi's "Finta" *Finta pazza*', *Journal of the American Musicological Society*, 36 (1983), 303–11.

had arranged to give' (L. 95 [96]). Such occasions had already prompted Monteverdi to set to music the *Lamento d'Apollo*, performed in the Palazzo Bembo in Carnival 1620—this was later combined with a danced eclogue, most probably on the subject of Apollo and Daphne—and also the *Combattimento di Tancredi et Clorinda* (for Mocenigo, like *Licori finta pazza*, and performed in Carnival 1624). The projected *Armida abbandonata* (1626), left incomplete, was also intended for a similar context. Unless Strozzi was lying for personal gain, it seems that *Licori finta pazza innamorata d'Aminta* was also still on the drawing-board—however advanced the project—and that it had never actually been performed. As Monteverdi said, it was 'so far neither set to music, nor printed, nor ever acted on the stage; for as soon as the author had completed it he himself straightway gave me, with his own hands, a copy of it' (L. 92 [93]), 'confessing that in writing this play he did not achieve the degree of perfection he had in mind' (L. 95 [96]).

In its first version, then, the text came to some 400 lines with no division into acts (L. 92 [93]: 'If the aforementioned Signor Giulio gets to know that it might be to His Most Serene Highness's taste, I am quite sure that with extreme promptness of thought and deed he will put it in order—divided into three acts'). As for the characters, we know only those of the title, Licori and Aminta, who are also cited in another of Monteverdi's letters (L. 93 [94]), referring to a scene of this 'little work' (*operina*). These names suggest a pastoral setting in the manner of the *favola boschereccia*. Moreover, the promises made by Monteverdi to have the text enlarged in terms of scenes and characters to avoid excessive monotony in the handling of the plot suggests that these two characters took up most if not all the recitative dialogue (as the intended destination of the piece required and as had also occurred in the similar other 'little works' by Monteverdi listed above).[2] Indeed, the text must have focused primarily on the character of Licori and on her rendition of feigned madness—as already stated in the title—which was given something of a dramatic framework by making it the central strategem of the manœuvres of the nymph to 'marry' her shepherd-lover. Here we seem to be dealing with that most common of occurrences in Arcadia, the changing of love first rejected into one requited, used as a pretext for an actress's set-piece, one of those 'scene di forza' typical of the professional baggage of the great theatrical players of the time.

Printed plays of the sixteenth and seventeenth centuries, and surviving collections of scenarios of professional *comici dell'arte*, offer abundant evidence

---

[2] For example, in L. 93 [94] Monteverdi announces his intention 'to see whether Signor [Strozzi] can improve it with other novelties, such as additional characters', precisely so as to avoid the danger of too little variety of action. In a following letter (L. 95 [96]) the composer says that Strozzi shares this concern: 'He also admits that as far as the part of Licori is concerned, he will make her come in later, and not in almost every scene.'

of the success achieved by this kind of dramatic situation in the period: a large number of titles and plots are founded on just such mad-scenes. The obvious source of this interest in madness is of course Ludovico Ariosto's famous epic, *Orlando furioso*. The insanity of the character Nastagio is the central event of Raffaello Borghini's *L'amante furioso*, a comedy written in France in 1579–80 and performed in Fabriano before the Accademia dei Disuniti in Carnival 1580; and Fileno is rendered mad by his nymph's rejection of his love in *La pazzia*, a *favola pastorale* by Giovanni Donato Cucchetti written for the wedding of Marfisa d'Este (1589). *I pazzi amanti* by Lodovico Riccato was performed in Venice in 1596, and *L'amante ardito* in 1600; among its cast is Gerindo, a 'mad shepherd' (*pastor pazzo*).[3] Two separated lovers go mad in Giovan Battista della Porta's *La furiosa*, published in Naples in 1600, and the madness of Camillo plays a significant part in Francesco d'Isa's *La Ginevra* from the beginning of the seventeenth century. *Il pazzo finto* and *La pazzia* are two comedies by Cristoforo Sicinio (respectively Rome, 1603; Venice, 1604), who was also the author of *La pace di Marcone* (Venice, 1604), which contains a number of mad elements. Again in Venice, the anonymous *La pazzia saggia* was performed in 1605. Lodovico Riccato wrote another comedy, *Le pazzie amorose* (Padua, 1608), and Livio Rocco *La pazzia di Panfilo* (Ferrara, 1614); and both Lelio and Filena feign madness in the first (the comic) act of *La centaura*, the monumental theatrical work by Giovanni Battista Andreini printed in Paris in 1622.

As for the scenarios of the *commedia dell'arte*, Flaminio Scala's *Il teatro delle favole rappresentative* (Venice: Pulciani, 1611) includes the tragedy *La forsennata principessa* (*Giornata* xli) and two comedies, *La finta pazza* (*Giornata* viii) and *La pazzia d'Isabella* (*Giornata* xxxviii)—the latter shares only the title with the play performed in Florence by Isabella Andreini in 1589, which had a significant part to play in the establishment, circulation, and subsequent popularity of this topos. The *Pazzia di Scapino* was printed in Bologna by Antonio Pisarri at an unknown date. Manuscript collections of scenarios by Basilio Locatelli (1618 and 1620; in Rome, Biblioteca Casanatense), with their rich assortment of mad-scenes, pay eloquent testimony to the growth of this tradition in the early seventeenth century: *La pazzia di Doralice, Li finti pazzi, Orlando furioso, Li tre matti, La finta pazza, La pazzia di Filandro, La pazzia di Dorindo*, and *La giostra* (which includes a mad-scene for Donna Agna).[4] From professional *comici*, we also find some texts written out in full

[3] See Angelo Solerti, 'Le rappresentazioni musicali di Venezia dal 1571 al 1605 per la prima volta descritte', *Rivista musicale italiana*, 9 (1902), 503–58 at 523–4, 535.

[4] See Vito Pandolfi (ed.), *La commedia dell'arte: Storia e testo*, v (Florence: Sansoni, 1959), 225–6, 232, 236–8, 248. On the general theme of madness in the theatre of this period, see *Folie et déraison à la Renaissance: Colloque international tenu en novembre 1973 sous les auspices de la Fédération Internationale des Instituts et Sociétés pour l'Étude de la Renaissance* (Brussels: Éditions de l'Université de Bruxelles, 1976); and Vanna Gentili, *La recita della follia: Funzioni dell'insania*

(and thus with some literary pretensions): in manuscript (in Milan, Biblioteca Nazionale Braidense) *La pazzia di Arianna*, by 'Lavinia comica Gelosa' (Marina Dorotea Antonazzoni), dated 1622, and in print *La pazzia* (Bologna: Ferroni, 1624) by 'Dottor Graziano comico Unito' (Pietro Bagliani).

With Strozzi and his *Licori finta pazza innamorata d'Aminta*, the theme of madness entered the world of opera, the newest genre to reach the theatre. That his obvious point of reference was the professional world of spoken drama is later made clear by Giovanni Faustini, who in the preface to his *L'Egisto* (1643) reveals his own embarrassment in the face of a subject successful to the point of abuse:

> Se tu sei critico, non detestare la pazzia del mio Egisto come imitazione d'un'attione da te veduta altre volte calcare le scene, trasportata dal comico nel dramatico musicale, perché le preghiere autorevoli di un personaggio grande mi hanno violentato a inserirla nell'opera per sodisfare al genio di chi l'ha da rappresentare.

> (If you are a critic, do not despise the madness of my Egisto as the imitation of an action seen at other times treading the boards, transferred from the comic to the musical drama, since the all-powerful requests of a great person have forced me to include it in the work to satisfy the inclination of him who has to stage it.)

In contemporary comedy and in the *commedia dell'arte*, mad-scenes were regularly presented as *bravura* pieces, required by convention to be ridiculous in whole or in part. Such scenes appear in comedies or in pastorals—the latter is by far the most common setting—and also in serious contexts. Flaminio Scala gives an excellent example in *La forsennata principessa*, a 'tragedy' in which Alvira first

> ragiona sopra il dolore che sente per lo ucciso amante e sopra l'allegrezza per vedersi innanzi la testa del suo nimico, e facendo varii pensieri contrastando diventa furiosa, pazza e delira stracciandosi le chiome e squarciandosi i panni d'attorno corre fuora della città verso il mare . . .[5]

> (speaks of the grief she feels for her murdered lover and of the joy of seeing before her the head of her enemy, and contrasting these various thoughts she

nel teatro dell'età di Shakespeare (Turin: Einaudi, 1978). For opera, see Ellen Rosand, 'Iro and the Interpretation of *Il ritorno d'Ulisse in patria*', *Journal of Musicology*, 7 (1989), 141–64; ead., 'Operatic Madness: A Challenge to Convention', in Steven Paul Scher (ed.), *Music and Text: Critical Inquiries* (Cambridge University Press, 1992), 241–87. See also Anne E. MacNeil, 'Music and the Life and Work of Isabella Andreini: Humanistic Attitudes toward Music, Poetry, and Theater in the Late Sixteenth and Early Seventeenth Centuries' (Ph.D. diss., University of Chicago, 1994).

[5] Flaminio Scala, *Il teatro delle favole rappresentative* (Venice: Pulciani, 1611), facs. edn. ed. Ferruccio Marotti (Milan: Il Polifilo, 1976), fo. 128ᵛ.

becomes mad: frantic and delirious, tearing her hair and rending her garments she runs outside the city towards the sea . . .)

Later (at the end of Act II), she returns 'doing and saying many mad things, continually gibbering over Tarfè's head and the betrayal done [to her]'.[6] She finally throws herself from 'a very high rock' (un altissimo scoglio)[7] and drowns. Each time, however, her outbursts are topped by the same ridiculous jokes and extravagant eccentricities adopted by madmen and madwomen in contemporary comedy, far removed from the mad-scenes of classical tragedy, as of Ajax in Sophocles, Heracles in Euripides and Seneca, and Orestes in Euripides (Iphigenia among the Taurians, Orestes). They are also somewhat distanced from the great model provided by Ariosto's Orlando furioso, of which scant use could be made: although the actions there involved extreme, abnormal gestures, they were almost entirely without speech. As for Scala's Alvira:

'Io non mi maraviglio che l'acqua del fiume sia dolce e quella del mare salata, perché l'insalata va sempre col suo olio filosoforum e con lo stretto di Gibiltarra o vuoi di Zibilterra, Che l'uno e l'altro nome li vien detto, pure come piacque al suo fatal destino, quella poveretta dell'Orsa maggiore si calzò li stivali d'Artofilace et andò a pigliar ostreghe e cappe longhe nel golfo di Laiazzo in ver Soria, che la cosa sia o non sia, sia voga, voga sia, e sia col malanno che Dio vi dia, e nella vostra tasca vi sia la mala pasca, e con usate tempre vi sia anche il mal sempre, e tutto 'l dì su l'asen. . . . Oh che gran specchio mi si rappresenta innanzi agli occhi. Io in questo specchio vedo il sole tutto infocato arrostir nello spiedo ad un fuoco di ghiaccio quel traditore del prenc. di Marocco per haver rubbata una gallina ad un gallo all'osteria del Moro. Ah ah ah, tu ci arrivasti pure. Pigliate del lardo vecchio e pergottatelo ben bene, ponetevi sopra del sale e datelo a mangiare ad una brigata d'astomi. Su su, cavalieri d'onore, di qua si salta il periglio, so varco, questa è la strada di Montefiasconi, questa è la vera via de Mestri e de Marghera, questo è 'l famoso carro di Fusina e questa è la vera caldara dei maccheroni dove entro v'erano le brache del Gonella, sapientissimo filosofo. Addio, addio, brigata, addio.' Ciò detto salta nel mare, s'affoga e non si vede più.[8]

('I'm not surprised that river-water is sweet and sea-water salty, because the salad always goes with its philosopher's oil, and with the strait of Gibraltar or if you wish, Zibilter ['Sybil's land'], for both one and the other name is given

[6] Ibid., fo. 129ʳ: 'facendo e dicendo molte cose da pazza, e sempre motteggiando sopra la testa di Tarfè e del tradimento fatto'.
[7] Ibid., fo. 129ᵛ.
[8] Ibid. As one might expect, it is almost impossible to produce an English translation that makes any sense, or for that matter one that captures fully the resonances (from mythology, literature, current proverbs, and homilies, etc.) readily perceivable by even a modern Italian audience. The same applies to many of the translations below.

it, and as pleased her fatal destiny, that poor wench of the Great Bear pulled
on the boots of Arctophylax and went to gather oysters and razor-shells in the
Gulf of Ajaccio towards Soria, whether it be or be not, whether it is fashion,
fashion let it be, and let it be with the misfortune which God gives you, and
may there be a curse on your purse, and with the usual tempers may there
always be evil for you, and all the day on the donkey. . . . Oh how great a
mirror appears before my eyes. In this mirror I see the sun all aflame roasting
on the spit on a fire of ice that traitorous Prince of Morocco for having
robbed a hen from a rooster at the Moor's Inn. Ah, ah, ah, you came then.
Take some old lard and beat it well, place salt on it, and give it to a gang of
Astomi [the mouthless folk] to eat. Up, up, knights of honour, from here one
avoids danger. This is the passage, this is the road to Montefiascone, this is
the true way to Mestre and to Marghera, and this is the famous ferry to
Fusina, and this is the true macaroni pot within which were the long johns
of Gonella, a very wise philosopher. Farewell, farewell, lads, farewell.' Having
said this she jumps into the sea, drowns, and is never seen again.)

By transferring one of these comic mad-scenes to the musical stage,
Strozzi was experimenting with comedy in the field of opera, a dimension
heretofore entirely marginal, limited for the most part to satyric characters
(Fileno in the lost *La disperatione di Fileno* by Laura Guidiccioni and Emilio
de' Cavalieri of 1590; Bacco (Bacchus) in Stefano Landi's *La morte d'Orfeo*
of 1619; the satyrs in Andrea Salvadori's *La Flora* performed to music by
Marco da Gagliano and Jacopo Peri in Florence in 1628), to those drawn
from the underworld (Caronte (Charon), again in *La morte d'Orfeo*), or else
to those evidently borrowed from the *commedia dell'arte* (in *La Ferinda* by
Giovanni Battista Andreini of 1622, and in Giulio Rospigliosi's *L'Egisto o
Chi soffre speri* of 1637 and 1639, and his *San Bonifatio* of 1638). However,
Licori finta pazza innamorata d'Aminta is focused entirely on the demented
ravings of the protagonist (the 'thousand comical situations' noted by Monteverdi), placing the comic dimension at centre-stage. Strozzi thus challenged the composer's genius to broach a kind of theatrical music hitherto
scarcely explored, inclined as this music was to favour large-scale scenes of
emotional pathos.

Monteverdi's letters are the only source of information we have concerning Licori's madness. In the final five-act version (L. 97 [98]) of Strozzi's
text, it begins in Act III (L. 99 [100]). Licori feigns madness in at least three
contexts, 'first, when the camp is being set up . . . second, when she pretends
to be dead; and third, when she pretends to be asleep' (L. 94 [95]); in the
last episode, Aminta also takes part with a 'discourse' delivered to the 'sleep-
ing' nymph (L. 93 [94]). During her pretended delirium, Licori acts as 'first
a man and then a woman', speaking of 'war . . . peace . . . death, and so

forth' (L. 92 [93]); and the chosen interpreter (Margherita Basile) had to take care to act as 'a brave soldier, timid and bold by turns' (L. 99 [100]). But if we compare Monteverdi's remarks with the part of Deidamia in Strozzi's *La finta pazza*, as transmitted by the Venetian edition of the libretto printed by Giovan Battista Surian (1641), the parallels become clear. Act II, Scene x, Deidamia's first entrance as a madwoman, opens with warlike shouts with which—to follow Monteverdi's Licori—'the camp is being set up': Deidamia pretends to be first a warrior ('a brave soldier') and then Helen of Troy ('first a man and then a woman', in effect), speaking of 'war' and later of love ('peace', and so on). The scene when Deidamia, feigning sleep, is the addressee of a 'discourse' from Achille (III. iv) is strongly reminiscent of Monteverdi's account. So not all of Strozzi's earlier text seems to be lost: *La finta pazza* could well have contained some sections of it with adaptations and expansions as appropriate, and particularly the section marking the beginning of her mad-scene.

It is worth noting that there is no mention of Deidamia's madness in the classical source which Strozzi probably had chiefly in mind when describing the adventures of Achilles on Skyros (in the absence of Euripides' lost tragedy on the subject), the second book of Statius' *Achilleis*: here the hero seeks the hand of Deidameia from Lycomedes on his own initiative, and the most one finds is an emotional lament by Deidameia on the imminent departure of her beloved. Even less useful, from this point of view, were the fleeting references in Ovid, who does not even mention Deidameia in recalling this episode in Achilles' life in the *Metamorphoses* (xiii. 162 ff.), and he cites her only briefly in the *Ars amatoria* (i. 689 ff.). It does indeed seem that the idea of exploiting her calculated delirium and making it an instrument for the resolution of her story (she thereby tells her father both of her passion for Achilles and of her pregnancy so as to marry her lover) is due primarily to the casual way in which Strozzi felt able to transfer to Deidamia the artful ravings of Licori. However, it is significant that Strozzi grafts his clear borrowing of a leading-lady's set-piece on to an established myth already complete within itself, the tale of Ulysses and Diomedes arriving on Skyros to unmask Achilles (paralleling Orestes and Pylades landing among the Taurians in search of Iphigenia in Euripides' tragedy, and Ubaldo and Carlo infiltrating Armida's garden to secure Rinaldo's repentance in Tasso's *Gerusalemme liberata*). Here Strozzi must have had in mind the possibility of exploiting an exceptional singer-actress, Anna Renzi (the need for a remarkable performer had already been clear to Monteverdi; see L. 92 [93]), as the vehicle for the eventual realization of his ideas of more than a decade before, that is, of transferring into music the mad-scenes of the *commedia dell'arte*.

We know in considerable detail how those scenes worked thanks to

surviving texts, both those drawn from literary comedy and those compendia
or sets of instructions which constitute the scenarios of the *commedia dell'arte*.
The latter also often provide lengthy extracts of such monologues, perhaps
as an *aide-mémoire* or to provide suggestions for new inventions of the same
kind. A chief ingredient was the nonsensical conjunction of ideas from
different sources—for the most part often appearing paradoxical or idiotic—
in a teeming accumulation of small, illogical fragments. These mad-scenes
also involved confused actions and strange appearances. Flaminio Scala calls
for 'Isabella dressed as a madwoman' (*Isabella vestita da pazza*) in *La pazzia
d'Isabella*,[9] and as we have seen, Alvira in *La forsennata principessa* 'becomes
mad: frantic and delirious, tearing her hair and rending her garments'. But
above all, these scenes focus on haphazard speech and emphatic, long-
winded monologues during which the unfolding of the events represented
in the play is slowed or entirely halted. In a prototype of the genre, *La
pazzia d'Isabella* of 1589, Isabella Andreini first

> come pazza se n'andava scorrendo per la cittade, fermando or questo ed ora
> quello, e parlando ora in spagnuolo, ora in greco, ora in italiano, e molti altri
> linguaggi, ma tutti fuori di proposito, e tra le altre cose si mise a parlar francese
> et a cantar certe canzonette pure alla francese . . . Si mise poi ad imitare li
> linguaggi di tutti i suoi comici, come del Pantalone, del Graziano, dello
> Zanni, del Pedrolino, del Francatrippa, del Burattino, del Capitano Cardone
> e della Franceschina.[10]
>
> (as a madwoman went running through the city, stopping now one person
> and now another, and speaking now in Spanish, now in Greek, now in Italian
> and many other languages, but all without reason, and among other things she
> began to speak French and to sing certain canzonettas in the French style . . . She
> then began to imitate the speech of all her colleagues in the troupe, such as
> Pantalone, Graziano, Zanni, Pedrolino, Francatrippa, Burattino, Captain
> Cardone, and Franceschina.)

Here the comic use of different languages also signified the temporary loss
of identity of her own theatrical role and thus the blocking of the dramatic
elements associated with it.[11]

---

[9] Ibid., fo. 117^r. Images of deranged madmen can be seen in the vignettes included in
the scenarios of *La pazzia di Doralice* and *Li dui finti pazzi* in the Corsini Manuscript (reproduced in Pandolfi (ed.), *La commedia dell'arte*, v, after p. 256).

[10] Giuseppe Pavoni, *Diario . . . delle feste nelle solennissime nozze delli serenissimi sposi il sig.
duca Ferdinando Medici e la sig. donna Christina di Lorena* (Bologna: Giovanni Rossi, 1589), 29–
30 (cited in Scala, *Il teatro delle favole rappresentative*, ed. Marotti, p. lxxv). Pantalone *et al.* are
standard *commedia dell'arte* characters. As late as Grazio Braccioli's *Orlando furioso* (1713), the
paladin Orlando, while raving, speaks in French (II. iv–v).

[11] See Cesare Molinari, *La commedia dell'arte* (Milan: Mondadori, 1985), 122; and Roberto
Tessari, *La commedia dell'arte nel Seicento: "Industria" e "arte giocosa" della civiltà barocca* (Florence: Olschki, 1969), 185.

The fundamental element of mad monologues was absurdity, the silly nonsense also typical of roles not marked by mental infirmity but likewise tending towards clownish exaggeration, perhaps mixed with the grotesque deformations of the 'lingua graziana' (the language used by the character Graziano): not for nothing did Francesco Gabrielli (the 'Scapino' mentioned by Monteverdi in L. 123 [124]) give his play based on madness the long title *Pazzia di Scapino con spropositi pazzeschi et canzoni burlevoli* (*Scapino's Madness with Mad Absurdities and Burlesque Songs*). As we have seen, Scala's Isabella and Alvira string together a shower of absurdities thrown meaninglessly together. Such sequences are often created by a taste for insistent rhymes, drawn from modern speech in clear opposition to the supposed period of the dramatic action. Here we find references to music, particularly the world of dance and popular song, to literary sources, to cookery, and very often to the world of mythology overturned and made comic. Such effects had been typical of some dialect genres of the sixteenth century, and they were now being adopted by the authors of the new genre of heroicomedy.

'Io mi ricordo, l'anno non me lo ricordo, che un arpicordo pose d'accordo una pavaniglia spagnola con una gagliarda di Santin da Parma, per la qual cosa poi le lasagne, i maccheroni e la polenta si vestirono a bruno non potendo comportare che la gatta fura fusse amica delle belle fanciulle d'Algieri. Pure come piacque al califfa d'Egitto fu concluso che domattina sarete tutti duo messi in berlina', seguitando poi di dire cose simili da pazza . . . Isabella da pazza dice al Capit. di conoscerlo, lo saluta e dice d'haverlo veduto fra le 48 imagini celesti che ballava il canario con la luna vestita di verde, et altre cose tutte allo sproposito, poi col suo bastone bastona il Capit. . . . Isabella arriva pian piano e si pone in mezo a Pantal. et a Gratiano dicendo che stieno cheti e che non facciano romore perché Giove vuol stranutare e Saturno vuol tirare una coreggia. Poi seguitando altri spropositi domanda loro se havrebbono veduto Oratio solo contro Toscana tutta . . .[12]

('I recall—but the year I forget—that a harpsichord placed in concord a Spanish pavan with a galliard by Santin da Parma, as a result of which the lasagne, macaroni, and polenta put on mourning weeds since they could not bear the fact that the wild-cat should be a friend of the beautiful girls of Algiers. But as it pleased the Caliph of Egypt, it was decided that tomorrow morning you will both be put in the pillory', [she says,] proceeding to utter other things typical of a madwoman . . . As a madwoman, Isabella says to the Captain that she knows him; she salutes him and says that she saw him among the 48 heavenly images, dancing the canary with the moon dressed in green, and other entirely absurd things, and then with her cudgel she beats the Captain . . . Isabella enters unhurriedly and places herself between Pantalone and Graziano, saying that they should be quiet and not make a noise because

[12] Scala, *Il teatro delle favole rappresentative* (1611), fo. 117ʳ.

Jove wants to sneeze and Saturn wants to let off a fart. Then continuing with other absurdities, she asks them whether they had seen Horatius alone against the whole of Tuscany . . .)

At the end of the seventeenth century the 'Esempio di sproposito in prosa' ('Example of Absurdity in Prose') which Andrea Perrucci includes among his 'Soliloquii delle parti toscane' ('Soliloquies of non-dialect roles') for the use of lovers 'in some madness, either true or feigned' (*In qualche pazzia, o vera o finta*)[13] consists precisely of such mythological jiggery-pokery, which one is advised to use to excess, since part of the comic effect stems from meandering speech:

> E quanto più spropositi si diranno, saranno più belli. Per provvedersene, ne daran mille belle forme i cervelli bisbetici del Burchiello e del Doni . . .[14]

> (And the more absurdities are uttered, the more beautiful they will be. To supply oneself with them, the crabbed brains of Burchiello and Doni will provide a thousand beautiful models . . .)

In extending his feigned madness to music, Strozzi drew chiefly on the conventions lying at the heart of similar scenes in the spoken theatre, that is, the use of one or more almost entirely comic set-pieces during which the actor/actress involved temporarily puts aside the role appropriate to him/her (in Deidamia's case, that of first lover) to play variously the part of a heroic champion ('Guerrieri, all'armi, all'armi'; 'Warriors, to arms, to arms'), then a mythical seductress ('Elena bella io sono'; 'I am beautiful Helen'), an amateur stage-director ('Ch'a me non manca l'arte . . .'; 'For to me the art is not lacking . . .'), a new Icarus ('Applicatemi l'ali . . .'; 'Fix the wings on me . . .'), and in the end a Diana-like huntress ('Alla caccia, alla caccia, al monte, al bosco'; 'To the hunt, to the hunt, to the mountain, to the wood'). Even Nastagio in Borghini's *L'amante furioso* (III. iii) strikes in rapid succession the pose of a gallery of different characters (prince, soldier, lawyer, merchant, poet), while Ardelio and Vittoria, who go mad in Della Porta's *La furiosa* (III. ii), rapidly assume the linguistic mantles of this or that character, according to the lesson already presented by Isabella Andreini:

ARDELIO. Esto non soffrire yo, por vida de mi rey, y se no callays te dare de garotes.
BIZOZERO. Adesso contrafa un servo spagnolo che havemo in casa.
VITTORIA. Caperrone sbregognato, che malannagia l'arma [= l'alma] delle muorti tuoi.
AGATIO. Et ella un servo napolitano nostro.

---

[13] Andrea Perrucci, *Dell'arte rappresentativa premeditata ed al'improvviso* (1699), ed. Anton Giulio Bragaglia (Florence: Sansoni, 1961), 177.
[14] Ibid. 178.

(ARD. I will not stand for it, by the life of my king, and if it doesn't suit you, I will kill you. BIZ. Now he acts like a Spanish servant whom we have in the house. VIT. Shameless goat, a curse on the soul of your ancestors. AG. And she our Neapolitan servant.)

Among the recurring themes, military images could already be found, for example, in Borghini and also in two texts by Lodovico Riccato. In *I pazzi amanti* (III. i), we see:

ELIODORO. Chi mi tien legato? Lasciami, che 'l Turco con tutti i suoi bascià a mia destruttione han fatto lega. Il prete Gianni volando se ne viene senza braccia zoppicando in mio favore: la lega è fatta. Tocca tamburo: alle mani, alle mani . . .

(Who holds me bound? Let me go, for the Turk with all his pashas has formed an alliance for my destruction. The priest Gianni comes flying without arms hobbling in my favour: the alliance is made. Strike the drum: to blows, to blows . . .)

and in *Le pazzie amorose* (IV. iii):

A la guerra, a la guerra: su, su, tutti, Pastori, capre e becchi; ferma, ferma, Che vò partirmi: a l'arma, a l'arma. Ecco il silentio . . .

(To war, to war: up, up, shepherds all, nanny- and billy-goats. Stop, stop, for I want to leave: to arms, to arms. Behold the silence . . .)

There are similar images in Andreini's *La centaura* (I. x). Given that in the spoken theatre the dramatic circumstances always favoured mimicry and the opportunity for onomatopoeic effects, it is easy to see how they offered the composer a convenient resource for word-painting. Thus it is not surprising that, following the unperformed 'warlike madness' of Licori but before that of Deidamia, Prospero Bonarelli also had recourse to this traditional component of mad-scenes in one of his texts for music, *La pazzia d'Orlando*, printed in Venice in 1635:[15]

ORLANDO. Su su, all'armi, all'armi,
risoniamo la tromba.
Su, tamburri: che fate?
Ah battete, sonate:
non vedete, voi là,
che mi vien contro il tartaro et il moro,

[15] This text has only the title in common with, *La pazzia d'Orlando ovvero L'acquisto di Durlindana*, a *balletto* danced in Carnival 1638 at the Teatro Barberini alle Quattro Fontane (see Frederick Hammond, 'Girolamo Frescobaldi and a Decade of Music in Casa Barberini: 1634–1643', *Analecta musicologica*, 19 (1979), 94–124 at 116–17).

> e del campo nimico
> hanno ambo i corni Angelica e Medoro?

(Up, up, to arms, to arms, | let's sound the trumpet. | Up drums, what are you doing? | Ah beat, play: | don't you see, you there, | moving against me the Tartar and the Moor, | and that of the enemy camp | Angelica and Medoro hold both wings?)[16]

Mythology also has a large part to play in these comic, metamorphic rantings, prolonging and extending a burlesque tradition also found in learned styles involving dialect and macaronics, and in the new genre of heroi-comedy.[17] The protagonist of Livio Rocco's *La pazzia di Panfilo*, for example, believes himself to be first Cadmus, and then Orpheus in the underworld (IV. iii, v), and so it continues (see v. ii). Similarly, mythological nonsense appears prominently in the first and the fourth of Francesco Gabrielli's *spropositi pazzeschi* in the *Pazzia di Scapino*. Other examples can be found in the texts by Scala cited above, and likewise those by Riccato. For example, in the latter's *I pazzi amanti* (III. i):

ELIODORO. Gran meraviglie veggio qui sopra: il Sole ha aperto hosteria, la Luna gli apparecchia le mense, Mercurio è entrato, Giove mi fa un brindese. Bon pro ti faccia. Ah ah: Amore è ubriaco e Venere tien camera locante.

(What wonders do I see above: the Sun has opened a hostelry, the Moon kits out its tables, Mercury has come in, Jove offers me a toast—'I give you good health.' Ah, ah: Cupid is drunk and Venus keeps a room for personal services.)

And in *Le pazzie amorose* (IV. iii), Giacinto says:

> T'accorgi, babuino, che nell'aria
> vanno a caccia le selve.
> Mira quel grillo armato
> che dà la fuga a le cicale. Hor vedi:
> colui è Giove che nel letto giace
> ammalato di rabbia, e Bacco appresso
> che gli scaccia le mosche e acciò che dorma
> Vener gli grata i piedi.
>
> .   .   .   .
>
> A te m'inchino e riverente abbraccio
> il tuo leggiadro manto. Udite Orfeo
> ch'al suon de la sua lira

---

[16] The last line doubtless involves a pun: horns are also a sign of cuckoldry, and Orlando is in love with Angelica, who has fallen for Medoro.

[17] See Paolo Fabbri, 'Andrea Gabrieli e le composizioni su diversi linguaggi: La giustiniana', in Francesco Degrada (ed.), *Andrea Gabrieli e il suo tempo* (Florence: Olschki, 1987), 249–72.

> tira a sé tutte l'acque.
> Oh oh, Mercurio e Pane che gli vanno
> lieti cantando inanti, ecco di dietro
> Apollo con le Muse.

(See, booby, that in the air | the woods go to hunt. | Look at that armed cricket | which puts the cicadas to flight. Now see: | that is Jove who lies abed | sick with frenzy, and Bacchus at his side | who chases away the flies, and so that he can sleep | Venus scratches his feet. | . . . | I bow to you and reverently embrace | your graceful mantle. Listen to Orpheus | who to the sound of his lyre | draws all the waters to him. | Oh, oh, Mercury and Pan go | before him singing happily, and lo behind | Apollo with the Muses.)

Similarly, the mad Filena in Andreini's *La centaura* (i. v) starts by quoting a popular song:

> Tien giù le mani, vè, se non che. Chi t'ha fatto quelle scarpette, che te stan sì bene Gerometta, che te stan sì ben. Me le ha fatte quel ciabattino di Marte al suono di timpani e di gnaccare con tanta melodia che Teucro re di Cipro crepava di doglia di corpo. Il capo di Medusa scoppiava delle risa vedendo il drago esperido che faceva contrapunto sopra la groppa del monton Frisso, e duo sonagli da sparviere cantavano la guerra che fecero i Giganti contra le gelatine fredde, e quella ribalda della fantesca di Proserpina pelava un zampetto di porco con tanta leggiadria che non si conosceva l'Asia dall'Europa. In quello Titone si risolse di salutar l'Aurora, e facendosi ferrare dai piè di dietro per passar il mar delle Zabacche, comparve l'ombra del re Mida tutta lampeggiante d'oro in oro, accompagnata da quelle sue orecchiacce d'asino che faceva un sole, che mai non fu veduta la maggior pioggia. Intanto il re Minos pestava la salsa et un alchimista tirò una correggia così grande, che 'l mar Oceano havendo la renella pisciò l'isola del Giapone e della China e del Perù. Ma zitto, zitto, che quei sordi non ci sentano.

(Hands down, you, or else . . . Who made you those shoes that suit you so well, Girometta, that suit you so well? They were made for me by that cobbler Mars to the sound of drums and nakers with such melody that Teucer, King of Cyprus, died of bodily grief. Medusa's head burst with laughter seeing the Hesperidean serpent making counterpoint on the back of Phrixus' ram, and two falconers sang of the war made by the Giants against the cold jellies, and that scoundrel of a maidservant of Proserpina peeled a pig's trotter with such grace that you couldn't tell Asia from Europe. Then Tithonus decided to greet Aurora, and making himself shoes from the back feet to cross the sea of the Zabacche, there appeared the ghost of King Midas all shining of gold, accompanied by those huge ass's ears which made a sun, for never had greater rain been seen. Meanwhile King Minos was pestling the sauce and an alchemist let rip such a big fart that the sea Oceanus, having gravel, pissed out the

island of Japan and China and Peru. But hush, hush, lest those deaf people
hear us.)

Strozzi's *La finta pazza* harks back to this kind of mythological horseplay.
But the text also exploits the tradition of deforming or subverting serious
literature for comic ends, with such hyperbole as Deidamia's 'inner lament'
(*racchiuso pianto*) that 'makes a lake' (*fa lago*) of the 'grieving heart' (*mesto cor*)
as she weeps for fear of drowning in it. Certainly, these are the ravings of
an unbalanced mind, but the result is not so dissimilar to the tendency towards extravagant metaphor in contemporary lyric poetry. Thus the raving
Fileno in Giovanni Donato Cucchetti's *La pazzia* (IV. ii) gives vent to an
anadiplotic display of nonsense which does nothing more than exaggerate
the witticisms and *concettismo* of contemporary madrigals:

> Dunque pensar vogl'io, ma che pensiero
> il mio sarà? Sarà d'amor: su, dunque,
> ché tutto in preda mi darò al pensiero.
> Io vo pensar che la mia donna è donna:
> dunque havrai danno s'ella è donna? Danno?
> Che danno? Anzi piacer, perché si piega
> la donna più che tenerella pianta.
> Horsù, mi vò partir: ma dove vai?
> Da la mia cara ninfa. E che parole
> sei per formar, tu non ci pensi adunque?
> Anzi sì, anzi no: deh pensa prima,
> che fa mestier d'antiveder le cose.
> Horsù, s'ella dirà: dove sei stato,
> pastor, sì lungo tempo, che dirai?
> Dirò: son stato in cielo fra i beati.
> Nol crederà: se dirò in terra? In terra?
> Terra non è dove che alberga lei,
> ma paradiso sì, forse diratti.
> E c'hai veduto in ciel? C'ho visto in cielo?
> Ho visto il sol, dirò, di te men bello.
> Ma se men vado a lei, che porterolle?
> Perché gl'è vera e natural usanza
> di tutte donne a dimandar tacendo.
> Deh ninfa, le dirò tutto gioioso,
> canzon ti canterò che mai megliore
> pastor cantasse in boscareccia stanza.
> Non vò canzon, dirà, son le canzoni
> fatte per fuggir l'otio, et io dirolle:
> altro non ho, che t'ho donato il core.
> Dunque che bado più? Fia ben che vada,

anzi megl'è ch'io resti: io vado, io resto,
anzi giusto non è, anzi conviene.

.   .   .   .   .   .

E se levar vogl'io
la cagion del mio mal, del mio tormento,
che mi levi di vita fa bisogno,
perché lo star in vita è la cagione
d'amar, e amando sto in affanno: adunque
per uscir di passion forz'è ch'io muoia,
e certo vò morir. Ah traditori,
traditori assassini. Oh da la strada,
portatemi quell'ali, che li segua.
Io vengo, io vengo: olà, fermate il passo.

(So I would think, but my thought | will be of what? It will be of love. Up, then, | for I will give myself wholly as prey to my thought. | I am thinking that my woman is a woman: | so shall I be harmed if she is a woman? Harm? | What harm? Rather pleasure, for | woman is more pliant than a tender plant. | So, I want to go. But where are you going? | To my dear nymph. And to what words | you are to utter will you not give some thought? | Perhaps yes, perhaps no. Ah, think first, | for it is right to plan things in advance. | So, if she will say, 'Where have you been, | shepherd, for so long a time?', what will you say? | I shall say: 'I have been in heaven among the blessed.' | She won't believe it. If I say 'on earth'? On earth? | Earth is not where she lives, | but paradise, yes. Perhaps she will say to you, | 'And what have you seen in heaven?' 'What have I seen in heaven? | I have seen the sun', I will say, 'less beautiful than you.' | But if I go to her, what shall I take her? | For it is a true and natural custom | of all women to ask in silence. | 'Ah nymph', I shall say, all happy, | 'I will sing you a song such as | a shepherd never sang better in rustic rhyme.' | 'I don't want a song', she will say, 'for songs are | made to put rest to flight.' And I shall say to her: | 'I have nothing else, for I have given you my heart.' | So why do I delay? It would be good if I went, | although it is better that I stay. I go, I stay, | even if it isn't just, it is expedient. | . . . | And if I wish to remove | the cause of my ill, of my torment, | it is necessary for me to take my life, | for to remain alive is the cause | of loving, and in loving I remain in torment: so | to escape my passion, I am forced to die, | and certainly I wish to die. Ah traitors, | traitorous assassins. Oh clear the way, | bring me those wings so that I may follow her. | I'm coming, I'm coming: hey, stand still.)

No less revealing is Deidamia's canzonetta 'Verga tiranna ignobile', the *versi sdruccioli* of which invoke powerful literary resonances in terms of denoting a rustic or eccentric quality, as had already been seen in Cristoforo Sicinio's *Il pazzo finto* (I. viii: 'Fermatora a questa cantonitrico, | che mo' mo' vi vengo a sciogliora . . .') and in Gabrielli's 'canzon', 'O spinetta infamissima', in Scapino's third *sproposito*.[18]

Among the images incongruously exploited as 'normal' by these comic lunatics, there tends to be a strong preference for those relating to music, with citations of instruments, dances, individual performers, and popular tunes: this is doubtless because of the potential for striking visual and aural effects. We have already seen (above, p. 165) Flaminio Scala's references to the harpsichord, the 'Spanish pavan with a galliard by Santin da Parma' (a celebrated lutenist who died at the beginning of the seventeenth century), and the canary. In Act III, Scene ii of Della Porta's *La furiosa* (1600, pub. 1618) Ardelio and Vittoria sing together *terze rime* concluded by an echo ('Vittoria mia che col tuo sole illustri'), which causes a slight altercation:

ARDELIO. Tu non canti bene e fai discordar ancor me.
VITTORIA. Anzi sei tu che non fai la gorga a proposito.

(ARD. You do not sing well, and you make me discordant too. VIT. But it's you who do not make the right sound.)

The speech of Filena in Andreini's *La centaura* given on p. 169 opens with the song 'La Girometta' and then alludes to the 'sound of drums and nakers' and to a comic 'counterpoint'.[19] In a following scene (I. x), a new entrance of a madman is marked by another popular song:

LELIO. Chiella, chiella? Eh, eh, eh.
FILENA. Eh, eh, eh. (*Qui Lelio e Filena rideranno tutti ad un tempo, poi canteranno questa canzone: 'Le belle tette c'ha la mia Rossina do viva l'amor Dò Rossina bella, fa la la lella, viva l'amore che morir mi fa.' Di nuovo rideranno insieme e faranno ij.*)

(LEL. Who's there, who's there? Eh, eh, eh. FIL. Eh, eh, eh. (*Here Lelio and Filena will both laugh at the same time, and then they will sing this song: 'The*

---

[18] On the use of *versi sdruccioli* (with the accent on the antepenultimate syllable) in texts for music, see Wolfgang Osthoff, 'Oper und Opernvers: Zur Funktion des Verses in der italienischen Oper', *Neue Zürcher Zeitung*, 8 Oct. 1972, 51–2 (a translation of an expanded version of the text is published as 'Musica e versificazione: Funzioni del verso poetico nell'opera italiana', in Lorenzo Bianconi (ed.), *La drammaturgia musicale* (Bologna: Il Mulino, 1986), 125–41); id., 'Händels "Largo" als Musik des Goldenen Zeitalters', *Archiv für Musikwissenschaft*, 30 (1973), 175–89; Silke Leopold, '"Quelle bazzicature poetiche, appellate ariette": Dichtungsformen in der frühen italienischen Oper (1600–1640)', *Hamburger Jahrbuch für Musikwissenschaft*, 3 (1978), 113–21; ead., 'Madrigali sulle egloghe sdrucciole di Iacopo Sannazaro: Struttura poetica e forma musicale', *Rivista italiana di musicologia*, 14 (1979), 75–127; Lorenzo Bianconi, *Il Seicento* (Storia della musica, iv; Turin: EDT, 1982), esp. 214 (*Music in the Seventeenth Century*, trans. David Bryant (Cambridge University Press, 1987), 215).

[19] On the musical tradition of the *Girometta* and of the *Franceschina–Bustachina*, see Warren Kirkendale, 'Franceschina, Girometta, and their Companions in a Madrigal "a diversi linguaggi" by Luca Marenzio and Orazio Vecchi', *Acta musicologica*, 44 (1972), 181–235.

beautiful titties which my Rossina has: long live love. To beautiful Rossina, fa la la lella, long live the love which makes me die.' Again they laugh together and repeat the song.))

Tintinnaco, the 'mad servant' (*servo pazzo*) in Sicinio's *La pazzia* (1604), also sings snatches of well-known songs (I. i):

E mi che non ghe penso la la dirido. Cappelleto paga l'hoste ninoste, bufoste, chi ha niente di caldaroste da vendere? La femina, e l'ingegno li dicea, cavava i sassi e li dava alla gente.

(And I, who do not think of it, *la la dirido*. The cavalier pays the landlord, nin-lord, buf-lord—who has no roast to sell? The woman, and her wit told her, pulled out the rocks and gave them to the people.)

And later he receives a proposal from another character to sing something with him (I. vi):

cantiamo una canzona insieme, che io farò quella voce sottile, fastidiosa, minuta mi re mi fa mi che ci va tanto bene.

(let's sing a song together, for I will produce that subtle, scrupulous, precise voice *mi re mi fa mi* which suits us so well.)

He also recalls the 'moresca' and the 'organs' (II. vi), and his friend Sicinio the 'hat-dance' (*ballo del cappello*; IV. vi), then singing and sol-faing cheerfully (V. ii):

Oi, a, o la, chi mi fa dar novella d'Aurelia mia bella, ut re mi fa sol fa fa mi re mi fa.

(Oy, ah, ola, who makes me tell of my lovely Aurelia: *ut re mi fa sol fa fa mi re mi fa.*)

These musical topoi were to last a long time, often reusing literally the same clichés. Francesco Torretti's *La pazzia di Clorinda* (1645) provides a notable example. In Act III, Scene vii, Clorinda exclaims:

Oh che musica soave io sento! Zitti tutti: oh bene, oh oh oh, non mi maraviglio adesso, e' sono i poeti greci che su 'l liuto di Santin da Parma cantan varie canzoni su l'aria della Girometta.

(Oh what sweet music I hear! Hush all: oh good, oh oh oh, I don't wonder now: they are the Greek poets who to the lute of Santin da Parma sing various songs on the tune of the *Girometta*.)

And later, in Act III, Scene x, she sings:

Anima mia che vai dal corpo sciolta, a riveder la donna di Ruggier dolente, senza parola per non spaventarla, la la diridon.

(My soul, you who go free from the body, to see again the woman of sad Ruggiero, without a word so as not to frighten her, *la la diridon*.)

Similarly, Ariaspe, who feigns madness in Giacomo Castoreo's *Il pazzo politico* (1659), says (I. xiii):

> Una cicalla
> col contrapunto delle peracotte
> sfidò 'l grillo a cantare,
> ma un poco raffredata
> mancò nel passeggiar la sore ute,
> onde l'altro addirato
> la rimesse così con le battute.

(A cicada | with the counterpoint of the stewed pears | challenged the cricket to sing, | but with a slight cold | it missed its passages *la sol re ut*, | whence the latter, grown angry, | set it right with beatings.)

Finally, the principal character of *La pazzia politica di Roberto re di Sicilia* by the academician Rinato Tirinto (1689) sings what is almost an aria (I. viii):

> Alba, sorgi: homai sparì
> della notte il fosco horrore.
> Alba, sorgi e porta il dì.

(Dawn, rise: already disappeared | is the dark horror of the night. | Dawn, rise and bring the day.)

Strozzi's use of these same techniques for Deidamia in *La finta pazza*, then, forms part of a long tradition: she, more than any other representative of the role, likes to display her inclination for strophic canzonettas (to be performed complete, without cuts). This makes great play of the novelty of having that mixture of poetry, stage-machines, and song that is early seventeenth-century opera both support and represent the act of madness, a modern mania for turning a mirror on life that is invoked in her second entrance as a madwoman.

No less rich in traditional resonances invoking these comic precedents are various specific stylistic features of Deidamia's part, such as the series of close-spaced internal rhymes ('Ti picchi? ti rannicchi? t'incrocicchi?') and her taste for lists. Take, for example, her catalogue of mythological adversaries: 'La fiera d'Erimanto, | l'Erinne acarontea, | il Piton di Tessaglia, | la Vipera lernea' ('The Erymanthian Boar, | the Erinnys [the Fury] from Hades, | the Python of Thessaly, | the Lernaean Hydra'). Similarly, she apostrophizes an imaginary Paris with a litany of ornithological epithets (compare Riccato's *I pazzi amanti*, III. vii): 'Cutrettola, fringuella, oca, frusone,

| barbaggianni, babbusso' ('Wagtail, chaffinch, goose, hawfinch, | barn owls . . .'). Such long lists—we have seen other examples in Alvira's monologue given on pp. 161–2—had already formed the mainstay of mad-scenes in Raffaello Borghini's *L'amante furioso*, as the following (from the first such scene in II. xii) reveals:

> NASTAGIO. O vè spilunca, o vè quanto fuoco, o i' veggo Plutone in sedia, o vè quanta gente che gli va a offerire. I soldati gli offeriscono sangue mutato in fuoco, i dottori libri stracciati cangiati in oro fonduto, i mercatanti denari conversi in carboni accesi, i gentilhuomini vesciche piene di vento divenute fredissimo gielo, e le donne lisci et ornamenti trasformati in fummo e filiggine, e perciò le donne danno disturbi, debiti, danni, dishonestà, difficultà, diffidenze, deformità, dimenticanze, debolezze, dishonori, disaventure, distruttioni, derisioni, disperationi, doglio, durezze, disgratie, discipline, dolori, dispetti, digiuni, disagi e disordini. . . . Giove fece nozze con Giunone, Nettuno con Teti, Plutone con Proserpina, Venere con Vulcano, o che vergogna, e Apollo non tolse moglie, o bella cosa. . . . Dimmi un poco buon compagno, non ti pare un buon guadagno che le leggi sieno come tele di ragno et il povero come il rigagno et il ricco come Alessandro Magno?

(Oh there's a cave, oh there's so much fire, oh I see Pluto enthroned, oh there are so many people who bring him offerings. Soldiers offer him blood changed to fire, scholars torn books changed into molten gold, merchants coins changed into burning coals, gentlemen bladders full of wind turned into coldest ice, and women beauty creams and jewellery turned into smoke and soot, and thus the women make disturbances, debts, damages, dishonesties, difficulties, diffidences, deformities, delusions, debilities, dishonours, disadventures, destructions, derisions, despairs, distress, duresses, disgraces, disciplines, discomforts, disparagements, denials, disquiets, and disorders. . . . Jove marries Juno, Neptune Tethys, Pluto Proserpina, Venus Vulcan—oh what shame—and Apollo does not take a wife—o fine thing. . . . Tell me something, good friend, does it not seem to you a good reward that the laws are like spider webs, the poor man like the gutter and the rich man like Alexander the Great?)

A similar sequence of names in Francesco Gattici's *Gli pensieri fallaci* (V. v) ends up as a comic and meaningless catalogue of nonsense rhymes:

> PAZZO. Cicerone pittore, Oratio fabbro, Petrarca cacciatore, Platone alchimista, Diogene uccellatore, Aristotele sarto, Virgilio hortolano, Ovidio speciale, Plutarco fornaro, Seneca marangone. . . . Ah galant'hom, ah homo da ben, le mie pillole, le mie pillole, dico: reubarbo, agarico, mel rosato, liqueritia, polvere di scena, capelvenere, ogli, acque, conserve, paste, polveri, unguenti, sughi, impiastri, bocconi, bevande. . . . trent'uno, gilè, primiera: ti toglio la berretta nera. Pane, castagne, noci, vue [= uve] agreste: ti straccio ancor la veste. Quaglie, starne, galline con il galetto: ti faccio un siroppo al fazzoletto.

(Cicero the painter, Horace the smith, Petrarch the hunter, Plato the alchemist, Diogenes the fowler, Aristotle the tailor, Virgil the gardener, Ovid the apothecary, Plutarch the baker, Seneca the carpenter. . . . Ah gallant man, ah good man, my pills, my pills, I say: rhubarb, mushroom, pink honey, liquorice, senna powder, maidenhair fern, oils, waters, conserves, confections, powders, unguents, sauces, poultices, morsels, drinks. . . . *Trent'uno, Gilè, Primiera* [all card-games]: I take off your black hat. Bread, chestnuts, walnuts, wild grapes: I also tear off your jacket. Quails, partridges, hens with the cockerel: I make you handkerchief-syrup.)

And chains of phonic tics are scattered through the account of Flavio, the fake lisper and scheming 'madman' who is the protagonist of Sicinio's comedy *Il pazzo finto* (III. viii):

havete da sapele che sbrag sbreg sbrig sbrog sbrug era nipote calnale di fac fec fic foc fuc, che fu flustato perl Roma da lac lec lic loc luc perlche havea robbato un paro di gnac gnec gnic gnoc gnuc. Di modo che havendo io in mano un certo gaf gef gif gof guf, ne feci un cambio con chetta stamegna.

(You should know that sbrag sbreg sbrig sbrog sbrug was the carnal nephew of fac fec fic foc fuc, who was flogged through Rome by lac lec lic loc luc since he had stolen a pair of gnac gnec gnic gnoc gnuc. So that having in hand a certain gaf gef gif gof guf, I made an exchange with him this morning.)

In mixing together these essential ingredients of the quick-fire speeches and punch-lines that formed the staple diet of comic actors, Strozzi placed within his text some of those non-verbal theatrical elements which were used to characterize these mad-scenes, as for example the gestures and mimicry connected with the sudden changes of the mad character and with his high-wired speech.[20]

From Strozzi and Sacrati's *La finta pazza* onwards, the theme of madness enjoyed a success in opera that appears almost uninterrupted for the rest of

---

[20] These devices were all well known to Monteverdi, who for his part had underlined the necessity for a performer alive to these matters: 'It will now be up to Signora Margherita [Basile, who was to sing the part of Licori] to become a brave soldier, timid and bold by turns, mastering perfectly the appropriate gestures herself, without fear or favour' (L. 99 [100]). Similarly, 'the part of Licori, because of its variety of moods, must not fall into the hands of a woman who cannot play first a man and then a woman, with lively gestures and different emotions. Therefore the imitation of this feigned madness deserving consideration (provided it is in the present, not in the past or future), it must consequently derive its support from the word, not from the sense of the phrase. So when she speaks of war she will have to imitate war; when of peace, peace; when of death, death, and so forth. And since the transformations take place in the shortest possible time, and the imitations as well—then whoever has to play this leading role, which moves us to laughter and to compassion, must be a woman capable of leaving aside all other imitations except the immediate one, which the word she utters will suggest to her' (L. 92 [93]).

the seventeenth century. To be sure, we need more systematic data to evaluate fully the fluctuating fortunes of the theme, although the tradition does appear to be unbroken.[21] But whatever the case, after mid-century, the texts which I have examined seem to reveal a general tendency to limit the signifying of madness to an increasingly restricted number of verbal and physical gestures. Take two characters seen on the stage at the same time as Deidamia—Iarba in Busenello's *Didone* and Lilla in Ferrari's *La ninfa avara* (both 1641)—who are rendered genuinely mad as a result of their amorous misadventures. They display their delirium in a variety of traditionally imbecilic ways. Iarba first of all 'rends his garments' (*si straccia l'habito*), exploding in a tirade of curses, self-pitying and raging (II. xii), continuing with raving speech that also contains allusions to music (II. xiii):

> meritevole sei
> che in suono d'[e]f fa ut
> ti canti in un l'Arcadia e 'l Calicut.

(You are indeed praiseworthy | who in the sound of F *fa ut* | sing at the same time of Arcadia and Calicut.)

to dance (III. ii)

> Ma guarda quante mosche per quest'aria
> battono la canaria.
> DAMIGELLA. È il tuo cervel che vola
> e batte con le piume una chiaccona.

(But look how many flies in this air | beat the canary. | DAM. It is your brain that takes wing | and beats a *ciaccona* with its feathers.)

to gambling (the card-games 'a spade o coppe' and the 'mora' also noted in III. ii), and to literature (the allusions in this same scene to a *letterato* 'modenese', perhaps Fulvio Testi or Maiolino Bisaccioni), including a journalistic extract of grotesque 'avvisi di Parnaso' ('news from Parnassus'; again III. ii).

Ferrari's Lilla has a verbose monologue (II. iii) rich in extravagant lyric metaphors and also word-plays ('Che tanti amori? Che tanti umori?'; 'What great amours? What great humours?'). She takes the shepherd Ghiandone for Orpheus, asking him to lend her melodious assistance worthy of his fame:

> Cantami un poco in tuono d'effaut
> s'è più bella l'Arcadia o Calicut.

---

[21] On the French fortunes of the theme of madness in the mid-17th c., note the discussion in Giovanni Morelli (ed.), *Scompiglio e lamento: Simmetrie dell'incostanza e incostanza delle simmetrie; L'Egisto di Faustini e Cavalli (1643)* (Venice: Teatro La Fenice, 1982), 607.

(Sing for me a little in the key of F *fa ut* | whether Arcadia or Calicut is the more beautiful.)

she says, like Iarba. This leads to his singing a silly song with *double entendres*.

Similarly, in Act III, Scene v of Faustini's *L'Egisto* (1643) Egisto enters with a canzonetta in a long chain of *quinari* and *quaternari sdruccioli* (III. v: 'Celesti fulmini') and continues his speechifying in an imaginary argument with Amor. Then he believes himself to be talking to Charon as if attempting to repeat Orpheus' descent to Hades. The identification becomes complete in Act III, Scene ix:

> Rendetemi Euridice
> Orfeo son io . . .

(Give Eurydice back to me | I am Orpheus . . .)

and is abandoned only for a further and more sudden metamorphosis in the same scene:

> Io son Cupido
> che per la terra
> vo' mascherato . . .

(I am Cupid | who through the land | goes masked . . .)

In this his second appearance as a madman, and after his emotional lament on the death of Eurydice, Egisto, too, turns himself into a lively hawker of clownish mythological news:

> Fatevi in giro, udite
> novelle di là su . . .

(Roll up!—hear | news from up there . . .)

then a public storyteller of absurdities:

> Io vo' narrarvi un caso . . .

(I want to tell you a tale . . .)

then a magistrate:

> Pensato e ripensato,
> pur di novo ripenso,
> ho stabilito e ancora
> stabilisco, ratifico e confermo . . .

(Having considered and reconsidered | now I consider again; | I have decided and again | I decide, ratify, and confirm . . .)

then Cupid (see the canzonetta given above). He finally bursts into irrational laughter:

> Siete, siete pur sciocchi, ah ah ah ah.

(You are, you are indeed fools, ha ha ha ha.)

For that matter, in announcing Egisto's misfortune in the preceding scene, the servant Cinea describes to Ipparco in effect the whole kaleidoscopic repertory of the lunatic (III. viii):

> Signor, l'hospite Egisto
> l'intelletto ha travolto,
> è divenuto stolto,
> hor di furor ripieno
> la campagna trascorre,
> hor s'arresta e discorre
> a sterpi, a tronchi, a venti
> con vari e impropri accenti,
> hor tace e bieco mira,
> né conosce mirando,
> hor geme et hor sospira,
> hor ride e va cantando
> sciocche e immodeste rime
> e talvolta di Clori il nome esprime.

(Sire, the guest Egisto | has lost his mind; | he has become mad; | and now full of fury | he runs through the countryside; | now he stops and speaks | to brushwood, to tree trunks, to winds | with varied and improper sounds; | now he is silent and looks grim; | nor does he recognize what he sees; | now he weeps and now sighs, | now he laughs and goes about singing | stupid and immodest rhymes; | and sometimes he utters the name of Clori.)

Later texts instead tend to reduce the range of expressions in the representation of madness, focusing on fewer resources. In the simulation that gives the title to Giovanni Andrea Moniglia's *Il pazzo per forza* (1658), Flavio once more has recourse to mythological raving (I. xxvii), and he sings ariettas with contemporary references drawn from the world of dance:

> Ballando la boré,
> cantando il saltarello,
> si muova snello il piè.

(Dancing the bourrée, | singing the saltarello, | one moves the graceful foot.)

But more widespread is the practice of having the madman identify with mythological characters. Aurelio Aureli, for example, exploits this device both in *Le fortune di Rodope e Damira* (1657; II. xx: Damira pretends to see in Batto first Theseus and then Actaeon) and in *Gli amori d'Apollo e di Leucotoe* (1663; II. xiv, xv, and xxviii: the love-sick Eritreo, like Faustini's Egisto, believes himself to be in the underworld and, a new Orpheus, he takes Orillo for Charon). In Domenico Gisberti's *Caligula delirante* (1672), the emperor sees himself as Alcides (II. xiv) and Endymion (III. viii), suffering from mythological hallucinations that persuade him that he loves Diana and should be jealous of Paris (III. ix–x).

Among all these images, the most often used are those which take as their theme the world of Hades and which implicitly propose an equivalence between the chief character and Orpheus. For example, in Matteo Noris's *Totila* (1677; I. x and II. xvi–xvii), the general Publicola, rendered mad by his defeat, imagines himself beyond the grave; he later lusts after the servant Desbo, calling him a seductive Narcissus, only to withdraw immediately in horror because, he says, he has changed into a frightening monster (III. v). The same occurs with Eurillo in Domenico Filippo Contini's *Gli equivoci nel sembiante* (1679; III. vi), who describes himself surrounded by an army of terrifying monsters from Hades, with whom he identifies himself in his ravings:

> Sono Aletto che viene
> dalle tartaree rive,
> sono il Re delle pene,
> son la Morte che vive.

(I am Alecto, coming | from the Tartarean banks, | I am the King of Torments, | I am Death who lives.)

There are other examples. In Antonio Franceschi's *Didone delirante* (1686; III. xviii), Didone (Dido), while trying to persuade Anna, Sicambre, and Dirce to dance with her, is disturbed by an imaginary apparition of the monster Typhon which suddenly changes itself into Amor. In Gasparini's *Lo schiavo fortunato in Algeri* (1688), Rosaura, disguised as Orgonte, takes the role of a raging Megaera arrived 'Dalle rive d'Acheronte' ('from the banks of the Acheron') accompanied by the 'latrati | del trifauce mastino' ('barking | of the three-throated mastiff'; II. xiv). In *Amore fra gl'impossibili* by the Arcadian Amaranto Sciaditico (1697), Lucrina imagines herself to be a range of mythical characters (in the last scene of Act I and the third and last scenes of Act II), and also thinks that she has dealings with demons and witches (II. ii). Similarly, the hero of Carlo Sigismondo Capece's *L'Orlando overo La gelosa pazzia* (1711; I. xi and II. viii) believes himself faced with legendary beings from the world of the dead, as also occurs in Grazio Braccioli's *Orlando furioso* (1713; II. vi).

Often these delusions concerning the underworld were accompanied by arias in *versi sdruccioli*, the metrical sign of eccentricity, absurdity, and exaggerated behaviour (see above, p. 171). Indeed, Orlando's madness in Adriano Morselli's *Carlo il Grande* of 1688 is denoted almost exclusively by a close succession of *sdruccioli*: 'Pazzo forse son io, che non conosca | le mamme candide, | il labro morbido, | il crine lucido . . .'—'Perhaps I am mad, for not recognizing | the white breasts, | the soft lip, | the shining hair . . .' Other examples include:

Le fortune di Rodope e Damira: 'Fuggite rapidi' (II. xxi)
Totila: 'Arpie de l'Erebo' (I. xi) and 'Su, stringetevi' (II. xvi)
Gli equivoci nel sembiante: 'Ancora, ancor non sento | di Cerbero i latrati, | Tesifone e Megera, | Furie pallide esangui . . .' (III. vi; with the *sdruccioli* occurring unusually at the beginning of the line)
Lo schiavo fortunato in Algeri: 'Sì, s'ardano' (II. xiv)
Amore fra gl'impossibili: 'Lasciva femina' (final scene of Act I)
L'Orlando overo La gelosa pazzia: 'Già latra Cerbero' (I. xi)
Orlando furioso: 'Scendi nel Tartaro' (II. vi)

A further development of this idea was to have the character behave like a Fury, rushing around the stage brandishing a torch (Lucrina in *Amore fra gl'impossibili*, in the second and last scenes of Act II) and ending up by setting things alight, as with Rosaura/Orgonte in *Lo schiavo fortunato in Algeri* (II. xiv) and Gernando in Domenico David's *Amor e dover* (1697; II. ix). Apart from this, mad behaviour was also signalled by sudden laughter (see Aureli's *Le fortune di Rodope e Damira*, II. xx, and *Gl'amori d'Apollo e di Leucotoe*, III. xv, as well as Gisberti's *Caligula delirante*, III. viii), and by hallucinations of battle, which could always be guaranteed to make an effect. Here the madman on stage believes himself to be at the centre of epic deeds of war, as occurs to Eurillo in *Gli equivoci nel sembiante* (III. vi):[22]

---

[22] Similar images appear in contemporary spoken theatre. Torretti's *La pazzia di Clorinda*, for example, contains the following passage (V. vi) full of military sounds imitated vocally, which make one think of the effects exploited by Monteverdi in his setting of Strozzi's canzonetta 'Gira il nemico insidïoso Amore' included among the 'canti guerrieri' of his *Madrigali guerrieri, et amorosi . . . Libro ottavo* (Venice: Alessandro Vincenti, 1638):

CLORINDA. Tappa tappa ta, tappa tappa ta, tara tara ta, tappa tappa ta, tarra tarra ta.
BECCAFICO. Torn'in drè, poltron, torn'in drè, poltron.
CLORINDA. Butta sella, butta sella, butta sella, tu tu tu tu tu, tutt'a cavallo, tutt'a cavallo, tutt'a cavallo.
BECCAFICO. Non tremate, padrone, fatevi animo.
CAPITANO. Che bellico invito sento io nell'orecchio rimbombarmi?

(CLOR. *Tappa tappa ta, tappa tappa ta, tara tara ta, tappa tappa ta, tarra tarra ta.* BECC. Turn back, coward; turn back, coward. CLOR. Saddle up, saddle up, saddle up, a-a-a-a-a-all

> Ma dove sto, qual suono
> di bellici stromenti
> sfida a guerra il mio core? . . .

(But where am I, what sound | of warlike instruments | challenges my heart
to war? . . .)

As regards these techniques, in the second half of the seventeenth century
they are most clearly articulated in those texts which have a mad character
not merely as a temporary event on the stage but as the main theme of the
plot. In the anonymous *Il savio delirante* (1695), Arpago lets loose mythological absurdities like wildfire (III. xii), laughs and moves about uncontrollably
(ibid.), sings and sol-fas, and behaves like a Fury with torch in hand, setting
fire to his library (III. x). Similarly, in the course of two scenes in Noris's
La finta pazzia d'Ulisse (1696; I. xi, II. xii) Ulysses performs a veritable
panoply of mad actions: he speaks in *versi sdruccioli* ('Tuo raggio lucido'), he
'falls . . . as if dead' (*cade . . . come morto*), he 'pretends to weep in torrents'
(*finge dirottamente piangere*), he laughs, he takes on mythological roles, he is
inflamed with warlike fury ('Date a l'armi: guerra ed armi'; 'Take up arms:
war and arms') interrupted by mad laughter, again he speechifies on mythological topics, he 'reads singing' (*legge cantando*) a book, and he 'takes the
lighted torch from the hand of the temple-servant and exits running' (*Leva
di mano al servo del tempio la torcia accesa e parte correndo*).

Still more significant examples are to be found in those texts which
provide some kind of instruction in how to perform a mad-scene. In Cristoforo
Ivanovich's *Coriolano* (1669), the servant Momerco, wishing to feign insanity, provides a quick-fire succession of the various ways of pretending lunacy
(III. iii):

SILENIO.	Arresta il passo.	
MOMERCO.		Ohimè,
	me 'l presagiva il core.	
SILENIO.	Di che temi? Su, parla.	
MOMERCO.		Un non so che
	mi fa tremar, signore.	
SILENIO.	Chi sei?	
MOMERCO.	Dir non lo so.	

to horse, all to horse, all to horse. BECC. Don't be frightened, sir, take courage. CAP.
What warlike invitation do I hear strike my ear?)

As for references to the underworld and the assumption of mythological roles, there are many
examples in the other texts destined for the spoken theatre cited in the course of this essay.

SILENIO.	(Costui volsco non è.)
	Di che patria tu sei?
MOMERCO.	Non so del padre il nome.
SILENIO.	Io nol ricerco.
MOMERCO.	(Vorrebbe ch'io dicessi: io son Momerco.
	O questo no!)
SILENIO.	Ma come
	la tua patria si noma?
MOMERCO.	(Vorrebbe che dicessi: io son di Roma.
	O questo no!)
SILENIO.	Favella.
MOMERCO.	Odi, signore.
	Pluto è in ciel, Giove è in mar e sta Nettuno
	giù ne l'inferno: io solo
	governo questo mondo.
SILENIO.	Che parli?
MOMERCO.	Io son Alcide, hor che del cielo
	sovra gli homeri miei sostento il pondo.
SILENIO.	(Un pazzo costui parmi.)
MOMERCO.	Su presto, a l'armi, a l'armi.
	Marte pugna, e Vulcano:
	un brando ha questi, e quei martelli in mano.
SILENIO.	Olà, costui si prenda.
MOMERCO.	Guarda che non gli offenda:
	ho la pelle de l'Idra
	e di Medusa il capo. Ogn'uno in pietra
	si cangerà di voi, se non s'arretra.
SILENIO.	Ha sembiante da spia:
	s'arresti, su.
MOMERCO.	Non sia
	chi mi tocchi: intendete?
	Ah, ah, ah, ah: mirate,
	che Venere con Marte è colta in rete. (*Fugge.*)

(SILENIO.	Hold your step.
MOMERCO.	Alas,
	my heart predicted it.
SILENIO.	What are you frightened of? Up, speak.
MOMERCO.	An I-don't-know-what
	makes me tremble, Sire.
SILENIO.	Who are you?
MOMERCO.	I don't know how to say.

SILENIO.   (This is no Volscian.)
            From what country do you come?

MOMERCO.   I don't know my father's name.

SILENIO.   I didn't ask it.

MOMERCO.   (He would have me say that I am Momerco.
            Oh this, no!)

SILENIO.   But what
            is your country called?

MOMERCO.   (He would have me say that I am from Rome.
            Oh this, no!)

SILENIO.   Speak.

MOMERCO.   Listen, Sire.
            Pluto is in heaven, Jove is in the sea, and Neptune stands
            below in the underworld: I alone
            rule this world.

SILENIO.   What are you saying?

MOMERCO.   I am Alcides, for now
            I bear the weight of the sky on my shoulders.

SILENIO.   (This chap seems a madman to me.)

MOMERCO.   Up, quickly, to arms, to arms.
            Mars fights, and Vulcan:
            the latter has a dagger, and the former hammers in hand.

SILENIO.   Hey there, take this man.

MOMERCO.   Make sure I don't cross them:
            I have the skin of the Hydra,
            and the head of Medusa. Each of you
            will be changed into stone if you don't pull back.

SILENIO.   He looks like a spy:
            arrest him, now.

MOMERCO.   Let no one
            touch me: understand?
            Ah, ah, ah, ah: look,
            there's Venus caught with Mars in the net.   [*He flees*])

Similarly, in Aureli's *Helena rapita da Paride* (1677), Elisa teaches the jealous
Euristene how to feign lunacy (II. ix), becoming so absorbed in the lesson
as to assume herself some of the typical signs of madness (for example,
ariettas in *versi sdruccioli*):

EURISTENE.   Partì Paride?

ELISA.   Dimmi:
              da Paride che vuoi?

EURIST.   Dentro il suo petto
immerger questo acciaro: amante core
soffrir non può rivalità in amore.

ELISA.   Frena la cieca destra: io ti prometto,
se il mio consiglio apprendi,
ch'avran ristoro i tuoi penosi incendi.

EURIST.   Deh, amica, e quando?

ELISA.   Ascolta. A l'or che incontri
il tuo nume superbo, onde sospiri,
finger tu dei da l'amoroso affanno
scema la mente, e dei mentir deliri,
ch'io a l'ora poi forza darò a l'inganno.
Chi sa? forse, chi sa? de' tuoi martori
così pietade avrà l'idol che adori.

EURIST.   Seguirò il tuo consiglio, e per un volto
sarà Euristene e delirante e stolto.

ELISA.   Spirto ci vuole
e al tutto si arriva.
Certi ridicoli
giovini semplici
d'animo timido
e di cor tenero
a grandi imprese
aspirar sogliono,
ma non ottengono
mai quel che vogliono.
Vuol esser stimolo
d'un'alma viva:
spirto ci vuole
e al tutto si arriva.

(EURIST.   Has Paris gone?

ELISA.   Tell me:
what do you want with Paris?

EURIST.   Within his breast
to sink this sword: a loving heart
cannot suffer rivalry in love.

ELISA.   Stay your blind right hand: I promise you,
if you take my counsel,
that your harsh burning will have relief.

EURIST.   Ah friend, and when?

ELISA.   Listen. At the moment when you meet your
proud goddess for whom you sigh,

you must pretend that by the torment of love
your mind has gone, and you should feign delusions,
and then I will strengthen your deceit.
Who knows? Perhaps, who knows? On your torments
the idol you adore will thus take pity.

EURIST.   I will follow your advice, and for once
Euristene will be both delirious and stupid.

ELISA.   One needs spirit
and one gains everything.
Certain clowns,
simple youths
of timid soul
and tender heart
to great enterprises
are wont to aspire,
but they never obtain
that which they want.
One needs the stimulus
of a lively soul:
one needs spirit
and one gains everything.)

In the following scene (II. x), Euristene makes his play, showing how well
he knows the ways and means of feigned madness:

Con insanie e deliri
mi fingerò in amor gionto a l'estremo:
sovente chi è in catena il capo ha scemo.

Fingerò mille follie
per amore d'un bel volto.
Dentro il laccio che mi strinse
sarò Ulisse che si finse
più d'Oreste insano e stolto:
fingerò mille follie
per amore d'un bel volto.
Un Alcide che delira
per novella Deianira
da ciascun io sarò tolto:
fingerò mille follie
per amore d'un bel volto.

(With madness and delusions | I will feign myself brought to an extreme by
love: | often he who is enchained has a weak head.

I will feign a thousand madnesses
for the love of a fair face.
Within the noose that binds me
I will be Ulysses who pretended
to be more insane and stupid than Orestes:
I will feign a thousand madnesses
for the love of a fair face.

    For an Alcides who raves
for a new Deïaneira
I shall be taken by all:
I will feign a thousand madnesses
for the love of a fair face.)

And we see just how capable he is of bringing Elisa's suggestions to life in Act II, Scenes xvii and xxiv, when he begins his mad act in earnest, taking Enone for Diana and Elisa for a harpy, and then feigning the usual trip to the underworld ('Su le rive d'Acheronte | giungo amante disperato . . .'; 'At the banks of the Acheron | I arrive, a despairing lover . . .').

The most extended, and perhaps the best, example of all these lessons in madness is presented by Perillo in Act II, Scenes xii–xiii of Adriano Morselli's *Falaride tiranno d'Agrigento* (1684); the text is given in full in the Appendix. But no less significant, as we move into the eighteenth century, is the increasing absence of ranting and raving for mere theatrical effect: the representation of madness shifts progressively in favour of seriousness and even pathos. This is already apparent in David's *Amor e dover*, and still more in the case of Rosmene in Silvio Stampiglia's *Imeneo in Atene* (1723). Here we see a tendency towards regularity and the tragic through which the mad-scene was to abandon the world of simple comedy to become a characteristic of the newly emerging *comédies larmoyantes* of the second half of the eighteenth century.

                                              (Translated by Tim Carter)

Adriano Morselli, *Falaride tiranno d'Agrigento* (1684), Act II, Scenes xii–xiii

Perillo instructs Irene in the ways of madness:

PERILLO.   Leno ti vide?

IRENE.   Il dissi.

PERILLO.   Per mentir quel fellone
vo' che pazza ti finga.

IRENE.   Parli forse da vero?

PERILLO.   Ed è saggio il pensiero.

IRENE.   Già inferma, or delirante.

PERILLO.   Dirò che il male asceso
intorbidò i fantasmi.

IRENE.   Io far da pazza! E come?

PERILLO.   Ti rabbuffa le chiome,
empi d'orrore il volto,
con la destra minaccia,
batti col piè l'arena:
voci sconcie e interrotte,
gemiti, gridi e pianto . . .

IRENE.   Piano, piano, che far non saprò tanto.

PERILLO.   Gl'esempii, o figlia, attendi
e meco a finger prendi.

IRENE.   (So ch'avrò buona scuola.)

(Qui Perillo incomincia.)

PERILLO.   Armi, armi,
trombe e timpani
fendete l'aria,
spargete armonici
i vostri carmi,
armi, armi.

IRENE.   (Quasi m'intimorisce.)

PERILLO.   Ma son già stanco: io vò seder al fine
fra l'armi e le ruine.

(Siede per terra.)

O dolce libertà.
Su l'erba tenera

con sonno placido
il petto indomito
respirerà:
o dolce libertà.

(*Salta in piedi.*)

Presto, via: dammi l'arco.
Mira sovra quel faggio

augel selvaggio
al suon de l'onda
tra fronda e fronda
cantando va:
o dolce libertà.

Basta così.

IRENE.   Voglio ancor io provarmi.

Armi, armi,
trombe e timpani
fendete l'aria,
spargete armonici
i vostri carmi:
armi, armi.

Mira, mira quel faggio
che furioso il turbine crollò.

PERILLO.   Siedi prima fra l'erbe.

IRENE.   O questo no.

Augel selvaggio
al suon de l'onda
tra fronda e fronda
cantando va:
o dolce libertà.

PERILLO.   Ma vien Fallari appunto.

IRENE.   Fantasie più bizzarre
mi soministra il capricioso ingegno.
Attendi.

Scena 13

FALARIDE.   (Ecco l'indegno.)

PERILLO.   (*A Falaride*)

L'infermità de l'infelice Irene
in pazzia terminò.

IRENE.   Ch'io mi sieda fra l'erbe? O questo no.

FALARIDE. Stolta Irene?

IRENE.   Tu menti:
son di me più insensati i tronchi e i marmi.

                            Armi, armi . . .

FALARIDE. (La misera m'affligge.)

IRENE.   (*Prende Falaride per mano.*)
Sai tu ch'io sono?

FALARIDE.   Irene.

IRENE. Mi fai ridere: io sono
cantatrice sirena
che in musici concenti
snoda le labra.

FALARIDE.   (O miserella.)

IRENE.   Senti.
                    (*Prende per mano anco il padre.*)

              Bel mestiero è far da stolto
              ed i semplici ingannar.
              Havrò doppio il core e il volto,
              veder tutto e non parlar:
              bel mestiero è far da stolto
              ed i semplici ingannar.

PERILLO. (Ella non può far meglio.)

IRENE. Ma dove, dove siamo?

FALARIDE. In casa di Perillo.

IRENE. Ah, ah, ah: tu vaneggi.
Quest'è un teatro: mira
colui che attento e fisso
sorridendo ci ascolta,
quell'altro che nel palco
tiene a l'amica il lume
che legge il dramma, e quello
che attende a bocca aperta le canzoni.

FALARIDE. (Che strane illusioni!)

IRENE. Vedo sguardi furtivi,
moti, sorrisi e vezzi.
E tu li vedi?

FALARIDE.   Io nulla.

IRENE. O che balordo!

FALARIDE.   (Oh misera fanciulla!)

IRENE. Gentile a fè, gentile.

FALARIDE.	E cosa?
IRENE.	In quella parte estinto il debil lume voglion star a l'oscuro: sai perché?
FALARIDE.	Perché?
IRENE.	Basta: è morta già Penelope la casta.
PERILLO.	(Come pronto ha l'ingegno!)
IRENE.	Guardatevi, fuggite.
FALARIDE.	(Qualche larva novella.)
IRENE.	La gran stella di Giove dal soffitto si svelle e già minaccia di caderne adosso.[23]
FALARIDE.	(Più resister non posso.) *(Parte con Perillo.)*
IRENE.	Quando genio non havrò schermirò tutti così. Già fra tanti bei sembianti un sol guardo il cor m'aprì: quando genio non havrò schernirò tutti così.

(PERILLO.	Did Leno see you?
IRENE.	I already said so.
PERILLO.	To deceive that felon I want you to pretend to be mad.
IRENE.	Do you really speak the truth?
PERILLO.	And the idea is a wise one.
IRENE.	Once ill, now delirious.
PERILLO.	I shall say that the increased sickness brought on hallucinations.
IRENE.	I play the madwoman! And how?
PERILLO.	You ruffle your hair, fill your looks with horror,

---

[23] For similar references to the theatre, compare also Selim, the feigned madman in *La fortuna invidiata nella prosperità d'Osimano, con la pazzia politica di Selim*, an 'opera tragica' in prose by Giacomo Morri (Bologna: Giacomo Monti, 1669). As well as the usual absurdities drawn from mythology (I. i) and the standard changes of identity (as a doctor in II. vi and an astrologer in II. xix), he imagines himself to be a playwright and director, the creator first of a 'dramma' (II. xviii) and then of a 'tragedia' (III. viii).

threaten with your right hand,
stamp your feet on the ground:
words distorted and interrupted,
groans, cries, and weeping . . .

IRENE.   Easy, easy, I shan't be able to do so much.

PERILLO.   Wait, my daughter, for examples
and learn to feign with me.

IRENE.   (I know that I shall have a good teacher.)

[*Here Perillo begins*]

PERILLO.   Arms, arms,
trumpets, timpani
cleave the air,
scatter your harmonic
charms,
arms, arms.

IRENE.   (I'm almost afraid.)

PERILLO.   But I am already tired. I wish finally to sit
amid the arms and the ruins.

[*He sits on the ground*]

O sweet liberty.
On the soft grass
with peaceful sleep
my indomitable breast
will rest:
o sweet liberty.

[*He jumps to his feet*]

Quick, here: give me the bow.
See on that beech

the woodland bird
to the sound of the water
from branch to branch
goes singing:
o sweet liberty.

That'll do.

IRENE.   I, too, want to practise.

Arms, arms,
trumpets, timpani
cleave the air,
scatter your harmonic
charms:
arms, arms.

Look, look at that beech
which the raging wind shook.

PERILLO. First sit on the grass.

IRENE.   Oh this, no.

The woodland bird
to the sound of the water
from branch to branch
goes singing:
o sweet liberty.

PERILLO. But here comes Fallari himself.

IRENE. Still more bizarre fantasies
does my capricious wit suggest to me.
Wait.

Scene 13

FALARIDE.   (Here's the unworthy fellow.)

PERILLO.   [*To Falaride*]

The illness of the unhappy Irene
ended in madness.

IRENE. That I should sit on the grass? Oh this, no.

FALARIDE. Irene insane?

IRENE.   You lie:
Tree-trunks and statues are less feeling than I.

                 Arms, arms . . .

FALARIDE. (The wretched woman affects me.)

IRENE.   [*She takes Falaride by the hand*]
Do you know who I am?

FALARIDE.   Irene.

IRENE. You make me laugh: I am
the singing siren
who in musical harmonies
loosens the lips.

FALARIDE.   (O wretched woman.)

IRENE.   Listen.
        [*She also takes her father by the hand*]

It is a fine job to play the dunce
and to deceive the simpletons.
I will have a double heart and countenance,
to see all and not to speak:

                it is a fine job to play the dunce
                and to deceive the simpletons.

PERILLO.	(She couldn't do better.)
IRENE.	But where, where are we?
FALARIDE.	In Perillo's house.
IRENE.	Ah, ah, ah: you're raving.
	This is a theatre: look
	at him who laughing and transfixed
	listens to us, smiling,
	and that other one who in the stalls
	holds the light for his girl-friend
	who reads the drama, and that one
	who waits open-mouthed for the songs.
FALARIDE.	(What strange illusions!)
IRENE.	I see furtive glances,
	gestures, smiles, charms.
	And do you see them?
FALARIDE.	Me, nothing.
IRENE.	O what an idiot!
FALARIDE.	(Oh wretched girl!)
IRENE.	Softly, in faith, softly.
FALARIDE.	And what?
IRENE.	Over there,
	the feeble light extinguished,
	they want to stay in the dark:
	do you know why?
FALARIDE.	Why?
IRENE.	Enough:
	chaste Penelope is already dead.
PERILLO.	(How ready is her wit!)
IRENE.	Look out, flee.
FALARIDE.	(Some new phantom.)
IRENE.	The great star of Jove
	emerges from the ceiling
	and now threatens to fall on top of us.
FALARIDE.	(I can no longer endure it.) *[He leaves with Perillo]*
IRENE.	When I haven't the talent
	I will mock everything thus.
	Already among so many

fine beauties
just one look opened my heart:
when I haven't the talent
I will mock everything thus.)

9

Steffani's Solo Cantatas

৵৵৵

COLIN TIMMS

In this connection one should also mention Agostino Steffani [1654–1728], who likewise through his teacher Ercole Bernabei is to be counted with the Roman school and who, though his life, as is well known, extends far into the eighteenth century, nevertheless remains throughout a spiritual child of the seventeenth. Indeed, Steffani is perhaps the most distinguished name in the whole field of vocal chamber music. It must be admitted, however, that the master figures so prominently as the specialist of the chamber duet that, by comparison, his few surviving solo cantatas hardly come into the reckoning. At this point in our account, therefore, he can receive little but a general mention, for the notable refinement that he achieved in melodic expression overall, which indirectly—i.e. through its influence on his contemporaries—then bore fruit in the form of the solo cantata too.

THUS wrote Eugen Schmitz in his pioneering history of the secular solo cantata (1914).[1] The picture has changed very little since then. There has been no major reassessment of the history of the solo cantata as a whole,[2] nor of Steffani's place within it. Studies of the composer and his music have focused, quite rightly, on his chamber duets and operas, and on his role as a representative of Italian music at the courts of Munich, Hanover, and Düsseldorf.[3] His solo cantatas, like his sacred works, have largely been ignored.

[1] *Geschichte der Kantate und des geistlichen Konzerts: Geschichte der weltlichen Solokantate* (Leipzig, 1914; repr. Hildesheim: Olms, 1966), 92–3.

[2] Literature to 1976 is listed in *The New Grove Dictionary of Music and Musicians*, ed. Stanley Sadie (London: Macmillan, 1980), iii. 702. Major contributions since then include: Piero Mioli, *A voce sola: Studi sulla cantata italiana del XVII secolo*, i: *Firenze, Venezia, Roma* (Archivum musicum: Collana di studi, D; Florence: SPES, 1988); Fabio Carboni, Teresa M. Gialdroni, and Agostino Ziino, 'Cantate ed arie romane nel tardo Seicento nel Fondo Caetani della Biblioteca Corsiniana: Repertorio, forme e strutture', *Studi musicali*, 18 (1989), 49–192; Luca Zoppelli (ed.), *Studi e ricerche sulla cantata da camera nel barocco italiano* (I Quaderni della Civica Scuola di Musica, 9; Milan: Ricordi, 1990); Teresa M. Gialdroni, 'Bibliografia della cantata da camera italiana', *Le fonti musicali in Italia: Studi e ricerche*, 4 (1990), 31–131.

[3] For the literature on Steffani, see *New Grove*, xviii. 97–8, and *The New Grove Dictionary of Opera*, ed. Stanley Sadie (London: Macmillan, 1992), iv. 532. More recent studies include:

Whereas most of Steffani's church music was printed in his lifetime, providing the basis for a reasonably reliable statement of his output in that field, the vast majority of his secular works remain in manuscript, presenting greater difficulties to any would-be cataloguer. As a result, there is no complete list of his solo cantatas and thus no firm foundation for any account of his contribution to this repertory. A number of attempts have been made, nevertheless, at a listing of these works. The incipits of seven 'scherzi a 1 voce con istromenti'—six of them in Modena and the other at the Royal College of Music in London—were appended by Alfred Einstein to his thematic index of Steffani's chamber duets (1905).[4] In his article on the composer in *Die Musik in Geschichte und Gegenwart* (1965), Gerhard Croll added the cantata 'Occhi miei, lo miraste', which had been discovered in Hanover and edited in 1919, and the collection 'Trastulli', four manuscript volumes in Munich that were said to contain 'Italian cantatas (and several arias from [the opera] *Briseide* [Hanover, 1696]), most for soprano or bass with one or two instruments and continuo'.[5] My own list of Steffani's works in *The New Grove* includes the six 'scherzi' in Modena and 'Occhi miei, lo miraste', but omits the Royal College 'scherzo' and gathers up everything else in the vague formulation, '*c*80 arias and cantatas attrib. Steffani, most for S, insts, bc . . . perhaps not all authentic'. Clearly it is time for an attempt to be made at defining his output of solo cantatas and arias more precisely.

The results of this attempt are summarized in the Appendix below, in which cantatas and arias are listed according to reliable or unreliable attributions or as spurious works. The 'reliable' arias come from Steffani's Hanover operas of 1689–95 and thus need little comment. There is some discussion of 'unreliable' arias, most of which also belong to operas or other larger works, but it is the cantatas that form the central concern of this essay.

CANTATAS WITH INSTRUMENTS AND CONTINUO

It is somewhat disappointing to have to admit that of fifteen solo cantatas ascribed to Steffani, only seven can be attributed reliably to him. Six of these

---

Candace Ann Marles, 'Music and Drama in the Hanover Operas of Agostino Steffani (1654–1728)' (Ph.D. diss., Yale University, 1991); Colin Timms, 'Bass Patterns in Steffani's Chamber Duets', *Studi corelliani*, 4 (1990), 85–107; id., 'The Fate of Steffani's *I trionfi del fato*', in Chris Banks, Arthur Searle, and Malcolm Turner (eds.), *Sundry Sorts of Music Books: Essays on the British Library Collections Presented to O. W. Neighbour on his 70th Birthday* (London: British Library, 1993), 201–14.

[4] *Ausgewählte Werke von Agostino Steffani (1654–1728), erster Teil*, ed. Alfred Einstein and Adolf Sandberger (Denkmäler der Tonkunst in Bayern, 11, Jg. vi/2; Leipzig: Breitkopf & Härtel, 1905), pp. xxv–xxvi.

[5] *Die Musik in Geschichte und Gegenwart*, ed. Friedrich Blume (Kassel: Bärenreiter, 1949–79), xii. 1213.

call for instruments in addition to continuo; the other is for continuo alone. The six cantatas with instruments are all to be found in Modena, Biblioteca Estense, MS Mus. F. 1102, the only early source in which they are known to survive.[6] The manuscript is a small oblong octavo comprising fifty-two folios of good-quality music paper in six fascicles of eight leaves and one of four. The paper is ruled with eight staves per side and the music copied in a single, neat, professional hand throughout. The volume is bound in card boards covered with pink satin. The title-page and contents are as follows:[7]

SCHERZI
DELL'
ABBATE STEFFANI

fo. 1[r]   Spezza Amor l'arco e li strali
            ('Canto solo. i. Piffero. i. Fagotto')

     16[r] Il più felice e sfortunato amante
            ('Alto solo con 2. Violini')

     23[v] Guardati, o core, dal dio bambin!
            ('Canto solo con 2. Violini')

     31[r] Fileno, idolo mio, | ove lungi da me ti stai, mio bene?
            ('Canto solo con 2. Violini')

     37[v] Lagrime dolorose, | da gli occhi miei venite
            ('Basso solo con 2. Flauti')

     45[r] Hai finito di lusingarmi
            ('Canto solo con 2. Pifferi')

The manuscript has clearly been in Modena since the late seventeenth century, for it is listed in the *Repertorio de libri musicali sì manuscritti come stamp[a]ti di S[ua] A[ltezza] S[erenissima]*, an inventory that represents virtually the entire collection of Francesco II d'Este, Duke of Modena from 1674 to 1694.[8] One of the foremost patrons of the arts in late Seicento Italy, Francesco was also a major collector of music and other books. He was particularly active in this respect in the 1680s, much copying and binding being completed

---

[6] The entire manuscript is published in facsimile in *Cantatas by Agostino Steffani 1654–1728*, ed. Colin Timms (The Italian Cantata in the Seventeenth Century, 15; New York and London: Garland, 1985), 1–53.

[7] In this essay, text incipits of cantatas and arias generally comprise one or two complete lines of verse, as appropriate; vertical strokes mark divisions between lines. Punctuation is editorial, abbreviations are expanded, and orthography and the use of capital letters modernized; but the original spelling is retained.

[8] E. J. Luin, 'Repertorio dei libri musicali di S. A. S. Francesco II d'Este nell'Archivio di Stato di Modena', *La bibliofilia: Rivista di storia del libro*, 38 (1936), 418–45.

between 1684 and 1690.[9] It is largely thanks to him that the Biblioteca Estense today is such an important centre for the study of Italian Baroque music.

It seems doubtful, however, that Steffani's 'scherzi' were composed for Francesco's court. Although cantatas with instruments were by no means unknown in Modena, the instruments required were normally strings.[10] While three of the 'scherzi' call for two violins apiece, the others are scored for a variety of wind instruments—'flauti' (recorders), 'pifferi' (shawms or oboes), and a bassoon. Two cornettists appear to have been employed as members of Francesco's *cappella* in 1677–89 and 1689 respectively, but no other wind-players are listed at all.[11] If their scoring is anything to go by, it seems more likely that the 'scherzi' were written for Munich, where Steffani was educated and employed between 1667 and 1688. 'Pifferi' and 'flauti' (and bassoon) are mentioned in all but the first of his Munich operas, and pairs of them are used in alternation in *Alarico il Baltha* (1687).[12] 'Pifferi' do not appear in his Hanover operas, where their place is taken by 'hautbois' and the bassoon is called a 'basson'.[13]

A further clue to the date of Steffani's 'scherzi' is the fact that the words of one of them, 'Fileno, idolo mio', were set also by Atto Melani (1626–1714).[14] Although either composer could conceivably have found the text elsewhere, it is more likely that one of them adapted it from the other's work. The fact that Melani's setting contains seven more lines than Steffani's[15]—and that its composer was twenty-eight years older—suggests that his cantata is earlier than Steffani's 'scherzo'. Furthermore, if cantata texts enjoyed only brief popularity in a limited geographical area before

[9] Alessandra Chiarelli, *I codici di musica della Raccolta Estense: Ricostruzione dall'inventario settecentesco* (Quaderni della Rivista italiana di musicologia, 16; Florence: Olschki, 1987), 7.

[10] See e.g. the works discussed in Owen Jander, 'The Cantata in Accademia: Music for the Accademia de' Dissonanti and their Duke, Francesco II d'Este', *Rivista italiana di musicologia*, 10 (1975), 519–44.

[11] Victor Crowther, 'A Case-Study in the Power of the Purse: The Management of the Ducal *Cappella* in Modena in the Reign of Francesco II d'Este', *Journal of the Royal Musical Association*, 115 (1990), 207–19 at 218–19; see also id., *The Oratorio in Modena* (Oxford: Clarendon Press, 1992), 16–17.

[12] Hugo Riemann, 'Agostino Steffani als Opernkomponist', in *Ausgewählte Werke von Agostino Steffani (1654–1728), dritter Teil (zweiter Band der Opern)*, ed. id. (Denkmäler der Tonkunst in Bayern, 23, Jg. xii/2; Leipzig: Breitkopf & Härtel, 1912), pp. xix–xxi; *Ausgewählte Werke . . . zweiter Teil: 'Alarico'*, ed. id. (Denkmäler der Tonkunst in Bayern, 21, Jg. xi/2; Leipzig: Breitkopf & Härtel, 1911), 81–2.

[13] See e.g. *Le rivali concordi*, facs. ed. Howard Mayer Brown (Italian Opera 1640–1770, [14]; New York and London: Garland, 1977), Act II, p. 17.

[14] Facs. edn. in *Cantatas by Alessandro Melani 1639–1703 and Atto Melani 1626–1714*, ed. Robert Lamar Weaver (The Italian Cantata in the Seventeenth Century, 11; New York and London: Garland, 1985), 157–63.

[15] See ibid. 190; and *Cantatas by Agostino Steffani*, ed. Timms, 219.

falling into oblivion, as appears to have been the case, it follows that both composers probably encountered this text in the same place and around the same time.

Melani's activities as a singer, composer, and secret agent are somewhat reminiscent of Steffani's more distinguished career as an organist, composer, diplomat, and bishop. In 1644 Melani made his first visit to Paris, where he later sang in Italian opera and became a gentleman of the chamber to Louis XIV. In 1661, however, he fell from grace and was exiled from France. He was eventually restored to favour and returned there in 1679, having spent the intervening years mainly in Rome. Although Steffani's base during Melani's period of exile was Munich, he, too, was in Rome in 1672–4 and visited Paris in 1678–9, returning to Munich via Turin. If the words of 'Fileno, idolo mio' were accessible to both composers around the same time, these are the periods and places in which they are most likely to have been so.

Although Steffani's 'scherzi' were probably composed in the 1670s and 1680s, we have still to establish when the Modena volume was copied and given to the Duke. That the title-page of the manuscript, at least, was probably written in Germany in the 1680s or 1690s is suggested by the spelling of the composer's name and by his title. He started to adopt 'Steffani' in Munich: he had been baptized as 'Stievani', which Italians usually rendered as 'Stefani', and adopted a double 'f' to indicate to Germans that the stress should be placed on the first syllable. Also, he was appointed 'abbate' of Lepsingen, a sinecure between Augsburg and Nuremberg, in December 1682: thereafter, he was generally known as 'abbate' Steffani until he became Bishop of Spiga (nomination 1706; consecration 1707). Since the volume of 'scherzi' belonged to Francesco II, it must have been copied before the Duke's death. The period of copying is therefore narrowed to 1683–94.

This must also be the period when the manuscript was given to the Duke. There is no indication from Steffani's Munich years of a link between him and the Modenese court, but there is a strong hint of one from the start of his period in Hanover. Steffani left Munich in May 1688, visited Venice that month, and was in Hanover by 27 June.[16] On 30 January 1689 he directed the première of his first Hanover opera, *Henrico Leone*. Among the performers were the tenor Antonio Borosini and the violinist Giuseppe Galloni, both of them 'borrowed' from Modena.[17] Borosini had been employed there

---

[16] Alfred Einstein, 'Agostino Steffani, I. Münchener Zeit. 1654–1688', *Kirchen-musikalisches Jahrbuch*, 23 (1910), 1–36 at 35–6; Rosenmarie Elisabeth Wallbrecht, *Das Theater des Barockzeitalters an den welfischen Höfen Hannover und Celle* (Quellen und Darstellungen zur Geschichte Niedersachsens, 83; Hildesheim: August Lax, 1974), 176.

[17] E. J. Luin, 'Antonio Giannettini e la musica a Modena alla fine del secolo XVII', *Atti e memorie della R. deputazione di storia patria per le provincie modenesi*, 7th ser., 7 (1931–2), 145–230 at 175–6.

from 1686 and was to return to Hanover in 1693 (and 1696).[18] Although the release of these musicians was requested by Duke Ernst August of Hanover, Borosini must have been known to Steffani, at least by repute. If the composer did not visit Modena in May or June 1688, he could conceivably have done so in 1686, when little is known of his whereabouts, or in 1690 or 1692.[19] In other words, the manuscript of his 'scherzi' could have been taken to Modena by Borosini in 1689 or 1693, or by Steffani between 1686 and 1692. It may have been presented to Francesco II as a token of the composer's gratitude for the loan of the Duke's tenor in 1689, and may also reflect the dynastic connection between Hanover and Modena which was being investigated during this period by Leibniz.[20]

Be that as it may, the volume was a very handsome gift. The 'scherzi' are arranged in a sequence according to their vocal and instrumental requirements:

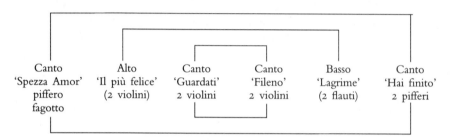

Canto   Alto   Canto   Canto   Basso   Canto
'Spezza Amor' 'Il più felice' 'Guardati'   'Fileno'   'Lagrime'   'Hai finito'
piffero   (2 violini)   2 violini   2 violini   (2 flauti)   2 pifferi
fagotto

The desire for this pattern may explain why the works were not placed in alphabetical order: five of them begin with consecutive letters of the Italian alphabet (F, G, H, I, L), and the sixth, 'Spezza Amor', may have been included because its scoring completes the symmetrical arrangement. The existence of a group of pieces beginning with consecutive letters makes one wonder whether Steffani composed a 'scherzo' for every letter of the alphabet. This is not such an improbable idea as it may seem. Similarly abstract or intellectual feats were performed in his two printed books of sacred music: his *Psalmodia vespertina* (1674) includes a Latin epigram, probably by the composer, incorporating a double acrostic based on his name, while his

---

[18] Winton Dean, 'Borosini, Antonio', *New Grove*, iii. 63; T. W. Werner, 'Agostino Steffanis Opemtheater in Hannover', *Archiv für Musikforschung*, 3 (1938), 65–79 at 70.

[19] Georg Fischer, *Musik in Hannover* (Hanover: Hahn, 1903), 22, states that Steffani was in Venice in Apr. 1690. In 1692 he went to Padua: 'Dall'anno precedente 1692. sino al presente giorno, è notorio che io non sono stato in Patria che due soli giorni nel 1709' (letter from Steffani to Count Girolamo Frigimelica-Roberti, 15 Oct. 1717; Rome, Sacra Congregatio pro Gentium Evangelizatione seu de Propaganda Fide, Archivio, Fondo Spiga, vol. 61).

[20] His research resulted specifically in his *Lettre sur la connexion des maisons de Brunsvic et d'Este* (Hanover: Samuel Ammon, 1695).

Sacer Ianus quadrifrons (1685) comprises twelve motets for three voices and continuo, each of which can be performed in four ways.[21] Both these collections, like, I believe, his six surviving 'scherzi', date from his Munich years.

The 'scherzi', furthermore, are extremely accomplished and appealing examples of Steffani's musical art. The recitative displays his acute sensitivity to the rhythm of words and frequently bursts into flower in the shape of a cavata.[22] While the arias are cast in a variety of metres and tempos, they also impress by their assured handling of tonality and harmony and by the richness of the counterpoint between instruments and voice. The instruments are used with discrimination and help to articulate the musical forms, which are, in any case, extremely varied and interesting. Above all, perhaps, the 'scherzi' exhibit the melodic refinement mentioned by Schmitz: Steffani's idiom combines the 'classical' beauty of his contemporary Corelli with the warmth and suppleness characteristic of vocal music, enriching both with voluptuousness of harmony and texture and producing a blend that appeals to heart as well as head. All in all, his 'scherzi' would surely have delighted any connoisseur who was fortunate enough to hear them performed.

The seventh 'scherzo' in Einstein's thematic index, 'All'or ch'in grembo all'ombre', is the only other cantata with instruments known to be ascribed to Steffani. The source, Royal College of Music MS 1026,[23] contains just this cantata and an incomplete copy of his chamber duet 'Inquieto mio cor'. The presence of the duet has no bearing on the authenticity of the cantata, however, for the two works are in different hands and occupy separate manuscripts bound together after copying. The cantata, which takes up six folios, is entitled 'Cantata à Voce Sola | + con duoi Violini'; the voice is alto, and the violins are apparently replaced by flutes or recorders in one of the arias (fo. 3ᵛ), where the abbreviation 'flut.' is written above the upper instrumental part. The work is in the hand of the non-Italian copyist active in early eighteenth-century England who wrote out at least twelve other manuscripts of cantatas, oratorios, and operas by Bononcini, Ariosti, and others.[24] The ascription to 'Stephani' is in a different hand and carries no authority. The true composer may be represented instead by the remains of

---

[21] The epigram, and the preface to *Sacer Ianus quadrifrons*, are given in Gaetano Gaspari, *Catalogo della Biblioteca del Liceo musicale di Bologna* (Bologna, 1890–1943; repr. Bologna: Forni, 1961), ii. 314 and 499 respectively.

[22] See Colin Timms, 'Cavata', *New Grove Dictionary of Opera*, i. 790.

[23] Not MS 1927, as stated in *Ausgewählte Werke . . . erster Teil*, ed. Einstein and Sandberger, p. xviii.

[24] Including Oxford, Bodleian Library, Mus. d.20–21, reproduced in facsimile in *Cantatas by Giovanni Bononcini 1670–1747*, ed. Lowell Lindgren (The Italian Cantata in the Seventeenth Century, 10; New York and London: Garland, 1985); see also the editor's introduction, last paragraph, and his n. 29.

Ex. 9.1. 'All'or ch'in grembo all'ombre', mvt. 1

(... the mortal enjoys in sleep's feathers and in the thousand lights of the day's rays at heaven's behest . . .)

the word at the top of the page which has largely been trimmed off. The absence of a descender suggests that this ascription, if such it was, did not give Steffani's name in any of its various spellings.

The musical evidence for the attribution of 'All'or ch'in grembo all'ombre' is no more compelling. Although in terms of general style the cantata appears to be within his range, several details point elsewhere. The instrumental introduction here is called a 'sinfonia'; in the Modena manuscript, such movements are entitled 'preludio'. Whereas the longest Modena 'scherzo' consists of three arias separated by recitative (ARARA), this cantata comprises seven movements (RARARAR). The first recitative includes, by Steffani's standards, some poorly stressed word-setting (Ex. 9.1) and ends with a short ritornello, a pairing not found in his 'scherzi'. Furthermore, the bass of one of the arias descends to bottom B', a pitch avoided in his vocal chamber music and rarely encountered in his operas (his lowest note is normally C). Thus neither the manuscript nor the music provides good reason for attributing this cantata to Steffani.

The contents of the four volumes of 'Trastulli' in Munich, Bayerische Staatsbibliothek, Mus. MS 178, are entirely unascribed. Ten of the arias in Vol. 2 come from *Briseide* (Hanover, 1696) and are included in section II.B of the catalogue below. The possibility that this opera was composed by Steffani appears to be the main reason why the 'Trastulli' as a whole were attributed to him: Croll followed Riemann in regarding *Briseide* as authentic.

After looking again at the sources of information on opera at Hanover in the late seventeenth century, however, Philip Keppler challenged this attribution and suggested, plausibly, that the work may have been composed by Pietro Torri.[25] To the points made by him may be added the fact that its librettist (Francesco Palmieri) was not Steffani's normal collaborator at Hanover (Ortensio Mauro), and that, unlike Steffani's authentic three-act operas for that court, *Briseide* was not taken up a few years later in Hamburg. If Steffani did not compose the opera, there is apparently no reason for attributing the 'Trastulli' to him. Indeed, according to Robert Münster, the entire contents of these four volumes were both composed and copied by Torri.[26] If this is the case, they have no further place in a study of Steffani's cantatas; nor do the pieces selected from them and published under his name.[27]

CANTATAS WITH CONTINUO ONLY

'Occhi miei, lo miraste' is the only other cantata that may be regarded as reliably attributable to Steffani. It survives in vol. 76 of the Kestner collection in the Hanover Stadtbibliothek, a seventeenth-century Italian manuscript that was given to Hermann Kestner in 1873. Although it was described in print by T. W. Werner in 1918–19,[28] this interesting manuscript appears to have attracted little attention since then. An oblong octavo measuring 24 × 9.5 cm. and with four staves per side, it exhibits the long narrow format typical of Italian cantata and aria manuscripts of the mid-seventeenth century. The contents are as follows:

p.   1   Già la vermiglia aurora | di bianche perle ricamato havea
         ('Del S. Ercole Bernabei')

    25   Occhi miei, lo miraste
         ('Del S. Agostino Stefani')

    61   Non mi guardate | che mi ferite
         ('Del S. Giuseppe Ant[oni]o Bernabei')

    85   Dell'ardore ch'il core distempra
         ('Del Sig. Aless[andr]o Stradella')

[25] Philip Keppler, 'Agostino Steffani's Hannover Operas and a Rediscovered Catalogue', in Harold Powers (ed.), *Studies in Music History: Essays for Oliver Strunk* (Princeton University Press, 1968), 341–54 at 348–9.
[26] Private communications, 12 Apr. and 5 July 1978.
[27] Agostino Steffani, *Eight Songs for Solo Voice, One or Two Woodwinds and Continuo*, ed. Gertrude Parker Smith (Smith College Music Archives, 11; Northampton, Mass.: Smith College, 1951), nos. 1–6, 8.
[28] T. W. Werner and Alfred Einstein, 'Die Musikhandschriften des Kestnerschen Nachlasses im Stadtarchiv zu Hannover', *Zeitschrift für Musikwissenschaft*, 1 (1918–19), 441–66 at 449.

101 Dove fugisti ed in che loco
('Del S. Aless. Stradella')

116 Da mille pene e mille | stanco, afflitto, doglioso
('Del S. Aless.o Stradella')

156 Non so s'io mi fido
('Del S. Anton[io] Franc[esc]o Tenaglia')

172 Stelle, se omai v'offesi
('Del S. Alless[andr]o Melanie')

188 Speranza bugiarda | di farmi più sperar
('Del S. Ant[oni]o Masin[i]')

200 S'io la duro, la duro così
('Del S. Carlo Ambrosio Lonati')

Although Werner styled all ten of these pieces as cantatas, 'Dell'ardore ch'il core distempra' is listed as an aria in the latest catalogue of Stradella's works,[29] and others, too, may be regarded as arias rather than cantatas. 'Dell'ardore' and 'Da mille pene e mille' are the only ones known also from other sources: both are included in the Stradella catalogue, though not on the basis of this manuscript. 'Dove fugisti', 'Non so s'io mi fido', and 'Stelle, se omai v'offesi', on the other hand, do not appear in published lists of their composers' cantatas,[30] and the remaining five pieces also may be *unica*. Most important, perhaps, there seems to be no conflicting ascription elsewhere for any of the pieces in the volume.

The repertory of the manuscript provides further grounds for trusting the ascriptions and also offers clues to the provenance of the works. All the composers worked in Rome in the 1670s—with the possible exception of Tenaglia, whose career after 1661 is unknown.[31] Steffani went there in 1672 to study with Ercole Bernabei, with whom he returned to Munich in 1674. Giuseppe Antonio Bernabei followed his father north in 1677, in which year Stradella, another pupil of Bernabei, and Lonati also left Rome. Masini died there in 1678, but Alessandro Melani remained there until his death in 1703 (and had dealings with Hanover in 1691).[32] In view of all this, it seems very likely that

---

[29] Carolyn Gianturco and Eleanor McCrickard, *Alessandro Stradella (1639–1682): A Thematic Catalogue of his Compositions* (Stuyvesant, NY: Pendragon, 1991), 174.

[30] Eleanor Caluori, 'Tenaglia, Francesco Antonio', *New Grove*, xviii. 686; Robert Lamar Weaver, *Alessandro and Atto Melani* (Wellesley Edition Cantata Index Series, 8–9; Wellesley, Mass.: Wellesley College, 1972).

[31] Caluori, 'Tenaglia', *New Grove*, xviii. 685.

[32] On 3 and 17 Nov. he wrote from Rome to Magliabechi in Florence about certain books to be procured in Rome for Leibniz; see Robert Lamar Weaver, 'Materiali per le biografie dei fratelli Melani', *Rivista italiana di musicologia*, 12 (1977), 252–95 at 287.

Ex. 9.2. Steffani, 'Occhi miei, lo miraste', mvt. 1

(. . . yes, they were given to the winds! Ah! ah, traitor . . .)

the works in the volume were composed in Rome in the 1670s and that the manuscript itself was produced there at around the same time. If so, the ascriptions are probably to be trusted.

This conclusion is supported in Steffani's case by the evidence of 'Occhi miei, lo miraste', a cantata for high soprano (from c' to bb'') and continuo based on five portions of text (RARAR). The setting contains nothing that he could not have composed and a great deal that is highly characteristic of his style. The recitatives display phrase repetition, occasional melismas, and cadences in which the vocal line ends over the dominant chord (Ex. 9.2, from the first section), as well as Steffani's usual sensitivity to verbal rhythm. The change of key signature in Ex. 9.2 is not a standard feature of his style but is prompted by the meaning of the words (and reversed after fifteen bars, when they allow). The opening and closing recitatives end with cavatas, the first composed of vigorous non-imitative counterpoint between voice and bass, and the second entirely of imitative counterpoint in which the 'counter-subject' is inverted to illustrate the word 'contrari' (Ex. 9.3). Both kinds of counterpoint are used in the first aria, where the bass takes up a phrase from the voice and repeats it in the manner of an ostinato.[33] Imitation is occasionally

---

[33] On ostinatos in Steffani, see Hugo Riemann, 'Basso ostinato und Basso "quasi" ostinato: Eine Anregung', in *Festschrift zum 90. Geburtstage Sr. Excellenz des wirklichen geheimen Rates Rochus Freiherrn von Liliencron* (Leipzig: Breitkopf & Härtel, 1910), 193–202; id., 'Agostino Steffani als Opernkomponist', pp. xvi–xvii; Timms, 'Bass Patterns in Steffani's Chamber Duets'.

Ex. 9.3. Steffani, 'Occhi miei, lo miraste', mvt. 5

(... that love and jealousy are two opposites ...)

Ex. 9.4. Steffani, 'Occhi miei, lo miraste', mvt. 2

(... to wither the vines ...)

created by an extra note in the continuo part (Ex. 9.4, from the first aria), which also keeps moving under pedals in the voice. The other aria is in 12/8, a metre found elsewhere in Steffani's works and which affords opportunities for cross-rhythms resembling hemiolas. The opening phrase of this aria (Ex. 9.5a) recalls that of one of his chamber duets, 'Gelosia, che vuoi da me?' (London, British Library, RM 23.k.8, fo. 79ʳ), set to the same word (Ex. 9.5b), while the setting of the line 'non è albergo di mostri il mio core' begins identically with the movement 'Conducetemi verso il porto' in the duet 'Tu m'aspettasti'.[34] These similarities may not be very significant, but they strengthen the feeling that the works were composed by one and the same person.

Of the other cantatas ascribed to Steffani, 'Piange la bella Clori, e del suo pianto' has the strongest claim to authenticity. The source is a manuscript in the Harry S. Truman Presidential Library at Independence, Missouri, appended to a Walsh print of Bononcini's *Camilla*.[35] How the manuscript reached this unlikely location is explained as follows:

On September 25, 1951, the prime minister of Italy, Alcide de Gasperi, sent Truman a photographic facsimile of the autograph manuscript of Verdi's *Falstaff*

---

[34] See *Cantatas by Agostino Steffani*, ed. Timms, 160 ff.
[35] I am grateful to Professor Lowell Lindgren for drawing my attention to this manuscript and for providing information on its contents.

Ex. 9.5. *a* Steffani, 'Occhi miei, lo miraste', mvt. 4; *b* Steffani, 'Gelosia, che vuoi da me?', mvt. 1

(*a*)

(Jealousy, jealousy, be gone from me . . .)

(*b*)

(Jealousy, what do you want . . .)

and a most intriguing, beautifully bound edition of excerpts from Giovanni Bononcini's *Il trionfo di Camilla* (1696). The opera, extremely popular in its day, was first performed in English at the Royal Theater, Drury Lane, London, in 1706. Truman's edition with its fine Dublin-style binding dates from this period. Appended to the end of the book are 216 handwritten pages of arias, cantatas, and minuets composed by Scarlatti, Caldara, Steffani, Mancini, Bononcini, and others—a valuable example of the spread of Italian vocal styles to the other side of the channel.[36]

The manuscript contains twenty-four Italian cantatas and fourteen arias. The music was composed mainly in late seventeenth-century Italy, although the works by Steffani and Wilderer were probably written in Germany, and the cantatas by Greber and Haym could have originated in early eighteenth-century London. The upright format of the volume, with twelve staves to a page, is also northern in style. Two hands can be distinguished, and misspellings suggest that the Steffani copyist was not an Italian.[37]

The composer is credited with nine pieces:

[36] Elise K. Kirk, *Music at the White House: A History of the American Spirit* (Urbana: University of Illinois Press, 1986), 264.
[37] e.g. 'aqua' for 'acqua' (p. 128), and 'sgardo' for 'sguardo' (p. 196).

p.   12   La natura è troppo frale
          ('Menuetto. del S^re Abbate Steffani.')

     82   Alma di donna | più spesso impiaga
          ('Menuetto, del S^re. Abbate Steffani.')

    102   La speranza come rosa
          ('Menuetto, del S^re Aogostino Steffani.')

  125–6   I tuoi vanni, arcier volante
          ('Aria, del S^re. Abbate Aogostino Steffani.')

 127–32   Piange la bella Clori, e del suo pianto
          ('Cantata. del S^re. Abbate Steffani.')

    132   Nume implacabile, | arcier terribile
          ('Arietta. del S^re Abbate Steffani.')

  175–6   Ciò che passa per veleno
          ('Chaconnette. del S^r. Abbate Steffani.')

  195–6   Se riveggo il bell'ond'ardo
          ('Aria, del S^re. Abbate Steffani.')

    204   Mi dà piacer vitale
          ('Arietta. del S^re. Abbate Steffani.')

The ascriptions are all in the same hand as the music and words, and most of them are demonstrably correct.[38] Apart from 'Alma di donna', the origin of which is unknown, all the arias come from Steffani's Hanover operas of the 1690s—'La speranza come rosa' from *La superbia d'Alessandro* (1690); 'Nume implacabile' from *Le rivali concordi* (1692); 'La natura è troppo frale', 'I tuoi vanni', 'Ciò che passa', and 'Se riveggo' from *La libertà contenta* (1693); and 'Mi dà piacer' from *I trionfi del Fato* (1695). This being so, it is tempting to assume that 'Alma di donna' and 'Piange la bella Clori' are also authentic Steffani works from a similar time and place.

The text of the cantata is short and unusual in design. The opening nine lines of recitative are followed only by a five-line aria and a final mixed stanza of four lines:

[Recit.]   Piange la bella Clori, e del suo pianto
              cade ogni stella ad affogarmi il core . . .

Aria   Pupillette care, care,
                            non piangete, io v'amerò.

---

[38] The misspelling of the composer's first name is also found in London, Royal Academy of Music, MS 43, fo. 63^v, where the same writer correctly ascribed a copy of 'Mio cor, preparati a giubilar' to 'Aogostino Steffani'. The aria (*recte* 'Cor mio') comes from his opera *La libertà contenta*.

> Già durano i pianti assai,
> serenate i vostri rai,
> altrimente io morirò.

[Arioso]   Ma se poi
              vi diletta il pianger tanto,
              consacrate il vostro pianto
              alla mia libertà, persa per voi.

Nevertheless, the cantata appears to be complete: the text makes sense as it stands, and the setting displays tonal unity and formal balance. The last line of the opening recitative is set in 3/2 as an imitative, bipartite cavata forming a tonal complement to the preceding recitative—a standard pattern in Steffani. The arioso, in ABB' form, begins in E flat and visits C minor and B flat before ending in G minor, the key from which the recitative departs and of the aria. Perhaps the most striking feature, however, is the florid ornamentation that is found in every movement, including the first (Ex. 9.6*a*) and last (Ex. 9.6*b*) phrases of the work. Steffani's writing for the voice, one of the high points of the bel canto style of the late seventeenth and early eighteenth centuries, is well known for its virtuosity. He was particularly fond of the kind of syncopation employed in Ex. 9.6*b*, even if it does not add up, using it in his operas and in the solo movements of his chamber duets.[39] Its presence in 'Piange la bella Clori' strengthens the credibility of this attribution.[40]

Most of the remaining cantatas ascribed to Steffani are to be found in MS G. Mus. 463 at the Guildhall Library, London, of which the title-page reads as follows: 'Italian Songs M.S. | by – (chiefly Cantatas) | Stephano | Scarlatti | Gregorij | Bononcini | Augustini | Gasperini | Pasquino | Franchi – 1692 | Carissimi'; at the back of the volume (reversed), there is

---

[39] See e.g. *Le rivali concordi*, Act I, pp. 8 and 42, and the recitative 'Se scendi a solcar l'onda' in the chamber duet 'Navicella, che ten' vai' (*Cantatas by Agostino Steffani*, ed. Timms, 73). The latter (adapted) appears in Pier Francesco Tosi, *Observations on the Florid Song*, trans. John Ernest Galliard (2nd edn., London, 1743; repr. London: William Reeves, 1967), pl. VI, no. 9, as an example of the 'Strascino or Dragg'. Further on Steffani's virtuosic writing, see Rodolfo Celletti, *A History of Bel Canto*, trans. Frederick Fuller (Oxford: Clarendon Press, 1991), 55–9.

[40] This is further strengthened by Professor Lindgren's discovery, revealed in a paper ('The Italian Cantata in England before Handel') presented at the Sixth Biennial Conference on Baroque Music, Edinburgh, 7–10 July 1994 (after this essay had been written), that most of the manuscript, including 'Piange la bella Clori', was copied by Johann Sigismund Cousser, probably in London in about 1706. During the 1690s, while Steffani was directing opera at Hanover, Cousser was doing the same at nearby Wolfenbüttel; he subsequently took Steffani operas to Hamburg, Augsburg, and Stuttgart. Incidentally, there is no connection (after the first four words) between the text of this cantata and that of Orazio Tarditi's madrigal 'Piange la bella Clori' (words by 'Cavaliero Anselmi') published in RISM 1624[11]: I am grateful to John Milsom for checking this source in Christ Church, Oxford.

Ex. 9.6. Steffani (attrib.), 'Piange la bella Clori': *a* mvt. 1; *b* mvt. 3

(*a*)

(The fair Chloris weeps . . .)

(*b*)

(. . . lost for you.)

also some keyboard music, apparently by John Loeillet.[41] The catalogue of the Gresham Music Library describes this manuscript as an early eighteenth-century copy in several hands;[42] it also states that it is of Italian provenance,

---

[41] According to a pencilled note, 'This appears to be Six suits of Lessons for the harpsichord or spinnet composed by John Loeillet (whose name erased appears below?).'

[42] *Gresham Music Library: A Catalogue of the Printed Books and Manuscripts Deposited in Guildhall Library* (London: Corporation of London, 1965), 73.

but the verbal texts of the contents are often so corrupt that this seems rather doubtful. The format of the volume—upright (20 × 31.5 cm.), with twelve staves to a page—is atypical of Italian manuscripts, while the binding—full calf with vestiges of gold-stamped designs front and back—points to England or Germany. This impression is reinforced by a watermark on a front flyleaf depicting a lion rampant holding scythe and sheaf, surrounded by a double circle and surmounted by a crown—a mark that is frequently found in north European papers of the late seventeenth and early eighteenth centuries.[43]

The manuscript seems to have been planned as an ordered collection. The 'pars prima' (pp. 1–25) is devoted to 'Stephano', to whom the first five works are ascribed:

p. 1 O martirio d'amor, che mi trafiggi!
       ('Pars Prima Del Sign[r] Stephano')

    5 Qual subterea mole il sol lampeggia
       ('Pars Prima Del Sign[r] Stephano')

   12 Alle lacrime, homai, occhi lucenti
       ('Del Sign[r] Stephano')

   18 Desiava gioire | sotto riche cortine
       ('Del Sign[r] Stephano')

   24 M'influisse il nume arciero
       ('Del Sign[r] Stephano')

The next ten pieces (pp. [26]–[47]) are credited to (Giovanni Lorenzo) Gregori, in whose *Cantate da camera a voce sola*, op. 3 (Lucca, 1699) all but one of them appear.[44] The 'Pars Tertia Del Sign[r] Gio. Bononcini' occupies pages [48]–[60]. This is followed by a veritable miscellany of works ascribed to various composers, including those named on the title-page. 'Stephano' is credited with the following group:

p. [104] Tenerezze, deh cessate
   [106] In ogni loco | d'amor il foco
   [108] Se non piange afflitto un seno
   [109] Misero core, | tu chiedi amore
   [112] Non vivo che ti disperi

---

[43] W. A. Churchill, *Watermarks in Paper in Holland, England, France etc. in the XVII and XVIII Centuries and their Interconnection* (Amsterdam: Menno Hertzberger, 1935), nos. 111, 115, 117 (closest), and 118.

[44] The exception is the aria 'Il raggio che tu scocchi', which does not appear in the list of contents given in Emil Vogel, Alfred Einstein, François Lesure, and Claudio Sartori, *Bibliografia della musica italiana vocale profana pubblicata dal 1500 al 1700* (Pomezia: Staderini, 1977), i. 811. It could, however, be a part of one of Gregori's cantatas.

[113]   Per lusinghe, vezzi e pianti
[114]   Ama, confida e spera
[114]   Bei crini d'oro
[116]   Bionde chiome, ch'ornate
[117]   L'empio arciero acceso dardo

Of the five works in the 'pars prima' of the volume, 'O martirio d'amor, che mi trafiggi!', the final aria of 'Qual subterea mole il sol lampeggia' ('Sembra caro l'infante Cupido'), and 'Desiava gioire' are also ascribed to 'Stephano' in another manuscript of the period, Westminster Abbey MS C. G. 63. Although this source is correct in some of its attributions,[45] it does not provide strong corroboration for the ascriptions to Steffani. Indeed, 'O martirio d'amor' also survives in a seventeenth-century Italian manuscript in Vienna, Österreichische Nationalbibliothek, MS 17763, where it is ascribed to Giovanni Maria Pagliardi (1637–1702).[46] If this cantata were by Steffani, it would be unique in his output in having a devotional Italian text. The final strophe is labelled '3a' in the Westminster Abbey volume, and the continuo line at this point in the setting (which is largely in recitative and arioso styles) is adapted from that at the beginning of the piece. It thus recalls the strophic-bass technique employed in cantatas of the early and mid-seventeenth century, and suggests that this work was composed by someone earlier than Steffani. Pagliardi is an obvious candidate.

If 'O martirio d'amor' is not by Steffani, doubt is cast on the other ascriptions to him in the Guildhall and Westminster Abbey manuscripts, and corroboration must be sought in the music itself. The evidence of 'Desiava gioire' and 'Qual subterea mole' is inconclusive: if they are not particularly characteristic of him, they nevertheless contain nothing that he could not have written. The least convincing features of 'Desiava gioire' (RARA) are: in the second recitative, a downward leap of an augmented fourth in the vocal line and a cadence in which a vocal fourth above the bass does not resolve on to the leading note (a kind of cadence found in the works of slightly earlier composers);[47] and, in the closing aria, the prominence of parallel motion and appoggiaturas (Ex. 9.7). In 'Qual subterea mole' (RARAA)

---

[45] e.g. those to Carissimi and Merula; see William Barclay Squire, 'Musik-Katalog der Bibliothek der Westminster-Abtei in London', *Monatshefte für Musikgeschichte*, 35 (1903), Beilage, 1–45 at 39.

[46] *Tabulae codicum manu scriptorum praeter Graecos et Orientales in Bibliotheca Palatina Vindobonensi asservatorum*, x (Vienna, 1899; repr. Graz: Akademische Druck- u. Verlagsanstalt, 1965), 53. I am grateful to Dr Günter Brosche for confirming that this setting is identical to the one in the Guildhall and Westminster Abbey manuscripts.

[47] See e.g. *Cantatas by Marc'Antonio Pasqualini 1614–1691*, ed. Margaret Murata (The Italian Cantata in the Seventeenth Century, 3; New York and London: Garland, 1985), 23 (bars 5–6) and 36 ('Raddoppiatemi', bars 6–7).

Ex. 9.7. 'Desiava gioire', mvt. 4

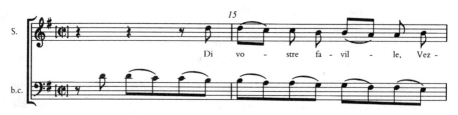

(. . . of your sparkle, beautiful eyes, soften the harshness . . .)

Ex. 9.8. 'Qual subterea mole', mvt. 2

(. . . nor do I know how to seek relief from my suffering . . .)

the first aria ignores the strophic structure of the text and includes a cadence
that contrasts major and minor thirds in a manner reminiscent of Carissimi
(Ex. 9.8).[48] The most doubtful feature of this cantata, however, is the final
aria, 'Sembra caro', which also survives separately in other manuscripts.
Steffani was fond of ostinato basses, and very resourceful in his use of them,
but the bass of this aria seems more instrumental in character than is normal
for him, and its treatment appears rather inflexible and ungracious.

The remaining two pieces in the 'pars prima' of the Guildhall manuscript
are even less likely to be authentic. The extraordinary chromatic progressions
at the beginning of 'Alle lacrime, homai, occhi lucenti' (RARA) are reminiscent of the 'impassioned, even bizarre, chromaticism' for which Pagliardi

[48] As in e.g. 'In un mar di pensieri'; see Giacomo Carissimi, *Six Solo Cantatas for High
Voice and Keyboard*, ed. Gloria Rose (London: Faber, 1969), 44 ff.

and his Florentine contemporaries are known.[49] Other doubtful features include broken figuration and parallel motion on the word 'costante' in the first aria, an unprepared accented minor seventh in the second recitative, and the dominant seventh chord (last inversion) which ends that section and leads directly into an arioso. 'M'influisse il nume arciero' is not a cantata but a da capo aria. The melody displays little invention, while the bass contrasts an active (but independent) figure with spineless parallel motion. A mechanical sequence opens the B section, and an impression of sterile repetitiveness is created by the aria as a whole.

Although the second group of works ascribed to 'Stephano' in the Guild-hall manuscript begins with an aria ('Tenerezze, deh cessate') from *I trionfi del Fato*, there is no good reason for attributing the following pieces to him. The last three items constitute a solo cantata ('Bei crini d'oro') known from other sources to be by Giovanni Bononcini.[50] The aria 'Misero core', recitative 'Non vivo che ti disperi', and aria 'Per lusinghe, vezzi e pianti' may also belong together in a single cantata, but they all include features uncharacteristic of Steffani and seem to have been written by a later composer. The remaining three pieces are isolated arias: none of them comes from any of his known works, or survives in any other source, and their attribution to Steffani is questionable on musical grounds as well.

Only two further pieces require discussion here. The source of 'Va girando intorno al suolo' (British Library, Add. MS 29963) is a large oblong volume containing cantatas and arias by various composers and copied by various hands.[51] Among the composers named are Astorga, Bononcini, Mancini, and Scarlatti. One anonymous recitative and aria with strings, possibly from an opera, is dated '18 Agosto 1712'—the only obvious pointer to the date of the collection as a whole. The ascription to Steffani of 'Va girando' (fo. 64ʳ) is not in the hand of the cantata itself and is therefore to be viewed with suspicion. One's doubts are confirmed by the style of the music, which seems a little too late for him. What is intriguing, however, is that 'Va girando' and the next cantata in the volume, the anonymous 'Detto lungi da te sott'alto cielo' (fo. 68ʳ), are in the large, bold hand of the professional scribe who in the early eighteenth century made fair copies of Hanover operas of the 1680s and 1690s, of an anonymous chamber duet appended to a volume of Steffani, and of duets and trios by Handel.[52] Though probably not by

[49] John Walter Hill, 'Pagliardi, Giovanni Maria', *New Grove*, xiv. 93.

[50] Facs. edn. in *Cantatas by Giovanni Bononcini*, ed. Lindgren, 126–9.

[51] Augustus Hughes-Hughes, *Catalogue of Manuscript Music in the British Museum* (London: British Museum, 1906–9), ii. 509.

[52] Colin Timms, 'Gregorio Piva and Steffani's Principal Copyist', in Ian Bent (ed.), *Source Materials and the Interpretation of Music: A Memorial Volume to Thurston Dart* (London: Stainer & Bell, 1981), 181–2, 189.

Steffani, 'Va girando' (and 'Detto lungi da te') may therefore have originated around the same time at the Hanoverian court in Germany or England.

The source of 'Vuoi saper perchè nel core' (Schwerin, Wissenschaftliche Allgemeinbibliothek (Mecklenburgische Landesbibliothek), Mus. 4725) is also a large oblong volume containing cantatas and arias (in German as well as Italian) by various composers.[53] Some of the music suggests a north German provenance. The first cantatas in the book are by Ruggiero Fedeli, who between 1691 and 1722 held posts in Berlin, Hanover, Kassel, Brunswick, and Wolfenbüttel. There follows a cantata ('Cieco nume, tiranno spietato') by Giovanni Bononcini, who visited Berlin in 1702–3. Two of the Italian arias come from Hanover operas—'Luci belle a pena viste' from Steffani's *I trionfi del Fato* (1695) and 'Mirando i tuoi begl'occhi' from Luigi Mancia's *La costanza nelle selve* (1697)—while three of the German arias belong to Keiser's *Die wunder-schöne Psyche*, which was performed in Hamburg on 20 October 1701 for the birthday of Queen Sophie Charlotte of Prussia. 'Vuoi saper perchè nel core' (p. 69) carries the heading 'Cantat[a] del Sig.ͤ Steffani', possibly in the same hand as the words of the piece, but it turns out to be only an aria. Like Pietro Torri's setting of the same text,[54] however, it may have been the first movement of a cantata in ARA form. The existence of Torri's cantata suggests that the text was known in northern Europe and strengthens the possibility that it was set also by Steffani. Although the Schwerin aria contains nothing that is specially characteristic of his style, it could nevertheless have been written by him and may be all that remains of a lost càntata.

The surviving corpus of solo cantatas attributable to Steffani is thus very small and seems to date from the earlier part of his composing career. 'Occhi miei, lo miraste' appears to have been written in Rome in 1672–4; 'Fileno, idolo mio' may date from the same period or from 1679, and his other 'scherzi' were probably written at Munich in the 1670s and 1680s. 'Piange la bella Clori', if authentic, is the only sign that he also composed solo cantatas in Hanover.

One cannot help feeling that a considerable number of cantatas must have been lost. If this is the case, these also probably date from his Munich period: other Munich works are now missing, including an opera, a serenata, and

---

[53] Otto Kade, *Die Musikalien-Sammlung des großherzoglich Mecklenburg-Schweriner Fürstenhauses aus den letzten zwei Jahrhunderten* (Schwerin: Sandmeyer, 1893), ii. 189. I am grateful to Dr Raimund Jedeck for supplying a list of contents of the manuscript.

[54] British Library, Add. MS 38036; Oxford, Bodleian Library, Mus. d.5. Torri's cantata comprises an aria 'Vuoi saper perchè nel core', recitative 'Dunque nel petto mio', and aria 'Cangia voglia, sì, sì'.

a tourney. If he had written a quantity of solo cantatas at Hanover, one would have expected to find them carefully preserved in the Royal Music Library, along with his chamber duets and operas. The 'scherzi' in Modena may have survived because they were given away: other cantatas from his Munich years may have been included among the 'carte di Musica' that passed to his relatives after his death and then were lost.[55]

The cantatas that survive confirm that Steffani's musical education in Rome was not restricted entirely to sacred composition. The principal fruits of his studies with Ercole Bernabei were his *Psalmodia vespertina* and other sacred pieces still in manuscript. His chamber duets show that he was also familiar with the secular field and that he learnt from examples by predecessors and contemporaries. 'Occhi miei, lo miraste' reinforces this impression, for the music and its source place him in the context of the leading Roman cantata composers of the 1670s. A glance at the two settings of 'Fileno, idolo mio' would demonstrate the stylistic differences between Melani's generation and Steffani's. In addition to melodic refinement, Steffani's 'scherzo' displays a greater command of counterpoint, a clearer sense of tonality, a sharper distinction between recitative and aria, and, paradoxically, a keen appreciation of the value of a cavata. The inclusion of pairs of instruments in his 'scherzi' enabled him, furthermore, to create many varied and satisfying structures, both in individual movements and in works as a whole. Obbligato instruments were relatively rare in Italian cantatas before the 1670s but were used increasingly frequently in those from the later Baroque period. Steffani was active during these years of transition and contributed to the development. It would be extremely difficult, on the basis of the six 'scherzi' in Modena, to argue that he made a major contribution to the genre, but we can at least be grateful for this collection of delightful miniature masterpieces.

---

[55] 'Le carte di Musica passarono in mano degli Eredi, che non ne tennero quel conto, che meritavano', in Giordano Riccati, 'Notizie di Monsig. Agostino Steffani', *Nuova raccolta d'opuscoli scientifici e filologici*, 33 (1779), 26. See also Alfred Einstein, 'Notiz über den Nachlaß Agostino Steffani's im Propaganda-Archiv zu Rom', *Zeitschrift der Internationalen Musik-Gesellschaft*, 10 (1908–9), 172–4.

Solo Cantatas and Arias Ascribed to Steffani

This appendix represents the first published attempt at a list of the secular solo cantatas and arias (with sources) ascribed or attributed to Steffani, including isolated copies of arias from operas and the arias from 'Trastulli' (Munich, Bayerische Staatsbibliothek, Mus. MS 178) that have been published under his name. It does not, however, attempt to list all the anonymous copies of arias from his larger works. The catalogue is divided into three main sections: reliable and unreliable attributions, and spurious works. The allocation of a piece to one or other of the first two sections is a matter of judgement based on the nature and provenance of the source(s) and the evidence of the music itself. When the judgement is difficult, the work is regarded as 'unreliable', this being the safer conclusion to reach. It follows, however, that the 'unreliable' category includes pieces that may well be authentic together with others that almost certainly are not.

Within each section the works are listed by genre, cantatas being separated from arias, and details of sources are repeated only when necessary. The entries for the cantatas give musical incipits (first vocal entry) and information on scoring; those for the arias do not supply such information, because isolated copies of arias often differ, in this respect, from each other or from the larger works to which the arias belong. The verbal incipits of cantatas and arias comprise one or two complete lines of verse, as appropriate; vertical strokes mark divisions between lines. Punctuation is editorial, abbreviations in the text are expanded, and orthography and capitalization are modernized; the original spelling is retained.

Libraries are cited by the following RISM *sigla*: *A-Wn*, Vienna, Österreichische Nationalbibliothek; *D-Bds*, Staatsbibliothek zu Berlin—Preußischer Kulturbesitz, Musikabteilung; *D-HVs*, Hanover, Stadtbibliothek; *D-Lr*, Lüneburg, Ratsbücherei; *D-Mbs*, Munich, Bayerische Staatsbibliothek; *D-SWl*, Schwerin, Wissenschaftliche Allgemeinbibliothek (Mecklenburgische Landesbibliothek); *F-Pn*, Paris, Bibliothèque nationale; *GB-Lbl*, London, British Library; *GB-Lam*, London, Royal Academy of Music; *GB-Lcm*, London, Royal College of Music; *GB-Lgc*, London, Gresham, College (Guildhall Library); *GB-Lwa*, London, Westminster Abbey; *GB-Ob*, Oxford, Bodleian Library; *I-MOe*, Modena, Biblioteca Estense; *I-Rc*, Rome, Biblioteca Casanatense; *US-CAh*, Cambridge, Mass., Harvard University, Houghton Library; *US-Cu*, Chicago, University of Chicago Music Library; *US-IDt*, Independence, Missouri, Harry S. Truman Presidential Library; *US-NYp*, New York, Public Library at Lincoln Center, Library and Museum of the Performing Arts. Other abbreviations in the catalogue are as follows:

A	alto
B	bass
b.c.	basso continuo

bn.	bassoon
DTB xi	*Ausgewählte Werke von Agostino Steffani (1654–1728), erster Teil*, ed. Alfred Einstein and Adolf Sandberger (Denkmäler der Tonkunst in Bayern, 11, Jg. vi/2; Leipzig: Breitkopf & Härtel, 1905)
DTB xxiii	*Ausgewählte Werke von Agostino Steffani (1654–1728), dritter Teil (zweiter Band der Opern)*, ed. Hugo Riemann (Denkmäler der Tonkunst in Bayern, 23, Jg. xii/2; Leipzig: Breitkopf & Härtel, 1912)
Garland	*Cantatas by Agostino Steffani 1654–1728*, ed. Colin Timms (The Italian Cantata in the Seventeenth Century, 15; New York and London: Garland, 1985) [facs. edn.]
MS(S)	manuscript(s)
piff.	piffero (pifferi)
rec.	recorders
S	soprano
SCMA xi	Agostino Steffani, *Eight Songs for Solo Voice, One or Two Woodwinds and Continuo*, ed. Gertrude Parker Smith (Smith College Music Archives, 11; Northampton, Mass.: Smith College, 1951)
vn.	violin(s)

I. RELIABLE ATTRIBUTIONS

A. Cantatas with instruments and continuo

1. *Fileno, idolo mio, | ove lungi da me ti stai, mio bene?* (S, 2 vn., b.c.)

Fi - le - no, i - do - lo mi - o

     Preludio
     [Recit]   Fileno, idolo mio
     [Aria]   Vieni, o sol, che solo adora
     [Aria]   Hor de l'alba i vaghi rai

Sources: I-MOe Mus. F. 1102, fos. 31ʳ–37ʳ; D-Mbs Mus. MS 5656 (copied from *I-MOe* in c.1900)
Editions: DTB xi; Garland

2. *Guardati, o core, dal dio bambin!* (S, 2 vn., b.c.)

Guar - - da - ti, guar - - da - ti

[Aria]	Guardati, o core, dal dio bambin!
[Recit]	Da quei begli occhi arcieri
[Aria]	Fugga pur l'impero
[Cavata]	Sono i frutti d'amor sospiri e doglie

Sources: I-MOe Mus. F. 1102, fos. 23ᵛ–30ᵛ; D-Mbs Mus. MS 5656
Editions: DTB xi; Garland

3. *Hai finito di lusingarmi* (S, 2 piff., b.c.)

[Aria]	Hai finito di lusingarmi
[Recit]	Più non m'abbaglia i lumi
[Aria]	Folle Amor, mendace nume
[Recit]	Così dicea Clorindo, | di Filli vezzosetta
[Aria]	Cara Filli, oh Dio, pietà!

Source: I-MOe Mus. F. 1102, fos. 45ʳ–52ᵛ
Edition: Garland

4. *Il più felice e sfortunato amante* (A, 2 vn., b.c.)

Preludio	
[Recit]	Il più felice e sfortunato amante
[Aria]	Moro, sì, ma non risolve
[Recit]	Ma s'è da un sì, da un no
[Aria]	Così dubbia e ria procella

Source: I-MOe Mus. F. 1102, fos. 16ʳ–23ʳ
Edition: Garland

5. *Lagrime dolorose, \| da gli occhi miei venite* (B, 2 rec., b.c.)

[Arioso]	Lagrime dolorose
[Recit]	E se 'l mio sole ascose
[Aria]	Occhi miei, dunque chiudetevi

[Recit]   Con si dogliosi accenti
[Cavata]   Che l'haver sempre i lumi in pianto absorti

Source: I-MOe Mus. F. 1102, fos. 37ᵛ–44ᵛ
Editions: Garland; SCMA xi (arioso only)

6. *Spezza Amor l'arco e li strali* (S, piff., bn., b.c.)

[Aria]   Spezza Amor l'arco e li strali
[Recit]   Così dicea Fileno, | che scoprir non potea del cor gli ardori
[Aria]   Zeffiretti placidetti, | che volate a' miei sospiri
[Recit]   E ragion vuol che sia
[Aria]   Fortuna crudele, | nemica d'Amore

Source: I-MOe Mus. F. 1102, fos. 1ʳ–15ᵛ
Edition: Garland

B. Cantata with continuo only

1. *Occhi miei, lo miraste* (S, b.c.)

[Recit]   Occhi miei, lo miraste
[Aria]   Ruggiada non cada (2: La spiga mendica)
Recit   E sarà vero, oh Dio, che la sua fede
[Aria]   Gelosia, va lungi da me
[Recit]   Queste due qualità non van del pari
[Cavata]   Ch'amore e gelosia son due contrari

Source: D-HVs Kestner Nachlass, vol. 76, pp. 25–60
Edition: in T. W. Werner and Alfred Einstein, 'Die Musikhandschriften des Kestnerschen Nachlasses im Stadtarchiv zu Hannover', *Zeitschrift für Musikwissenschaft*, 1 (1918–19), 441–66 at 457–66

C. Arias

1. Cara speme, se non m'inganni, D-Bds Mus. MS 21206: from *Henrico Leone* (Hanover, 1689)
2. Che folgori il cielo, GB-Lbl RM 23.f.4: from *Le rivali concordi* (Hanover, 1692)

3. Ciò che passa per veleno, *US-IDt* unnumbered MS bound in with a Walsh print of Bononcini's *Camilla*: from *La libertà contenta* (Hanover, 1693)

4. Cor amante, che farai, *F-Pn* Rés. Vma. 967: from *Orlando generoso* (Hanover, 1691)

5. Deh pietoso Amor m'addita, *F-Pn*: from *Orlando generoso*

6. I tuoi vanni, arcier volante, *US-IDt*: from *La libertà contenta*

7. La natura è troppo frale, *US-IDt*: from *La libertà contenta*

8. La sfrenata gioventù, *I-Rc* MS 2469: from *Henrico Leone*

9. La speranza come rosa, *US-IDt*: from *La superbia d'Alessandro* (Hanover, 1690)

10. La speranza tutti inganna, *F-Pn*, *US-CAh* MS 63: from *Orlando generoso*

11. Luci belle a pena viste, *D-SWl* Mus. 4725: from *I trionfi del Fato* (Hanover, 1695)

12. Ma voi, labra vezzosette, *D-Bds*: from *Henrico Leone*

13. Mi dà piacer vitale, *US-IDt*: from *I trionfi del Fato*

14. Mio cor, preparati a giubilar, *GB-Lam* MS 43: from *La libertà contenta* (Cor mio, preparati a giubilar)

15. Nume implacabile, | arcier terribile, *US-IDt*: from *Le rivali concordi*

16. Se riveggo il bell'ond'ardo, *US-IDt*: from *La libertà contenta*

17. S'ho perduto ogni mio ben, *F-Pn*: from *Orlando generoso*

18. Tenerezze, deh cessate, *GB-Lgc* G. Mus. 463: from *I trionfi del Fato*

II.   UNRELIABLE ATTRIBUTIONS

A. Cantatas

1. *Alle lacrime, homai, occhi lucenti* (A, b.c.)

Al – le   la - cri - me,   al – – le la – cri - me, ho - mai

[Recit]	Alle lacrime, homai, occhi lucenti
[Aria]	Mia bella crudele,	costante, fedele
[Recit]	O Filli amata, o adorata Filli
[Aria] ·	E l'idea del mio ben

Source: *GB-Lgc* G. mus. 463, pp. 12–17 ('Stephano')

2. *All'or ch'in grembo all'ombre* (A, 2 vn., b.c.)

Al - l'or   ch'in   grem - bo al - l'om   -   bre

Sinfonia
Recit   All'or ch'in grembo all'ombre
Aria   Ombre care, amichi orrori
Recit   Ma hoime [*sic*] ch'i cieli ancora
[Aria]   Se d'esser sordi, o cieli
Recit   Dunque il ciel d'un bel volto
Aria   Se tormento t'apporto l'amarti
Recit   Godi, dunque, spietata
Arioso   Che d'altro non è reo se non d'amore

Source: GB-*Lcm* MS 1026, fos. 1ʳ–6ᵛ ('Stephani')

3. *Desiava gioire* | *sotto riche cortine* (S, b.c.)

[Recit]   Desiava gioire
[Aria]   Cessate di ferirmi
[Recit]   Ma voi, fieri e spietati
[Aria]   Vezzose pupille, | di vostre faville

Sources: F-*Pn* Rés. Vma. 967, fos. 128ʳ–130ʳ; GB-*Lgc* G. Mus. 463, pp. 18–23
('Stephano'); *Lwa* C. G. 63, pp. 286–90 ('Stephano'). 'Vezzose pupille' only: *Lbl* Add.
MS 22099, fo. 78ʳ (unascribed); US-*Cu* MS f. 442, pp. 177–8

4. *O martirio d'amor, che mi trafiggi!* (S, b.c.)

[Arioso]   O martirio d'amor, che mi trafiggi!
[Arioso]   Giesù mio, se non sai che t'ami tanto
[Arioso]   Io so ben, che per me tanto penasti

Sources: A-*Wn* MS 17763, fos. 27ʳ–36ᵛ (Giovanni Maria Pagliardi); GB-*Lgc* G. Mus. 463,
pp. 1–4 ('Stephano'); *Lwa* C. G. 63, pp. 281–4 ('Stephano')

5. *Piange la bella Clori, e del suo pianto* (S, b.c.)

[Recit]   Piange la bella Clori, e del suo pianto
[Aria]   Pupillette care, care, | non piangete, io v'amerò
[Arioso]   Ma se poi | vi diletta il pianger tanto

Source: US-IDt unnumbered MS bound in with a Walsh print of Bononcini's *Camilla*, pp. 127–32 ('Abbate Steffani')

6. *Qual subterea mole il sol lampeggia* (S, b.c.)

[Recit]   Qual subterea mole il sol lampeggia
[Arioso]   Ma che giova ch'io l'adori
[Aria]   Son di giaccio [*sic*] s'io la miro
[Recit]   Dovrò dunque soffrir si fiero ardore
[Aria]   Tacerò, soffrirò, | ne mai scoprirò l'affetto celato
[Aria]   Sembra caro l'infante Cupido

Sources: GB-Lgc G. Mus. 463, pp. 5–11 ('Stephano'). 'Sembra caro' only: *Lbl* Add. MS 22099, fo. 77ᵛ ('Bononcini'); RM 23.f.4, pp. 169–71 ('Abbate Stefano'); *Lwa* C. G. 63, pp. 284–6 ('Stephano'); US-Cu MS f. 442, pp. 175–6 ('Stephano'); NYp *Mus Res. *MN. M292, pp. 157–60 (Steffani)

7. *Va girando intorno al suolo* (S, b.c.)

[Aria]   Va girando intorno al suolo
[Recit]   Augellino gentile, | quanto al vivo m'esponi
[Aria]   In mezzo a tante pene

Source: GB-Lbl Add. MS 29963, fos. 64ʳ–67ᵛ ('Steffani')

B. Arias

1. Agitati miei pensieri, D-Mbs Mus. MS 178: from *Briseide* (Hanover, 1696), probably by Pietro Torri
2. Alma di donna | più spesso impiaga, US-IDt unnumbered MS bound in with a Walsh print of Bononcini's *Camilla* ('Steffani')
3. Ama, confida e spera, GB-Lgc G. Mus. 463 ('Stephano')
4. Chi non gode di sua lode, D-Mbs; SCMA xi
5. Colà de gli Arcadi, D-Mbs; SCMA xi
6. Con placido incanto, D-Mbs; SCMA xi

7. Dolce auretta, che si grata, *D-Mbs*, *GB-Lam* MS 24, *Lbl* RM 23.f.10 ('Stefano'); SCMA xi: from *Briseide*

8. Festeggia, mio core, *GB-Lam*, *Lbl* ('Stefano'): from *Briseide*

9. Fulminato han Furie, *GB-Lam*, *Lbl* ('Stefano'): from *Briseide*

10. Godi, giubila, alma mia, *D-Mbs*, *GB-Lam*, *Lbl* ('Stefano'): from *Briseide*

11. Hai finito a tanti guai, *D-Mbs*, *GB-Lbl* ('Stefano'): from *Briseide*

12. Il pastorello sen' giace afflitto, *D-Mbs*; SCMA xi

13. In ogni loco | d'amor il foco, *F-Pn* Rés. Vma. 967, *GB-Lgc* ('Stephono')

14. Invisibile al mio core (with recitative 'Rivolgi gl'occhi a la mia strage, o sposo'), *GB-Lam*, *Lbl* ('Stefano'): from *Briseide*

15. Le follie di donna indegna, *D-Lr* K.N. 207/10 Nr. 7 (Steffani): from *Briseide*

16. M'influisse il nume arciero, *GB-Lgc* ('Stephano')

17. Misero core, | tu chiedi amore, *GB-Lgc* ('Stephano'): possibly the first movement of a cantata (see below, no. 21)

18. Morirai, ma l'ombra amata, *F-Pn* ('Stephani'), *GB-Lam*, *Lbl* ('Stefano'): from *Briseide*

19. Nel mio fiero penar, *D-Mbs*: from *Briseide*

20. Onde chiare, | imparate a non amare, *D-Mbs*; DTB xxiii: from *Briseide*

21. Per lusinghe, vezzi e pianti (with recitative 'Non vivo che ti disperi'), *GB-Lgc*: possibly the second and third movements of a cantata (see above, no. 17)

22. Quando venne nel mio core, *D-Mbs*, *GB-Lam*, *Lbl* ('Stefano'): from *Briseide*

23. Rendetemi al mio ben, *D-Mbs*, *F-Pn* ('Stephani'), *GB-Lbl* ('Stefano'): from *Briseide*

24. Securo che m'amate, *GB-Lam* MS 43

25. Se non piange afflitto un seno, *GB-Lgc* ('Stephano')

26. Una volta al fin saziatevi, *F-Pn* ('Stephani'), *GB-Lam* MS 24, *Lbl* ('Stefano'); DTB xxiii: from *Briseide*

27. Un core, o piante, o sassi, *D-Mbs*; SCMA xi: from *Briseide*

28. Vaghi rai del sol ch'adoro, *GB-Lam* MS 43

29. Vieni, o bella speranza cara, *A-Wn* MS 17767: from *Briseide*

30. Vieni, o cara amata sposa, *D-Mbs*, *F-Pn*; DTB xxiii; SCMA xi: from *Briseide*

31. Vuoi saper perchè nel core, *D-SWl* Mus. 4725 ('Steffani'): possibly the first movement of a cantata (lost)

III. SPURIOUS WORKS

A. Cantata

1. *Bei crini d'oro* (S, b.c.)

Bei cri - ni,   bei   cri - ni,   bei cri - ni d'o - ro

[Aria]   Bei crini d'oro

[Recit]   Bionde chiome, ch'ornate

[Aria]   L'empio arciero acceso dardo

Sources: GB-*Lgc* G. Mus. 463, pp. [114]–[118] ('Stephano') and many others

Edition: *Cantatas by Giovanni Bononcini 1670–1747*, ed. Lowell Lindgren (The Italian Cantata in the Seventeenth Century, 10; New York: Garland, 1985), 126–9

B. Aria

1. Amor porta le pene, GB-*Lbl* Add. MSS 22099 ('Stephano') and 31816 (lacking words; 'Steffani'), Eg. 2961 ('Sabatini'), L*wa* C. G. 63 ('Sabattina'), *Ob* Mus. Sch. E.389 (unascribed). Composed by Bernardo Sabadini for his opera *L'Eusonia* (Rome, 1697)

INDEX

Folle Amor, mendace nume I. A. 3
Fortuna crudele, | nemica d'Amore I.
   A. 6
Fugga pur l'impero I. A. 2
Fulminato han Furie II. B. 9

Gelosia, va lungi da me I. B. 1
Giesù, se non sai che t'ami tanto II.
   A. 4
Godi, dunque, spietata II. A. 2
Godi, giubila, alma mia II. B. 10
Guardati, o core, dal dio bambin! I.
   A. 2

Hai finito a tanti guai II. B. 11
Hai finito di lusingarmi I. A. 3
Hor de l'alba i vaghi rai I. A. 1

Il pastorello sen' giace afflitto II. B. 12
Il più felice e sfortunato amante I. A.
   4
In mezzo a tante pene II. A. 7
In ogni loco | d'amor il foco II. B. 13
Invisibile al mio core II. B. 14
Io so ben, che per me tanto penasti II.
   A. 4
I tuoi vanni, arcier volante I. C. 6

Lagrime dolorose, | da gli occhi miei
   venite I. A. 5
La natura è troppo frale I. C. 7
La sfrenata gioventù I. C. 8
La speranza come rosa I. C. 9
La speranza tutti inganna I. C. 10
La spiga mendica I. B. 1
Le follie di donna indegna II. B. 15
L'empio arcier acceso dardo III. A. 1
Luci belle a pena viste I. C. 11

Ma che giova ch'io l'adori II. A. 6
Ma hoimè ch'i cieli ancora II. A. 2
Ma s'è da un sì, da un no I. A. 4
Ma se poi | vi diletta il pianger tanto
   II. A. 5
Ma voi, fieri e spietati II. A. 3
Ma voi, labra vezzosette I. C. 12
Mia bella crudele, | costante, fedele II.
   A. 1

Mi dà piacer vitale I. C. 13
M'influisse il nume arciero II. B. 16
Mio cor, preparati a giubilar I. C. 14
Misero core, | tu chiedi amore II. B.
   17
Morirai, ma l'ombra amata II. B. 18
Moro, sì, ma non risolve I. A. 4

Nel mio fiero penar II. B. 19
Non vivo che ti disperi II. B. 21
Nume implacabile, | arcier terribile I.
   C. 15

Occhi miei, dunque chiudetevi I. A. 5
Occhi miei, lo miraste I. B. 1
O Filli amata, o adorata Filli II. A. 1
O martirio d'amor, che mi trafiggi! II.
   A. 4
Ombre care, amichi orrori II. A. 2
Onde chiare, | imparate a non amare
   II. B. 20

Per lusinghe, vezzi e pianti II. B. 21
Piange la bella Clori, e del suo pianto
   II. A. 5
Più non m'abbaglia i lumi I. A. 3
Pupillette care, care, | non piangete, io
   v'amerò II. A. 5

Qual subterea mole il sol lampeggia II.
   A. 6
Quando venne nel mio core II. B. 22
Queste due qualità non van del pari I.
   B. 1

Rendetemi al mio ben II. B. 23
Rivolgi gl'occhi a la mia strage, o
   sposo II. B. 14
Ruggiada non cada I. B. 1

Securo che m'amate II. B. 24
Se d'esser sordi, o cieli II. A. 2
Sembra caro l'infante Cupido II. A. 6
Se non piange afflitto un seno II. B.
   25
Se riveggo il bell'ond'ardo I. C. 16
Se tormento t'apporto l'amarti II. A. 2
S'ho perduto ogni mio ben I. C. 17

Son di giaccio s'io la miro II. A. 6
Sono i frutti d'amor sospiri e doglie I.
  A. 2
Spezza Amor l'arco e li strali I. A. 6

Tacerò, soffrirò, | ne mai scoprirò
  l'affetto celato II. A. 6
Tenerezze, deh cessate I. C. 18

Una volta al fin saziatevi II. B. 26
Un core, o piante, o sassi II. B. 27

Vaghi rai del sol ch'adora II. B. 28
Va girando intorno al suolo II. A. 7
Vezzose pupille, | di vostre faville II.
  A. 3
Vieni, o bella speranza cara II. B. 29
Vieni, o cara amata sposa II. B. 30
Vieni, o sol, che solo adora I. A. 1
Vuoi saper perchè nel core II. B. 31

Zeffiretti placidetti, | che volate a' miei
  sospiri I. A. 6

10

Tomaso Albinoni's *Pimpinone*
and the Comic Intermezzo

✒

MICHAEL TALBOT

THE *Pimpinone* of Tomaso Albinoni (1671–1751) belongs to a distinct group of some twenty sets of comic intermezzi written for the Venetian stage in the period 1706–9.[1] These short dramatic works, which pioneered an important new genre, included several that, like *Pimpinone*, immediately became repertory favourites performed year after year all over Italy and beyond. If *Pimpinone* is today somewhat better known than its companion pieces in the early intermezzo repertory, such as the intermezzi for the characters Lisetta and Astrobolo, or Pollastrella and Parpagnacco, or Palandrana and Zamberlucco, the main reason is probably that the publication, in 1936, of a modern edition of Telemann's later setting (1725) of the same libretto, slightly adapted and partly translated into German, stimulated curiosity about the original setting and its possible relation to Telemann's music.[2] Such speculation was eventually ended when a score of Albinoni's setting was tracked down and found to contain entirely different music (the very difference, of course, provoked further study directed towards a comparison of the two settings). But there was a separate and partly fortuitous reason why Albinoni's *Pimpinone* was singled out: it happens to be one of the very few sets of comic intermezzi from the first decade of the eighteenth century for

This essay is based on a paper entitled 'Il "Pimpinone" di Albinoni da Venezia a Napoli' read to the conference 'Il teatro musicale a Venezia e a Napoli nel Settecento' (Venice, 1985). I am grateful to Paul Everett for his helpful criticism of my revised manuscript.

---

[1] See Table 3 in Charles E. Troy, *The Comic Intermezzo* (Ann Arbor: UMI Research Press, 1979), 36–7. By a 'set' of intermezzi I mean the group of two or more intermezzi making up a single work. I regard as illogical, unhistorical, and potentially misleading the common modern use of the singular form, 'intermezzo', to refer to the whole composition (except in a purely generic sense, as in Troy's title) rather than to just one of its constituent portions.

[2] Georg Philipp Telemann, *Pimpinone*, ed. Theodor W. Werner (Das Erbe deutscher Musik, 1/vi; Mainz: Schott, 1936).

which the music survives and, additionally, where the identity of both librettist and composer is known for certain. The existence of these points of reference means that the original *Pimpinone* is a relatively easy work to place in literary and musical perspectives, especially since Albinoni and his librettist Pietro Pariati are figures already familiar from the scholarly literature. Almost by default, therefore, *Pimpinone* has become 'the' representative work of the Venetian comic intermezzo in the genre's earliest phase. In broad terms, this status is justified, but one must also bear in mind that in his intermezzi, as in his operas in general, Albinoni is a highly individual composer whose idiosyncrasies other prominent composers of early intermezzi such as Francesco Gasparini and Antonio Lotti do not share; similarly, Pariati's penchant for satire as distinct from farce—a preference that looks forward to the 'classic' phase of the comic intermezzo as represented by Gennaro Antonio Federico's text for Pergolesi's *La serva padrona*—is unusual for its time. One is grateful for these distinguishing characteristics, for the early Venetian comic intermezzo often seems colourless and lacking in finesse when set against Neapolitan *scene buffe* of the same period, not to mention the later, stylistically more complex works in the same genre by such composers as Giuseppe Maria Orlandini, Pergolesi, and Telemann.

Pariati's contribution to *Pimpinone* has been discussed, in the context of its adaptation by Johann Philipp Praetorius for Telemann's setting, by several writers, including Hellmuth Christian Wolff and Reinhard Strohm.[3] The non-musical aspects of *Pimpinone* also receive attention in general studies of the comic intermezzo by Gordana Lazarevich, Irène Mamczarz, Ortrun Landmann, and Charles Troy, as well as in a recent essay by Strohm.[4] However, there are fewer discussions informed by a knowledge of the music, despite the fact that as early as 1925 Robert Haas noted the existence of a score in the Österreichische Nationalbibliothek, Vienna.[5] A later study by Wolff compares Albinoni's and Telemann's settings, and my own *Albinoni: Leben und Werk* and *Tomaso Albinoni: The Venetian Composer and his World*

---

[3] Hellmuth Christian Wolff, *Die Barockoper in Hamburg (1678–1738)* (Wolfenbüttel: Möseler Verlag, 1957), i. 115–18, 332–5; Reinhard Strohm, *Die italienische Oper im 18. Jahrhundert* (Wilhelmshaven: Heinrichshofen, 1979), 120–4.

[4] Gordana Lazarevich, 'The Role of the Neapolitan Intermezzo in the Evolution of Eighteenth-Century Musical Style: Literary, Symphonic and Dramatic Aspects 1685–1735' (Ph.D. diss., Columbia University, 1970), 153, 271, 349 n., 350, 375; Irène Mamczarz, *Les Intermèdes comiques italiens au XVIIIe siècle en France et en Italie* (Paris: CRNS, 1972), 53, 97, 213; Ortrun Landmann, *Quellenstudien zum Intermezzo comico per musica und zu seiner Geschichte in Dresden* (diss., University of Rostock, 1972), 180–97; Troy, *The Comic Intermezzo*, 82; Reinhard Strohm, 'Pietro Pariati librettista comico', in Giovanna Gronda (ed.), *La carriera di un librettista: Pietro Pariati da Reggio di Lombardia* (Bologna: Il Mulino, 1990), 73–111.

[5] Robert Haas, 'Die Musik in der Wiener Stegreifkomödie', *Studien zur Musikwissenschaft*, 12 (1925), 3–64 at 5.

deal with *Pimpinone* briefly in the context of Albinoni's operas as a whole.[6] A more extensive commentary is contained, however, in my preface to a critical edition of the intermezzi published in 1983.[7]

Needless to say, the present essay draws heavily on that preface. But I have tried to pay special attention to aspects relating to a production of *Pimpinone* in Naples in 1709—aspects that bring out the difference between Venetian and Neapolitan operatic practice at that time—and to develop more fully than before some observations on the way in which *Pimpinone*, in the company of a handful of other intermezzi, existed for many years as a repertory work in the modern sense. Finally, I shall discuss at greater length the style of Albinoni's music for *Pimpinone*.

The comic intermezzo arose at the beginning of the eighteenth century from the confluence of two distinct elements well established in opera of the previous century: the *intermedio* (or *intermezzo*) and the comic scene. The idea of inserting successive portions of one sectional work into the interstices of another was a favourite Baroque constructional principle that was not limited to vocal or dramatic music. Albinoni's own *Baletti e sonate a tre*, op. 8 (1722), intercalate chamber sonatas (the *baletti*) among church sonatas of a more contrapuntal character, an arrangement that the composer likens in his preface to the relationship of comic intermezzi and opera: 'E perche conobbi che il passare da un Canone all'altro poteva forse dar un po di noia a riguardo dello stesso Metodo presi espediente d'intrecciare doppo di ciaschuno d'essi Canoni qualche altro Componimento di gusto e stile diverso, come appunto trà gl'atti delle Tragedie si frameschiono [*sic*] gl'Intermezzi' ('And because I knew that passing [directly] from one canon to the next risked becoming a little boring on account of the sameness of technique, I adopted the expedient of inserting after each of these canons some other compositions in a different style and taste, exactly as intermezzi are intercalated between the acts of tragedies'). In seventeenth-century opera such contrasting *intermedi*, though always lighter in tone, are not necessarily comic. However, opera in this period often admitted comic characters who, in addition to their interaction with the principals, were given comic monologues and dialogues forming distinct scenes. The reforms introduced at the beginning

---

[6] Hellmuth Christian Wolff, '*Pimpinone* von Albinoni und Telemann—ein Vergleich', *Hamburger Jahrbuch für Musikwissenschaft*, 5 (1981), 29–36; Michael Talbot, *Albinoni: Leben und Werk* (Adliswil: Kunzelmann, 1980), 165–6; id., *Tomaso Albinoni: The Venetian Composer and his World* (Oxford: Clarendon Press, 1990), 222–6.

[7] Tomaso Albinoni, *Pimpinone: intermezzi comici musicali*, ed. Michael Talbot (Recent Researches in the Music of the Baroque Era, 43; Madison, Wis.: A-R Editions, 1983). The preface contains, as an appendix, a catalogue of productions of *Pimpinone* that lists the locations of extant musical and literary sources and provides transcriptions of the title-pages of librettos.

of the eighteenth century and associated with the circle around Apostolo
Zeno purged *opera seria* of the comic element. But since the public and also
the singers specializing in comic roles did not wish to be deprived of them,
the former comic scenes, now termed 'intermezzi', were removed to conventional points in the host work where they would encroach least on the
main action. Their preferred position was between acts. However, when
there were three intermezzi, as in *Pimpinone* and most sets of intermezzi
contemporary with it, obviously they could not all occupy an entr'acte
position in a three-act opera: in such cases, the normal solution was to place
Intermezzi I and II after Acts I and II respectively, and to insert Intermezzo
III somewhere around the middle of Act III.

Most sets of intermezzi present a unified scenario. In this respect a single
comic intermezzo, though corresponding in structure and duration to an
enlarged operatic scene, functions dramatically as one act of a larger work.
Although the characters of comic intermezzi were only rarely related to those
of the opera with which they were performed—an important development
that allowed any set of intermezzi to be presented alongside any opera, and
also allowed them to have a contemporary subject without any incongruity
—the stereotypes of the old-style *scene buffe* persisted. In particular, the two-
actor combination of the *paggio* and *vecchia* or (reversing the age-relationship)
the *servetta* and *vecchio* proved durable, as *Pimpinone* demonstrates. It must be
emphasized that the singers who performed the first comic intermezzi were
the same as those who had earlier specialized—and, where local practice
permitted, were still specializing—in *scene buffe*, and that public taste in the
comic sphere underwent no sea change as a result of the reform of opera.
Dramatically and stylistically, the comic intermezzo makes no clean break
with the *scena buffa* tradition.

The literary texts of the first Venetian intermezzi were not printed and
cannot, therefore, have circulated very widely. It soon came to the notice
of the censors that alterations were being made in performance to intermezzo texts previously approved; to prevent this abuse, they decreed on 1
October 1707 that the texts of comic intermezzi were to be printed in the
same way as opera texts.[8] One doubtless unintended effect of this ruling was
to raise the level of interest in the new genre among bibliophiles. Bonlini's
opera catalogue, admittedly, rejects comic intermezzi disdainfully and contains a short essay justifying their exclusion.[9] However, the publisher Antonio
Groppo included them in his manuscript 'master-catalogue', and a statement
in his better-known printed opera catalogue indicates that he intended to

---

[8] Venice, Museo Civico Correr, MS P. D. 348, fo. 23[r].
[9] *Le glorie della poesia e della musica* (Venice: Buonarrigo, [1730]), 149–50.

issue a separate catalogue of intermezzi (although none is known today).[10] The catalogue by the continuers of Allacci lists a good number of them.[11] In most cases, the librettos of early comic intermezzi were published without any indication of authorship, probably because the low literary status of the genre in its early years made the authors fear for their reputations. But as time went on and the genre became more firmly entrenched, anonymity became less common.

We know for certain that Pietro Pariati (1665–1733) was the librettist of *Pimpinone* only because he revived it, to accompany his drama *Sesostri*, in 1717 at the Viennese court (where he served as *Kaiserlicher Kammerdichter*); for this production the text was slightly adapted (the character Vespetta is renamed Grilletta) and given an entirely new musical setting by Francesco Conti, who also wrote the music for *Sesostri*. The title-page of the combined libretto was possibly the source from which the revised *Drammaturgia di Lione Allacci* derived its information on the authorship of the original *Pimpinone* text.[12] It remains significant, however, that none of the literary or musical sources associated with the original setting by Albinoni identifies Pariati as the author.

Until recently there has been only one full-length study of this important literary figure's life and works: Naborre Campanini's *Un precursore del Metastasio* (Florence: Sansoni, 1904). Campanini lists four librettos of *Pimpinone* in his appended bibliography but fails to discuss the work. This is particularly unfortunate, since Pariati's gift for comic writing seen in the *tragicommedie* of his Viennese period must have been sharpened by his earlier experiences as a writer of comic intermezzi. Although one suspects that he was the anonymous author of several other sets of Venetian intermezzi contemporary with *Pimpinone*, no confirmation exists: such attributions as have been made to him (e.g. for the intermezzi of Pollastrella and Parpagnacco first performed at the Teatro S. Cassiano in 1708 with *Flavio Anicio Olibrio*) seem to lack supporting evidence.[13]

---

[10] Antonio Groppo, *Catalogo purgatissimo di tutti i drammi per musica recitatisi ne' teatri di Venezia dall'anno MDCXXXVII sin oggi*, in Venice, Biblioteca Nazionale Marciana, MS It. VII. 2326 (= 8263), 1741–67; id., *Catalogo di tutti i drammi per musica* (Venice: Groppo, 1745), 8.

[11] *Drammaturgia di Lione Allacci accresciuta e continuata fino all'anno MDCCLV* (Venice: Pasquali, 1755).

[12] Ibid., col. 629.

[13] Lazarevich, 'The Role of the Neapolitan Intermezzo', 350; Mamczarz, *Les Intermèdes comiques italiens*, 449. Strohm goes so far as to argue that the authorship of no fewer than six of the early Venetian sets of intermezzi besides *Pimpinone* can be attributed, with varying degrees of probability, to Pariati ('Pietro Pariati librettista comico', 82–6). I find his line of reasoning unconvincing in the final analysis, since it relies entirely on general propositions that cannot be assumed to apply to particular cases.

The confirmation of Albinoni's authorship of the original music for *Pimpinone* is, surprisingly, more problematic. The composer is not cited either in the libretto of the original production at the Teatro S. Cassiano in autumn 1708 or in any of the subsequent librettos that (for reasons given below) we are able to associate with the same musical setting. Groppo and Allacci are similarly silent. Even the scores of *Pimpinone* preserved in Vienna and Münster lack an attribution, although the separate parts in Schwerin for the opening aria of Intermezzo I, 'Chi mi vuol? Son cameriera', are marked 'dell'opera Sign. Albinoni'.[14] Given the rigorous distinction between 'opera' and 'intermezzo' observed in this period, the inscription is likely to mean merely that this aria and its intermezzo were inserted into an Albinoni opera. It so happens that one of the eight other Albinoni arias in the Schwerin source is 'Stelle ingrate' from his *L'Astarto* (I. ix), with which *Pimpinone* was originally performed. But this fact, possibly coincidental, brings one no closer to discovering who wrote the music for *Pimpinone*.

Several writers have stated or tacitly assumed that the composer of the opera for which a set of intermezzi was originally written was normally also the one responsible for the intermezzi themselves. What little independent evidence there is supports this observation at the level of a generalization. But it obviously cannot be used to establish authorship conclusively in individual cases. Moreover, one must bear in mind that the generalization holds only for cases where both the opera and the intermezzi were newly composed. Failure to recognize this simple point has resulted in some entirely arbitrary attributions for later productions of *Pimpinone*. Thus the music for the 1711 production at the Ruspoli private theatre in Rome has been credited to Antonio Caldara, who composed the opera, despite the evidence of the Münster score prepared for Ruspoli: this has exactly the same music as the Vienna score derived from the 1709 production in Naples, with which Caldara was unconnected.[15] The music for the 1725 production in Venice, accompanying Giuseppe Maria Buini's *Li sdegni cangiati in amore*, has, through a curious additional error, been attributed to Marc'Antonio Ziani, who set an earlier version of this opera's libretto;[16] and the same Buini has been made the composer of the score used in Bologna in 1728, where it partnered his *Il Malmocor*.[17] To complete this picture of confusion, one must mention that

[14] Vienna, Österreichische Nationalbibliothek, MS 18057; Münster, Santini-Bibliothek, MS 798a; Schwerin, Wissenschaftliche Allgemeinbibliothek (Mecklenburgische Landesbibliothek), Mus. 4721.

[15] See Mamczarz, *Les Intermèdes comiques italiens*, 205, 509; Ursula and Warren Kirkendale, 'Caldara, Antonio', in *Dizionario biografico degli italiani*, xvi (Rome: Istituto della Enciclopedia Italiana, 1973), 563.

[16] Mamczarz, *Les Intermèdes comiques italiens*, 290, 454.   [17] Ibid. 195, 454, 517.

the music for the original 1708 production has been attributed to Gasparini,[18] and that of the 1740 production in Ljubljana (Laibach) to Buini.[19] This is not to say that the texts of comic intermezzi were never set to new music—the versions of *Pimpinone* by Conti and Telemann prove the reverse—but it is clear that the revival of intermezzi with different operas by different composers did not of itself necessarily generate new settings.

On what grounds, then, can the original *Pimpinone* be attributed to Albinoni? Beyond the circumstantial evidence of its first performance with *L'Astarto* there remains only the evidence of style. But since, as I have already said, Albinoni's musical language is highly individual, one can be bolder than usual in arguing for authorship by reference to stylistic criteria. Fortunately, two dramatic works by Albinoni from the same period survive: the first three acts of *Engelberta* (Gasparini supplied the last two) performed at the Teatro S. Cassiano in Carnival 1709, and the serenata *Il nascimento de l'Aurora* (c.1710). Both works offer a valid comparison with *Pimpinone*, if allowance is made for the peculiarities of the intermezzo style.

I shall return to the music of *Pimpinone* below. First, however, the background to its frequent revival needs to be examined. If we exclude Conti's setting of 1717 and its revivals in Brunswick in 1720 and 1731, as well as Telemann's setting of 1725 and its revival of 1730, there remain twenty-six productions for which the original music is known to have been used or may have been used (see Table I). The frequent revival of *Pimpinone* would not have been possible if its musical material—the prerequisite for any production—had not circulated in a manner radically different from that of operas. After the production of an opera, the one or more scores (excepting those specially copied out for collectors or for presentation to a patron) remained in the possession of the impresario or the composer (sometimes the same person, as we know from Vivaldi's case). Consequently, the initiative for a revival normally came from one of those two quarters rather than from singers, who had no access to the complete musical material. Since the recruitment of a cast was not usually carried out with the precise requirements of a pre-existing score in mind, most revivals entailed the recomposition of certain sections to take account of changed vocal ranges, different capabilities, additional singers, and similar factors. In these conditions, operas could only exceptionally become repertory works in the modern sense, capable of revival without significant alteration.

With comic intermezzi, however, the performing material remained in the hands of the singers themselves, to whom responsibility for the performance

[18] Lazarevich, 'The Role of the Neapolitan Intermezzo', 153, 349 n., 350, 376.
[19] Dragotin Cvetko, *Musikgeschichte der Südslawen* (Kassel and Ljubljana: Bärenreiter and Založba obzorja, 1975), 86.

TABLE I. *The productions and casting of Albinoni's Pimpinone*

Year and Season	City and Theatre	Host Work	Vespetta	Pimpinone
1708, aut.	Venice, S. Cassiano	*L'Astarto* (Albinoni)	Santa Marchesini	Giovanni Battista Cavana
1709, car.	Venice, S. Cassiano	*Il falso Tiberino* (Pollarolo)	Santa Marchesini	Giovanni Battista Cavana
1709, win.	Naples, Royal Palace	*Engelberta* (Orefici–Mancini)	Santa Marchesini?	Giovanni Battista Cavana?
1709	Libretto pub. in Milan[a]			
1711, car.	Rome, Ruspoli theatre	*La costanza in amore vince l'inganno* (Caldara)	Annibale Pio Fabbri	Giovanni Battista Cavana
1711, May	Ferrara, S. Stefano	*La fede tradita e vendicata* (Gasparini)	Rosa Ungarelli	Giovanni Battista Cavana
1712, May	Vicenza, Grazie	*Peribea in Salamina* (Pollarolo)	Santa Marchesini	Giovanni Battista Cavana
1713, car.	Florence, Cocomero	*Il tiranno eroe* (Albinoni?)	Anna Maria Bianchi	Filippo Rossi
1713	Forlì	*La Giuditta di Baviera* (Orlandini)	Rosa Ungarelli	Francesco Bernasconi
1714, car.	Parma, Ducale	*La fede nei tradimenti*	Rosa Ungarelli	Angelo Cantelli
1715	Udine, Mantica	unknown	unknown	unknown
1716, car.	Turin, Carignano	*Arideno* (Fiorè)	Rosa Ungarelli	Antonio Ristorini
1717, spr.	Bologna, Formagliari	*Lucio Vero* (Perti?)	Rosa Ungarelli	Antonio Ristorini
1718	Florence, Pergola	unknown	Rosa Ungarelli?	Antonio Ristorini
1718	Fano, Fortuna	*Il tradimento traditor di sé stesso* (Lotti?)	Giovanni Battista Perugini	Domenico Manzi
1722, Oct.	Munich, Court	*I veri amici* (Albinoni)	Rosa Ungarelli	Antonio Ristorini
1723, car.	Pesaro, Sole	unknown	unknown	unknown
1724, car.	Lucca, S. Girolamo	*Lucio Papirio* (pasticcio) or *Rodelinda* (Canuti)	Maria Giovanni Pioli	Pietro Pertici
1724, spr.	Parma, Court	*Il Venceslao* (Capelli)	Rosa Ungarelli	Antonio Ristorini
1725, car.	Venice, S. Moisè	*Li sdegni cangiati in amore* (Buini)	unknown	unknown
1725, aut.[b]	S. Giovanni in Persiceto, Accademici Candidi Uniti	unknown	Antonia Bertelli	Pellegrino Gaggiotti
1728, car.[b]	Bologna, Marsigli Rossi	*Il Malmocor* (Buini)	Maria Penna	Pellegrino Gaggiotti
1728, aut.	Brussels, Monnaie	*Griselda* (Orlandini)	Rosa Ungarelli	Antonio Ristorini
1731, Mar.–Apr.	Moscow, Court	*Le cocu imaginaire* and *L'amant trahi* (spoken comedies)	Margherita Ermini	Cosimo Ermini
1740, car.	Ljubljana, Provincial Palace	*Artaserse* or *Rosmira* (both Hasse)	Antonia Bertelli	Giovanni Michieli

[a] Possibly a purely 'literary' libretto not connected with any staged performance.
[b] Titled *La serva astuta*.

was subcontracted, as it were. Once the small team of comic singers, ordinarily only two or three, had been engaged, it would have some latitude in deciding which pieces from its repertory to perform. Understandably, this repertory was conservative, relying heavily on tried and tested favourites. Once a given set of comic intermezzi had entered the repertory of such a team (in the case of *Pimpinone*, a contralto and a bass), there was rarely an overriding reason to alter the music drastically for a new performance. True, individual arias and ensembles could be added, subtracted, and replaced in the course of time, as we shall see; but the recitative, constituting the bulk of the work, offered little margin for improvement and remained substantially the same. Entirely new settings of an old libretto, such as those produced for *Pimpinone* by Conti and Telemann, are associated with a break in the performing tradition where singers were learning the lines for the first time.

The central core of the performing tradition of *Pimpinone* is formed by two pairs of singers: Santa Marchesini and Giovanni Battista Cavana, through whom it was first put into circulation, and Rosa Ungarelli and Antonio Ristorini, whose tours brought it north of the Alps. The 1711 production in Ferrara is a crucial link between the two pairs, suggesting how Ungarelli acquired the music from Cavana, subsequently passing it on to Ristorini. Charles Troy, who provides valuable information on the careers of all four singers, notes that after 1709 Marchesini remained most of the time in Naples, while Cavana continued to tour widely (exceptionally, the two linked up again for tours in 1712 and 1716–18).[20] This obliged Cavana to introduce his repertory to other partners, so beginning the fragmentation— but also the wider diffusion—of the performing tradition. The 1711 production at the Ruspoli theatre presented a particular problem in view of the papal interdict on female singers; it was solved by giving the role of Vespetta to the young Annibale Pio Fabbri (1697–1760), whose voice had evidently not yet broken. For the reasons outlined above, it is likely that all the productions involving one or more of the singers Marchesini, Cavana, Fabbri, Ungarelli, Cantelli, Bernasconi, and Ristorini used Albinoni's music except in the case of additional or substituted numbers. We can at present be less sure about the other productions. For the later years, we can identify another cluster of singers who probably sang a common version: Bertelli, Gaggiotti, Penna, and Michieli. But there is no evidence so far that any of these teamed up with singers in the first group.

The printed librettos of *Pimpinone*, which survive for most of the productions listed in Table I, offer further clues to the evolution of the performing

[20] Troy, *The Comic Intermezzo*, 48.

tradition. The derivation of each printed text is not always easy to establish, since so many different factors may come into play. The text printed in 1708 differs considerably in minor details from that set by Albinoni (not counting other modifications stemming from the composer himself);[21] it was presumably revised by Pariati before publication. The 1708 published text was reproduced closely (but with an extra aria for Pimpinone in Intermezzo I, 'La favorita | Di Pimpinon') both in the libretto printed in Milan in 1709 and, more unexpectedly, in the libretto for the 1712 production in Vicenza. These are librettos that maintain a purely literary tradition.[22] On the other hand, in the early years after 1708 a form of text corresponding closely to that supplied to Albinoni probably travelled around in manuscript with the singers, serving as the copy-text for several of the printed librettos; the 1711 libretto for Rome seems to be the one closest to the archetype, since the 1709 libretto for Naples contains a few unique and puzzling deviations. As printed librettos multiplied, they came increasingly to be used as copy-texts for further librettos; that of the second Parma production (1724) follows that of the first (1714) closely, and the two librettos for Bologna (1717 and 1728) are similarly related. To complicate matters, editors or printers had their own ideas about orthography and sometimes retouched the text after their own taste; in the 1718 libretto for Florence—the most radical such case—the letter E is supplied wherever possible to the end of infinitives that lack it. It is instructive to list, in diplomatic transcription, the various forms of line 53 (Intermezzo I) found in the two extant musical scores and seventeen of the librettos (see Table II).

These readings for just one line out of more than 280 already point to some of the relationships that a wider examination confirms. But while most of the variants are capable of explanation through literary source-criticism alone without reference to changes in the sung text as it evolved over the same period, an exception must be made for alterations to the words of arias and duets, which were usually, but not invariably, reflected in the libretto for the same production. As the Milan libretto shows, even at an early stage there was felt to be an imbalance between the first intermezzo, with only one aria, and the remaining two, each with a pair of arias. Most librettos after 1715 have an extra aria for Pimpinone ('Ella mi vuol confondere') inserted after line 58, which removes the imbalance.[23] After 1716 many

---

[21] e.g. line 245 in the Vienna score reads 'Non si può! Quella roba è mia', whereas the full, metrically correct form given in the libretto is 'Non si può! Quella roba è roba mia.'

[22] However, the tradition spread to musical sources when the text, adapted (one presumes by Pariati himself) at certain points, was set by Conti in 1717. The score of this setting is preserved in Vienna, Österreichische Nationalbibliothek, MS 17120, and Vienna, Gesellschaft der Musikfreunde, Q1205.

[23] The libretto of 1715 for Udine is the first of those known to include the new aria.

TABLE II. *Readings of line 53 in Intermezzo I*

Year	City	Source	Reading
1708	Venice	lib.	Buona cosa è'l servir un'uomo, e solo.
1709	Milan	lib.	Buona cosa è'l servir un'uomo, e solo.
1709	Naples	score	buona Cosa è'l servir un huomo, e solo.
1709	Naples	lib.	Buona cosa è'l servir un'huomo, e solo.
1711	Rome	score	buona cosa el' servir un huomo e solo.
1711	Rome	lib.	Buona cosa è'l servir un'huomo, e solo.
1711	Ferrara	lib.	Buona cosa servir un Uomo, e solo.
1712	Vicenza	lib.	Buona cosa è'l servir un'uomo, e solo.
1714	Parma	lib.	Buona cosa è il servir un Uomo solo.
1715	Udine	lib.	Buona cosa è'l servir | Un Uomo, e solo.
1716	Turin	lib.	Buona cosa, il servir un huomo, e solo.
1717	Bologna	lib.	Buona cosa è il servir' un'Uomo, e solo.
1718	Florence	lib.	Buona cosa è il servire un'Uomo, e solo,
1722	Munich	lib.	Buona cosa è il servir un Uomo solo.
1724	Parma	lib.	Buona cosa è il servir un Uomo solo.
1725	Venice	lib.	Buona cosa è il servir un'uomo, e solo.
1725	S. Giovanni in Persiceto	lib.	Buona cosa è il servir un'uomo, e solo.
1728	Bologna	lib.	Buona cosa è il servir' un'uomo, e solo.
1740	Ljubljana	lib.	Buona cosa è il servire un uomo, e solo!

librettos replace Vespetta's opening aria with a new text beginning 'Eh non giova l'esser buona' (the 1722 libretto for Munich has instead an aria beginning 'Alle volte io non vorrei'). Rather oddly, the 1725 libretto for Venice has on the one hand a strong resemblance to the 1711 libretto for Ferrara (even retaining Vespetta's opening 'Chi mi vuol? Son cameriera'), but on the other, it contains some accretions from later in that decade (including 'Ella mi vuol confondere'). At first sight, its text-form seems eclectic, hinting at a new musical setting, but another possibility is its derivation from a 'missing link' of *c.*1715 that had already added 'Ella mi vuol confondere' while not yet replacing 'Chi mi vuol? Son cameriera'. This 1725 libretto, incidentally, was the one taken by Praetorius as the basis for his adaptation of the text for Telemann.

Most intermezzo librettos were published separately from that of the host work. This makes good sense when one considers that a single set of intermezzi could serve two or more different operas within one season, while, conversely, a single opera might be accompanied during its run by more than one set of intermezzi. Also, perhaps collectors preferred opera and intermezzo librettos to be issued separately. 'Combined' librettos that insert each intermezzo into the appropriate gap in the opera text are comparatively rare; the only example for *Pimpinone* is the libretto printed for the guests invited by Ruspoli to see *La costanza in amore vince l'inganno*.[24] A compromise arrangement, where the intermezzi occupy a separate gathering at the end of the opera but share its pagination and binding, is more common for private (including court) theatres; this happens with *Engelberta* (1709, Naples) and *I veri amici* (1722, Munich). What is particularly interesting about the *Engelberta–Pimpinone* libretto—and also about an alternative form of that libretto (held by the Library of Congress in Washington) which has the intermezzi *Melissa schernita* in place of *Pimpinone*—is that the intermezzi are not simply dissolved into the opera as quasi-comic scenes *alla napolitana*, a fate suffered by the version of the intermezzi for Lisetta and Astrobolo that Marchesini and Cavana performed in Naples during the same season; in the latter case, Lazarevich informs us that 'the four intermezzi were converted into five comic scenes, and the comic characters were reintroduced into the accompanying opera, *Astarto*'.[25] One senses in the Neapolitan production of *Pimpinone* a certain mismatch between what the local public were used to and expected from Marchesini and Cavana (who, although not locally born, had both made their careers in Naples) and what the two comic singers, fresh from their Venetian experience, wished to provide. *Pimpinone*, which satirizes contemporary Italian life and fashion, could not conceivably be merged with *Engelberta*: it had to be played as an independent dramatic composition or nothing. But the activity of the following years suggests that the Neapolitan public was not ready in 1709 to accept the new genre fully. Reinhard Strohm has pointed out that the term 'intermezzo' was not used in Naples until around 1715, when the first imported intermezzi (he is evidently discounting the group of 1709) played alongside native operas, and that it was only in 1724 that a librettist working in Naples penned comic intermezzi to accompany his own opera, Metastasio's *L'impresario delle Canarie* for *Didone abbandonata*.[26]

Neapolitan conservatism is reflected even more in the Vienna score, which, following a common practice applied to works performed on the emperor's name-day, was copied, probably at source, for deposit in the imperial music library. One learns from the libretto that Antonio Orefice composed all the music for *Engelberta* up to Act II, Scene xi, and Francesco Mancini the remainder. The first two intermezzi of *Pimpinone* appear in

---

[24] This is also the only libretto to specify scenery: a courtyard with colonnades.

[25] Lazarevich, 'The Role of the Neapolitan Intermezzo', 74.

[26] Strohm, *Die italienische Oper im 18. Jahrhundert*, 116–17.

the score exactly in the manner of traditional Neapolitan comic scenes: Intermezzo I has become 'Scena 15.a' of Act I, and Intermezzo II has become 'Scena XX' of Act II. Intermezzo III, however, is described as such and appears without any scene number of its own after Act III, Scene vi. Short of actually altering original scene numbers in the opera, the copyist has done his best to submerge the separate identity of *Pimpinone*. As for the Münster score, from the Santini collection, this was copied for Ruspoli by Tarquinio Lanciani, whose collaborator and probable relative, Francesco Antonio Lanciani, receipted the invoice for the work on 28 February 1711.[27] Only a volume containing Act I of *La costanza in amore vince l'inganno* followed by Intermezzo I of *Pimpinone* survives; there were presumably two further volumes, each containing one act and one intermezzo. The musical text of Intermezzo I corresponds astonishingly closely to the Vienna score, even reproducing minor errors: it is quite possible that both manuscripts were transcribed from the same source, which might well have been a copy owned by one of the singers.

As a prelude to the discussion of Albinoni's music for *Pimpinone*, something must be said about Pariati's text. Since the theme and plot of the intermezzi have been discussed quite fully in the preface to my edition and in other writings, only a few salient points need mention here. The story concerns three episodes in the relationship of a young servant girl, Vespetta, and a rich citizen, Pimpinone. In Intermezzo I Pimpinone engages Vespetta as his maid, rashly believing her assurances about her capacity for hard work, efficient housekeeping, and discretion in private matters. In Intermezzo II Vespetta, who has proved herself indispensable to Pimpinone in the running of his house, threatens to leave because of rumours about the nature of her service; Pimpinone swallows the bait, agreeing to marry her and to put up the dowry himself. In Intermezzo III, Vespetta, flouting her earlier promises to behave as a decorous *cittadina*, declares her intention to live in the style of a noblewoman and to enjoy all society's pleasures: dancing, theatre-going, gaming, and the rest. She brushes aside Pimpinone's reproaches and successfully calls his bluff when he threatens to take a stick to her. The relationship between the two characters exploits all the antitheses familiar from the *servetta–vecchio* tradition: male and female, youth and age, guile and gullibility, assertiveness and cowardice. However, a new, satirical element comes into play by virtue of the fact that Pimpinone is the custodian of the traditional *cittadino* virtues of sobriety and plain living, while Vespetta, after her marriage, aspires to higher social spheres inappropriate for a *cittadina*, let

---

[27] See Ursula Kirkendale, *Antonio Caldara: Sein Leben und seine venezianisch–römische Oratorien* (Graz and Cologne: Böhlau, 1966), 58, 105–6, 365.

alone an erstwhile *popolana*. The fact that its characters belong to the lower social orders should not mislead us into imagining, anachronistically, that *Pimpinone* is conceived as entertainment for the rising middle class; if anything, it is a theatre-piece designed to confirm the nobility's belief in its higher, separate status at a time in Venetian history when an increasing lack of correlation between rank and wealth was causing social strains.

The literary superiority of the early Venetian intermezzo over its Neapolitan counterpart (the *scena buffa*) is rightly emphasized by Lazarevich.[28] But her generalizations about the typical musical differences between the two local traditions are perhaps too sweeping, both as statements of fact and as value-judgements, even if much of what she says has relevance for *Pimpinone*. She writes (p. 353):

> The text underlay in the intermezzi of Gasparini and the early 18th-century Venetian composers (with the exception of Orlandini) was not conducive to as successful a union of text and music as in the Neapolitan intermezzo. The Venetian form seldom created a true buffo line in which the rhythm and shape of the melodic motive are guided by the inflections of the words (as exhibited with Sarro in this period). Most of the arias in the Venetian intermezzo were merely set in dance-like patterns which created a lighter effect. Consequently, musical characterization was not so successful in the Venetian as it was in the Neapolitan intermezzo. Dance rhythms in 3/8 and 12/8 meter were applied to almost every aria, which resulted in a certain monotony. The duets were no more than *arie a due*. None of Scarlatti's miniature dramatic clashes were present. The arias that were not in dance rhythm were frequently square cut and devoid of grace.

And later (p. 356):

> The Neapolitan phrase exhibited melodiousness, musical poetry, melodic inventiveness, and a variety of sentiments, including the mock pathetic and the dramatic. The Venetian intermezzo phrases were relatively colorless, dance-like, with little contrast of mood or quality. While to the Neapolitan composer the unity of text and music was of some importance, to the Venetian the text of an aria was of secondary value, something to be fitted in after the music was composed.

It is quite true that dance-rhythms are perceptible in the arias and duets of *Pimpinone*, but that is a general characteristic of the Venetian opera style of the time. The essential point is rather that the Neapolitans evolved a highly distinctive style for their comic scenes and intermezzi, while the Venetians were

---

[28] Lazarevich, 'The Role of the Neapolitan Intermezzo', 356–7.

content to make a less radical adaptation of their normal operatic idioms. In the closed numbers of *Pimpinone*, the drive for concision is paramount. Antecedents and consequents are often of equal length (see below, Ex. 10.3), whereas in the normal operatic style consequents tend to be extended with *Fortspinnung* devices such as sequence. In place of long vocal melismas, one finds the repetition of pithy phrases set in syllabic, *parlando* style. Ritornellos, where present, are brief to the point of perfunctoriness, and the *Devise* (Hugo Riemann's term for the preliminary statement, by the voice, of an opening motto) is altogether absent, despite its frequent appearance in the arias of Albinoni's other dramatic works from the same period. Lazarevich's epithets 'square cut' and 'devoid of grace' are not out of place, although one wonders just how important it is for comic intermezzi to demonstrate grace. However, *Pimpinone* does not bear out her observation about the preponderance of 3/8 and 12/8 metres: most of its closed numbers are in common time, and the only movement employing one of those metres is the duet in Intermezzo I.

Pace Lazarevich, *Pimpinone* is certainly not devoid, in places, of effective characterization. What could be more appropriately vespine, for instance, than the jagged rhythms, darting in and out, of Vespetta's opening aria in Intermezzo I, 'Chi mi vuol? Son cameriera'? This opening (Ex. 10.1) also exemplifies the general comments on style made in the preceding paragraph. But although stated in too forceful terms, Lazarevich's claim that the literary text in Venetian intermezzi is of 'secondary' value receives some support from the word-setting in *Pimpinone* (and, if one is to be honest, from Albinoni's dramatic music as a whole). The opening of the vocal line, doubled throughout by first violins, in Vespetta's 'Voglio far come fan l'altre' from Intermezzo III has a rhythmic organization entirely suited to writing for instruments but barely compatible, in its pattern of length and accent, with the text (Ex. 10.2).

The penultimate chord of Ex. 10.2 contains one of the many individual touches that, taken together, argue for Albinoni's authorship. Like many of his generation, including Vivaldi, Albinoni often employed *bassetti*—bass lines lying one, even two, octaves above the normal register; in string ensembles, such 'little basses' were played on violins or violas without continuo support. Unlike his contemporaries, however, Albinoni often harmonized a *bassetto* as if it were actually sounding in the normal octave; in other words, it is treated as being a fifth below an upper part even though it sounds a fourth above. This results in an abundance of 6-4 chords treated as if they were in root position. The most radical examples of this rather unorthodox approach are found in Albinoni's *Concerti a cinque*, op. 5 (1707); however, a particularly close parallel is the opening of Bonoso's aria 'Da te parto' from Act I, Scene

Ex. 10.1. Albinoni, *Pimpinone*, Intermezzo I, 'Chi mi vuol? Son cameriera?'
(Vespetta), opening ritornello

i of Albinoni's own setting (jointly with Gasparini) of *Engelberta* (1709).[29]
Similarly, the four-bar ritornello of Pimpinone's aria 'Guarda un poco in
quest'occhi di foco' from Intermezzo II (Ex. 10.3) illustrates two further
personal fingerprints: the use of the supertonic chord in first inversion as a
substitute for the subdominant chord in a quasi-plagal cadence (bar 2, third
beat) and a fondness for intertwining two upper parts that, although having
a similar contour, eschew direct imitation. The second violin 'teases' the first
violin, so to speak, by echoing or anticipating its prominent notes. In the
context of a comic intermezzo, such playfulness, suggestive of repartee, is
especially apt.

Albinoni has two basic strengths—as a tunesmith and as a contrapuntist.
The examples already given here attest to his facility as a melodist, but for

[29] See the example in Hellmuth Christian Wolff, 'Neue Quellen zu den Opern des
Tommaso Albinoni', *Studi musicali*, 8 (1979), 273–89 at 283.

Ex. 10.2. Albinoni, *Pimpinone*, Intermezzo III, 'Voglio far come fan l'altre'
(Vespetta), first vocal period

(I want to do as the others do, dance well, speak French, dress up, be
flirtatious, but with decorum, however.)

evidence of his contrapuntal gifts we have to turn to the duets, whose lively
interchange (or near-simultaneous presentation) of different motifs profits
from Pariati's witty handling of stichomythia.[30] These duets are far from
being the mere *arie a due* suggested by Lazarevich's description. However,
their counterpoint is not normally imitative counterpoint of a textbook
kind: it revels in the combination of lines of contrasted character, in juxtaposing repetitive (e.g. sequential) lines and non-repetitive ones. The 'organized anarchy' of this kind of counterpoint can at its best produce exactly the
kind of realistic effect that Lazarevich associates (rightly) with the more progressive Neapolitan comic style. Consider the opening bars of the final duet
(Ex. 10.4): here the incessant overlapping of phrases of varied length conveys

---

[30] For an illuminating discussion of the way in which the rhyme, metre, and syntax of
Pariati's text facilitated, and even suggested, the musical characteristics of Albinoni's setting
see Strohm, 'Pietro Pariati librettista comico', 88–91.

Ex. 10.3. Albinoni, *Pimpinone*, Intermezzo II, 'Guarda un poco in quest'occhi di foco' (Pimpinone), opening ritornello

the message that normal conversation between Vespetta and Pimpinone has come to an end and that we are instead witnessing a slanging match in which each attempts to shout down the other. Only a certain stiffness of rhythm betrays the duet's Venetian rather than Neapolitan provenance.

If the music of Albinoni's later intermezzi, *Malsazio e Fiammetta* (1726, Rome) and *Il Satrapone* (1729, Pavia and Prague) had survived, we would be able to judge whether the promise shown in *Pimpinone* was fulfilled in them. This we must, unfortunately, doubt, for although Albinoni tried with some success to imitate the style of melody introduced by Neapolitan composers during the 1720s, his harmonic language and approach to musical form remained rooted in the practice of his youth; as a result, his later operatic music, of which only a few fragments are extant, appears to lack the stylistic integrity of his earlier works.

Ex. 10.4. Albinoni, *Pimpinone*, Intermezzo III, concluding duet, opening period

(V: If ever again . . .   P: (Cursed be . . .)   V: What! What are you saying?
P: Nothing, nothing.   V: If we ever quarrel like this again, that will be the end
of our marriage.   P: (Cursed be the day when [I got involved with such a
devil.] . . .)

Albinoni's *Pimpinone* is no masterpiece. It is outclassed in every respect by
Telemann's setting, even when allowance is made for its earlier date and for
the relatively unformed nature of the genre at the time when it was composed. Historically, however, it is of far greater importance than the later
score in both dramatic and musical terms. No set of comic intermezzi from
the first generation (1706–9) seems to have been performed so often and so
widely.[31] For its part, Pariati's libretto is the model to which many later texts
on the master–maidservant theme can be traced, as is evident from the many

[31] Compare the revivals of *Pimpinone* with those of other contemporary intermezzi listed
in Troy, *The Comic Intermezzo*, 141–52 (App. A: 'Some Frequently Revived Intermezzi').

parodies of its verse.[32] From Venice to Naples and from Brussels to Moscow, *Pimpinone* spearheaded the triumphant advance of the comic intermezzo, preparing the ground for the further syntheses that were to bring into being the *opera buffa* of later decades.

[32] See Mamczarz, *Les Intermèdes comiques italiens*, 97.

11

The Neapolitans in Venice

༥Ⴚ༒

REINHARD STROHM

THE supremacy of Neapolitan composers in eighteenth-century Italian opera is an established myth in the history of music. Already discussed by contemporary critics (see below), the concept of 'Neapolitan opera' later influenced music historiography for two centuries. Compounding the issue, Francesco Florimo in 1880 propagated the more specific concept of a 'scuola musicale di Napoli' which linked the notion of Neapolitan supremacy to the conservatoire training received by Neapolitan (and immigrant) composers.[1] The idea of a 'Neapolitan school' in the stylistic sense became the working basis for historical interpretation and source studies in the era of Hermann Kretzschmar, Hugo Riemann, Hermann Abert, and Rudolf Gerber, whose work was paralleled in Britain by Edward J. Dent and Frank Walker. Most of these writers actually questioned the label 'Neapolitan'. In 1961 the history and problems of the concept were surveyed, under the slightly more cautious formula of a 'Neapolitan Tradition in Opera', by Edward O. D. Downes and Helmut Hucke in a widely noted IMS round-table.[2] But despite many shifts of opinion concerning the question of geography, international musicology in the early 1960s still favoured an approach which grouped together chronology, geography, and the classification of musical style, an approach which remains apparent in the second edition of Donald J. Grout's

---

[1] Francesco Florimo, *La scuola musicale di Napoli e i suoi conservatorii* (Naples, 1880–3; repr. Bologna: Forni, 1969). Classifications based on stylistic 'schools' were then used in art criticism and history; the term was adopted by Raphael Georg Kiesewetter in his influential 'Die Verdienste der Niederlaender um die Tonkunst' of 1829. It is also likely that Florimo inherited the specific concept of a 'Neapolitan school' from German scholarship: for example, Francesco Degrada ('L'opera napoletana fra Seicento e Settecento', in *Storia dell'opera*, ed. Guglielmo Barblan and Alberto Basso, i/1: *L'opera in Italia* (Turin: UTET, 1977), 237–332), cites Emil Naumann, 'Alessandro Scarlatti und die Schule von Neapel', in *Italienische Tondichter von Palestrina bis auf die Gegenwart* (Berlin, 1876).

[2] Helmut Hucke and Edward O. D. Downes, 'Die neapolitanische Tradition in der Oper/The Neapolitan Tradition in Opera', in *International Musicological Society: Report of the Eighth Congress, New York 1961*, ed. Jan LaRue (Kassel: Bärenreiter, 1961), i. 253–84, ii. 132–4.

successful history of opera[3] and in individual studies by Helmut Hucke, Daniel Heartz, Edward O. D. Downes, and others. In 1967 Heartz, while acknowledging the problems of a stylistic–geographical periodization of opera, still favoured the notion of a Neapolitan-led renewal around 1720–40.[4] Partly concurring with this view, I myself proposed in 1976 that regional traditions such as that of Naples were relevant only until *c.*1730–40, and that after that time a more general Italian operatic language had developed, which by force of tradition remained known as 'Neapolitan'.[5] Since the late 1970s, however, the whole question has seldom been mentioned. This is not because more detailed style studies or newly uncovered documents have made it redundant, but because the whole principle of style periodization in music has gone out of fashion.

Meanwhile, scholars such as Francesco Degrada and Michael Robinson had turned their attention to the socio-cultural and economic conditions in Naples itself which made such developments in style possible in the first place,[6] a successful approach encouraged by the work of Neapolitan cultural historians such as Benedetto Croce and Ulisse Prota-Giurleo. In the 1980s studies of theatre and social history became more relevant for opera history in general. There was increasing interest in the libretto, as a historical document and occasionally even as a literary work. The types of material studied with the greatest zeal now included librettos, singers, scenography, costume, dramaturgy, theatre management, and patronage. Much of this research was not focused geographically. The exploration of individual repertories and composers intensified only with respect to some subgenres such as the comic intermezzo, or with the best-known authors such as Handel, Alessandro Scarlatti, Vivaldi, or Pergolesi. The standard *dramma per musica*, and the average 'Neapolitan' composer such as Vinci, Leo, Sarro, or Porpora, did not benefit from this expansion of interest. Studies of Johann Adolf Hasse, prompted by his bicentenary in 1983, had little to say about his most successful operas, and in any case they remained silent on the question of style periodization, and indeed on the Neapolitan tradition with which he ought

---

[3] Donald J. Grout, *A Short History of Opera* (New York, 1947; 3rd edn., New York: Columbia University Press, 1988).

[4] Daniel Heartz, 'Opera and the Periodization of Eighteenth-Century Music', in *International Musicological Society: Report of the Tenth Congress, Ljubljana 1967*, ed. Dragotin Cvetko (Kassel: Bärenreiter, 1970), 160–8; see also id., 'Approaching a History of 18th-Century Music', *Current Musicology*, 9 (1969), 92–5.

[5] Reinhard Strohm, *Italienische Opernarien des frühen Settecento (1720–1730)* (Analecta musicologica, 16; Cologne: Arno Volk Verlag, 1976).

[6] See e.g. Degrada, 'L'opera napoletana fra Seicento e Settecento'; Michael Robinson, *Naples and Neapolitan Opera* (Oxford: Clarendon Press, 1972).

to be associated.[7] Pietro Metastasio also received attention in bicentenary conferences of 1982, but his Neapolitan background was again neglected.[8]

Apart from these fluctuations of scholarly fashion, we can still reasonably ask what happened to Italian opera—especially *opera seria*—in the eighteenth century, and whether a qualified case for 'Neapolitan leadership' can be made after all. I believe it can. First, it has always been acknowledged that around 1730 composers, librettists, and singers trained in Naples suddenly started to dominate the *opera seria* repertory in Venice and elsewhere. Second, many eighteenth-century observers of Italian opera perceived changes of style and the emergence of a new outlook among composers as well as librettists. They approached the matter in terms of geography: for Diderot, Rousseau, Algarotti, Burney, Grétry, Schubart, and Vogler, it was the good taste of the 'Neapolitans' which had helped eighteenth-century opera emerge from Baroque dust.[9] It is probably no accident that the term 'Baroque' itself was used in Paris in 1746 to characterize, pejoratively, an old-fashioned style of music, presumably represented by composers such as Albinoni and Vivaldi.[10] Already in 1739 the Chevalier de Brosses had noted on a visit to Naples the excellence of Leonardo Leo's *La Frascatana*.[11] As is well known, Leo's music rivalled Pergolesi's in the Parisian performances leading to the *querelle des bouffons*; Hasse, Latilla, Rinaldo, and Auletta were heard there too. As if to increase the Parisians' awareness of Italian composers and genres, in 1754 Francesco Algarotti, reflecting the taste of the Prussian court, cited Leonardo Vinci's *Didone abbandonata* as a model setting of a *tragedia per musica*.[12] Thus

[7] But see Friedrich Lippmann, 'Hasses Arienstil und seine Interpretation durch Rudolf Gerber', in *Colloquium 'Johann Adolf Hasse und die Musik seiner Zeit' (Siena 1983)* (Analecta musicologica, 25; Laaber: Laaber Verlag, 1987), 17–65, for a thoughtful assessment of past efforts; and also Hellmuth Christian Wolff, 'Johann Adolf Hasse und Venedig', in Maria Teresa Muraro (ed.), *Venezia e il melodramma nel Settecento* (Florence: Olschki, 1978), 295–308. Hasse's reworkings of arias by Alessandro Scarlatti are discussed with a view to the problem of a 'Neapolitan tradition' in Reinhard Strohm, 'Hasse, Scarlatti, Rolli', in *Studien zur italienisch–deutschen Musikgeschichte, 10* (Analecta musicologica, 15; Cologne: Arno Volk Verlag, 1975), 220–57.

[8] Many publications of the years 1982–4 are reviewed in Giovanna Gronda, 'Metastasiana', *Rivista italiana di musicologia*, 19 (1984), 314–32.

[9] For surveys, see Heartz, 'Opera and the Periodization of Eighteenth-Century Music'; Degrada, 'L'opera napoletana fra Seicento e Settecento', 237–40. The full story still needs to be told.

[10] See Claude V. Palisca, 'Baroque', in *The New Grove Dictionary of Music and Musicians*, ed. Stanley Sadie (London: Macmillan, 1980), ii. 172–3.

[11] 'Je porterai cet opéra en France . . .'; see Charles de Brosses, *Lettres familières*, ed. Yvonne Bézard (Paris, 1931), i. 431.

[12] He especially praised the music of the last act for its accompanied recitatives: '. . . lo stesso Virgilio si sarebbe compiaciuto . . . tanto è animata e terribile' ('Virgil himself would have been pleased . . . so lively and awe-inspiring was it'); see Francesco Algarotti, *Saggio sopra*

a relatively small group of composers, all trained in Naples, was singled out for modernity and 'naturalness': a legend was taking shape that equated 'Neapolitan opera' with good taste.[13] We should note that this legend originated in the metropolises of northern and western Europe, and not in Italy (nor, incidentally, in Vienna or Dresden). But why did the critics of Paris, Berlin, London, and other centres hail a small cluster of Naples-trained opera composers when there were dozens of other Italians to choose from?

This 'European' acclaim of the 1750s and 1760s was the delayed effect of earlier, equally specific successes—those obtained by some of the same Neapolitans on the Venetian operatic stage in the preceding thirty years. The process began with Metastasian *drammi per musica* in Neapolitan settings performed in Venice in the 1720s and early 1730s, and continued with the Neapolitan intermezzi and *opere buffe* of the 1730s and 1740s. Historical connections between this 'inner Italian' expansion and later European fame are easily drawn. European cities received most of their Italian repertory from Venice, by way of performances attended during the Grand Tour, of manuscript circulation, and of the activities of travelling opera troupes which were mostly Venetian or north Italian in origin (the Mingotti and Bambini companies, to name just two). The structure of the Italian opera circuit itself made it almost impossible to succeed abroad without previously having attracted the interest of Venetian impresarios. The full story of the spread of the Neapolitan *commedia per musica* across the peninsula and then abroad has only recently been told by Piero Weiss.[14] The fact is that serious opera around 1720–50, dominated by Metastasio's *drammi per musica*, travelled on exactly the same north–south routes as *opera buffa*, and was partly carried by the same travelling companies. The operatic music of Leo, Vinci, Porpora, and Hasse found its way to the European centres after it had first been heard in Venice, and after Porpora and Hasse had found employment in that city. Although foreign consumers were of course able to obtain scores or librettos from Naples, Rome, or Parma 'at source' (witness Handel or de Brosses), to have dominated a carnival season in Venice was presumably the most powerful recommendation an opera could receive. Finally, the engagement of Italian opera composers at foreign courts also tended to follow Venetian successes. Even Niccolò Jommelli, trained in Naples in the 1730s and brought

---

l'opera in musica, ed. Giovanni Da Pozzo (Bari: Laterza, 1963), 162 (citing from the 2nd edn. of 1763).

[13] Neapolitan church music and vocal chamber works—for example by Scarlatti, Pergolesi, and Durante—were awarded the same critical acclaim. Eighteenth-century forgeries, a good measure of popularity, included oratorios and sacred music by Vinci, Hasse, and Pergolesi.

[14] 'La diffusione del repertorio operistico nell'Italia del Settecento: Il caso dell'opera buffa', in Susi Davoli (ed.), *Civiltà teatrale e Settecento emiliano* (Bologna: Il Mulino, 1986), 241–56.

to Vienna from Rome in 1749, is no exception, for it was in Bologna and Venice in the early 1740s that he became famous in his special field, that of *opera seria*. It almost seems that whatever the artistic contribution of Neapolitan composers, eighteenth-century opera history was made, rather, by Venetian impresarios.

What needs to be explained, however, is how Neapolitan composers came to conquer the Venetian *palcoscenico* in the first place. Here I shall attempt to shed some light on the early years of this story, mainly from the angle of operatic practice and business. Although not primarily concerned with questions of style, this factual account may reveal some of the mundane foundations of a grand historiographical theory, while in a sense confirming it.

The chronological outlines of this story are straightforward.[15] Between the time of the 'Febi armonici' (the 1650s) and 1707, no composer or librettist employed or trained in the Spanish-governed Kingdom of Naples had more than one opera performed on the Venetian stage. This is not surprising, since there were few resident opera composers or librettists employed in Naples before the early eighteenth century. Even Alessandro Scarlatti, a native of Palermo and the famous *maestro della Real Cappella*, had to wait (or chose to wait) until 1707 for Venetian performances of two his operas. The opera repertory of the Teatro S. Bartolomeo and the Royal Palace in Naples was a mixture of local and imported material, with Venetian imports dominating. Such imported works were invariably adapted to local requirements. There were also active connections—in terms of repertory and also, to some extent, of singers—between Naples and Rome until public opera was forbidden in the Papal States (in 1698). But in this respect, too, the operas performed in Naples, and their composers, where more often of Roman origin than vice versa. *Gli amanti generosi* (1705) by Francesco Mancini, then vice-*maestro* of the royal chapel, surprisingly reached London's Haymarket Theatre in 1710 and Genoa in 1711, but it never appeared in Venice.

Between 1707 (when the Austrians conquered Naples) and 1720, matters changed inasmuch as the activities of native or locally trained opera composers were now increasing rapidly. Domenico Sarro, Francesco Mancini, Antonio Orefice, Giuseppe Vignola, Nicola Fago, Nicola Porpora, Leonardo Leo, and Carmine Giordano began to emulate Alessandro Scarlatti. Neapolitan

[15] The main source for the following performance statistics is Taddeo Wiel, *I teatri musicali veneziani del Settecento* (Venice, 1897; repr. Leipzig: Peters, 1979); see also Lorenzo Bianconi, 'Funktionen des Operntheaters in Neapel bis 1700 und die Rolle Alessandro Scarlattis', in Wolfgang Osthoff and Jutta Ruile-Dronke (eds.), *Colloquium Alessandro Scarlatti, Würzburg 1975* (Tutzing: Schneider, 1979), 91–116.

singers also appeared more regularly in Venice and elsewhere in the north, as, for example, the famous Nicolò Grimaldi (Nicolini), who obtained the title of Knight of the Order of St Mark. A wave of emigration was fuelled by the War of the Spanish Succession (1700–14); in this context, some singers (Matteo Sassani) and composers (Giuseppe Porsile) got as far as Venice and Vienna. But not a single *dramma per musica* of Neapolitan origin was heard in Venice between 1707 and 1720. Sarro managed to have his inter-mezzi *Barilotto e Slapina* performed at the Teatro S. Angelo in 1712 (although nowhere else), but this is an isolated event as yet unexplained. On the other hand, of the seventy-six *drammi per musica* publicly performed in Naples between 1707 and 1720, about sixteen were imported from Venice, and about six from other centres, including London (Handel's *Rinaldo*). The remainder were local settings, about thirty of texts imported from Venice and about ten from other centres. Most of the imported works were adapted by local artists, however, an activity that seems to have provided a livelihood for several minor librettists and composers, and which perhaps created some of the know-how needed for the reversal of fortunes that followed in the 1720s.

The last Venetian opera performed in Naples for a long time to come was *Tito Manlio* by Carlo Francesco Pollarolo, adapted (for perhaps the twentieth time) in 1720 by the local musician Ignazio Prota. From 1721 until 1736, when again the government changed, no Venetian opera was performed in Naples,[16] although of the seventy local settings, around thirty used Venetian librettos. In Venice, on the other hand, of the seventy-eight *drammi per musica* assigned to the years 1721–36 in Wiel's catalogue, as many as thirty were by composers educated in Naples: Porpora (7), Hasse (7), Leo (5), Vinci (4), Sellitto (2), Araia (2), and Fiorillo, Sarro, and Broschi (1 each). It is more difficult to define Neapolitan origins for librettos. In any case, eighteen librettos were based on *drammi* by Metastasio—twelve of them on those written during his residence in Naples (1720–9)—and two had been written for Naples by the Roman poet Silvio Stampiglia, who had long-established contacts with the city (where he died on 26 January 1725). At least as regards operatic composition, the relationship between Naples and Venice was thus completely reversed in the third decade of the century. It seems to be this process which decided the future of operatic styles—even though the genres of comic intermezzo and *opera buffa* were not yet involved —and which later gave rise to the international fame of Italian and 'Metastasian' opera throughout Europe.

---

[16] Leonardo Leo provides an only partial exception; he revised his own *Argeno* (1728, Venice) for a performance in Naples in 1731.

A postscript to the above statistics leads directly into our story. In addition to Metastasio and Stampiglia, another 'southerner'—a native Neapolitan, even—contributed a total of twenty-two newly written or arranged librettos to the Venetian stage in the years 1710–36. This was Domenico Lalli, born in Naples in 1679 (his real name was Sebastiano Biancardi). He was a cashier at the Banco di SS. Annunziata when, apparently in 1706, the discovery of an enormous gap in the bank's balance forced him to flee the city, leaving his wife and family behind. The story of his flight, subsequent wanderings—mostly undertaken in the company of the aristocratic composer Emanuele d'Astorga—and final arrival in Venice in 1710 under a new name has been told by Roberto Pagano on the basis of Lalli's own autobiography (printed in Venice in 1732).[17] Lalli was able to consolidate his position in Venice thanks to his acquaintance with influential Venetian families and to his friendship with the famous librettist Apostolo Zeno, a contact which led to the production of his first *dramma per musica*, produced at the Teatro S. Cassiano in autumn 1710, entitled *L'amor tirannico*. Other aspects of Lalli's Venetian career include his libretto *Elisa* (S. Angelo, autumn 1711), according to Bonlini the first 'true musical comedy' seen in Venice; his collaborations and apparent litigations with Antonio Vivaldi; and his increasingly influential position as the house poet of the Grimani theatres (S. Giovanni Grisostomo and S. Samuele). In this capacity, he brought Vivaldi together with the budding librettist Carlo Goldoni to prepare the opera *Griselda* (S. Samuele, 1735).[18]

As a resourceful poet and hack, theatre manager, and career-maker, Domenico Lalli hardly surprises us by also being involved with the arrival of Neapolitan opera in Venice in Carnival 1723. Around that time, Lalli had made himself popular at the Bavarian court as well: he was commissioned to write opera librettos for the wedding of the electoral Prince Karl Albert in Munich in 1722. One of these works was *I veri amici*, a reworking of a libretto by Francesco Silvani loosely based on Pierre Corneille's *Héraclius*.[19] The music was by Tomaso Albinoni, who composed other works for the wedding celebrations, and with whom Lalli often collaborated in these years. The Munich opera was repeated in slightly revised form in Venice (Teatro S. Angelo) in the following carnival. Interestingly, of the several arias newly

[17] *Scarlatti Alessandro e Domenico: Due vite in una* (Milan: Mondadori, 1985), 253–7.

[18] For a translation of Goldoni's own account, see Michael Talbot, *Vivaldi* (London: Dent, 1978), 81–3.

[19] On the libretto, see Anna Laura Bellina, 'Dal mito della corte al nodo dello stato: Il "topos" del tiranno', in Lorenzo Bianconi (ed.), *Antonio Vivaldi: Teatro musicale, cultura e società* (Florence: Olschki, 1982), ii. 297–313, esp. 305–9. Silvani's libretto had been written for the Teatro S. Cassiano in 1713 and repeated elsewhere, including Naples (Carnival 1716, with music by Antonio Maria Bononcini). Bibliographers give Lalli's name in addition to that of Silvani for the 1713 production, but I rather suspect that Lalli's revision originated in 1722.

inserted into the score at this time two survive with musical settings ascribed
not to Albinoni but to Leonardo Leo.[20] No doubt these settings originated
for the S. Angelo production, since the musical copies also name the singers
performing the arias on that occasion (Nicolò Grimaldi and Antonia Cavazzi).
Moreover, in the libretto of the other S. Angelo opera of the season,
Timocrate, Leonardo Leo is named as the composer, with the exaggerated
title of 'primo organista della Real Cappella di Napoli'.[21] This libretto was
also by Lalli, this time derived from Thomas Corneille via *Amor vince l'odio,
overo Timocrate* by Antonio Salvi, first given at Florence in 1715. Of Leo's
setting of *Timocrate*, only two arias and a duet have survived.[22]

Before proceeding further, three observations are in order. First, there
may have been a previous connection between Lalli (b. Naples, 1679) and
Leo (b. S. Vito (near Bari), 1694). Leo was educated in 1709–12 at the Conservatorio de' Turchini, Naples, under Nicola Fago and Andrea Basso, and
had produced some oratorios before composing his very first opera, *Pisistrato*,
in May 1714 for the Teatro S. Bartolomeo. This opera uses one of the least-
known librettos by Lalli, printed in Venice for a performance at the Teatro
'Al Dolo' (in Venice?) in June 1711 (Lalli later had the *dramma* revived in
1736 in an adaptation by Goldoni). It is not impossible that Lalli was acquainted with Leo and had sent him his libretto. Second, it is worth noting
the dedicatees of the two Lalli/Leo librettos of the S. Angelo season in 1723:
Timocrate, the first carnival opera, was offered to an apparent patron of Lalli's,
Prince Johann Philipp Franz von Schönborn, Bishop of Würzburg; and *I veri
amici* was dedicated by 'N. N.' (either Lalli or the impresario) on 23 January
1723 to Fra Camillo, Duke of Pola, Receiver General of the Order of the
Knights of Malta in Venice.[23] It must be doubted, however, that either
dedicatee had a hand in the *scrittura* for Leo. Third, by way of caution, we
should keep in mind that Venetian opera-houses were often frequented by
'foreign' composers in those years, and particularly the Teatro S. Angelo:
Leonardo Leo may have gone almost unnoticed in the influx of Bolognese,

[20] Münster, Santini-Bibliothek, MS 2362, fos. 9 and 23. Sources for most of the following
operas are cited in Strohm, *Italienische Opernarien*, ii.

[21] He had held the position of 'supernumerary organist' of the royal chapel since 1713 but
was made first organist only in 1725.

[22] One aria, 'Mi va serpendo in seno', is transcribed and discussed in Strohm, *Italienische
Opernarien*, i. 42–4 (text), and ii, no. 104 (music).

[23] Some information is available on the musical interests of this prelate, who had close
connections with Johann Baptist Colloredo-Wallsee, the Imperial ambassador to Venice.
These two patrons commissioned much music for political and other occasions from com-
posers, including Albinoni, but not, so far as is known, other operas; see Eleanor Selfridge-
Field, *Pallade Veneta: Writings on Music in Venetian Society 1650–1750* (Venice: Fondazione
Levi, 1985), 332.

Florentine, and other north Italian musicians, some of whom had in fact been satirized in Benedetto Marcello's *Teatro alla moda* of 1720. It seems that Lalli had some kind of official role in the S. Angelo productions throughout the years 1719–26, and perhaps the opening to non-Venetian artists— including the composers Orlandini, Chelleri, and Porta, and the Belisani/ Buini opera troupe—was a necessary prelude to the invitations extended to Neapolitans.[24] In any case, it does not seem that Leo's contribution left the special mark on Venetian opera that his involvement might have led one to expect.

The next appearance of a Neapolitan composer in Venice happened under seemingly very different circumstances. I believe that it was connected with the Venetian librettist Benedetto Pasqualigo. Since 1718 this 'nobile veneto'—a member of the Accademia degli Animosi (as 'Merindo Fesanio') and a self-promoter of some skill—had been providing the Venetian stage with his special brand of classicizing dramas, sometimes even with tragic endings, on Greek mythological subjects. Extraordinary success was gained by his *Antigona* of 1718 (S. Cassiano) with the music of the Florentine Giuseppe Maria Orlandini; this opera had to be revived four times in the following seasons in Venice alone. Their 'tragedia da cantarsi', *Ifigenia in Tauride* (1719, S. Giovanni Grisostomo), tried to follow up on the success. But neither this nor Pasqualigo's other librettos based on literary classics— such as *Il pastor fido* (1721, S. Angelo; after Guarini), *Cimene* (1721, S. Angelo; based on Corneille's *Le Cid*), nor even *Giulio Flavio Crispo* (1722, S. Giovanni Grisostomo) and *Mitridate re di Ponto, vincitor di se stesso* (1723, S. Giovanni Grisostomo), both based on Racine (*Phèdre* and *Mithridate*, respectively) and both set to music by the Parmesan composer Giovanni Maria Capelli—seem to have engaged Venetian audiences. This perhaps explains Pasqualigo's attempt, in Carnival 1725, to better his lot with 'Neapolitan' imports. There is evidence that the Grimani family, owners of the Teatro S. Giovanni Grisostomo, supported Pasqualigo's plans, and that he even acted as their literary adviser for this season. The first three librettos used in the autumn/carnival season at this theatre in 1724–5 were all ostensibly noble, classical, or otherwise highly reputed literary works, answering to the standard notions of *gravità e decoro* considered by some contemporaries to be a trend of the times. The autumn opera, *Il trionfo della virtù* by Pietro d'Averara, was based on the Roman Republican subject of Lucius Sulla and

[24] On non-Venetian singers and composers in Venice in these years, see Sergio Durante, 'Alcune considerazioni sui cantanti di teatro del primo Settecento e la loro formazione', in Bianconi (ed.), *Antonio Vivaldi*, ii. 427–81; and Eleanor Selfridge-Field, 'Marcello, Sant'Angelo, and "Il teatro alla moda"', ibid. 533–46.

P. Cornelius Scipio.[25] The first carnival opera—in Venice, usually the main event of the season—was a revival of Pasqualigo's tragedy *Ifigenia in Tauride*, dedicated by him to a young son of Giovanni Carlo Grimani, Vincenzo, and rewritten for a new setting by Leonardo Vinci. The second carnival opera was a new effort by Pasqualigo, a heroic drama *Berenice* based on Corneille's *tragicomédie* (rather than Racine's *tragédie*) on this Roman Imperial subject. It involved a new *scrittura* for the formerly so successful Orlandini. A third carnival opera followed: the Neapolitan *maestro*, Vinci, was asked to set— perhaps at short notice—*Partenope* by the famous Arcadian Silvio Stampiglia, now renamed *La Rosmira fedele*. This libretto was dedicated by the impresario (not Pasqualigo) to Don Nicolò del Tocco, Duke of Sicignano—apparently a Neapolitan nobleman.[26]

If it is correct that *Ifigenia in Tauride*, like *Berenice*, was intended chiefly to serve Pasqualigo's poetic and aesthetic ambitions, why was *La Rosmira fedele* put on? This *dramma per musica* was definitely not a 'grave and noble' work. The opera was produced 'in the last days of carnival', as mentioned in a letter of 24 February 1725 from Apostolo Zeno to his brother Pier Caterino. Three carnival operas were not the norm at the Teatro S. Giovanni Grisostomo, but examples occurred from time to time, especially if the second opera did not 'draw'. On this occasion, however, an additional (perhaps the only) motivation must have been the death of the famous Stampiglia, a founding member of the Arcadian Academy, in Naples on 26 January 1725. Apostolo Zeno's letter of 24 February in fact comments on Stampiglia's death, also assessing his merits as a librettist.[27] It seems that audiences were talking about the poet, whose name was better known in Venice than his works.

Partenope had been written by Stampiglia in 1699 for and about Naples, being a love-and-adventure story loosely woven around the legendary foundation of the city by the eponymous heroine. Many revivals in other cities followed, including one in Venice in 1708 with music by Antonio Caldara.[28]

[25] The composer of this opera, the little-known Giovanni Francesco Brusa, earned praise for his next opera, *L'amore eroico* (spring 1725, S. Samuele), in Johann Mattheson's journal *Critica musica* (Hamburg, 1725), ii. 286–7.

[26] A certain Leonardo Tocco, Prince of Montemiletto, had been the addressee of Silvio Stampiglia's previous libretto, *Imeneo*, at his wedding to Camilla Cantelmi in Naples in 1723. This had been set to music by Nicola Porpora; Marianna Benti was the prima donna.

[27] Apostolo Zeno, *Lettere*, ii (Venice, 1752), 181. According to Zeno (who succeeded him as Imperial court poet), Stampiglia had been more *ingegnoso* than *dotto*, and his librettos had more *spirito* than *studio*: in other words, he was a lightweight poet and not a classicist. I am grateful to Dott. Mario Armellini for helping me to identify Zeno's letter.

[28] For the various librettos and musical settings, see Robert S. Freeman, 'The Travels of Partenope', in Harold Powers (ed.), *Studies in Music History: Essays for Oliver Strunk* (Princeton University Press, 1968), 356–85.

But it is remarkable that in the whole time between 1700 and 1725—when *Partenope* was presented again—no other libretto by this very popular author had been heard in Venice. Stampiglia was not a natural preference of the Venetian theatres, and certainly for the 1720s he lacked some of the fashionable *gravità e decoro*.[29] This and the demonstrative homage to Naples implied in the 1725 production—plot, poet, musician, and dedicatee all being from that city—fit together if the opera was meant to honour the poet, more out of respect and curiosity than from aesthetic inclination. One also wonders whether the visit of Don Nicolò del Tocco had any bearing on the choice of opera.

The fact that Vinci was chosen among the many Neapolitan composers to 'represent' his city on the most noble Venetian stage is of some historical significance.[30] His reputation, barely established in Naples and Rome by one opera each in 1724, was now spreading across Europe almost overnight. In Handel's pasticcio *Elpidia* (London, Haymarket Theatre, 11 May 1725), the composer presented—partly on advice given from Venice by the opera manager Owen Swiney—a musical anthology of the three S. Giovanni Grisostomo operas of this carnival, drawing at least fourteen arias from Vinci's *Ifigenia in Tauride* and *Rosmira fedele*, plus perhaps the overture from the former work. Only three arias were taken from Orlandini's *Berenice*.[31] Apparently, Swiney had sent a skeleton score or aria collection to London, calling the product

---

[29] Wiel lists a total of only six Venetian operas on librettos by Stampiglia in the whole of the 18th c.: three versions of *Partenope* (1708, 1725, and 1753), two of *Imeneo* (1726, 1750), and one of *Camilla regina de' Volsci* (1749). The seventh, a *Cirene* given in 1742, is probably not authentic.

[30] Charles Burney noted that 'in 1725 the Venetian theatre first heard the natural, clear, and dramatic strains of Leonardo Vinci, in his two operas of *Ifigenia in Aulide* [*sic*] and *La Rosmira Fidele* [*sic*]'; see Burney, *A General History of Music from the Earliest Ages to the Present Period (1789)*, ed. Frank Mercer (London, 1935; repr. New York: Dover, 1957), ii. 108. Much valuable information on Vinci's operas is offered in Kurt Sven Markstrom, 'The Operas of Leonardo Vinci, Napoletano' (Ph.D. diss., University of Toronto, 1993).

[31] For the music and sources of Handel's first pasticcio, see Reinhard Strohm, 'Handel's Pasticci', in id., *Essays on Handel and Italian Opera* (Cambridge University Press, 1985), 164–211, esp. 167–9, 200–1. For Swiney's involvement, see Elizabeth Gibson, *The Royal Academy of Music 1719–1728: The Institution and its Directors* (New York and London: Garland, 1989), 362 ff., 372 ff. (letters by Swiney of 15 Mar. 1726 and 23 Jan. 1727). I now suspect that the material sent by Swiney may have been connected with the preparations for the opera *I rivali generosi* (i.e. *Elpidia*) given with music by Giuseppe Vignati at the Teatro S. Samuele in May 1726 but perhaps already planned in 1725, although the libretto does not have many arias in common with Handel's. It is worth mentioning here that Swiney detested the libretto of *Partenope*: 'it is the very worst book (excepting one) that I have ever read in my life: Signor Stampiglia . . . endeavours to be humourous and witty, in it: If he succeeded in his attempt, on any stage in Italy, 'twas, meerly, from a depravity of Taste in the audience—but I am very sure that 'twill be received with contempt in England' (letter of 13 Aug. 1726; Gibson, *The Royal Academy*, 369).

Elpidia as if it were a completed opera score using that libretto (Zeno's *I rivali generosi* of 1697). He later asked to be reimbursed for having '*Elpidia*' copied, and for giving a present (*regalo*) to Vinci, presumably for being allowed to copy arias from both of Vinci's operas. Swiney's and Handel's choice proved successful, and Handel's later pasticcios seem to confirm that he preferred Vinci's music to all other contemporary Italian operas.

Vinci did have a recent connection with Stampiglia: for the autumn season of 1724 in Naples, he arranged (together with Leo) a pasticcio on Stampiglia's *Turno Aricino*, which had been revised by the poet's son, Luigi Maria Stampiglia; and Vinci also set his *Eraclea*, revised for the occasion by the author himself. But Vinci was not the most obvious choice for the Venetian initiative. A much more senior member of the royal chapel, Domenico Sarro, had set *Partenope* in 1722 in a new version likewise provided by Stampiglia himself, and with great success: it was repeated in Rome in Carnival 1724. Sarro was the only Neapolitan opera composer of these years who could rival the reputation of Alessandro Scarlatti while being considered a representative of the modern style. Not by coincidence, he was the first composer to set Metastasio's *Didone abbandonata*, in Naples in 1724. But in fact *Didone abbandonata* was given in Venice in the 1725 carnival season at the Teatro S. Cassiano with new music by Albinoni. It seems that Metastasio was present, having revised his text for the occasion: the libretto contains a dedicatory sonnet by the poet addressed 'to the Ladies of Venice'. Sarro's setting of *Didone abbandonata* was given in Venice only in 1730 and remained his only work ever heard there (see also below).

If the decision to put on *Partenope* was caused by Stampiglia's death, then the *scrittura* for the music came to Vinci by a stroke of luck and at short notice: he was in Venice anyway; his *Ifigenia* had been a success; and he had some experience of Stampiglia's poetry. The preferment of Vinci over Sarro may seem rather unfair when one notes that Vinci used his senior rival's music to carry out the commission. It is Vinci's own autograph score of 1725 that betrays him.[32] Most of the recitatives of his opera are borrowed or derived from Sarro's score of 1722, with the clear intent of copying as much as possible from the original (keys, rhythms, bass lines, etc.) and adjusting only as much as necessary (the tessitura for those singers who in the Venetian performance had a different register). Also, the few, short sinfonias and acclamatory choruses are virtually identical with Sarro's. This is scarcely a common phenomenon in early eighteenth-century opera (or perhaps better,

---

[32] By another strange coincidence, this is the only surviving autograph of an *opera seria* by Vinci (in London, British Library, Add. MS 14232). It is inscribed *Partenope*, thus using Sarro's original title, and signed by Vinci. On the libretto, music, and autograph score, see Markstrom, 'The Operas of Leonardo Vinci', 86–95.

research in recitative composition is so little advanced that we have yet to uncover a similar case). An obvious explanation, although not an excuse, would be pressure of time: Vinci does seem to have had more time, by contemporary standards, for the preparation of his *Ifigenia* (the *Avvisi di Napoli* inform us with reference to 29 November 1724 that the composer was already in Venice).[33] Perhaps Sarro had in fact been invited to offer his *Partenope* at the end of carnival but for some reason could not come, leaving Vinci to take advantage of the opportunity. That said, however, I suggest that the goddess Fortune favoured the right contestant. Lack of space forbids me to discuss the music in detail here, but Vinci's achievement should not be left in doubt. Musically, neither the recitatives nor the choruses counted in a *dramma per musica*, only the arias. Vinci's arias in this opera are consistently superior to Sarro's.[34] His mastery of declamatory verse-setting as well as of graceful melody, and his superbly characterized, dramatically compelling music were at that point the best Naples had to offer. Perhaps music history would have developed somewhat differently if Sarro had been chosen in 1725, but even a Venetian success would not ultimately have made up for the fact that Hasse and Pergolesi, to name but two, were to follow the style of Vinci and not that of Sarro.

Pietro Metastasio's *Didone abbandonata*, the *tragedia per musica* given at the same time at the Teatro S. Cassiano was, of course, another début of a Neapolitan artist in Venice. It also was a drama with an unhappy ending (*funesto fine*), like several other earlier Venetian librettos (for example, by Pasqualigo and Salvi).[35] The Teatro S. Cassiano, the only one competing with the social prestige of the Grimani theatres, had taken up the 'noble' literary and classicist orientation also pursued by Pasqualigo: his *Antigona* was repeated there in the autumn season of 1724. But instead of using Sarro's music for *Didone*, the impresario commissioned a setting from a well-tried Venetian composer, Albinoni. S. Cassiano had its pathetic and classicist librettos, whereas S. Giovanni Grisostomo had these plus its *galant* and dramatic Neapolitan music. The combination—one indeed of historic

---

[33] See Ulisse Prota-Giurleo, 'Leonardo Vinci', *Il convegno musicale*, 2 (1965), 3–11.

[34] See e.g. the comparison of their respective settings of 'Al mio tesoro' and 'Ardi per me fedele' (from *Didone abbandonata*) in Strohm, *Italienische Opernarien*, i. 45–50 (text), and ii, nos. 105–7 (music). The score of *Ifigenia in Tauride*, unfortunately, is lost, although single arias survive in full score, including those used for the London *Elpidia*.

[35] See Reinhard Strohm, '"Tragédie" into "Dramma per musica": iii', *Informazioni e studi vivaldiani*, 11 (1990), 11–26. The following Venetian operas of these years had tragic endings: A. Salvi, *Amore e maestà* (*Arsace*), 1718 (M. A. Gasparini); B. Pasqualigo, *Ifigenia in Tauride*, 1719 (G. M. Orlandini); P. Suarez, *Leucippe e Teonoe*, 1719 (A. Pollarolo); A. Piovene, *Nerone*, 1721 (G. M. Orlandini); B. Pasqualigo, *Giulio Flavio Crispo*, 1722 (G. M. Capelli); G. Piazzon, *Antigono tutore di Filippo*, 1724 (G. Porta; T. Albinoni).

significance—was going to succeed. By the end of 1725, the upper-class theatres of Venice were prepared to accept other imported, tragic, and classical dramas, written as well as composed by southerners.

Before we follow Venetian audiences into the next season, it may be worth mentioning that other opera-houses seem to have staged 'homages' to Stampiglia in 1724–7. Neapolitan composers were asked for new settings of his famous librettos in several centres in and outside Naples. After the revival of Sarro's *Partenope* at the Teatro Pace in Rome and the Vinci/Leo settings performed in Naples, all in 1724 (see above), Sarro composed *Tito Sempronio Gracco* for the Teatro S. Bartolomeo in January 1725, when the poet was still alive; Vinci composed *Il trionfo di Camilla* for Reggio Emilia in May 1725; Leo set the same drama for the Teatro Capranica, Rome, in Carnival 1726; and Vinci produced *La caduta dei Decemviri* for Naples in autumn 1727.

In the season of 1725–6, the Grimani theatres adopted a distinct preference for Metastasio and his Neapolitan circle. This circle, it can now confidently be stated, included the poet's friend and muse, the famous soprano Marianna Benti Bulgarelli *detta* La Romanina, and the 'Cavaliere' of St Mark's, Nicolò Grimaldi. Benti was a member of the Neapolitan royal chapel and the main performer in settings of Metastasio's early librettos: the serenatas *Angelica* (Porpora, 1720), *Endimione* (Sarro, 1721), *Gli orti Esperidi* (Porpora, 1721), and *La Galatea* (Comito, 1722), and the *drammi per musica* *Siface* (Feo, 1723) and *Didone abbandonata* (Sarro, 1724). For many of her major roles in the early to mid-1720s, she sang opposite Nicolò Grimaldi; both appeared together in the first three productions of *Didone abbandonata* (see below). But their association began in the seasons of 1717–18, when their shared repertory included two appearances in the main roles of a famous *tragedia per musica* by Antonio Salvi which must be called a forerunner of *Didone abbandonata*:

> *Eumene*, Salvi/Albinoni, S. Giovanni Grisostomo, autumn 1717
> *Arsace*, Salvi/M. A. Gasparini, S. Giovanni Grisostomo, carnival 1718
>   (Statira; Arsace)
> *Astianatte*, Salvi/A. Bononcini, S. Giovanni Grisostomo, carnival 1718
> *Rinaldo*, Hill/Handel (rev. Leo), S. Bartolomeo, 1 Oct. 1718
> *Arsace*, Salvi/Sarro, S. Bartolomeo, Dec. 1718 (Statira; Arsace)

Benti and Grimaldi collaborated again in Naples in the 1723 season, and from 1724 onwards all their 'co-productions' concerned Metastasio and a small group of mostly Neapolitan composers:

> *Siface*, Metastasio/Feo, S. Bartolomeo, May 1723 (Viriate; Siface)
> *Silla dittatore*, Cassani/Vinci, S. Bartolomeo, 1 Oct. 1723

Amare per regnare, Passarini/Porpora, S. Bartolomeo, Dec. 1723

Didone abbandonata, Metastasio/Sarro, S. Bartolomeo, carnival 1724
(Didone; Enea)

Didone abbandonata, Metastasio/Albinoni, S. Cassiano, carnival 1725
(Didone; Enea)

Didone abbandonata, Metastasio/Porpora, Reggio Emilia, fiera 1725
(Didone; Enea)

Siface, Metastasio/Porpora, S. Giovanni Grisostomo, carnival 1726
(Viriate; Siface)

Siroe, Metastasio/Vinci, S. Giovanni Grisostomo, carnival 1726 (Emira;
Siroe)

Siroe, Metastasio/Sarro, S. Bartolomeo, carnival 1727 (Emira; Siroe).

This last production apparently saw Benti's final public appearance. Grimaldi, however, went on singing at a rapid pace until his death at the beginning of 1732.[36] With other partners—in Venice, often the young soprano Lucia Facchinelli—he performed the role of Enea also in Sarro's *Didone abbandonata* in Venice, 1730, and that of Siroe also in Porta's setting in Milan, 1727, and with Vinci's music in its Venetian revival in 1731. He created other Metastasian roles—Catone (*Catone in Utica*), Ezio (*Ezio*), Scitalce (*Semiramide riconosciuta*), and Artabano (*Artaserse*)—for their Venetian premières. Other favourite characters included the tragic one of Arsace (see 1718, above)—which he repeated in Milan in 1725 (set by Brusa) and Faenza in 1726 (Orlandini)— as well as Theseus in Pariati's *Arianna e Teseo* (1721, Naples, Leo; 1728, Venice, Porpora; 1728, Florence, Porpora).[37] In addition, it is worth remembering that Grimaldi had performed in both Leo operas given at the Teatro S. Angelo in Carnival 1723: he was involved from the start in the performance of Neapolitan music in Venice. And one other singer belonged, with Benti and Grimaldi, to a kind of team for Metastasian opera: Domenico Gizzi 'napolitano', a member of the royal chapel. He sang the *secondo uomo*, Araspe, in four different productions of *Didone*: in Naples (1724), Venice (1725), Reggio (1725), and Rome (1726; Vinci). He also sang in Metastasio's *Angelica* (1720, Naples) and in *La Galatea* (1722) with Benti, and in three later Metastasian operas in Venice with Grimaldi.

The S. Giovanni Grisostomo season of 1725–6 offered only two *drammi per musica*, both in carnival and both by Metastasio (the only ones extant at the time besides *Didone*), *Siface* and *Siroe*. There was not even an autumn

[36] See Eugenio Faustini-Fasini, 'Gli astri maggiori del "bel canto" napoletano', *Note d'archivio*, 12 (1935), 297–316.

[37] He thus repeated the same dramatic roles, regardless of whether the music was the same or different; there are in fact other examples, contradicting prejudices about the exclusive importance of the music for the singers.

production to contrast with them. *Siface* was given first, in a setting by Porpora of the poet's early effort based on an old libretto by Domenico David. New research on both the librettos and the music of this drama suggests that Porpora composed two versions of his setting in 1725–6:[38] one was performed in Milan, the other at the same time in Venice. For the Milan score, however, the composer used a number of his older arias to suit the singers, almost as in a self-pasticcio. For Venice, the original text by Metastasio, first set by Francesco Feo for Naples in 1723, was largely restored, even including the original *argomento*. It is almost certain that this was due to the poet himself, and that he had been asked to contribute to the production in person. That he was in Venice in that carnival season is shown by a letter he wrote to his brother from Venice (16 February 1726): 'Il mio Siroe è alle stelle molto più che non fece la Didone l'anno scorso.'[39] This also implies that Metastasio had seen the production of *Didone* in 1725, the year before Vinci's *Siroe*. What Metastasio reports here clinches the main argument of this essay: the reputations of Stampiglia and Metastasio, of Naples in general, and of Benti and Grimaldi were insufficient for full Venetian success without the music of Leonardo Vinci.

Siroe re di Persia is a problematic libretto and by no means one of Metastasio's best: the gloomy, psychologically depressing atmosphere contrasts with the somewhat light-hearted handling of disguise, agnition, and the happy ending. The influence, again, of Salvi's *Arsace* (Siroe, like Arsace, spends most of his time in prison) and certain Racinian motives (for example, the jealousy between two terribly unequal brothers, as in *Mithridate*) may have been obvious to contemporaries. But Vinci's music demonstrated a unity of conception between declamation, painting of affections, and dramatic pace which, I believe, was achieved through direct collaboration with the poet and presumably the lead singers. As I have described elsewhere,[40] this collaboration may well have started in Naples in the autumn of 1725 concerning both *Didone abbandonata*, given in Rome in January, and *Siroe*, given in Venice in February. The question is: who or what caused these two first *scritture* for this poet–composer partnership which was to flourish until Vinci's

---

[38] Elena Zomparelli, 'Il *Siface* di P. Metastasio' (tesi di laurea, University of Rome, 1988).

[39] 'My *Siroe* is being raised to the stars much more than *Didone* was last year'; see Pietro Metastasio, *Tutte le opere*, ed. Bruno Brunelli, iii (2nd edn., Milan: Mondadori 1954), no. 25. Johann Joachim Quantz reported in his autobiography that *Siroe* was more successful than *Siface*; he evaluates the singers and mentions that the two composers were present (see Markstrom, 'The Operas of Leonardo Vinci', 158 nn. 73 and 79). Further remarks by Burney on the Venetian season of 1726 confirm the notion of rivalry between Vinci and Porpora; see Burney, *General History of Music*, ed. Mercer, ii. 108; Markstrom, 137–47.

[40] Strohm, 'Leonardo Vinci's *Didone abbandonata* (Rome 1726)', in id., *Essays on Handel and Italian Opera*, 213–24.

death in 1730? We may wonder about the fact that the main venue of the partnership's successes, the Teatro delle Dame in Rome, was the property of the Order of the Knights of Malta, whose Receiver General Fra Camillo Pola has been mentioned above as a patron of Lalli and perhaps Leo in 1723. I suggest, rather, that both the librettist and the composer had independently attracted the interest of patrons and impresarios in Rome and Venice, and that the two rival *scritture* were coincidental.[41] Not that they remained isolated. Barely recruited to the 'Neapolitan fashion', the Venetians already had to compete with Rome, as well as with Naples itself and with secondary centres of the Italian circuit such as Reggio Emilia or Florence, for these coveted productions. In successive seasons from 1726 to 1732, Venice and Rome produced rival performances of the following librettos, composers, or plots (revivals are omitted):[42]

> *Didone abbandonata*, Venice, carnival 1725, Albinoni; Rome, carnival 1726, Vinci
>
> *Siroe*, Venice, carnival 1726, Vinci; Rome, carnival 1727, Porpora
>
> *Catone in Utica*, Rome, carnival 1728, Vinci; Venice, carnival 1729, Leo
>
> *Ezio*, Venice, autumn 1728, Porpora; Rome, carnival 1729, Auletta
>
> *Semiramide riconosciuta*, Rome, carnival 1729, Vinci; Venice, carnival 1729, Porpora
>
> *Artaserse*, Rome, February 1730, Vinci; Venice, February 1730, Hasse
>
> *Alessandro nell'Indie*, Rome, carnival 1730, Vinci; Venice, carnival 1732, Pescetti
>
> *Mitridate*, Venice, carnival 1730, Zeno/Giay; Rome, carnival 1730, Vanstryp/Porpora
>
> *Annibale*, Rome, carnival 1731, Vanstryp/Giacomelli; Venice, autumn 1731, Vanstryp/Porpora

The non-Metastasian operas of 1730 and 1731 were apparently considered as continuations of Metastasio's Italian series (the poet had by then left for Vienna).[43] The other *drammi* are all by Metastasio and constituted all his

---

[41] Charles Burney (*Memoirs of the Life and Writings of the Abate Metastasio* (London, 1796), 36) reported that the Venetian ambassador to Rome brought about the commission to Metastasio for Venice after hearing Sarro's *Didone abbandonata*; see Markstrom, 'The Operas of Leonardo Vinci', 136 (who notes that Burney erroneously gives the place of performance of Sarro's opera as Rome instead of Naples).

[42] Most of these performances took place at the Teatro delle Dame, Rome, and the Teatro S. Giovanni Grisostomo, Venice; exceptions are *Didone* (Venice: S. Cassiano), *Mitridate* and *Annibale* (Rome: Teatro Capranica), and *Annibale* and *Alessandro* (Venice: S. Angelo).

[43] The two librettos by the Roman Arcadian Filippo Vanstryp are both directly modelled after Racine and Corneille and are thus classicist works in the tradition just described.

Italian output. Venice and Rome had both 'adopted' him, and it is no less significant that the first edition of his collected works was begun in 1732 by Bettinelli in Venice.

In many cases, competition alone may provide a motive for the choice of the same work in Venice. The choice of composers also seems to result partly from competition, and not only from policy or patronage. Metastasio usually collaborated with Vinci in Rome until the latter's death in 1730. But there seems to be no particular reason why Porpora interrupts Vinci's series in 1727: probably the Roman impresario got to him first this time. In Venice, composers changed more often: only Porpora was chosen twice in the season 1728–9.

One reason why Porpora plays a somewhat special role in Venice is that since 1726 he had been *maestro del coro* of the Ospedale degl'Incurabili there. This position was surely due to his fame as a singing teacher rather as an opera composer. But Porpora was just the man to exploit any of his chances to the full. The *scrittura* for *Siface*, his Venetian operatic début, may have been due to his Neapolitan connections with Metastasio: he had set the early serenatas *Angelica* and *Gli orti Esperidi* (see above). There is also a possibility that he, rather than Francesco Feo, had originally been asked to set the libretto of *Siface* in 1723 for Naples.[44] Furthermore, by 1724 at the latest Porpora shared Leonardo Leo's privilege of being a friend of Domenico Lalli. Porpora and Lalli already may have collaborated in Naples; they certainly did so after 1720, as in the opera *Damiro e Pitia*, written for Munich in 1724. By that time, Porpora had composed or at least reworked twelve *drammi per musica* for Naples, Rome, and Vienna, although his most successful dramatic work of those years was to become the above-mentioned serenata (*componimento drammatico*) to a text by Stampiglia, *Imeneo* of 1723. When Cardinal Pietro Ottoboni, reconciled with his native city, arrived in Venice for an extended visit in the summer of 1726, the Consiglio dei Dieci decreed that an opera was to be performed in his honour on 20 September at the Grimani Teatro S. Samuele: this was Porpora's *Imeneo*, now rewritten in three acts (rather than two *parti*) and retitled *Imeneo in Atene*.[45] I suggest that Domenico Lalli was the reviser of the libretto. The performance presumably happened at the request of the Cardinal himself, and one singer of his personal household, Domenico Rizzi, appeared in the main role of Tirinto. Did the Cardinal also choose either the librettist or the composer? It is not

---

[44] Metastasio remembered Porpora as late as 1772 in connection with the first performance; see Strohm, *Italienische Opernarien*, ii. 160–1.

[45] For the Ottoboni visit, see also Selfridge-Field, *Pallade Veneta*, 45, and Michael Talbot, 'Vivaldi's Manchester Sonatas', *Proceedings of the Royal Musical Association*, 104 (1977–8), 20–9 at 27.

known whether Porpora had any previous connections with him, but Lalli apparently did.[46] What is more, Lalli dedicated his next libretto, *Argeno*, to Ottoboni in 1728. Porpora, in turn, had scored a moderate success with *Siface* at the Teatro S. Giovanni Grisostomo in the preceding carnival; his position at the Incurabili would have recommended him to the civic authorities to represent the Republic. From then on, the graceful Stampiglia serenata took flight in Porpora's setting, and Porpora and Lalli gained influence at the Grimani theatres.

To be sure, Lalli had other 'friends' as well. One of them was the north Italian composer Giovanni Porta, who since 1717 had already set five librettos from Lalli's pen, the last an *Ulisse* for the Teatro S. Angelo in Carnival 1725. I suspect that the next Venetian opera by Porta, with which S. Giovanni Grisostomo opened its 1726–7 season, *Il trionfo di Flavio Olibrio*, was an adaptation by Lalli of Zeno's *Flavio Anicio Olibrio*. (It is also possible that the earlier of two settings by Porpora of this libretto, given at the Teatro S. Bartolomeo in 1711, also had some traces of Lalli in it.) Porta also composed the second carnival opera in 1727, *Aldiso* (libretto by Claudio Nicola Stampa), but Porpora received the honourable task of writing the first, *Meride e Selinunte* after Apostolo Zeno. It appears that all these librettos were adapted by Lalli. The librettos of *Aldiso* and *Meride* were printed with the old-style (*more veneto*) date of '1726'. Of Porpora's opera, some of the most important sources are in London, including the autograph (British Library, Add. MS 16111) and a copy presumably brought from Venice by a member or associate of the Royal Academy, which then became part of a collection owned by Handel's young friend William Savage (Royal Academy of Music, MS 80). Owen Swiney, writing to the Duke of Richmond, praised the production of *Flavio Olibrio* and commented critically on the cast of the season.[47]

It seems, nevertheless, that the season as a whole did not go very well for the Grimani theatres,[48] and that for this reason the 'Neapolitan element' was

---

[46] See Pagano, *Scarlatti Alessandro e Domenico*, 260.

[47] See Gibson, *The Royal Academy of Music*, 371–2. (letter of 29 Nov. 1726).

[48] In a letter of 23 Feb. 1727 to Madame de Caylus, Antonio Conti praised Vivaldi's operas at the Teatro S. Angelo, but said of the competition: 'Le nouvel Opéra de San Crisostomo a mieux reussi que l'autre par la magnificence des décorations mais la composition est si détestable et la musique si triste que j'y ay dormi pendant un acte' ('The new opera of S. Grisostomo had better success than the old one for its magnificent stage-sets, but the poetry is so contemptible and the music so boring that I slept for a whole act'); see Remo Giazotto, *Antonio Vivaldi* (Turin: ERI, 1973), 214. This suggests that the first S. Giovanni Grisostomo opera, *Meride e Selinunte*, was unsuccessful, and that in the second, *Aldiso* (by Giovanni Porta), the libretto and music still did not please Conti. For clarifications about this correspondence, see Karl Heller, *Vivaldi: Cronologia della vita e dell'opera* (Florence: Olschki, 1991), 45, and Michael Talbot, 'Vivaldi and the Empire', *Informazioni e studi vivaldiani*, 8 (1987), 31–50 at 39–40.

increased again in 1727–8. Only two operas were given, but both settings were commissioned from Neapolitan composers. The libretto of Porpora's *Arianna e Teseo*, in autumn, was a reworking of Pietro Pariati's *Teseo in Creta* (1715, Vienna) following, with slight alterations, a revision made by an unknown librettist for the Teatro S. Bartolomeo in Naples in 1721. Here, Leonardo Leo had arranged the music as a pasticcio, with many arias of his own, and in 1729 he returned to the libretto, giving it a new setting all of his own for the Roman Teatro Pace. (This libretto became the immediate model for Handel's *Arianna in Creta*.) Porpora's music for Venice is a remarkably good effort for him: it was repeated in Florence the following summer but not in London in 1733–4 when Handel, for the King's Theatre, used Pariati's libretto (Porpora, for the Opera of the Nobility, had to set an *Arianna in Nasso* by Paolo Rolli instead). Nevertheless, the only musical sources of Porpora's Venetian opera are in England, including his autograph of the second act (British Library, Add. MS 14114). One wonders if any understanding with Leo had been reached before using the version of the text already arranged for him in Naples. Leo's new opera of this season, *Argeno*, represented a renewal of his collaboration with Lalli as librettist (who, as we have seen, dedicated the libretto to Cardinal Pietro Ottoboni). This opera seems to have been very successful, playing for the whole carnival season. Owen Swiney reports on the success obtained in this and the preceding opera by Nicolò Grimaldi, who had returned to the Teatro S. Giovanni Grisostomo.[49] Leo's score is found in a number of places, among them, again, the William Savage collection (Royal Academy of Music, MS 74), and it seems possible that Handel once considered the work for use as a pasticcio.[50] Leo himself seems to have been pleased with the libretto, which offers a wide range of violent emotions in an exotic (East Asian) context: he reused it for a largely new setting (*Argene*) for Naples in 1731.[51]

In the Venetian season of 1728–9, all the protagonists of our story are assembled: Lalli and Metastasio, Porpora and Leo, and Nicolò Grimaldi. Also, the main topics are all there: rivalry with Rome, librettos of *gravità e decoro*, and immediate transmission abroad. But another ingredient can now be added: a new star castrato. Many contemporary witnesses identify the first appearance in Venice of Carlo Broschi *detto* Farinelli as the main event of

---

[49] Gibson, *The Royal Academy of Music*, 377 (letter of 13 Feb. 1728).

[50] This is apparently the *Argeneo* mentioned in Thomas Kerslake's sales catalogue of scores from Handel's estate: see Hans Dieter Clausen, *Händels Direktionspartituren ('Handexemplare')* (Hamburg: Wagner, 1972), 17. In fact, Handel used only one aria from Leo's *Argeno* ('Tuona il ciel'), in his pasticcio *Ormisda*, but this may suggest in any case that he had access to the score.

[51] Also in 1731, Leo composed a totally new setting of Lalli's *I veri amici* for Rome under the title *Evergete*.

the season. The Teatro S. Giovanni Grisostomo had of course outflanked other competitors in hiring him. This ex-pupil of Porpora, often presented in librettos as 'napolitano', had rather a late début in Venice: perhaps he was kept away by the jealousy of other singers and their protectors. Whatever the case, however, his resounding success overshadowed, according to contemporary reports, even the appearances of Faustina Bordoni and Senesino at the Teatro S. Cassiano.

Several British customers were in Venice this season, including Handel, who in fact tried to hire Farinelli for London. One of the directors of the Royal Academy, Sir John Buckworth, seems to have attended the three main operas at the Teatro S. Giovanni Grisostomo—Porpora's *Ezio*, Leo's *Catone in Utica*, and Porpora's *Semiramide riconosciuta*—since he owned full scores of all of them (now in the William Savage collection: Royal Academy of Music, MSS 79, 75, and 81 respectively). Buckworth must have lent the score of *Catone* to Handel, who used it to prepare his pasticcio of the same title in 1732.[52] The libretto of *Semiramide riconosciuta* was dedicated to Buckworth by Domenico Lalli. Likewise, the dedications of *Ezio*, played in autumn, and of *Catone in Utica*, the first carnival opera, were signed by Lalli.[53]

The significance of these dedications is that all three librettos were new works by Metastasio. Since the Venetian success of his *Siroe re di Persia* of 1726, the poet had not produced a new drama for Venice. His *Catone in Utica*, given with Vinci's music in Rome in January 1728, had not reached Venice that carnival. But while presenting it as the first carnival opera in 1729, the Teatro S. Giovanni Grisostomo also got hold of the two new librettos which Metastasio was just preparing for the same Roman season. *Ezio* reached Venice even before it was premièred in Rome at the Teatro delle Dame on 26 December 1728 (with music by Pietro Auletta). Lalli revised the libretto, Porpora set it to music, and the opera was put into rehearsal all before the end of November (the dedication of Lalli's libretto is dated 20 November 1728). *Semiramide riconosciuta* reached the stage shortly thereafter (in February 1729) in Vinci's setting for Rome. It is almost certain that Metastasio had authenticated and directed the Roman versions of these operas. We can only speculate how the Venetians got hold of his newest dramas: with Lalli's help, and possibly with a large thank-offering to the new star librettist. Why they were so keen to produce these works can no longer be in doubt.

[52] See Strohm, 'Handel's Pasticci', 179–82.
[53] *Ezio* was dedicated to Count Harrach, the Austrian ambassador who later became Viceroy of Naples, and *Catone* to the Neapolitan Don Domenico Marzio Pacecco Carafa, Prince of Mataloni.

It is also certain that Leonardo Leo was allowed to use a revision of
Catone in Utica which the poet himself later acknowledged and printed.[54]
Like *Didone abbandonata*, this drama had a tragic ending (Cato's suicide), the
staging of which had been criticized in Rome in 1728. Metastasio then
wrote a new version in which the suicide happens off-stage. Although Leo's
setting of the revised *Catone* was later used by Handel (where the ending is
further conventionalized), its effect in Venice was perhaps spoilt by the
casting. Nicolò Grimaldi excelled in the title-role, and Domenico Gizzi, the
Neapolitan castrato mentioned above as a partner of Grimaldi and Benti,
sang Cesare. But both were overshadowed by Farinelli's showmanship in the
secondary role of Arbace, for which additional arias were inserted having
little to do with the drama. The editions of the libretto identify these with
asterisks, probably out of respect for Metastasio. Some of these arias—not all
of them by Leo—were circulated widely. In *Ezio* and *Semiramide*, however,
the forces of the same three singers were much better balanced, but fewer
of Porpora's arias attained any popularity. This is perhaps confirmed by the
last S. Giovanni Grisostomo opera this season, *L'abbandono d'Armida*, a pasticcio
arranged by Antonio Pollarolo exclusively for the last night of carnival from
famous arias heard earlier in Venice. Of its total of fourteen arias, four are
drawn from *Catone*, but only two from *Semiramide*, and one from *Ezio*. Interestingly, Handel chose as the basis for his pasticcio *Semiramide riconosciuta*
(1733) the homonymous opera by Vinci, not by Porpora, although he must
have had easy access to the latter. To use eighteenth-century metaphors, if
Vinci was a true painter of the affections, then Porpora was a skilful deco-
rator. As for Leo, his achievement is for some reason underrated today. But
then, he does not seem to have quite seized his chance. Perhaps the opportunity of presenting a Metastasian 'first' in Venice was spoilt for him by the
imbalanced casting and by his own difficulties, discernible elsewhere, with
heroic subjects. Be that as it may, both Leo and Porpora were nearing the
end of their luck with the fickle Venetians. Although the next season at the
Teatro S. Giovanni Grisostomo was artistically controlled by Lalli like none
before, neither composer appeared in it. Obviously, Lalli and his superiors
wanted still newer musical attractions.

With one exception, the pattern of 'discovery' or promotion of Neapolitan
opera seria composers in Venice changed around 1730. From then on for decades to come, Venetian *scritture* for new *opere serie* always strike a fair deal
between southern and northern artists: Riccardo Broschi (1730), Sellitto
(1733), Araia (1734), Fiorillo (1736), Pergolesi (1738), etc. alternate with the

---

[54] See Metastasio, *Tutte le opere*, ed. Brunelli, i (2nd edn., Milan: Mondadori, 1953),
1399 ff., and Strohm, *Italienische Opernarien*, ii. 185.

northerners Cordans (1728), Pescetti and Galuppi (1728), Giacomelli (1729), Ciampi (1729), Giay (1730), Courcelle (1732), Schiassi (1735), and so forth. Established local composers such as Albinoni and Vivaldi still dominate the minor opera-houses. Of course, such even-handedness would have been unthinkable around 1720, when the southern element simply was not there.

The one composer who did not fit even the new pattern was Johann Adolf Hasse. I believe that in this last case of a spectacular Neapolitan success, ulterior motives and personal influences once more helped a great musical talent along. Hasse's training with Alessandro Scarlatti (1724) and his operatic career in Naples (1725–9) had been rather brief when he was able to attract the Venetian *scrittura* for Metastasio's newest libretto, *Artaserse*, late in 1729. As in the season of 1728–9, the impresario managed to get hold of the freshly written drama and to have it performed at almost the same time as Vinci's 'official' première in Rome (4 February 1730): I estimate that Hasse's setting for Venice was premièred as soon as two weeks later. The stream of revivals flowing from both Vinci's and Hasse's *Artaserse* settings is in itself the single most substantial tradition in eighteenth-century *opera seria*.

Hasse's setting was already the fourth opera at the Teatro S. Giovanni Grisostomo this season. The others (see also above) were: Francesco Ciampi's *Onorio*, a humble work actually revived in London in 1735 (Opera of the Nobility); Riccardo Broschi's *Idaspe* (first carnival opera), whose major interest was the arias for the composer's brother Carlo, i.e. Farinelli; and *Mitridate* by the Turin composer Giovanni Antonio Giay. All three libretti were written (*Onorio*) or adapted by Lalli; his transformation of Zeno's *Mitridate* into a classical five-act drama was especially ambitious. No doubt the fact that the Teatro Capranica was putting on a *Mitridate* directly derived from Racine (see above) was an influence. For Hasse, Lalli delegated much of the rewriting of the aria texts to an assistant he had been using since 1728, Giovanni Boldini, who succeeded in giving Hasse the basis for such epochal successes as 'Pallido il sole' and 'Lascia cadermi in volto'.[55] To avoid offending Metastasio, a second edition of the libretto was distributed with his unaltered text, to which the revised libretto explicitly refers. One wonders whether this was Metastasio's condition for giving his new drama away: he may have felt that the asterisks in Leo's *Catone* libretto did not suffice to protect his authorial claims.

Further observations, including the striking similarity between some of Hasse's and Vinci's settings of the same aria texts (for example, 'Amalo, e se al tuo sguardo'),[56] give the impression that there was some connection

---

[55] On these pieces, see Daniel Heartz, 'Hasse, Galuppi and Metastasio', in Muraro (ed.), *Venezia e il melodramma nel Settecento*, 309–39.

[56] See Strohm, *Italienische Opernarien*, i. 141–3, 149 (text), and ii, nos. 73 and 74 (music).

between Metastasio, Hasse, and Vinci over the planning of both operas. This was technically possible—all three were still resident in Naples in late 1729—and certainly Metastasio later expressed his high esteem for both composers' music. Hasse had the asset—in the poet's eyes—of composing for Grimaldi and Farinelli; Vinci could rely on Carestini and on Metastasio's darling soprano, Giacinto Fontana. This hypothesis may further imply that Metastasio himself had given Hasse some help in obtaining the Venetian *scrittura*, since he was obviously asked first for his permission to use the libretto.

Later this spring Hasse married Faustina Bordoni, with whom he collaborated for the first time in his opera *Dalisa*, given in May at the Teatro S. Samuele. The libretto of this superfluous little opera had been revised and dedicated (to Edward Coke) by Domenico Lalli. In *Artaserse*, however, Faustina's arch-rival, the Florentine Francesca Cuzzoni, was the prima donna. Faustina had been a mainstay of the Teatro S. Giovanni Grisostomo from 1718 until 1725, when she created all three title-roles of the Pasqualigo–Orlandini–Vinci season. On her return from London in 1728, however, she accepted a contract with the Teatro S. Cassiano, together with Senesino. This may have lost her the engagement at the Teatro S. Giovanni Grisostomo in Carnival 1730, which she spent in Turin (in fact, singing Porpora). My suspicion about who brought her back into the fold of the Grimani theatres, and thus possibly acquainted her with Hasse, focuses on Domenico Lalli.

Porpora and Leo had fallen from favour at the Grimani theatres. Lalli continued to supervise the productions at least as regards the texts, but his signature on the librettos of Sarro's *Didone abbandonata* (autumn 1730) and a revival of Vinci's *Siroe* (Carnival 1731, with additions by Galuppi and Pescetti) also hints at some manner of influence over the music. Indirect evidence—a letter written by Vivaldi on 29 December 1736—further suggests that some sort of control over S. Samuele and S. Giovanni Grisostomo productions around 1732–6 was in the hands of Michele Grimani.[57] Thus, the Grimani themselves probably favoured Hasse, who in 1732 produced Metastasio's *Demetrio* at the Teatro S. Giovanni Grisostomo, a particularly successful work, and Zeno's *Euristeo* at the Teatro S. Samuele. Of his many operas heard later in Venice, the most remarkable was a revision of his setting of Metastasio's *Alessandro nell'Indie* in 1736. Leo withdrew to Naples. Porpora found things to do in Turin and Rome, visiting the Teatro S. Angelo (in Vivaldi's absence) in autumn 1731 with an *Annibale* written in

---

[57] Vivaldi says that the manuscript scores of two operas requested from him were deposited at 'Ca' Grimani' with Michiel Grimani, and that it was not easy to have them copied. The two operas were, in my reconstruction of the events, Hasse's *Demetrio* of 1732 and his *Alessandro nell'Indie* of 1736. See Francesco Degrada and Maria Teresa Muraro (eds.), *Antonio Vivaldi da Venezia all'Europa* (Milan: Electa, 1978), 95–6.

Rome (see above); and from 1733 he was in the service of the Opera of the Nobility in London. In 1732 his post as *maestro delle figlie del coro* at the Incurabili had gone to Hasse, who managed to reconcile a foreign position (Dresden) with Venetian residency.

Setting librettos by Metastasio was something like a sports competition in which the winner could make music history, provided he was a Neapolitan. Vinci outclassed Sarro, Porpora, and even Leo in all the Metastasian operas before 1730,[58] when he had to accept a draw with Hasse, despite the latter's use of a Venetianized *Artaserse*. For the next twenty years or so, Hasse dictated the style of Metastasian opera from wherever he happened to work. The extent to which Hasse was as true a Neapolitan opera composer as all these others is still undetermined. But it is a fact that Venice promoted him, and Neapolitan opera, into the great operatic world of the Settecento.

The underlying question of this study—'who or what makes opera history?'—has not found a clear answer. We can see that the European critics who in the eighteenth century first conceived of the 'Neapolitan myth' were not only guided by taste (a taste which, by the way, nineteenth-century musicology did not share) but also swayed by box-office successes. These successes, in turn, can be traced with surprising precision to the 1720s, and to a tangle of mere accident, individual volition, personal relations, rivalries, and careerism, especially that of an exiled Neapolitan who promoted his compatriots. No major pattern of artistic policy or patronage emerges. Strategies were aimed at immediate success and lasted for one to three seasons. Little emerges from the study of the dedicatees of librettos. The impresarios —not known by name—remain in the background, whereas librettists and composers seem to be the driving force. Few individuals are involved: four composers and four librettists, one of the latter entirely passively. These artists—and to a lesser extent, the singers—seem to have to make their own beds in each new season, playing on audience expectations, which we can only identify in the areas of poetic taste and singing ability. But some of these artists had a luckier hand than others. What counted, at least in part, was an individual's ability to exploit his chances (Leo did not in 1723 and 1729; Vinci did in 1725, etc.), and also, perhaps, his sensitivity to broader trends of the times. Some of the final verdicts (but not necessarily those pursued by premature ambition) tend to coincide with the impressions gained by modern musicologists who have studied these scores. I wonder whether in this case the benefits of hindsight can find some contemporary justification: the 1720s may have been the historic moment when criteria of content

---

[58] Except for *Ezio*, which was not touched by Vinci and which remained a risky drama for any composer's reputation, even Handel's.

and quality—musical as well as poetic—started to 'show through' in the business of Italian opera. Patronage, opportunity, and status were still decisive, but those who wrote better librettos and scores at that historic moment became more successful than those who even then remained humble agents of an aristocratic pastime.

12

Vivaldi and the Pasticcio:
Text and Music in *Tamerlano*

ERIC CROSS

IN his seminal essay 'Towards an Understanding of the *Opera seria*',[1] Reinhard Strohm questions the validity of the concept of the individual 'work' when dealing with Italian operatic practice of the early eighteenth century. Instead, he advocates viewing operas of this period as 'productions', dominated less by the wishes of the composer than by the influence of the individual singers employed for that particular season. This undoubtedly reflects the relationship between singers and composers described in many contemporary sources, as well as their status in terms of financial reward.[2] But where does this leave the relationship between music and drama in *opera seria* of this period? Were composers (with the obvious exception of Handel, who, as Strohm points out, was working within a very different set of constraints) concerned in any way with a work's larger-scale structure and balance, and what was their approach at the level of the individual aria?

I am grateful to the Research Committee of the University of Newcastle upon Tyne for support in the preparation of this essay.

---

[1] In Strohm, *Essays on Handel and Italian Opera* (Cambridge University Press, 1985), 93–105.

[2] For example, the surviving accounts for Hasse's setting of Nicolò Minato's *Dalisa* in 1730 show that the prima donna, Faustina Bordoni, received 5,625 lire for creating the title-role. Her husband probably received about a quarter of that sum; a total of 2,380 lire was paid to the 'Maestri di musica', of which Hasse himself would presumably have received the lion's share. It is also interesting to note that Vivaldi's protégée, the mezzo-soprano Anna Girò, also sang in this production, though she was clearly regarded as the 'seconda donna', receiving only 1,320 lire. These figures are quoted in Nicola Mangini, *I teatri di Venezia* (Milan: Morsia, 1974), 105, where they are erroneously given in ducats. This is corrected by Michael Talbot, *Tomaso Albinoni: The Venetian Composer and his World* (Oxford: Clarendon Press, 1990), 203, although he suggests that Hasse would have received the full sum allocated to the *maestri*. Vivaldi himself claimed in a letter of 3 Nov. 1736 to Marquis Guido Bentivoglio that his normal fee was 100 *zecchini* (2,200 lire); see Adriano Cavicchi, 'Inediti nell'epistolario Vivaldi–Bentivoglio', *Nuova rivista musicale italiana*, 1 (1967), 45–79 at 50.

These questions become even more pertinent when discussing the pasticcio. By the beginning of the eighteenth century it was common for operatic revivals to contain foreign arias, and many leading composers were involved in producing pasticcios. Bearing in mind that the pressure for inserting new arias often came from the singers, it is not surprising that two of the best-known composers to compile pasticcios during the first half of the century—Handel and Vivaldi—also often acted as impresarios. Handel turned to the pasticcio for several works for the London stage in the 1730s, and Vivaldi, too, relied much more on the pasticcio during this decade. Both composers must have recognized that the new style cultivated by many of the younger composers, particularly those centred on Naples, was proving extremely popular with the general public. Its great emphasis on the voice and on vocal technique provided a showcase for modern virtuosos trained by teachers such as Porpora, and this new vocal style was closely tied up with the new literary taste for the lyrical poetry of Metastasio. Handel favoured arias by Leo, Vinci, and Hasse in his efforts to beat the rival Opera of the Nobility at its own game, although it is perhaps significant that his pasticcios did not attract large audiences, and that his own operas in fact generally had longer runs.[3]

The pasticcio clearly presents something of an aesthetic dilemma. According to Strohm:

> Probably it should not be judged by aesthetic standards that cannot also be applied to original operas of the period, for the unity of musical style, the integrity of characterization and the balance and cohesion of the drama are not necessarily either better or worse in pasticcios than in original works. The unity of an opera was not guaranteed simply by the fact that all its parts came from the same composer; rather it resulted from a clever arrangement of those parts to achieve a balance among various degrees of dramatic and lyric expression. An artistically capable arranger, when filling out and dressing up the work of another with insertions and additions for a repeat performance, was also able to achieve this unity. In London in 1732 the pasticcio *Catone* (music by Leo and others) was mistaken for a work by Handel; it is scarcely possible even for the expert listener to differentiate between an original and a pasticcio.[4]

One of Vivaldi's most interesting works to examine from this viewpoint is his pasticcio *Tamerlano*. Although the libretto and its background have recently been exhaustively documented,[5] this study says very little about the

[3] See Reinhard Strohm, 'Handel's Pasticci', in id., *Essays on Handel and Italian Opera*, 164–211.

[4] 'Pasticcio', *The New Grove Dictionary of Music and Musicians*, ed. Stanley Sadie (London: Macmillan, 1980), xiv. 289.

[5] In Anna Laura Bellina, Bruno Brizi, and Maria Grazia Pensa, 'Il pasticcio Bajazet: La "favola" del Gran Tamerlano nella messinscena di Vivaldi', in Antonio Fanna and Giovanni Morelli (eds.), *Nuovi studi vivaldiani* (Florence: Olschki, 1988), 185–272.

music. What does this opera suggest about Vivaldi's approach to the retexting of arias, or about the relationship between the original dramatic context of borrowed arias and their new context within Vivaldi's work? And how does his approach to the libretto relate to that of other composers?

The story of the fourteenth-century emperor Tamerlane and his defeat of the sultan Bajazet was a source for many different librettos during the early eighteenth century. Among these were Antonio Salvi's *Il gran Tamerlano*— first set by Alessandro Scarlatti for Pratolino in 1706 and later by Francesco Gasparini and two of his pupils as *Il Trace in catena* (1717, Rome)—and Agostin Piovene's *Tamerlano*, first performed with music by Gasparini at the Teatro S. Cassiano, Venice, in January 1711. The latter libretto was revised by Ippolito Zanelli to include the dramatic on-stage suicide by Bajazet, and this text was reset by Gasparini for Reggio Emilia as *Il Bajazet* (the dedication of the libretto is dated 29 April 1719). Although only nine arias from Gasparini's earlier setting survive, the complete 1719 score has come down to us in two copies. For this production many new aria texts were added, and some of the original 1711 texts were given completely new musical settings. According to the *Protesta* of the 1719 libretto, although the drama, now entitled 'Bajazet', was the same as that performed elsewhere under the title 'Tamerlano', the balance of the parts was altered, 'particularly as regards the arias, which always need to be accommodated to new musicians. . . . In having Bajazet seen more or less dying on the stage, after he has taken poison, we have followed the aforementioned French tragedian' ('particolarmente nell'Arie, che sempre esigono d'essere accomodate a' nuovi Musici. . . . Nel far veder Bajazet, e poco men, che spirar sulla Scena, dopo aver' egli preso veleno, si è seguito il sunnominato Tragico Franzese').[6]

Handel originally based his *Tamerlano*, first performed at the King's Theatre on 31 October 1724, on Piovene's early version of the text, but it is clear that at some point during the work's composition he became aware of both

---

[6] IL | BAJAZET | DRAMMA PER MUSICA | Da rappresentarsi nel teatro dell'Illustrissimo | Pubblico di Reggio in occasione della | Fiera l'Anno MDCCXIX (Reggio: Vedrotti, 1719), 6–7, in Venice, Fondazione Giorgio Cini, Gasparini A–B; reproduced in Howard Mayer Brown (ed.), *Italian Opera Librettos: 1640–1770* (New York and London: Garland, 1978), iii. The important influence of French tragedy on opera librettos at this time has recently been examined by Reinhard Strohm in '"Tragédie" into "Dramma per Musica"', *Informazioni e studi vivaldiani*, 9 (1988), 14–25; 10 (1989), 57–102; 11 (1990), 11–26; 12 (1991), 47–75. Although the libretto's tragic ending, emphasized in the 1719 version, is an important precedent for Metastasio's librettos such as *Didone abbandonata* and *Catone in Utica*, Piovene was by no means the first librettist to experiment in this fashion; for details of other operas with a *funesto fine* before 1730, see Strohm, in *Informazioni e studi vivaldiani*, 11 (1990), 15. The difficulty in deciding whether the tyrant or the sultan should be the central character is reflected in the 1735 setting, where the libretto is entitled *Il Tamerlano* while Vivaldi's score is headed *Il Bajazet*.

the 1719 libretto and score through the arrival of the tenor Francesco Borosini, who had sung Bajazet in Gasparini's opera and was to recreate the part for Handel. Thus Handel's text, prepared for him by Nicola Haym, is an amalgam of Gasparini's two librettos.[7] Vivaldi's setting, first performed at the Teatro Filarmonico, Verona, in Carnival 1735, owes much to the original 1711 libretto, although it has been shown that this text was transmitted through a Milanese production of 1727 (the cast included Anna Girò), with some additional influences from a Venetian version of 1723.[8]

The ways in which some of these different productions approached Piovene's libretto can be seen from Figs. 1–4.[9] In the original 1711 production, the hierarchy of the roles is clear from the number of arias (see Fig. 1). Asteria (sung by Santa Stella) is prima donna with a total of nine arias;[10] Tamerlano and Bajazet are next in line with five and six respectively; Andronico and Irene are clearly secondary characters with four each; and the minor figures of Leone, Tamur, and Zaida receive none at all. In 1719 (see Fig. 2) the role of Asteria (Marianna Benti Bulgarelli, called 'La Romanina') is reduced to six arias, now on a par with Bajazet (whose relative importance was increased for the distinguished tenor Francesco Borosini and reflected in the opera's change of title). Indeed, there is an equal weighting between all five main roles, while Leone and Clearco receive three and four arias respectively, and even Zaida is given one. Haym's arrangement of the text for

---

[7] For details of the relationship between the works of Gasparini and Handel, and the role played by Borosini, see J. Merrill Knapp, 'Handel's "Tamerlano": The Creation of an Opera', *Musical Quarterly*, 56 (1970), 405–30; Winton Dean and J. Merrill Knapp, *Handel's Operas 1704–1726* (Oxford: Clarendon Press, 1987), 527–71; and Judith L. Sheridan, 'Handel's "Tamerlano": A Contextual Study' (M.Phil. diss., University of Lancaster, 1988). The most recent study of Handel's score is Terence Best, 'New Light on the Manuscript Copies of "Tamerlano"', *Göttinger Händel-Beiträge*, 4 (1991), 34–45.

[8] Bellina *et al.*, 'Il pasticcio Bajazet', 210.

[9] This information is taken mainly from the printed librettos: TAMERLANO | TRAGEDIA | PER MUSICA | Da rappresentarsi | NEL TEATRO TRON | DI SAN CASSIANO | L'Anno 1710 (Venice: Rossetti, [1711]), in Venice, Biblioteca Nazionale Marciana, Dramm. 3531.4; the copy of *Il Bajazet* in the Fondazione Cini, Venice (see above, n. 6); TAMERLANO: | DRAMA. | Da Rappresentarsi | Nel REGIO TEATRO | di HAY-MARKET, | PER | La Reale Accademia di Musica (London, King's Theatre, 1724), in London, British Library, 162.g.41; reproduced in Brown (ed.), *Italian Opera Librettos: 1640–1770*,·iii; and IL | TAMERLANO | TRAGEDIA PER MUSICA | Da rappresentarsi | NEL NUOVO TEATRO | DELL'ACCADEMIA | FILARMONICA | Nel Carnovale dell'anno 1735 (Verona: Vallarsi, [1735]), in Milan, Biblioteca Nazionale Braidense, Racc. Dramm. 3653. The presence of several minor characters, particularly Zaida, in certain scenes is not always specified, although it is sometimes implied by the action.

[10] The figures for Asteria throughout include her short mid-scene aria text 'Folle sei', which occurs in Act III, Scene xi of the 1711 libretto. This text is given a fifteen-bar setting by Handel in his III. viii, although in Gasparini's 1719 setting it is reduced to a mere four bars in III. xiii. The text does not occur at all in Vivaldi's 1735 setting.

FIG. 1. Structure of Gasparini/Piovene, *Tamerlano* (Venice, 1711)

Act I

	1	2	3	4	5	6	7	8	9	10	11	12
Tamerlano			A			A						
Bajazet	A							A				
Asteria					A				A			A
Andronico				A								
Irene											A	
Leone												
Tamur												
Zaida												
stage sets	Guard-room of Tamerlano's palace				Apartments appointed for Bajazet and Asteria					Courtyard adjoining the garden		

Act II

	1	2	3	4	5	6	7	8	9	10	11	12	13	14
Tamerlano	A				A					T				
Bajazet								A		T	A			
Asteria			A			A				T				A
Andronico				A								A		
Irene							A						A	
Leone														
Tamur														
Zaida														
	Gallery which then opens ...				... to reveal Tamerlano's cabinet				Room with two thrones					

Act III

	1	2	3	4	5	6	7	8	9	10	11	12	13	14	15	Aria totals
Tamerlano				A											C	5 + T
Bajazet	A											A				6 + T
Asteria				A							a			A		9 + T
Andronico						A									C	4
Irene									A						C	4
Leone															C	0
Tamur															C	0
Zaida															C	0
	Part of the harem in which Bajazet and Asteria are held by soldiers							Imperial hall with a table laid for Tamerlano								

Key: Shading = on stage for at least part of the scene; A = aria; a = short aria/arioso; T = trio; Q = quartet; C = coro

FIG. 2. Structure of Gasparini/Piovene–Zanelli, *Il Bajazet* (Reggio Emilia, 1719)

Act I

	1	2	3	4	5	6	7	8	9	10	11	12	13	14	15
Tamerlano			A				A								
Bajazet	A								A						
Asteria											A				A
Andronico				A										A	
Irene											A	A			
Leone							A								
Clearco			A										A		
Zaida															
stage sets	Quarters for the guards who are holding Bajazet					Apartments appointed for Bajazet and Asteria					Court of the imperial palace adjoining the garden				

Act II

	1	2	3	4	5	6	7	8	9	10	11	12	13	14	15
Tamerlano	A			A							T				
Bajazet									A		T	A			
Asteria		A									T				A
Andronico			A										A		
Irene							A							A	
Leone								A							
Clearco						A									
Zaida															
	Gallery which then opens...			...to reveal Tamerlano's cabinet							Throne-room				

Act III

	1	2	3	4	5	6	7	8	9	10	11	12	13	14	15	16	17	18	*Aria totals*
Tamerlano				A														C	5 + T
Bajazet	A															a			6 + T
Asteria													a			A			6 + T
Andronico									A									C	5
Irene									A				A					C	6
Leone		A																C	3
Clearco								A										C	4
Zaida			A																1
	Courtyard of the harem adjoining the towers, where Bajazet and Asteria are held								Hall prepared for Tamerlano's meal									

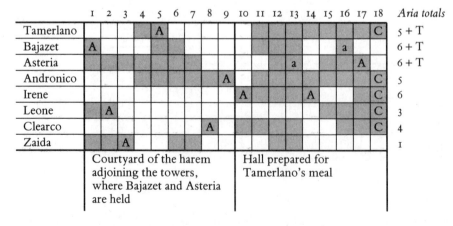

Handel (see Fig. 3) continues this weighting, with Borosini recreating the role of Bajazet in six arias, the same number as for Asteria and Andronico. Tamerlano and Irene are reduced to four each, while Leone has just one.[11] Vivaldi's libretto sees a further levelling process (see Fig. 4). Gone are the minor roles of Tamur (the head of Tamerlano's eunuchs), Zaida (Asteria's maidservant and confidante), and Leone (Andronico's confidant and Bajazet's general in 1719); all are replaced by Idaspe, who acts as Andronico's confidant and sings three arias. Andronico, Tamerlano, and Bajazet have four arias each, while Asteria has five, as one might predict, given that the role was sung by Anna Girò.

However, it is not just the number of arias which reflects the importance of individual characters. The length of time during which an actor remains on the stage can also influence the perception of his or her role. In Piovene's original libretto, there are seven different stage sets: Act I: Guard-room of Tamerlano's palace; Apartments appointed for Bajazet and Asteria; Court-yard adjoining the garden; Act II: Gallery which then opens (typically, by raising a curtain at the beginning of Scene v) to reveal Tamerlano's cabinet; Room with two thrones; Act III: Part of the harem in which Bajazet and Asteria are held by soldiers; Imperial hall with a table laid for Tamerlano.[12] This produces eight 'scene-complexes', counting the Act II transformation from gallery to cabinet (Scenes i–iv, and v–viii) as two (compare Fig. 1). Andronico is on the stage throughout the first (I. i–iv) and fourth (II. i–iv) of these scene-complexes, while Asteria (along with her maidservant Zaida) is similarly present during the second (I. v–ix) and sixth (II. ix–xiv). Irene and Tamur (in hiding for part of the time) are on the stage for the whole of the long final *mutazione* of Act III, and are joined from Scene ix by Tamerlano and Andronico.

The same pattern holds true for the 1719 libretto, although in Act III Irene departs after singing her aria in Scene xiv, so that the emphasis is placed slightly more on Tamerlano and Andronico. Haym's layout is similar, although Asteria, partly in hiding, is on the stage throughout the first section of the final act, which culminates not in a solo aria for Andronico but in his duet with Asteria. The part of Andronico, however, is emphasized in other ways. The first act now ends with a soliloquy for him (Handel, as an afterthought, added strings to accompany the recitative here),[13] so that four

---

[11] However, the part of Leone was expanded in 1731 when the fine new bass Montagnana took over the part from Boschi; see Dean and Knapp, *Handel's Operas*, 556.

[12] 'Corpo di Guardia del Palazzo del Tamerlano'; 'Appartamenti destinati à Bajazet, ed Asteria'; 'Cortile corrispondente al Giardino'; 'Galleria che poi s'apre con veduta del Gabinetto del Tamerlano'; 'Sala con due Troni'; 'Parte del Serraglio in cui sono custoditi da' Soldati Bajazet, ed Asteria'; 'Salone Imperiale che serve alle mense del Tamerlano'.

[13] See fo. 39ʳ of the autograph score, in London, British Library, RM 20.c.11.

Fɪɢ. 3. Structure of Handel/Piovene–Zanelli–Haym, *Tamerlano* (London, 1724)

Act I

	1	2	3	4	5	6	7	8	9
Tamerlano		A		A					
Bajazet	A					A			
Asteria					A		A		
Andronico			A						A
Irene								A	
Leone									
Zaida (unspecified)									
stage sets	The place where Bajazet is imprisoned			Apartments appointed for Bajazet and Asteria in Tamerlano's palace				A court in Tamerlano's palace	

Act II

	1	2	3	4	5	6	7	8	9	10	
Tamerlano	A								T		
Bajazet							A		T	A	
Asteria		A							T		A
Andronico			A				A			A	
Irene						A					A
Leone						A					
Zaida (unspecified)											
stage sets	Gallery leading to Tamerlano's cabinet			The curtain on the cabinet opens to reveal Tamerlano and Asteria			Throne-room				

Act III

	1	2	3	4	5	6	7	8	9	10	11	Aria totals
Tamerlano			A								C	4 + T
Bajazet								A		a		6 + T
Asteria	A				D			a				6 + D + T
Andronico					D		A				C	6 + D
Irene							A				C	4
Leone											C	1
Zaida (unspecified)												silent role
stage sets	Courtyard in the harem, in which Bajazet and Asteria are kept by soldiers					Imperial hall prepared for Tamerlano's meal						

FIG. 4. Structure of Vivaldi/Piovene–Vivaldi, *Tamerlano* (Verona, 1735)

Act I

	1	2	3	4	5	6	7	8	9	10	11	12
Tamerlano			A			A						
Bajazet	A											
Asteria								A				
Andronico				A								A
Irene											A	
Idaspe		A										

stage sets	Delightful place in the royal palace . . .	Royal apartments appointed for Asteria and Bajazet who are under guard

Act II

	1	2	3	4	5	6	7	8	9	10
Tamerlano					A					Q
Bajazet								A		Q
Asteria			A			A				Q
Andronico				A						
Irene							A			Q
Idaspe		A								

	Countryside with Tamerlano's pavilion which suddenly opens . . .	. . . to reveal Tamerlano and Asteria seated on two cushions	Battle-field with a throne . . .

Act III

	1	2	3	4	5	6	7	8	9	10	11	12	13	14	15	Aria totals
Tamerlano				A											C	4 + Q
Bajazet	A										A					4 + Q
Asteria						A								A		5 + Q
Andronico								A							C	4
Irene															C	3 + Q
Idaspe							A								C	3

	Garden on the banks of the River Euphrates	Room prepared for Tamerlano's meal . . .

of his arias, in addition to the Act III duet, come just before a change of set. Furthermore, he is given an extra aria ('Più d'una tigre altero') in II. viii; this extra emphasis doubtless reflects the casting of Senesino in the role. But even this extra exposure fails to turn Andronico into a convincing heroic figure.

Vivaldi's libretto, like Haym's, reduces the number of scenes in Act II, although the greatest change is at the end of this act. Haym follows Piovene in building tension through an unusually long stretch of recitative before releasing it in a fiery trio followed by a series of four arias, one for each character in turn.[14] Vivaldi, however, while following the 1711 recitative very closely, ignores Piovene's unusual conclusion and opts for the more immediate climax of a quartet for Asteria, Irene, Bajazet, and Tamerlano. The text for this ensemble, 'Sì crudel! questo è l'amore', is not found in any other *Tamerlano* libretto from this period,[15] but the reasons for Vivaldi's decision were no doubt practical: the quartet is taken from his favourite opera *Farnace*, originally produced in Carnival 1727 and frequently revived during the late 1720s and 1730s. Thus although a considerable amount of rewriting was necessary, the labour would still have been much less than that required by a setting of Piovene's text.

Another interesting point of comparison relates to the stage sets by Francesco Bibiena, Giannantonio Paglia, and Michel'Angelo Spada for the 1735 Verona production. Winton Dean and Merrill Knapp draw attention to the almost claustrophobic nature of Handel's setting, the entire action taking place within Tamerlano's palace,[16] yet Vivaldi's version moves the action into the open air for the majority of the seven *mutazioni*, there being no change of set for the end of Act I. Thus the stage sets are: Act I: Delightful place in the royal palace of Bursa (capital of Bithynia) occupied by Tamerlano after the defeat of the Turks; Royal apartments appointed for Asteria and Bajazet who are under guard; Act II: Countryside with Tamerlano's pavilion which suddenly opens to reveal Tamerlano and Asteria seated on two cushions; Battlefield with a throne on which are seated Tamerlano and Asteria in view of the whole army; Act III: Garden on the banks of the River Euphrates; Room prepared for Tamerlano's meal in view of the whole army.[17] The 1735 libretto also mentions ballets choreographed by Petrillo

---

[14] This is, in fact, the longest section of uninterrupted recitative in any Handel opera. Dean and Knapp (*Handel's Operas*, 538) suggest that Piovene may have borrowed the unusual structure of a trio followed immediately by several short arias from Handel's *Agrippina*, which was produced in Venice a year before Piovene's libretto for the same city.

[15] Bellina *et al.*, 'Il pasticcio Bajazet', 268.   [16] *Handel's Operas*, 537.

[17] 'Deliziosa nel Palazzo Reale di Bursa Capitale della Bitinia, occupata dal Tamerlano dopo la sconfitta de' Turchi'; 'Appartamenti reali destinati per abitazione d'Asteria, e Bajazette, custoditi da Guardie'; 'Campagna con Padiglione del Tamerlano, che s'apre all'improviso, e

Gugliantini. The insertion of ballets between the acts instead of comic intermezzi is typical of Vivaldi's preference in his later operas, again presenting
an interesting parallel with Handel, who incorporated substantial ballet and
choral scenes, with a strong leaning towards the French style, in his works
of the mid-1730s for Covent Garden.[18]

John Walter Hill has shown that many of Vivaldi's borrowed arias were
taken from previous roles for the same singer, particularly in the case of
Anna Girò.[19] There is little evidence, however, that most arias in his pasticcios
were chosen for this reason, so what factors, both musical and textual, might
have influenced his decisions here? According to Strohm,[20] rather more than
half the parody texts of Handel, Hasse, Vinci, and Vivaldi which he examined were closely connected to their original in affective content, and around
a third showed affective, semantic, and syntactical similarities. He concluded
that both Handel and Vivaldi placed more importance on similar textual
formulations than on the basic affect, so that more often different emotions
were expressed with similar words than similar emotions with different
words.

The sources of the poetic texts for Vivaldi's *Tamerlano* have been outlined
systematically by Bellina, Brizi, and Pensa, although their discussion of the
musical sources is sometimes flawed.[21] A study of some of these borrowed

vedesi Tamerlano, ed Asteria a sedere sopra due Origlieri'; 'Campo d'Armi con Trono, sopra
il quale siedono Tamerlano, ed Asteria a vista di tutto l'Esercito'; 'Giardino alle Rive del
Fiume Eufrate'; 'Sala preparata per le mense del Tamerlano a vista di tutto l'Esercito'. The
final phrase for the last set is presumably a printer's error, unless the room is to have a very
large window, and later in the libretto it is in fact changed to 'all'intorno di tutto l'Esercito'.
For a discussion of the relationship between the sets of *Tamerlano* and other productions at
the Teatro Filarmonico, see Maria Teresa Muraro and Elena Povoledo, 'Le scene della "Fida
ninfa": Maffei, Vivaldi e Francesco Bibiena', in Francesco Degrada (ed.), *Vivaldi veneziano
europeo* (Florence: Olschki, 1980), 235–52.

[18] These scenes, instigated by the arrival of the French choreographer and dancer Marie
Sallé, can be seen in Handel's works for the 1734–5 season, including *Oreste*, *Ariodante*, and
Alcina. Although Vivaldi's score for *Tamerlano* contains no ballet music, the pasticcio *Dorilla
in Tempe* (1734) has elaborate scenes with chorus and ballet at the ends of Acts I and II, the
latter involving a masque-like entertainment enacting a hunt.

[19] See Hill, 'Vivaldi's Griselda', *Journal of the American Musicological Society*, 31 (1978), 53–
82, and id., 'A Computer-Based Analytical Concordance of Vivaldi's Aria Texts: First Find-
ings and Puzzling New Questions about Self-Borrowing', in Fanna and Morelli (eds.), *Nuovi
studi vivaldiani*, i. 511–34.

[20] *Italienische Opernarien des frühen Settecento (1720–1730)* (Analecta musicologica, 16; Cologne: Arno Volk Verlag, 1976), i. 256.

[21] 'Il pasticcio Bajazet', 262–70. This includes a list of text incipits for the arias and details
of their derivations. The observations on the musical sources require the following additions/
corrections:

No. 6, 'Coronata di gigli, e di rose': only Acts I and II of the 1738 score of *Farnace* survive
in Turin, Biblioteca Nazionale Universitaria (hereafter *Tn*), Giordano 37, but the whole
opera appears in Giordano 36.

arias within their original contexts provides fascinating evidence of how the same music can function with a different text and within a new dramatic context. For example, the first scene of Act I ends with an aria for Bajazet. The score has two alternatives at this point.[22] 'Questa cara a voi confido' is clearly the original aria: its F major tonality follows logically from the C major cadence concluding the recitative, which was later changed to G minor when a new E flat major aria was added. The vocal line is written in the bass clef and demands a very wide range, from F to f', with trills and an arresting sequence of falling tenths, originally at the words 'il cerca al prato, il cerca al monte'. However, the poetic text obviously caused Vivaldi some problems, for there are three different versions for the first section of the aria. And at some point before the libretto was printed it was decided that the tenor Marc'Antonio Mareschi, who was to create the role of Bajazet, should sing instead a revised version of the aria 'Del destin non vi lagnate', which he had sung the previous carnival in Vivaldi's *L'Olimpiade*. In its original context, the aria is sung by King Clistene, who has offered the hand of his daughter Aristea to the victor in the Olympic Games. He ignores her pleas to postpone the contest and, unmoved by her complaints about the servile fate of women, advises her in his aria to accept her destiny: although women are seemingly subordinate to men, they are in fact the rulers, for beauty will always defeat strength in any contest.

The situation of Bajazet, the imprisoned sultan at the mercy of Tamerlano, has little in common with that of Clistene, and in fact the two texts are almost totally different except for the first line, 'Del destin non dee lagnarsi':

No. 15, 'Nasce rosa lusinghiera': although this text is not found elsewhere in Vivaldi's operas, the music does in fact reappear in *Giustino*, II. viii, and *Farnace*, III. iii (III. iv in the printed libretto).

No. 21, 'Sì crudel! Questo è l'amore': again, although the text is not found elsewhere in Vivaldi's operas, the music is taken from the quartet in *Farnace*, III. vii (viii).

No. 27, 'Veder parmi or che nel fondo': the attribution of this aria should not be 'ignoto', since the music reappears in both scores of *Farnace* for the aria 'Roma invitta, ma clemente' (II. xii).

No. 29, 'Vedeste mai sul prato': there is no reason for this aria to be attributed to 'Vivaldi?', since it is borrowed from Hasse's *Siroe re di Persia* (1733).

[22] *Tn* Giordano 36, fos. 150^r–153^v and 154^r–156^v. In this score, the recitatives, which are in Vivaldi's hand, are on numbered gatherings; the arias (though some are missing), in the hands of Vivaldi and nine different copyists, are written on a variety of paper-types and inserted into the score. See Paul Everett, 'Vivaldi's Italian Copyists', *Informazioni e studi vivaldiani*, 11 (1990), 27–86 at 39–41.

Tamerlano (1735), I. i   L'Olimpiade (1734), I. v
Bajazet (Marc'Antonio Mareschi)   Clistene (Marc'Antonio Mareschi)

<table>
<tr><td>

Del destin non dee lagnarsi
  chi ha nel petto un'alma forte,
  e l'aspetto della morte
  non paventa un cuor di Re.
Il morir solo m'avvanza
  e 'l mio caro amato pegno
  fido Prence a te consegno,
  tu poi l'ama ancor per me.

</td><td>

Del destin non vi lagnate
  se vi rese (rende) a noi soggette;[23]
  siete serve, ma regnate
  nella vostra servitù.
Forti noi, voi belle siete
  e vincete in ogn'impresa
  quando vengono a contesa
  la bellezza e la virtù.

</td></tr>
<tr><td>

(He should not complain of
destiny | who has in his breast a
brave soul, | and the face of
death | does not frighten the
heart of a king. || Only death
approaches me, | and my dear
beloved, | faithful prince, I
consign to you: | you can love
her also for me.)

</td><td>

(Do not complain of destiny | if it
has made (makes) you subject to
us; | you are servants, but you
rule | in your servitude. || We are
brave, you are beautiful, | and you
win in every contest | when there
come to do battle | beauty and
strength.)

</td></tr>
</table>

Clearly the keyword that links these two arias is 'destin': Bajazet is summon-
ing up his strength to face his destiny—death at the hands of his enemy—
just as Clistene exhorts Aristea to accept hers. The situation of a stern father
attempting to calm the fears of his daughter may also have led Vivaldi to
think of this aria when compiling his new score. Although both texts are in
regular *ottonari*, the rhyme-schemes are slightly different, ABAC BDDC
being altered to ABBC DEEC. This change is reflected in Vivaldi's new text
underlay for the opening of the second vocal section.[24] In *L'Olimpiade*, the

---

[23] 'Rende' in Vivaldi's autograph score in *Tn* Foà 39, fos. 1–140. All texts, unless otherwise stated, are taken from the printed libretto, with any significant differences in the score
given in parentheses.

[24] Although many of the arias in *Tamerlano* are in the hands of copyists, it was Vivaldi's
usual practice in his pasticcios to add the new poetic text himself, sometimes making slight
alterations/additions to the scribes' work and often adding extra dynamic markings. We do
not know who arranged the texts for Vivaldi's pasticcios, but it is clear from many of his
operatic scores that the composer frequently made textual alterations. The most substantial
evidence for this kind of activity is to be found in the cantata 'Nel partir da te, mio caro',
RV 661, in which several different beginnings to a section of recitative show Vivaldi con-
ceiving a new literary text along with the music; see Mary Meneve Dunham, 'The Secular
Cantatas of Antonio Vivaldi in the Foà Collection' (Ph.D. diss., University of Michigan,
1969), 63–4; Peter Ryom, *Les Manuscrits de Vivaldi* (Copenhagen: Antonio Vivaldi Archives,
1977), 93–4, and Michael Talbot, *Vivaldi* (London: Dent, 1978), 170. Bajazet's aria 'Del destin
non dee lagnarsi' appears to have been copied from the score of *L'Olimpiade*, for the musical
texts are virtually identical, although some missing A♮s have been corrected in bars 18–20,
and Vivaldi has added not only dynamic markings but also trills in the violin part on many

Ex. 12.1. Vivaldi, *L'Olimpiade*, I. v (Clistene); Vivaldi, *Tamerlano*, I. i (Bajazet)

Clistene: For - ti noi, voi bel - le sie - te, E vin - ce - te in o - gni im- pre - sa
Bajazet: Il mo - rir so - lo ___ m'av-van- za, E'l mio ca - ro a - ma - to pe- gno

(C: We are brave, you are beautiful, and you win in every contest . . .
B: Only death approaches me, and my dear beloved . . .)

whole opening line of text is repeated, followed by a repetition of the second half, 'non vi lagnate', which is expanded into a two-bar melisma. Although Vivaldi originally planned to do the same with his new text, he changed his mind as he went along, crossing out the repetition and substituting the second verse, so that the melisma now comes on 'forte', thereby emphasizing the rhyme with 'morte', a word sung to a four-bar melisma in the first vocal section and a five-bar one in bars 72–7. (In *L'Olimpiade*, these melismas underlined the *lagnate–regnate* rhyme.) The opening of the B section of the aria works less well, however. Here Clistene's juxtaposition of strength and beauty is reflected in the contrast between a strong G minor arpeggio and a gentler scalic passage. This contrast is completely inappropriate for 'Il morir solo m'avvanza', as is the emphatic five-bar phrase following, originally depicting the victory of feminine beauty but now simply setting Bajazet's reference to his daughter, the 'amato pegno' (see Ex. 12.1).

The following aria in *Tamerlano*, Idaspe's 'Nasce rosa lusinghiera', is also taken from one of Vivaldi's own works: it appears in *Giustino* (1724, Rome), where it is sung by the Emperor's sister Leocasta, and also in two versions of the much-reworked *Farnace* (1731, Pavia; 1732, Mantua):[25]

Tamerlano (1735), I. ii	*Giustino* (1724), II. viii	*Farnace* (1731), III. iii (iv)
Idaspe (Giovanni Manzoli)	Leocasta (Girolamo Bartoluzzi)	Gilade (Cristofforo Rapparini)
Nasce rosa lusinghiera	Senti l'aura, che leggiera	Scherza l'aura lusinghiera,
al spirar d'aura	và scotendo,	e scuotendo ramo e
vezzosa,	e ramo, e fronda,	fronda

of the longer notes. Despite the fact that the vocal part is given in the alto clef throughout, it is consistently written as if it were in the tenor clef, and its range of $G–f'$ is almost as wide as that of 'Questa cara a voi confido'.

[25] The score for the 1731 production survives in *Tn* Giordano 36, fos. 2–139. The aria appears in II. x of the 1732 production as opposed to III. iii of the 1731 score and III. iv of the corresponding libretto. The text is quoted here as it appears in the score. The aria from *Giustino* appears in Strohm's edition of the opera (Milan: Ricordi, 1991), 220–5.

e a quel dolce
  mormorio
va spiegando sua
  beltà.
Poscia al suol
  langue la rosa,
così fa bellezza
  altera
che mancando
  tosto và.

e con dolce
  mormorio
và spiegando il suo
  piacer.
Gigli, e Rose, onde
  superba
suole andar
  la Primavera,
d'ogni fonte in sù
  la sponda
tutti invitano à
  goder.

col suo dolce
  mormorio
và spiegando il
  suo goder.
Tale appunto son
  anch'io
di tua bellezza altera

cedo ai vezzi, ed al
  piacer.

(The delightful rose is born | at the breath of a charming breeze, | and to that sweet murmuring | unfolds its beauty. || Then the rose wilts to the ground; | thus it is with proud beauty | which soon fades away.)

(Hear the breeze which lightly | brushes both the branch and the leaf | and with sweet murmuring | displays its pleasure. || Lilies and roses, on which proud | Spring is wont to walk | from every stream on the bank | all invite to enjoy.)

(The delightful breeze plays | and brushing branch and leaf | with its sweet murmuring | displays its joy. || I, too, am precisely the same | and of your proud beauty | I yield to the delights and to pleasure.)

The dramatic situations have little in common. Leocasta tells the Empress Arianna, fresh from her rescue from the sea monster by Giustino, to enjoy the delights of nature; Gilade, captain of Queen Berenice's guard, sings of his love for Selinda; and Idaspe warns Prince Andronico that feminine beauty could be his downfall. The common ground between the texts is clearly the beauty of nature, and it is no coincidence that all three scenes are related to the outdoors: a palace garden (*Giustino*), rooms adjoining a garden (*Farnace*), and a *deliziosa* (*Tamerlano*).

It is interesting to see how the texts are transformed. The initial stanzas for *Giustino* and *Farnace* are very similar, with just minor alterations such as the substitution of 'scherza' for 'senti'. But whereas in *Giustino* the second stanza continues the images of nature with its 'lilies and roses' and its reference to spring,[26] in *Farnace* the second part personalizes the aria as Gilade

[26] The 'gigli, e rose' recall the closing chorus of Piovene's libretto, 'Coronata di gigli, e di rose', which Vivaldi used not only to end *Tamerlano* in 1735 but also to conclude *Farnace* as early as 1727, an indication that he must have known at least part of Piovene's text long before he set the whole work himself.

likens the beauty of nature to that of Selinda. The text of Idaspe's aria has
little in common with Leocasta's, save the image of the rose, now expanded
to dominate the aria, and the significant phrase 'dolce mormorio'. This is,
in fact, the key to the borrowing, for Vivaldi's music takes its cue from this,
with gently swaying violin figures permeating both sections of the piece,
and the composer's favourite sighing phrase at exactly this point in the text.
However, the new verses for *Tamerlano* appear to be derived from those of
Farnace: the opening line retains 'lusinghiera' but loses 'l'aura', so that it is
now unrelated to the incipit from *Giustino*, apart from its rhyme; the second
half again relates nature to the situation of the characters on stage and to the
'bellezza altera'; and this half is again reduced to three lines. As with the
retexting of the previous aria, there is an interesting change to the rhyme-
scheme. Leocasta's aria has the pattern ABCD EABD, and Gilade's the
pattern ABCD CAD (reversing the positions of 'piacer' and 'goder'),[27] while
Idaspe's text provides yet another layout of the B section: ABCD BAD.
Musically the versions in *Giustino* and *Farnace* are virtually identical, and
there are only minor differences in *Tamerlano*. Some of these may simply
reflect performance practice: certain dotted semiquaver figures are written as
even semiquavers, suggesting that the singer would 'bend' his semiquavers
to fit in with the predominant dotted string rhythms, while the pause on the
voice's opening unaccompanied 'Nasce' is a clear indication for a short
cadenza.

Another aria which Vivaldi borrowed from *Giustino* is 'La cervetta
timidetta'. Here it is sung by the Empress Arianna (III. vii), who is determined to warn her beloved Anastasio of Amanzio's treachery. She likens her
situation—recently banished by a furious and jealous husband—to that of the
timid little hind searching everywhere for her mate. In *Tamerlano* (II. vi), the
aria was sung by Anna Girò as Asteria, who is trying to convince Irene that
she is not her rival for the hand of Tamerlano. The image of the 'cervetta'
was a familiar operatic simile, and it appears elsewhere in Vivaldi's works.
For example, *La costanza trionfante degl'amori, e degl'odii*, first performed in
Venice in 1716 and later revised several times, contains the aria 'La timida
cervetta' (II. vi), which was reused in I. ix of *Teuzzone* (1718, Mantua): here
the image of the hind running through the forest in fear of the hunter calls
forth repeated-note figures similar to those found in the *Giustino* aria.[28]

---

[27] Vivaldi in fact writes 'goder' instead of 'piacer' in bars 50–1 and 53–4 of Leocasta's aria;
see *Giustino*, ed. Strohm, Critical Commentary, 107.

[28] The aria appears in *Tn* Foà 33, fos. 34^v–35^r and is discussed in Strohm, '"Tragédie" into
"Dramma per Musica"', *Informazioni e studi vivaldiani*, 10 (1989), 69–70. Gasparini's *Il Bajazet*,
performed a few months after *Teuzzone*, has an aria for Irene in I. xii, 'La violetta và
timidetta', whose B section also deals with Irene's jealousy and the loss of 'sposo, e trono'.
Here the text emphasizes Irene's timidity, in contrast to the more positive arias at this point
in the 1711 and 1724 versions.

Tamerlano (1735), II. vi
Asteria (Anna Girò)

La cervetta
  timidetta
  corre al fonte,
  al colle, al monte,
  trova al fine il suo diletto
  l'accarezza, si consola.
Cerchi Irene il suo diletto,
  ah! il suo ingrato
  sposo amato
  il mio cor nò non gl'invola.

(The little hind, | timid, | runs
to the spring, | to the hills, to
the mountain, | and in the end
she finds her beloved, | caresses
him and is consoled. || Let Irene
search for her darling. | Ah! may
her ungrateful | beloved
betrothed | not steal my heart.)

Giustino (1724), III. vii
Arianna (Giacinto Fontana)

La Cervetta
  timidetta
  corre al fonte
  al Colle, al Monte,
  e trovando il suo diletto
  l'accareza [*sic*], e lo consola:
Così spera anche il mio core;
  mà trovato il dolce amore
  pien di sdegno,
  fugge ingrato, e resto sola.

(The little hind, | timid, | runs
to the spring, | to the hills, to
the mountain, | and in the end
she finds her beloved, | caresses
him and consoles him. || Thus
my heart wishes for the same; |
but having found sweet love, |
full of scorn | it flees ungrateful,
and I stay alone.)

Both Irene and Arianna have been unjustly rejected by their betrotheds, though both display unwavering determination to achieve their goal, and in each text the B section personalizes the simile of the 'cervetta'. The aria, originally in B flat major for the soprano Giacinto Fontana, was transposed down a fifth for Anna Girò, necessitating some octave transpositions, mainly in the bass line. There are some differences in articulation and some extra dynamic markings, and several subdominants in the bass line leading to final cadences have been sharped, but otherwise the music is much the same. In the middle section, Vivaldi's original setting includes a melisma on 'sdegno', and a more fragmented texture at 'fugge ingrato' to emphasize 'flees'. The later version breaks up the melisma and, with its frequent repetitions of the last line, opts for more continuous text-setting; it also loses the impact of the Neapolitan inflections for 'sola' (see Ex. 12.2).

This aria, as Strohm points out,[29] became very fashionable, and Vivaldi also used material from it in several concertos (most notably, in the first movement of RV 189). Handel borrowed it for his pasticcio *Catone* of 1732, where it was originally intended to be sung by the soprano Celeste Gismondi in the role of Emilia.[30] Once again, the B section has a new text; here, again,

[29] *Giustino*, ed. Strohm, Introduction, 48.
[30] The score of *Catone*, an arrangement of Leo's setting of Metastasio's text dating from 1729, is reproduced in Howard Mayer Brown and Eric Weimer (eds.), *Italian Opera 1640–*

Ex. 12.2. Vivaldi, *Giustino,* III. vii (Arianna); Vivaldi, *Tamerlano,* II. vi (Asteria)

Ex. 12.2. (*cont.*)

(Ar: Thus my heart wishes for the same; but having found sweet love, full of
scorn it flees ungrateful, and I stay alone.   Ast: Let Irene search for her darling.
Ah! may her ungrateful beloved betrothed not steal my heart.)

Emilia is looking forward to being reunited with her husband, although this time it must be in Elysium, as Pompey has already been killed. In Handel's version, the melisma in bar 83 comes on the word 'pegno', while the isolated cries of 'fugge' in bars 89 and 90 are replaced by equally appropriate repetitions of 'vola' ('flies').[31]

One other aria in *Tamerlano* borrows its music from Vivaldi's earlier operas.[32] Bajazet's aria in the opening scene of Act III, 'Veder parmi or che nel fondo', is virtually identical with Pompeo's 'Roma invitta, ma clemente' from II. xii of *Farnace*, originally sung in Carnival 1727 by the tenor Lorenzo Moretti. Two scores of *Farnace* survive;[33] in the 1731 version, this aria is in C major for alto (Gaetano Fracassini), while in the later score, dated in Vivaldi's hand 'Ferrara 1738', it is in F major and in the tenor clef. Strangely, it is the alto version which appears in the score of *Tamerlano*, but presumably a similar tenor transposition was intended, as the aria's range is from *g* to *d″*.[34] The musical text is almost identical with that of *Farnace*, although, as usual, Vivaldi has added some extra dynamics to the copyist's score. The words, however, are substantially different:

1770, 71 (New York and London: Garland, 1983). It appears that Gismondi, who had just joined Handel's company, may have had a relatively free hand in her choice of arias. Before the libretto was printed, Vivaldi's aria was replaced by Porpora's 'Priva del caro sposo' from *Germanico* (1732, Rome), which was inserted at the appropriate point into the score. This aria also evokes images of nature, although here the turtle-dove flies to seek its mate. 'La cervetta timidetta' was also in the Italian repertory during 1732, for it was sung that year in III. iv of the Mantuan performance of Vivaldi's *Semiramide*, again with a different second stanza.

[31] Handel also follows a practice common elsewhere in Vivaldi by shortening the da capo ritornello, omitting bars 4–16. This is something which Vivaldi, in his turn, does to Handel's aria 'Già risonar d'intorno' (*Ezio*, III. xiii) when he borrows it with the parody text 'Già risvegliar à sdegno' for *Rosmira* (1738), I. xi; see Eric Cross, *The Late Operas of Antonio Vivaldi, 1727–1738* (Ann Arbor: UMI Research Press, 1981), i. 57.

[32] Asteria's 'Stringi le mie catene' (II. iii), which Girò sang a few months later a tone higher as 'Brami le mie catene' in the title-role of *Griselda*, recalls Zidiana's 'Vedi le mie catene' from *Teuzzone*, II. ix. The first halves of the texts are very similar, and, although the two musical settings are different (they are structured differently, and the ritornellos in the *Teuzzone* aria have much more semiquaver movement), the rhythm and, to some extent, the melodic shape of the opening vocal phrases are close, reflecting the fundamental rhythm of the words. According to Bellina *et al.*, 'Il pasticcio Bajazet', 239, the text 'Stringi le mie catene' goes back to the libretto of the Verona production of *Tamerlano* in 1715, thus predating Vivaldi's *Teuzzone* by some four years.

[33] A complete score predominantly in the hand of of copyists (*Tn* Giordano 36, fos. 2–139, for the production in Pavia in 1731), and an autograph of Acts I and II in Giordano 37, fos. 58–160, for the projected revival (1739) in Ferrara.

[34] By coincidence, an error in the printed libretto ascribes the aria, and Bajazet's previous speech, to 'Ta.'.

Tamerlano (1735), III. i
Bajazet (Marc'Antonio Mareschi)

Veder parmi or che nel fondo
  giù precipiti (precipita) di Stige
  sangue illustre ed innocente
  gonfie andar le rapid'onde
  abbattendo argini, e sponde
  all'orror di crudeltà.
Nel mirar sì ingiuste merci
    (morti)
  già s'infuria, e l'onda
    estolle,
  e di sdegno (sangue) e
    d'ira bolle.
Assorbir bensì vorria
  e star (trar) seco in Compagnia
  chi nemico è di pietà.

(I now seem to see in the depths
| thrown down into the Styx |
illustrious and innocent blood. |
The swift waves grow swollen, |
beating down embankments and
banks | at the horror of cruelty. ||
On seeing such unjust rewards
(deaths) | it grows angry, and the
water rises, | and it boils with
scorn (blood) and anger. | And it
wishes to overwhelm | and keep
in (drag into) its company | him
who is an enemy of pity.)

Farnace (1731), II. xii
Pompeo (Gaetano Fracassini)

Roma invitta, ma clemente
  non precipita nel Tebro
  sangue illustre, ed innocente,
  gonfia ben le rapid'onde
  sormontando argini, e sponde
  all'orror di crudeltà.
E se beve e Latte, e sangue

ei s'infuria, e l'onda estolle

e di sdegno, e d'ira bolle;

assorbir bensì vorria
e trar seco in compagnia
chi ricusa la pietà.

(Unconquered Rome, but
clement, | does not throw into
the Tiber | illustrious and inno-
cent blood; | [the river] swells its
swift waves | surmounting embank-
ments and banks | at the horror
of cruelty. || And if it drinks
both milk and blood | it grows
angry and whips up the waves, |
and it boils with scorn and anger.
| And it wishes to overwhelm
| and drag into its company |
him who renounces pity.)

The music seizes on certain images in the text for *Farnace*. The opening
trumpet-like figure in even crotchets represents the defiance of undefeated
Rome, while the following falling scale, with the strings in unison, graphi-
cally depicts the plunge into the Tiber—even though the text is '*non* precipita'!
(see Ex. 12.3). The image of waves overflowing the river banks inspires
many of the accompanying violin figures, such as the demisemiquaver
flourishes seen in Ex. 12.3. The final words of each section, 'crudeltà' and
'pietà', are set to a powerful unison scale sequence with vigorous dotted
rhythms: this is obviously inappropriate to the word 'pietà' itself, but it fits
the denial of pity present in both texts as well as serving to underline the
crudeltà–pietà rhyme between the two stanzas. In Bajazet's aria, the sentiments
are much the same, although the river has changed from the Roman Tiber

Ex. 12.3. Vivaldi, *Farnace*, II. xii (Pompeo); Vivaldi, *Tamerlano*, III. i (Bajazet)

(P: Unconquered Rome, but clement, does not throw into the Tiber . . .
B: I now seem to see in the depths thrown down into the Styx . . .)

to the infernal Styx. His determination to stand firm against Tamerlano is just as strong as Pompeo's to ensure that Rome is seen as merciful, and in each case there is a threat to innocent blood, be it Bajazet's daughter or Farnace's young son.

Thus far, all the examples of retexting examined have involved arias drawn from Vivaldi's own works. But what about those by other composers? The origins of many of the arias in *Tamerlano* have been known for some time,[35] but the relationship in each case between the new and the original

---

[35] See Strohm, *Italienische Opernarien*, ii. 283; Cross, *The Late Operas of Antonio Vivaldi*, i. 51–2; Bellina *et al.*, 'Il pasticcio Bajazet', 262–70. Many of the arias chosen by Vivaldi for incorporation into his score of *Tamerlano* have texts by Metastasio. The new, fashionable operatic styles of the late 1720s and 1730s were closely bound up with the ideals of Metastasian poetry, and although Vivaldi did set three Metastasio librettos himself, he appears to have been less in sympathy with modern literary developments than many of his contemporaries. One further such aria text which seems to have been included at some stage in *Tamerlano*

texts and between their dramatic contexts has yet to be examined. Three numbers—one for each act of Vivaldi's opera—were taken from Hasse's *Siroe re di Persia*, first performed at the Teatro Malvezzi, Bologna, in spring 1733 with Farinelli in the title-role.[36] Metastasio's libretto was first set by Leonardo Vinci for Venice in 1726; the Argument prefacing the libretto for Hasse's setting draws attention to the necessity of altering some of the original aria texts, not for poetic reasons but purely for the benefit of the singers:

> se alcune arie si sono mutate, non è già che ciò siasi fatto col pensiero di migliorare, che temerario cosa, e forse impossibile sarebbe, così quelle del suo primo egregio Autore sono proprissime, e leggiadrissime; ma per la necessità di avere a sostituire tali desinenze, che diano luogo alla Musica, di aprir maggior campo alla abilità di qualche Cantante.

> (if some arias are changed, it is not that this is done with the thought of improving them, which would be a foolhardy thing and perhaps would be impossible, since those of the first, distinguished poet are very appropriate and most graceful, but [it is done] because of the need to be able to substitute those terminations which give way to music so as to give a greater opportunity to the skill of some singer.)

The first of Hasse's arias is 'Vedeste mai sul prato', sung in I. vi by Tamerlano to Asteria. In the preceding recitative, he declares his love and his intention to marry her; if she persuades her father to accept the situation, he will gain his life and freedom. Yet another 'nature aria', the first section tells of the summer rain reviving the rose and the violet, while the second section draws the comparison with Asteria, who has given him cause for hope and love, and her father cause for peace and liberty. (This last idea refers back to the recitative, Tamerlano's suggestion that Asteria can grant her father 'libertade, e pace, e vita' deriving from Piovene's original 1711 text.) Towards the end of Act I of *Siroe*, everyone is accusing the hero of treachery. Princess Emira, who had previously joined in the accusations despite being in love with

is the aria 'Vil trofeo d'un'alma imbelle' from I. iii of *Alessandro nell'Indie*. This libretto was first set by Vinci for Rome in 1730, and in fact Vivaldi produced a revision of Hasse's 1731 setting (entitled *Cleofide*) for Ferrara in Carnival 1737. Halfway down fo. 231ʳ of the *Tamerlano* score, in the middle of a stretch of recitative in II. viii, a foreign hand has added the direction 'aria vil trofeo'.

[36] Of the surviving scores, that in Vienna, Österreichische Nationalbibliothek, MS 17256 has been reproduced in Brown and Weimer (eds.), *Italian Opera 1640–1770*, 33 (1977). The corresponding libretto from Bologna, Civico Museo Bibliografico Musicale, is reproduced in Brown (ed.), *Italian Opera Librettos: 1640–1770*, vol. 59. In Vivaldi's score, the first aria is in Vivaldi's hand, while the second and third, on fos. 215ʳ–218ᵛ and 260ʳ–267ʳ, are in the hand identified by Paul Everett ('Vivaldi's Italian Copyists', 40) as Scribe 52.

Siroe, suddenly begins to defend him, and her aria refers to her change of
heart. This double emotion of anger and mercy in the second stanza of
Metastasio's text cannot be applied to Tamerlano, but the new text in
Vivaldi's score in fact contains two pairs—hope and love, and peace and
liberty—which can be compared back to the rose and violet of the identical
first stanza.

Tamerlano (1735), I. vi
Tamerlano (Maria Maddalena
   Pieri)

Hasse: Siroe re di Persia (1733), I. xv
Emira (Vittoria Tesi)

. . .

. . .

In me così voi siete
   cagion di speme e amore
   e ancor al genitore
   di pace, e libertà.

Il cor non è cangiato (sdegnato)
   se accusa, ò se difende,
   una cagion mi accende
   di sdegno, e di pietà.

(In me you are thus | the cause
of hope and love, | and also to
your father, | of peace and
liberty.)

(My heart does not change (grow
angry) | if it accuses or defends. |
One reason enflames me | with
scorn and pity.)

The music for both settings is also identical.

Two scenes earlier in Hasse's opera, Siroe is accused and condemned of
treachery in turn by Laodice, who is in love with him, by his brother
Medarse, by his beloved Emira, and by his father Cosroe. In the aria 'La
sorte mia tiranna' (I. xiii) Siroe laments his fate, referring in turn to his
accusers: the pitiless Laodice ('un'Empia'), his brother ('un Germano'), Emira
(who is disguised as a friend, Idaspe ('l'Amico')), and his father ('il Genitor').
The middle part of the aria expounds Siroe's dilemma: although he has been
faithful, he cannot reveal that his brother is the real traitor. In Act II, Scene
iv of Tamerlano, Andronico, believing that he is losing Asteria to Tamerlano,
decides that Bajazet's help is his only hope. Beyond the injustice of cruel
fortune, it is difficult to see any similarity between his situation and that of
Siroe, and the main reason for the borrowing here was probably the attraction of including a popular aria from the repertory of the famous Farinelli.[37]
Vivaldi originally adapted the text to refer in turn to two people rather than
four. The opening two verses are identical except for the replacement
of 'tiranna' by 'spietata', but the later text continues 'Mi cruccia, e ognor
m'affanna | Asteria, Il Tamerlano | l'amata e il Traditor' ('There torment

---

[37] The aria is one of three in Vivaldi's score to be marked for Farinelli, although Riccardo
Broschi's 'Qual guerriero in campo armato' (from his Idaspe of 1730), used by Vivaldi in I.
xi, was also from the singer's repertory.

Ex. 12.4. Hasse, *Siroe re di Persia*, I. xiii (Siroe); arr. Vivaldi, *Tamerlano*, II. iv
(Andronico)

(S: . . . There accuse me and condemn me a pitiless woman, and a brother, my
friend, and my father . . . A: . . . There accuse and condemn me my beautiful
tyrant, [and] the traitor of bad faith . . .)

and trouble me Asteria, Tamerlano, my beloved, and the traitor').[38] This
suits the vocal line, which splits into short phrases for Siroe to address each
character in turn, but in the end Vivaldi must have decided to focus on
Andronico's relationship with Asteria, for he crossed out this text and returned to something closer to Metastasio's original with 'M'accusa, e mi
condanna | la bella mia tiranna, | d'infido il traditor' ('There accuse and
condemn me | my beautiful tyrant, | [and] the traitor of bad faith'). (See
Ex. 12.4.) The close of Hasse's aria provides a couple of unexpected harmonic twists: a chromatic slip in the vocal line on 'error' and an enharmonic
change in the bass line under a diminished seventh chord—a musical pun
to depict the text's fraud and deception ('frode ed inganno'). While Vivaldi's
version keeps 'error', his last line, 's'arma à mio danno', misses the point of
Hasse's setting (Ex. 12.5).[39]

   The last of the arias from *Siroe* is one of the opera's most famous, 'Spesso
tra vaghe rose', which frequently appeared in comic operas and intermezzos
such as the pasticcio *Il maestro di musica*, performed in Paris in the 1750s.[40]
This aria, with its florid melismas and frequent Lombard rhythms designed
to show off the famous Farinelli, comes from II. iii, where Siroe has been
arrested for apparently threatening to attack 'Idaspe'. The first stanza describes the cruel snake, lurking under beautiful roses to ensnare the hapless
traveller. The second part is addressed directly to Cosroe, warning his father
to believe him and not to trust 'Idaspe'. Again, while the A section needs

---

[38] Vivaldi may have had in mind here another Metastasio text which he had set the
previous year. Argene's aria in Act I, Scene vi of *L'Olimpiade* begins 'È troppo *spietato* | Il
barbaro fato | Mi cruccia m'affanna | La sorte tiranna . . .'. The first line of the second stanza
of 'La sorte mia spietata' refers back to the opening verse with its rhyme of 'ingrata'.

[39] The printed libretto here has the less appropriate 'sdegno ed inganno' ('scorn and
deception'). Neither line appears in Metastasio's original.

[40] See the Introduction to Brown and Weimer (eds.), *Italian Opera 1640–1770*, vol. 33,
where the first word of the aria is misprinted as 'Spresso'.

Ex. 12.5. Hasse, *Siroe re di Persia*, I. xiii (Siroe); arr. Vivaldi, *Tamerlano*, II. iv
(Andronico)

(S: . . . this becomes an error: such is the power of fraud and deception against
me. . . .   A: . . . this becomes an error: all cruelty arms itself for my
downfall. . . .)

no alteration, the B section is totally inappropriate. In his soliloquy in Act III, Scene viii of *Tamerlano*,[41] Andronico pledges his love for Asteria, and, despite Idaspe's earlier advice, he is prepared to abandon his kingdom for her. Thus the idea of betrayal—the snake-in-the-grass, or rather the snake-in-the-rose—is not particularly relevant, but Vivaldi's second stanza avoids personalizing the image, discussing instead the general conflicts between love and anger, mercy and cruelty, while ensuring that the isolated pairs of chords which Hasse uses to set 'Padre' still emphasize the addressee of the aria, Asteria ('Cara').

Tamerlano (1735), III. viii	Hasse: *Siroe re di Persia* (1733), II. iii
Andronico (Pietro Moriggi)	Siroe (Farinelli)
. . .	. . .
Tal'io fuggir non posso	Tal cela un menzoniero
l'amore, e la pietà,	aspetto di pietà,
furore, e crudeltà.	furore, e crudeltà;
E pur contento io sono	non può tradirti un figlio;
lasciar grandezza, e trono,	deh prendi il mio consiglio,
cara, per te adorar.	padre, non ti fidar.
(Thus I cannot flee | love and pity, | anger and cruelty. | And yet I am content | to leave grandeur and the throne, | beloved, to adore you.)	(Thus he who tells lies hides | his sense of pity, | anger and cruelty. | A son cannot betray you; | ah, take my advice, | father, and do not believe him.)

Two other texts in *Tamerlano* are taken from Geminiano Giacomelli's *Merope*, first performed at the prestigious Teatro S. Giovanni Grisostomo, Venice, in 1734. This was a revival of Zeno's libretto—first set by Francesco Gasparini in 1712—in an arrangement by Vivaldi's frequent collaborator, Domenico Lalli. Although the work was performed in Venice, the three main roles were taken by leading Neapolitan virtuosos: the tenor Francesco Tolve (Polifonte) and two of Porpora's most famous pupils, the castratos Farinelli (Epitide) and Caffarelli (Trasimede), both of whom were soon to be singing on the stages of London (the former for the Opera of the Nobility and the latter for Handel).[42] It is interesting that around this time

---

[41] The aria is mistakenly bound into III. iii of the score, but the libretto makes its correct location plain. The recitative of III. viii originally cadenced in B minor, but this was later altered to end in D minor for Hasse's aria, which is in B flat major.

[42] Two complete scores of the work have survived: Vienna, Gesellschaft der Musikfreunde, Q1404, and Brussels, Conservatoire Royal de Musique, 2110 FJG, Obl. Both scores match the printed libretto exactly (Venice: Rossetti, 1734); a facsimile of the Brussels score, together with a transcription of the libretto, has been published in the series Drammaturgia musicale

Vivaldi himself was thinking of putting on a production of *Merope*. He must have been strongly advocating a performance of this libretto at the Teatro della Pergola, Florence, during the 1735–6 season, for the surviving correspondence with the composer from Marquis Luca Casimiro degli Albizzi, who for many years acted as the theatre's impresario, contains three letters of July 1735 in which Albizzi states with increasing force that the planned opera, *Ginevra*, cannot be replaced by *Merope*.[43] Perhaps Vivaldi had plans to make use of further sections of Giacomelli's score. But although his plans for Florence did not come to fruition, Vivaldi had already incorporated the aria 'Sposa . . . non mi conosci' from *Merope* (III. vii) into Act II, Scene vii of *Tamerlano*.[44] It was originally sung by Farinelli as the young hero Epitide, the legitimate heir to the throne of Messenia who, having escaped the massacre of the royal family, has been living in exile. His attempts to rescue his kingdom from the tyrant Polifonte, who has also abducted his beloved Argia, result in increasing frustration, and, as Silvie Mamy points out,[45] he becomes less and less a hero and more and more the victim of circumstances—a vulnerable, fragile young man. In Act III, Epitide, who has been in disguise as 'Cleone' throughout the opera, reveals his true identity to his mother Merope. She, however, is unconvinced, still believing 'Cleone' to be responsible for her son's death, and in Scene vii Argia also claims not to recognize her lover. Thus Epitide believes that all those he loves have rejected him, and in a final expressive aria he gives way to despair and the contemplation of death. This aria is set in the tragic key of F minor, and its consistent use of staccato markings in the string parts is clearly associated by Giacomelli with the idea of death.[46] The opening syllabic setting of phrases interspersed with rests is typical of the *aria parlante* (a technique already seen in 'Stringi le mie catene'), but the vocal line later expands into a typically Farinellian melisma of nine bars on 'speranza'. Zeno's text, which Lalli leaves unchanged, links up with the preceding lines of recitative:

veneta, 18 (Milan: Ricordi, 1984), along with an introductory essay ('Il Teatro alla moda dei rosignoli') by Silvie Mamy providing valuable background to the work and its interpreters.

[43] See William C. Holmes, 'An Impresario at the Teatro la Pergola in Florence: Letters of 1735–1736', in Edmond Strainchamps and Maria Rika Maniates (eds.), *Music and Civilization: Essays in Honor of Paul Henry Lang* (New York and London: Norton, 1984), 127–40 at 132 and 137–8.

[44] Tamerlano's III. iv aria 'Barbaro traditor' also has a text taken from I. xi of *Merope* (Giacomelli's setting, that is—it is not in Zeno's original). The music, however, is very different, Giacomelli's aria being in C minor while Vivaldi's is in F major. It is interesting that the arias which seem to have caught Vivaldi's attention are two of the opera's three arias in a minor key.

[45] In her introduction to the facsimile, cited above, n. 42.

[46] Silvie Mamy makes the point, and also discusses the similarity between this aria and 'Mancare, oh Dio, mi sento', also in F minor, from Giacomelli's *Adriano in Siria* (1733); ibid.

EPITIDE. Il tuo sposo son io.
ARGIA.   Più non t'ascolto.
EPITIDE. Io son il figlio tuo.
MEROPE.   Tu me l'hai tolto.

(EP. I am your betrothed. | ARG. I listen to you no longer. | EP. I am your son. | MER. You have taken him from me.)

In Act II, Scene vii of *Tamerlano*, Irene takes comfort from Asteria's assurances that she is not her rival for Tamerlano's affections, and her final lines of recitative hint at a better future. Gasparini and Handel both take their cue from this: Gasparini's 1719 aria 'Ti sento, sì, ti sento' is a D major Allegro, while Handel's aria at this point is the ravishing siciliana 'Par che mi nasca in sen', both of which retain a degree of optimism.[47] Vivaldi's choice of Giacomelli's aria at this point clearly alters Irene's character, adding more weight with this powerful, tragic piece, but its inclusion doubtless had more to do with a desire to include one of Farinelli's recent and most effective arias. Vivaldi may have been influenced in his choice of this piece— and indeed others —by the contralto Maria Maddalena Pieri, who sang the role of Tamerlano. Pieri had sung for Vivaldi at the Teatro S. Angelo in 1726–7, as well as in Mantua in 1732, and had appeared alongside Farinelli on the stage of the Teatro S. Giovanni Grisostomo in 1729–30 in Hasse's *Artaserse*, Giay's *Mitridate*, and Riccardo Broschi's *Idaspe*. Thus she may well have remembered the impact of 'Qual guerriero in campo armato', sung by Farinelli in his brother's setting of *Idaspe*: it is an extraordinary virtuoso piece whose vocal line ranges from g to c''', using five different clefs (G_2, C_1, C_3, C_4, F_4), with vast leaps and repeated octave figures, and a massive melisma on 'battaglia'. This must have made an ideal show-piece for the impressive technique of Vivaldi's newcomer, the soprano Margherita Giacomazzi, who sang the aria as Irene in I. xi. Pieri's sister Teresa sang the part of Argia in Giacomelli's *Merope*,[48] and so may well have suggested reusing 'Sposa . . . non mi conosci', although it is perfectly possible that Vivaldi himself visited the rival Teatro S. Giovanni Grisostomo during a season in which he was working at the Teatro S. Angelo.

Whereas Epitide, in his despair, addresses 'Sposa . . . non mi conosci' alternately to Argia and Merope, the cause of Irene's despair is not on the stage in this scene. Thus the aria, instead of being addressed directly to her

---

[47] Handel's aria survives in two versions, one in C major for soprano with two clarinets (Handel calls them 'Cornetti') and one in G major for alto with flutes. The text is based on Piovene's original of 1711, although it is expanded from four lines to six.

[48] Not Maria Maddalena Pieri, as suggested in Bellina *et al.*, 'Il pasticcio Bajazet', 202 n. 47.

tormentors, is internalized—the opening 'sposa' now applies to the character herself:

Tamerlano (1735), II. vii
Irene (Margherita Giacomazzi)

Felice me, se 'l Soglio,
che ragione, ò beltà sì mai difende,
gratitudine almen'oggi mi rende.

Sposa—son disprezzata

   fida—son oltraggiata
   cieli che feci mai?
   E pure egl'è il mio cor
   il mio Sposo—il mio amor
   la mia speranza.

L'amo, mà egl'è infedel

   spero . . . mà egl'è crudel
   morir mi lascierai
   oh Dio! manca il valor, e la
     costanza.

(Happy, I, if the throne, | which ever defends reason and beauty, | at least today gives me gratitude. || As betrothed, I am scorned, | as faithful, I am abused: | heavens, what ever did I do? | And yet he is my heart, | my betrothed, my love, | my hope. || I love him, but he is unfaithful. | I hope . . . but he is cruel. | You will leave me to die, | oh God!—my strength and constancy fail.)

Giacomelli: *Merope* (1734), III. vii
Epitide (Farinelli)

Epitide ad Argia
Sposa . . . non mi conosci.
A Merope
   Madre . . . tu non m'ascolti.
   (Cieli, che feci mai?)
   E pur sono il tuo cor,
   il tuo figlio, il tuo amor,
   la tua speranza.
Ad Argia
Parla . . . ma sei infedel.
A Merope
   Credi . . . ma sei crudel.
   Morir mi lascerai?
   Oh Dio! manca il valor
     e la costanza.

((*To Argia*) My betrothed . . . you do not recognize me. | (*To Merope*) Mother . . . you do not listen to me. | (Heavens, what ever did I do?) | And yet I am your heart, | your son, your love, | your hope. || (*To Argia*) Speak . . . but you are unfaithful. | (*To Merope*) Believe . . . but you are cruel. | Will you leave me to die? | Oh God! my strength and constancy fail.)

Now both 'Sposa' and 'fida' refer to Irene herself, but both still suit the emphatic two-crotchet gesture to the interval of a perfect fifth (Ex. 12.6), and, indeed, there is a gain here in rhyme between the final vowels, something also found in the middle section with 'L'amo' and 'spero' (even if the use of the first person rather than the imperative weakens the effect). The exact reproduction of the third line and the closeness of the sixth retain

Ex. 12.6. Giacomelli, *Merope*, III. vii (Epitide); arr. Vivaldi, *Tamerlano*, II. vii (Irene)

Epitide:	Spo - sa,	non mi co - no - sci. Ma - dre, tu non m'a - scol - ti.
Irene:	Spo - sa,	son di-sprez-za - ta, Fi - da, son ol - trag - gia - ta,

(E: . . . My betrothed, you do not recognize me. Mother, you do not listen to me. . . . I: As betrothed, I am scorned, as faithful, I am abused . . .)

the emphatic setting of 'Cieli' and the long melisma for 'speranza', while the last line reproduces the unexpected Ab to underline 'la costanza'. Although Giacomelli's music is largely unchanged, Vivaldi once again adjusts the aria's ritornello structure: the original provides a written-out *dal segno* ritornello, in effect cutting after bar 1 of the opening ritornello to bar 12, although this necessitates omitting a bass suspension. Vivaldi's copyist, on the other hand, has written in 'DC', so Vivaldi has indicated a longer cut in the ritornello for the return of the first section—from the beginning of bar 4 to bar 16— as well as two shorter cuts of nine and two bars in the main vocal section.

Whereas Handel had at one stage considered including three duets and a trio in his *Tamerlano*,[49] Vivaldi's setting includes only one ensemble—the quartet at the end of Act II (II. x), for which he borrowed the much-used 'Io crudel? Giusto rigore' from the last act of *Farnace* (III. vii (viii)). The reuse of this number provides a fitting climax to a very long stretch of recitative and was probably suggested by certain similarities between the two dramatic situations, both of which involve a central character under sentence of death while others around him plead in vain for mercy. Farnace has been condemned to death, and he resolutely accepts his fate, rejecting the idea of clemency in the same manner as Bajazet. Tamiri, Farnace's wife, begs for mercy as does Asteria, while Berenice threatens death in a manner similar to Tamerlano. Only Irene is in a different situation: she accuses Tamerlano of being a pitiless tyrant, whereas Pompeo joins Berenice in rejecting mercy.[50] One factor facilitating this reuse of material was the identity of the singers in Vivaldi's production: Anna Girò had been the original Tamiri in Carnival

[49] The Act III duets for Tamerlano and Irene, and for Tamerlano and Andronico, were cut before the opera's first performance.

[50] The situation here is different from that of the trio 'Voglio strage' in Piovene's original libretto, in which Asteria joins Bajazet in welcoming death while Tamerlano rages at them. Gasparini set this trio in 1719 with a full da capo, although in Handel's version Tamerlano rushes off in fury before the customary middle section.

Ex. 12.7. Vivaldi, *Farnace*, iii. vii (viii) (Tamiri); Vivaldi, *Tamerlano*, ii. x (Asteria)

(T: Mother, Duke: o God! why? O God, why? . . .   A: Dead my father, o God! Why? O God, why? . . .)

1727 and had sung the role in a further three revivals, while Maria Maddalena Pieri had created the title-role in 1727 and had repeated it alongside Girò in Mantua five years later. But the *Farnace* score in which this quartet appears is that of the 1731 version.[51] For this production Girò again sang Tamiri, the other roles being taken by the tenor Antonio Barbieri (Farnace), his wife the soprano Livia Bassi Barbieri (Berenice), and the alto Gaetano Fracassini (Pompeo). In Carnival 1727 the soprano Angela Capuano had sung the part of Berenice and the tenor Lorenzo Moretti the role of Pompeo, so that the vocal ranges were identical with those of *Tamerlano*. Thus it seems likely that the 1735 version of the quartet comes close to the original 1727 setting.

As one might expect, given their common interpreter and similar dramatic situations, the parts for Tamiri and Asteria are very close. Tamiri's appeals to Berenice and Pompeo—'Madre, Duce'—are altered to 'Morte Il Padre', since there are no longer two characters to whom she can appeal for mercy. Her pleading phrases include new written-out appoggiaturas, possibly reflecting the way in which the version in *Farnace* might have been ornamented (see Ex. 12.7). Berenice's emphatic opening repetition of 'Io crudel?', as she claims that Farnace's death sentence is fully justified ('Giusto rigore ti condanna, ò traditore'; 'Just severity condemns you, o traitor'), is equally appropriate to Irene's harsh attack on Tamerlano: 'Sì crudel! Quest'è l'amore d'un

---

[51] *Tn* Giordano 36. The quartet is transcribed in Cross, *The Late Operas of Antonio Vivaldi*, ii. 165–76. John Walter Hill ('A Computer-Based Analytical Concordance of Vivaldi's Aria Texts', 519–20) suggests that Vivaldi also used the same music for the quartet 'Morte a me? Fiero rigore' in the 1738 Venetian version of *Armida al campo d'Egitto*. Although the music for Act II has been lost, the text in ii. xiv of the 1738 libretto is close enough to that of the *Tamerlano* quartet to indicate what Hill terms an 'elaborate parody'. It is not clear, however, why Hill quotes the version in *Tamerlano* rather than that in *Farnace*, which is closer in every way to the *Armida* text.

tiranno . . .' ('Yes, cruel one! This is the love of a tyrant . . .'). Irene's new line at bar 30, with repeated *d"*s for 'No non sà, che sia pietà' ('No, he knows not what pity is') anticipates the almost hysterical repeated notes which permeate her part later on, although Berenice's aggressive 'Morte attendi' ('Expect death') is completely unsuitable for Irene and so is given instead to Tamerlano. The defiant Bajazet is given a mixture of phrases drawn from the music for both Farnace and Pompeo, although his opening phrase of 'Mostro indegno, dispietato senza fè' ('Unworthy monster, pitiless, without faith') is set much more emphatically than Pompeo's related 'Non sei degno di mercè' ('You are not worthy of pity'). The A section of the quartet builds to more of a climax than in *Farnace*, with Asteria's pleas juxtaposed with homophonic phrases for the other three characters rejecting the idea of mercy. The short B sections are very similar: here all four characters sing together, and so there is no need for the careful rewriting necessitated by the earlier juxtapositions of individual lines.

The final pages of Vivaldi's *Tamerlano* draw heavily on Piovene's 1711 libretto and differ substantially from Gasparini's 1719 and Handel's settings. Whereas the 1719 and 1724 versions climax in Bajazet's powerful death scene, in the 1735 libretto his suicide is merely reported, and the dramatic focus of the opera instead becomes Asteria's reaction to this tragic news. She claims that although her father is dead, his hatred lives on in her, and her guilt at twice having failed to take Tamerlano's life leads her to contemplate suicide herself. The composer's continuous numbering of gatherings and the lack of any inserted sheets for the last three scenes of the opera suggest that Asteria's accompanied recitative and aria in Scene xiv were written out as he composed the rest of the recitative. Here Asteria is full of aggression towards Tamerlano; Vivaldi's recitative takes its cue from this, using short four-part crotchet chords separated by rests in the strings, a texture which emphasizes the short, aggressive opening phrases of text: 'È morto, sì, Tiranno, io stessa il vidi, è morto' ('He is dead, yes, tyrant; I myself saw him, he is dead'). The main points of articulation in the text, particularly at the ends of sentences, are marked with unison arpeggio figures whose final chromatic twists wrench the tonality into new, often unpredictable keys and impart a strong feeling of forward momentum (Ex. 12.8). The tonality swings around wildly, moving from an initial A minor to G minor, hinting at various keys on the way, then within five bars to C sharp minor, before finally settling in C minor as Asteria begs to die herself.

Her concluding aria, 'Svena, uccidi, abbatti, atterra', continues the mood of the recitative with its angry fragmented phrases. The voice is accompanied by staccato strings in unison with powerful falling scale passages and wide leaps covering the full extent of Girò's range. The text is identical with

Ex. 12.8. Vivaldi, *Tamerlano*, III. xiv

Strings in unison

that of Piovene's 1711 libretto: Asteria's furious first stanza contrasts with the
second addressed to her dead father. Vivaldi slows the tempo of the middle
section from presto to andante, dropping the dynamic to *piano*, and completely changing the texture. It is interesting that when Handel came to set
this scene, the two affects were turned around, Piovene's second stanza
being rearranged to form a new A section, thereby emphasizing Asteria's
grief rather than her desire for vengeance:[52]

Tamerlano (1711 and 1735), III. xiv	*Tamerlano* (1724), III. xiv
Svena, uccidi, abbatti, atterra.	Padre amato, in me riposa,
Piaghe, morte, strage, guerra	io quell'ombra generosa
sempre invita incontrerò.	a momenti seguirò.
E tu, Padre, in me riposa	E tu, crudo empio tiranno,
dietro l'ombra generosa	ogni tormento e affanno
a momenti volerò.	sempre invitta incontrerò.
(Make me bleed, kill me, beat me, fell me to the ground. | Wounds, death, slaughter, war | I shall always meet undefeated. || And you, father, rest in me; | after your noble spirit | I shall fly any moment now.)	(Beloved father, rest in me; | I that noble spirit | will follow any moment now. || And you, cruel, harsh tyrant, | every torment and suffering | I shall always meet undefeated.)

The first four bars of Vivaldi's aria are identical, apart from their transposition from A minor to F minor, with the opening of an aria written over
twenty years earlier for Act II, Scene xiii of *Orlando finto pazzo*.[53] Here
Grifone is also facing possible death, although in his case the powerful

---

[52] Gasparini's 1711 music for this aria (which survives in Staatsbibliothek zu Berlin—
Preußischer Kulturbesitz, Musikabteilung, Mus. MS 30330) also has a passionate first part (in
A major) and a contrasting slower middle section (in triple time); see Dean and Knapp,
Handel's Operas, 555. The 1719 score omits this scene completely, although it appears in the
libretto with a totally different aria text (whose opening phrase, 'Padre amato', anticipates
Haym and Handel) addressing in turn Andronico and Tamerlano. Handel's aria, fine though
it is, was removed before the first performance and does not appear in the 1724 libretto.
[53] The first six bars also appear, transposed into B flat major, in the violin part of the aria
'Quel torrente che s'inalza' from *Giustino* (II. vi).

Ex. 12.9. Vivaldi, *Orlando finto pazzo*, II. xiii

(a)

L'al - ma del for - te La pal - ma ot - tie - ne,

Se del - la sor - te Non hà ti - mor.

(The spirit of the brave wins the palm if he has no fear of fate . . .)

(b)

Strings

(c)

Grifone
and strings

L'al - ma del for - - te

unisons depict the strength of character needed to stand firm in the face of
misfortune: 'L'alma del forte | la palma ottiene, | se della sorte | non ha
timor' ('The spirit of the brave | wins the palm | if he has no fear of fate').
This aria opens immediately with the voice—Grifone's response to Ersilla's
threats is immediate and uncompromising—with the expected ritornello
held back until bar 9. Vivaldi states the whole of the first stanza of text four
times, each time setting it as an eight-bar phrase ending, apart from the first
statement, with a pause before the next repetition. These repetitions are
rounded off by an extension of the text which personalizes Grifone's situation, the four bars of repeated 'nò's balancing an earlier passage of four 'sì's:
'io che son forte, nò, nò, nò, nò, non hò timor'.

   Much of the music of Grifone's aria is based on short, two-bar cells which
Vivaldi repeats, often in sequence and sometimes in a varied form (Ex. 12.9).
The falling scale passage in bars 3–4 is developed in different ways, including
changing the first bar to a falling arpeggio (bar 28), but it reverts to its
original form in the aria's B section at bar 76 for the text 'sono i tormenti,

Ex. 12.10. Vivaldi, *Tamerlano*, III. xiv

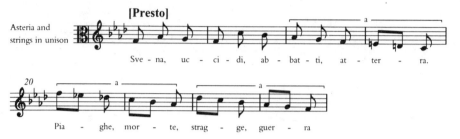

(Make me bleed, kill me, beat me, fell me to the ground. Wounds, death, slaughter, war . . .)

sono le pene'. These phrases are emphasized by repetitions in the violins, and in fact this section is typical of Vivaldi's arias from the 1710s in its frequent short instrumental interjections. Bars 5–6 also spawn two other two-bar phrases, one vocal and one instrumental, with identical rhythms but different melodic shapes (Ex. 12.9*b*, *c*). The falling sixth is often involved, although Vivaldi cannot make up his mind where to place the interval: some phrases leap between the first and second quavers and others between the second and third—indeed, at bar 59 he becomes so confused that the violins have one version while the bass line has the other. The same interval opens the B section, again setting 'sono i tormenti, sono le pene', with the aria's predominant unison texture soon giving way to simple two-part counterpoint.

Asteria's aria in *Tamerlano* begins with a staccato ritornello built on the same opening four bars as Grifone's aria, but after the initial vocal entry in bar 16 much of the rest of the aria is new (Ex. 12.10). The interval of a sixth has virtually disappeared from the aria, but the falling scale from bars 3–4 (bars 18–19 of the first vocal section) is now even more significant, being used increasingly towards the end of the A section until it completely dominates the vocal line. The rising sixth between bars 4 and 5 is extended to a more dramatic eleventh to emphasize 'piaghe', a word also highlighted by the first use of semiquavers in the voice, while octave leaps underline 'morte' and 'guerra'. (Although it may be just coincidence, it is worth noting that another semiquaver pattern which features prominently in the later ritornellos of this aria also appears in the bass line at bar 25 of Grifone's aria.) Vivaldi follows the customary practice of his later operas by setting the first stanza of text twice, repeating words and phrases, particularly the second time round, and framing the vocal sections with ritornellos. Despite the fact that the aria's regular *ottonari* imply elisions, he ignores these completely in this opening section, although he follows them more closely in the B section.

Ex. 12.11. Vivaldi, *Tamerlano*, III. xiv

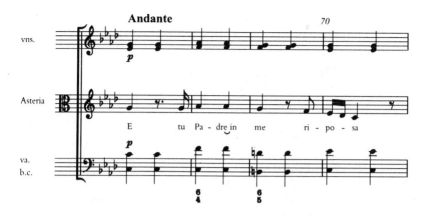

(And you, father, rest in me . . .)

Here there is a complete change as Asteria's thoughts turn to her dead father: the tempo drops to andante and the dynamic to *piano* as the strings provide a gentle, throbbing four-part accompaniment to a much more restricted melodic line (Ex. 12.11), a texture which remains constant apart from a short *forte* passage near the end in which 'dietro all'ombra generosa' is set to a unison falling scale with dotted rhythms.[54] This final aria thus exemplifies two of the opera's most crucial elements: the close relationship between Bajazet and his daughter, and their hatred of the cruel tyrant Tamerlano.

As we have seen, the factors which governed Vivaldi's choice of material for *Tamerlano* seem to have been very varied. In some cases, the reuse of a particular aria was clearly due to the singer involved; in other cases, a similar dramatic situation or a common idea in the text appears to have been the stimulus; and sometimes the cause was apparently just a desire to cash in on the success of an artist like Farinelli and to incorporate a fashionable style of music with which, to judge by his own musical style, Vivaldi himself seems to have had little sympathy. At the end of the opera, however, instead of merely borrowing a standard rage aria from another work, he chose to set Piovene's original text himself. This suggests that he was loath to leave the dramatic climax of the work in the hands of another composer. But it also enabled him to approach the end of the opera in what for him would have been an ideal fashion: with a scene that would reveal the acting talents of his beloved Anna Girò to the full.

[54] The aria 'Se in campo armato' from Vivaldi's *Catone in Utica* (1737; II. ix), another Veronese opera, has a similarly contrasting middle section; see Cross, *The Late Operas of Antonio Vivaldi*, ii. 141–2.

13

The Making of *Alcina*

WINTON DEAN

Alcina was the most successful of Handel's later operas, with eighteen performances in its first season (April–July 1735), three in November 1736, and two in June 1737. It is also by common consent one of the finest, and it has enjoyed much success in recent years, especially since the first modern British revival by the Handel Opera Society (with Joan Sutherland) in 1957. The opera has many attractions for audiences: quite apart from the quality of the music, it is (or should be) very spectacular in the theatre. Unlike most of Handel's operas, it employs all four vocal ranges, including a grateful tenor part and only one castrato; and the texture is varied by four true choruses (not mere ensembles for the soloists) and some captivating dances.

The story, based on an episode in Ariosto's epic poem *Orlando furioso* (Cantos VI–VII), is sufficiently familiar not to require a full summary here. The knight Ruggiero, held in thrall by the sexually voracious enchantress Alcina on her magic island, is rescued by his betrothed Bradamante, disguised as her warrior brother, and his old tutor Melisso by means of a magic ring, which opens his eyes to the true nature of his paramour. Alcina's former lovers, whom (like Circe) she has changed into animals, rocks, and trees, are restored to their human shape, and the enchanted island withers to a desert. A subsidiary plot concerning a desultory love affair between Alcina's general Oronte and her sister Morgana serves as an effective foil to the relationship of the central characters. The opera is dominated by the towering figure of Alcina, a genuinely tragic heroine, whose powers, hitherto invincible, cannot in the last resort command the love of the mortal with whom she is infatuated.

Thanks to the availability of Handel's autograph in the British Library, London (RM 20.a.4), and of his performing score in the Staats- und Universitätsbibliothek, Hamburg (MA 998), and to Reinhard Strohm's identification of the source libretto,[1] it is possible to trace the stages of the

---

[1] Reinhard Strohm, 'Händel und seine italienischen Operntexte', *Händel-Jahrbuch* (1975–6), 101–59 (trans. in id., *Essays on Handel and Italian Opera* (Cambridge University Press,

composition in some detail. There is abundant evidence that Handel not only chose his librettos with care, as we should expect, but played the dominant part in their adaptation. With rare exceptions, of which *Agrippina* (1709) and *Rinaldo* (1711) are the most notable, they were all old texts; many of them had been set repeatedly in Italy, and a number dated from well back into the seventeenth century. In adjusting them for his own purposes, Handel had the assistance of at least three Italian poets resident in London: Giacomo Rossi was his collaborator in three early operas, and Nicola Haym and Paolo Rolli in the fourteen operas (including the composite *Muzio Scevola*) of the first Royal Academy period (1720–8). Although Rolli was a poet of some repute, Haym, a professional musician who had adapted the librettos of *Teseo* and *Amadigi di Gaula* in 1713–15, was much the more adept in satisfying Handel's requirements and almost certainly more congenial to the composer (Rolli, a partisan of Bononcini, filled his letters with snide remarks about Handel). But Haym died in 1729, and no collaborator is known for Handel's remaining seventeen operas (with a single exception: the last of all, *Deidamia* of 1741, had a libretto by Rolli). There are one or two hints that Rossi may have been employed again, and Reinhard Strohm has conjectured that Haym prepared the libretto of *Orlando* (1733) before his death.[2] It is also conceivable that Handel sometimes did the job himself. This is certainly possible in the case of *Alcina*.

The source libretto, by an unknown author, is *L'isola di Alcina*, set by Riccardo Broschi, brother of the celebrated castrato Farinelli, for Rome in the carnival season of 1728. There the cast was headed by Farinelli as Ruggiero; and since a papal interdict banned women from the public stage in Rome, Alcina, Bradamante, Morgana, and Melissa (*sic*) were also played by castratos. Handel almost certainly acquired a copy of this libretto during his visit to Italy in 1729. He introduced one of its arias, 'Mi restano le lagrime', into the unfinished opera *Titus l'Empereur* (1731), part of whose music he adapted for *Ezio* in the following year. The words and music of 'Mi restano le lagrime' reverted to *Alcina* in 1735, but in a new setting. Oronte's Act I aria 'Semplicetto, a donna credi?' in both Broschi's and Handel's librettos originated in a cantata by Giovanni Bononcini, *Gl'amanti felici*.[3]

The changes made by or for Handel are less numerous and less drastic than usual in his adaptations—this was a good libretto which obviously

1985), 34–79). The opera is edited in *Georg Friedrich Händels Werke*, ed. Friedrich Chrysander, lxxvi (Leipzig: Breitkopf & Härtel, 1868; repr. Gregg, Ridgewood, NJ, 1965).

[2] *Essays on Handel and Italian Opera*, 266.

[3] See Lowell Lindgren, *A Bibliographic Scrutiny of Dramatic Works Set by Giovanni and his Brother Antonio Maria Bononcini* (Ann Arbor: UMI Research Press, 1974), 751, 901.

exerted a strong appeal—but they reveal very clearly the types of alteration he regularly introduced and the striking improvements they make to the drama. He scarcely altered the plot and the sequence of events, retaining all nine scene settings (three in each act) and the six characters of Broschi's opera, and only changing Melissa to Melisso to provide a role for the bass. (In Ariosto, Melissa, a benevolent sorceress, plays a much more important part in the story; Morgana is a minor figure, and Oronte and Oberto do not appear at all.) In accordance with his usual practice of throwing the central characters into relief, Handel reduced Morgana's quota from seven arias to four and that of Melissa(o) from three to one, and he slightly abridged those of Oronte and Bradamante from four to three. In Broschi's opera, in addition to the Act III trio, Bradamante had a duet with Ruggiero in Act II. Handel added the character of the boy Oberto as a late afterthought and gave an important role to the chorus. Whereas Broschi had only the conventional final ensemble for the soloists, Handel supplied four genuine choruses (for Alcina's courtiers, and for her victims as they return to life). This was a recent innovation in his operas, dating from within the past year, when he introduced choruses in the revival of *Il pastor fido* (1734) and then in *Ariodante* (1735). He was turning to account the small group of singing actors (we know their names from the autograph and performing score of *Alcina*) in John Rich's company at Covent Garden, to which Handel had moved from the King's Theatre in 1734. Dances already played a significant part in Broschi's opera at the same points as in Handel's, the second scene in Act I and the end of the second and third acts.

Of Broschi's thirty-four aria texts (including the duet and trio) Handel retained the exceptionally large number of twenty-four, nineteen of them for the same characters and five (with a few verbal changes) for different characters in different situations. Of the ten texts not retained, six disappeared as a result of the reduced quotas already mentioned, and three were replaced, two of them by stronger, more positive arias for Alcina herself. Ruggiero lost one inessential aria, 'Errante pellegrino', in Act I. Handel introduced nine new texts, three each for Oberto and the chorus (the fourth chorus is a setting of Broschi's final ensemble, 'Dall'orror di notte cieca'). The other three made striking contributions to the drama. Morgana's 'Tornami a vagheggiar', which brings Act I to an exhilarating conclusion, is a much improved version, words and music, of an aria in Handel's 1708 cantata 'O come chiare e belle'—another proof, if one were needed, of Handel's involvement in the construction of his librettos. 'Qual portento' in the first scene of Act II, Ruggiero's exclamation of amazement at the transformation wrought by the magic ring, derives its opening words from Broschi's recitative and is correctly described in Handel's autograph as a 'cavata',[4] i.e. a lyrical passage excavated from dialogue. The third new text, Bradamante's 'Vorrei vendicarmi' in the following scene, an indignant outburst as Ruggiero takes her for one of Alcina's phantoms, replaced the much milder and more plaintive 'Sì, son quella' (saying that she is the faithful woman he deserted for Alcina).

This is one of the five texts that Handel kept but transferred to other characters. It is much more effective in Alcina's mouth (Act I, Scene x) when Oronte has aroused Ruggiero's jealousy by telling him that Alcina is besotted with Ricciardo (the disguised Bradamante). 'All'alma fedel' (Bradamante, III. iv), the sense of which is that true faith will always be rewarded, was moved from Broschi's I. xiii, where it is sung by Melissa to Bradamante. Alcina's very moving 'Mi restano le lagrime' (III. v), when she has been deserted by Oronte as well as Ruggiero, is the last aria in Broschi's opera (III. xiii), after the climactic trio, and was sung by Morgana. No doubt Handel felt, correctly, that it would be wrong at this stage to divert the audience's attention (and sympathy) from the heroine to her sister. Oronte's 'Un momento di contento', a happy reflection after his reconciliation with Morgana in III. i, originated (with a different B section) as a conjugal duet for Ruggiero and Bradamante when the scales are removed from Ruggiero's eyes and he recognizes his wife (Broschi's II. xi). At this point in Handel's opera, immediately before Alcina's great incantation scene (the same text in both operas), Ruggiero sings the famous aria 'Verdi prati', looking back nostalgically at the enchanted landscape, the scene of so much happy dalliance, that he must now leave for ever. In Broschi's opera, it occurs not here but at the end of Act I and is sung not by Ruggiero but by Bradamante, in whose mouth it can carry none of the ironic overtones of Handel's wonderful setting, since she has never been subject to Alcina's magic powers.

This is not the only example of Handel achieving a stroke of rare genius by the simple process of transferring an aria from one character to another. In *Berenice* (1737), one of his least successful operas in which his dramatic powers are only fitfully engaged, the young Queen of Egypt has to choose between marrying for love or for political expediency to satisfy the imperial power of Rome. After struggling for two acts with the conflicting demands of conscience and desire, she submits to Rome. At this point in the source libretto, written by Antonio Salvi for Giacomo Antonio Perti in 1709, the Roman ambassador Fabio has an aria reflecting on the unpredictability of the blind capricious goddess Fortune ('Chi t'intende, o cieca instabile | capricciosa

---

[4] It is in Smith's hand, but he must have got the term from Handel.

Deità?'). Handel transferred the words to Berenice and turned a bystander's detached comment into a heart-rending *cri de cœur*. A long aria—almost a mad scene—of unique construction employing four different tempos expresses with extraordinary intensity the agony that her decision costs the young queen.

The autograph of *Alcina* throws further light on the composition of the opera. Handel was either pressed for time (he completed the score only eight days before the première) or seized with an overwhelming urge to tackle the main substance of the opera; for he abandoned his regular practice of writing out the words of the recitatives in their correct place between the arias. In the first two acts (the third was laid out in his usual manner), he composed the arias separately, beginning each one on a fresh page. Smith then prepared staves for the recitatives, supplying clefs and words, using any available space after the arias and sometimes continuing on odd scrap pages carrying discarded matter on the verso. These were inserted in the manuscript with cues when Handel had filled in the notes. (Perhaps for this reason he did not number each bifolium in his usual manner.) The only exception to this procedure is a brilliant aria for Ruggiero, 'Bramo di trionfar', in I. viii, composed in B flat major but marked for transposition to A, with its adjacent recitative in the usual place. This was a later insertion, in the position occupied by 'Errante pellegrino' in Broschi's opera (the aria and the continuation pages of the recitative are on paper ruled by a different rastrum from the rest of the autograph); but Handel cut it before performance, and (*pace* Clausen)[5] it was probably not copied into the performing score. The music was immediately adapted for the second setting of 'Through the land' in the oratorio *Athalia* (which received its London première on 1 April) and used again for 'Cease, O Judah, cease thy mourning', a late (1744) addition to *Deborah*. 'Bramo di trionfar' is included in Richard Bonynge's recording of *Alcina* (Decca MET.232–4, 1962).

The autograph contains no dances except the Musette and Menuet in the overture, but a cancelled annotation shows that Handel originally intended to use for the ballet in I. ii the big A major Chaconne composed for *Radamisto* in 1720 and transferred in 1734 to *Terpsicore*.[6] The F major setting of the chorus 'Questo è il cielo' in this scene is the original; the G major version, an insertion in the manuscript, was sung in the performances. There is a cue for dances at the end of Act I, but this idea was abandoned. For the ballet at the end of Act II Handel used the remarkable and elaborate scene representing the tortured dreams of the condemned Ginevra at the end

[5] Hans Dieter Clausen, *Händels Direktionspartituren ('Handexemplare')* (Hamburg: Wagner, 1972), 94; fo. 35 of the performing score does not seem to be an insertion.

[6] It is later found in G major with reduced scoring in the trio sonata op. 5 no. 4.

of the corresponding act of *Ariodante* but almost certainly not performed in that opera. This appears in the performing score of *Alcina*, simply lifted from *Ariodante* together with the close of Ginevra's preceding aria and her highly dramatic accompanied recitative, which concludes the act.

At a late stage, Handel decided to add the part of the boy Oberto for the young treble William Savage (he later became a bass), whose singing as Joas in *Athalia* must have impressed him (the *London Daily Post* reported on 3 April 1735 that he 'met with universal Applause'). The part is strictly superfluous, but Handel took advantage of the opportunity to add one telling detail: in II. vii Alcina (unless she is being duplicitous) shows a kindlier side to her nature, assuring Oberto that he will soon see his father again, immediately before being plunged into despair by the news of Ruggiero's defection. On the other hand, Oberto's instant recognition of a lion as his father comes dangerously close to bathos (in Ariosto, Astolfo is transformed not into a lion but into a myrtle-bush). The Oberto scenes are on fos. 16 and 86–90 of the autograph. They were copied as insertions in the performing score, which had already been prepared.

A few other details in the autograph may be worth mentioning. 'Di te mi rido' (I. iv), begun in *alla breve* time, is in F major, as in a very early aria collection, RM 19.a.12 (by the copyists known as S1 and S3), where it is marked andante. Chrysander printed it in G, one of the later transpositions for Gioacchino Conti. Handel originally intended to begin Act II with a sinfonia; 'Col celarvi' is probably an insertion (it is the only solo movement missing from RM 19.a.12). The violins in 'Mio bel tesoro' (II. vi) are muted. Abandoned openings of 'Sì, son quella' (I. x) and 'Pensa a chi geme' (II. i) remain in the manuscript. 'La bocca vaga' (I. xii) and 'Verdi prati' (II. xii), without tempo designation in Chrysander's edition, are clearly marked larghetto (or larghetta). Some changed tempo markings offer a possible clue to Handel's intentions in this respect: 'O s'apre al riso' was altered from allegro to andante; the G major 'Questo è il cielo' from andante to larghetto; 'Di, cor mio' from ?larghetto to andante larghetto; 'Chi m'insegna' from larghetto (or andante larghetto) to andante; 'Bramo di trionfar' from ?allegro to andante allegro; and 'Pensa a chi geme' from larghetto (autograph) to larghetto andante (performing score).

The cast at the first performance was: Alcina, Anna Strada del Pò (soprano); Morgana, Cecilia Young (soprano); Bradamante, Maria Caterina Negri (contralto); Ruggiero, Giovanni Carestini (mezzo-soprano castrato); Oronte, John Beard (tenor); Melisso, Gustavus Waltz (bass); Oberto, William Savage (treble). There were three cast changes in November 1736: Henry Theodore Reinhold (bass) succeeded Waltz, involving no pitch change in the music; Carestini was replaced by the soprano castrato Gioacchino Conti;

and Cecilia Young was succeeded by the mezzo-soprano Rosa Negri, sister of Maria Caterina. The performing score and a new libretto (called the third edition; there may have been two during the long 1735 run, although no second edition has yet turned up) make it possible to reconstruct what was performed. Handel considerably shortened the opera, especially in the second and third acts. All the dances except those in the overture were omitted—since Marie Sallé and her troupe were no longer available—together with the chorus 'Dall'orror di notte cieca'. Seven arias—'Pensa a chi geme', 'Vorrei vendicarmi',[7] 'Tra speme e timore', 'È un folle, è un vil affetto', 'Credete al mio dolore', 'Mi restano le lagrime', and 'Barbara! io ben lo sò'—were reduced to their A sections, and 'Col celarvi' was shortened by the omission of the last six bars, removing the second couplet of the text. These cuts, except in 'Col celarvi' and 'Pensa a chi geme', are indicated by brackets in Chrysander's score. In addition, Handel shortened the recitatives in three scenes, before and after 'È gelosia' in Act I, and at the start of Act III. The intention seems to have been to soften the bickering between Oronte and Morgana, but the excision of the entire recitative following 'È gelosia' removes an anomaly, a patch of unresolved recitative immediately before a set change (in Broschi's opera, Oronte concludes this scene with an aria). Only the first of these cuts is indicated by Chrysander.

In the recitatives for Ruggiero and Morgana, Handel added alternative notes (in ink or pencil) in the performing score, a higher tessitura for him, and a lower one for her.[8] Of Ruggiero's seven arias, 'Di te mi rido' (F to G), 'Col celarvi' (G minor to A minor), 'Mi lusinga il dolce affetto' (E flat to F), 'Mio bel tesoro' (G minor to A minor), and 'Stà nell'Ircana' (G to A) were put up a tone, 'La bocca vaga' (E to F) up a semitone, and 'Verdi prati' (E to G) up a minor third. Only 'Qual portento'[9] and Ruggiero's part in the trio remained at the original pitch. Rosa Negri was a singer of no great attainments, and her part of Morgana was reduced accordingly from four arias to one and a half. 'Tornami a vagheggiar' was transferred to Alcina with necessary adjustments to the preceding recitative; unfortunately, Chrysander gave preference to this dramatically inferior version. 'Ama, sospira'

[7] According to Clausen, this cut is not shown in the libretto; either this is a slip or he saw an otherwise unreported edition. Clausen is scrupulous in indicating insertions in the performing score, but he missed one (fo. 51, the new recitative before 'Tornami a vagheggiar', partly cancelled and amended by Handel).

[8] Chrysander, often inconsistent in such matters, prints the alternatives only in two widely separated phrases in his edition (pp. 37 and 75).

[9] According to Clausen, Handel marked 'Qual portento' for transposition up a tone, but cancelled the direction. This is not visible on a microfilm.

was cut,[10] and 'O s'apre al riso' transposed down a major third from A to F; 'Credete al mio dolore' (A section only) must also have been put down. The transposed arias were copied for the performing score by Smith and S1, with the upper instrumental parts represented by the top line only.

No libretto is known for the two performances in June 1737, but there was certainly one cast change, a more powerful and accomplished contralto replacing Rosa Negri as Morgana. Act II, Scene v, for Alcina, Morgana, and Ruggiero, was reorganized, and a new aria—'In mar tempestoso' from *Arianna in Creta* (1734) in its original key of D major—was inserted for Morgana, though not in the same place as 'Ama, sospira'. In III. i, 'Crede al mio dolore' was replaced by 'Vedrò frà poco', the superb final aria (composed for Faustina Bordoni) of Act II of *Admeto, re di Tessaglia* (1727), transposed down a tone from E to D. Both pieces were copied into the performing score by S1 without their verbal texts, and it is possible, as Clausen remarks, that they were sung with parodied words. Both are big virtuoso pieces, wholly out of scale in their new context and inappropriate in the mouth of Morgana. Handel was seriously ill at the time—he had had a probable stroke in the spring which immobilized the fingers of his right hand, and according to Lord Shaftesbury, who knew him well, his mind was affected in the summer. He was hardly in a condition to think seriously about changes to *Alcina*, and may have delegated the task to an assistant. The most likely singer of the two arias is Francesca Bertolli, who appeared in all Handel's operas this season (she had rejoined him after defecting to the Opera of the Nobility in 1733), including *Berenice* in May and June, whereas Rosa Negri seems not to have been available after the autumn of 1736.

---

[10] In the performing score, but not in Chrysander's edition, the B section of this aria is shown as cut. Since the aria was omitted entirely, this cut (and others) could have been made during the original run, as suggested by Clausen; but Handel could have shortened the aria in 1736 before deciding to omit it.

Index